PROVINCIALIZING EUROPE

A LIST OF TITLES

IN THIS SERIES APPEARS

AT THE BACK OF

THE BOOK

PRINCETON STUDIES IN

CULTURE / POWER / HISTORY

PROVINCIALIZING EUROPE

POSTCOLONIAL THOUGHT AND HISTORICAL DIFFERENCE

With a new preface by the author

Dipesh Chakrabarty

PRINCETON UNIVERSITY PRESS
PRINCETON AND OXFORD

Published by Princeton University Press, 41 William Street,
Princeton, New Jersey 08540
In the United Kingdom: Princeton University Press,
3 Market Place, Woodstock, Oxfordshire OX20 1SY

Reissue, with a new preface by the author, 2008
ISBN 978-0-691-13001-9

The Library of Congress cataloged the original edition of this book as follows

Chakrabarty, Dipesh.
Provincializing Europe : postcolonial thought and historical
difference / Dipesh Chakrabarty.
p. cm. — (Princeton studies in culture/power/history)
Includes bibliographical references and index
ISBN 0-691-04908-4 (alk. paper)—ISBN 0-691-04909-2 (pbk. : alk. paper)
1. Historiography—Europe. 2. Europe—History—Philosophy.
3. Eurocentrism. 4. India—Historiography. 5. Decolonization.
I. Title. II. Series.
D13.5. E85 C43 2000
901—dc21 99-087722

British Library Cataloging-in-Publication Data is available

This book has been composed in Sabon

Printed on acid-free paper. ∞

press.princeton.edu

Printed in the United States of America

7 9 10 8 6

For

Anne, Fiona, Robin

Debi, Gautam, Shiloo

IN FRIENDSHIP

Contents

Preface to the 2007 Edition ix

Acknowledgments xxiii

Introduction: The Idea of Provincializing Europe 3

PART ONE: HISTORICISM AND THE NARRATION OF MODERNITY

Chapter 1. Postcoloniality and the Artifice of History 27

Chapter 2. The Two Histories of Capital 47

Chapter 3. Translating Life-Worlds into Labor and History 72

Chapter 4. Minority Histories, Subaltern Pasts 97

PART TWO: HISTORIES OF BELONGING

Chapter 5. Domestic Cruelty and the Birth of the Subject 117

Chapter 6. Nation and Imagination 149

Chapter 7. *Adda*: A History of Sociality 180

Chapter 8. Family, Fraternity, and Salaried Labor 214

Epilogue. Reason and the Critique of Historicism 237

Notes 257

Index 299

Preface to the 2007 Edition
Provincializing Europe in Global Times

I

For all the criticisms that could be leveled at him, Roland Barthes' idea that a myth works by making the historical seem "natural" had something to it. Of course, by "historical," Barthes did not mean anything we could find in books about history, because, for him, such books would themselves belong to mythic systems of representation. "History," in Barthes's famous essay on "myth today," referred to the activity of living, an activity that, at least according to Barthes, was all about closing the gap to some degree (for it could never be fully closed) between the word and the world by orienting language more directly toward its referents "out there."[1] When caught up in the activity of living, words would mainly possess direct and practical connotation. "Europe" was not a word that ever bothered me in my middle-class Bengali childhood or youth as I was growing up in postcolonial Calcutta. The legacy of Europe—or British colonial rule, for that is how Europe came into our lives—was everywhere: in traffic rules, in grown-ups' regrets that Indians had no civic sense, in the games of soccer and cricket, in my school uniform, in Bengali-nationalist essays and poems critical of social inequality, especially of the so-called caste system, in implicit and explicit debates about love-match versus arranged marriages, in literary societies and film clubs. In practical, everyday living "Europe" was not a problem to be consciously named or discussed. Categories or words borrowed from European histories had found new homes in our practices. It made perfect sense, for instance, when radical friends in college would refer to someone—say, an obstructionist would-be father-in-law—as being full of "feudal" attitudes, or when we debated—for interminable hours over cheap cups of coffee or tea in inexpensive restaurants or tea shops where we generally overstayed our welcome—if the Indian capitalists were a "national bourgeoisie" or a "comprador" class playing second fiddle to foreign capital. We all knew, practically, what these words meant without having to put them under any kind of analytic microscope. Their "meanings" did not travel beyond the immediate environment in which they were being used.

Why, then, speak of "provincializing Europe"? The answer to this question has to do with the story of my own dislodgment from this everyday life in ways that were both metaphorical and physical. I will recount the story briefly, for the implications of it go, I think, beyond the merely autobiographical. My metaphorical dislodgment from my everyday middle-class life happened as I trained, in Marxist circles in the city, to be a professional historian for whom Marx's ideas were to be a conscious analytical tool. Words familiar from their everyday use (I should explain that I had been a student of science and business management before) now grew analytical wings, soaring into the level of what Barthes would have called "second- or third-order" metalanguages. Marxism, even more than liberalism, was the most concentrated form in which one encountered the intellectual pasts of Europe in Indian social-science circles.

It was about two decades ago, as I completed the manuscript for my book *Rethinking Working-Class History: Bengal 1890–1940*, that the question this book addresses began to formulate itself.[2] The roots of my effort in labor history went back to some passionate debates in Bengali and Indian Marxism of my youth about the world-historical role the proletariat might play in a country such as India that was, still, predominantly rural. There were obvious things to be learned from the Chinese and the Vietnamese revolutions. Yet, the more I tried to imagine relations in Indian factories through categories made available by Marx and his followers, the more I became aware of a tension that arose from the profoundly—and one might say, parochially—European origins of Marx's thoughts and their undoubted international significance. To call historical characters whose analogues I knew in everyday life as familiar types by names or categories derived from revolutions in Europe in 1789 or 1848 or 1871 or 1917 felt increasingly like a doubly distancing activity. There was, first of all, the distance of historical objectivity that I was trying to enact. But there was also the distance of comical misrecognition similar to what I had often experienced watching performances of Bengali plays in which Bengali actors, cast as colonial Europeans, acted out their heavily Bengali-accented imitations of how Europeans might have spoken Bengali, that is to say, their own stereotypes of how Europeans may have perceived us! Something similar was happening to my characters from Bengali and Indian history now clad, in my text, in the European costumes lent by the Marxist drama of history. There was a sense of comicality in my own earnestness that I could not ignore.

Yet in the discussion of Marx that I was an heir to in Calcutta—the discussion was always mediated, for historical reasons, by the available

English-language literature on the subject—there was no room for thinking about Marx as someone belonging to certain European traditions of thought that he may have even shared with intellectuals who were not Marxists or who thought in a manner opposed to his. This was not something that arose from a deficiency of reading. Calcutta had no dearth of bibliophiles. People knew nooks and crannies of European scholarship. But there was no sense of academic practices as part of living, disputed intellectual traditions in Europe. No idea that a living intellectual tradition never furnished final solutions to questions that arose within it. Marxism was simply "true." The idea of "uneven development," for example, so central to much of Marxist historiography, was treated as a piece of truth, at most an analytical tool, but never as a provisional way of organizing information, or as even something that was originally invented in the workshop of the Scottish Enlightenment. Marx was right (though he needed updating) and anti-Marxists were plain wrong if not immoral: such were the stark political antinomies through which we thought. Even a Weber did not get much of a serious look-in in the 1970s in the passionate scholarship of Indian historians of Marxist persuasion. There were, indeed, some gifted non-Marxist social scientists and historians in India. The names of Ashis Nandy and the late Ashin Das Gupta or Dharma Kumar easily come to mind. But in the heady and troubled days of a political and cultural *entente* between Mrs. Gandhi's India and the then-Soviet Union, it was Marxists who wielded prestige and power in the academic institutions of India.

My early unease—which later became a matter of intellectual curiosity—about the tension between the European roots of Marx's thoughts and their global significance did not have many takers among my Marxist friends in India, not then. The only significant dissident voice within the Marxist camp was that of Indian Maoism. The Maoist movement, known as the Naxalite movement (1967–1971) after a peasant revolt in the village of Naxalbari in West Bengal, suffered a catastrophic political defeat in the early 1970s when the government ruthlessly crushed the rebellion with an iron hand.[3] Maoism, it is true, had a vibrant intellectual presence in the early work of *Subaltern Studies*, a group with which I came to identify in the 1980s and later. But Maoism itself had become a soteriological formation by the time I began to train as a social scientist and its "corrections" or "modifications" of Marx's thoughts were practical. On the question of Marx's Europeanness, Maoists were incurious.

My theoretical unease was made more acute by my experience of physical displacement from my everyday life in India. This experience was another important influence on this project. I left India in December 1976 to pursue a doctoral degree in history at the Australian National University and have lived outside India ever since, though I have been involved in discussions with my Indian friends through annual visits, lectures, and regular publishing in India in both English and my first language, Bangla. Without the experience of migration, however—a profound combination of loss and gain, the opening up of new possibilities that do not necessarily compensate for the ones that get closed—I doubt that I would have written this book.

Until I arrived in Australia, I had never seriously entertained the implications of the fact that an abstract and universal idea characteristic of political modernity everywhere—the idea of equality, say, or of democracy or even of the dignity of the human being—could look utterly different in different historical contexts. Australia, like India, is a thriving electoral democracy, but Election Day there does not have anything of the atmosphere of festivity that I was used to in India. Things that in everyday life Australians assume to be essential to preserving the dignity of the individual—their personal space, for instance—are simply unpracticable in my poor and crowded India. Besides, the structures of sentiments and emotions underlying specific practices were things that I felt somewhat foreign to until, over time, I myself came to inhabit many of them.

Being a migrant made me see more clearly than I had in the past the necessarily unstable relation between any abstract idea and its concrete instantiation. No concrete example of an abstract can claim to be an embodiment of the abstract alone. No country, thus, is a model to another country, though the discussion of modernity that thinks in terms of "catching up" precisely posits such models. There is nothing like the "cunning of reason" to ensure that we all converge at the same terminal point in history in spite of our apparent, historical differences. Our historical differences actually make a difference. This happens because no human society is a *tabula rasa*. The universal concepts of political modernity encounter pre-existing concepts, categories, institutions, and practices through which they get translated and configured differently.

If this argument is true of India, then it is true of any other place as well, including, of course, Europe or, broadly, the West. This proposition has interesting consequences. It means, firstly, that the distinction I have drawn above between the figurative (how a concept is *visualized* in practice) and the discursive sides of a concept—its abstract purity, as it were—is itself a partial and overdrawn distinction. As Ferdinand de Saussure taught us a long time ago, one can distinguish between the "sound-image" of an idea and its "concept-image" only in an artificial manner. The two sides merge into each other.[4] If this is true, as I think it is, a second important conclusion follows. It is that the so-called universal ideas that European thinkers produced in the period from the Renaissance to the Enlightenment and that have since influenced projects of modernity and modernization all over the world, could never be completely universal and pure concepts (so long as they were expressible in prose—I am not concerned here with symbolic language like algebra). For the very language and the circumstances of their formulation must have imported into them intimations of pre-existing histories that were singular and unique, histories that belonged to the multiple pasts of Europe. Irreducible elements of those parochial histories must have lingered into concepts that otherwise seemed to be meant for all.

To "provincialize" Europe was precisely to find out how and in what sense European ideas that were universal were also, at one and the same time, drawn from very particular intellectual and historical traditions that could not claim any universal validity. It was to ask a question about how thought was related to place. Can thought transcend places of their origin? Or do places leave their imprint on thought in such a way as to call into question the idea of purely abstract categories? My starting point in all this questioning, as I have said before, was the silent and everyday presence of European thought in Indian life and practices. The Enlightenment was part of my sentiments. Only I did not know it as such. Marx was a household Bengali name. His German upbringing was never commented upon. Bengali scholars translated *Das Capital* without the slightest hint of any philological concerns. This recognition of a deep—and often unknown—debt to European thought was my point of departure; without that there could be no "provincializing Europe." One aim of the project was, precisely, to be aware of the specific nature of this debt.

The global relevance of European thought, then, was something I took for granted. Nor did I question the need for universalistic thinking. It was never, for instance, an aim of this book to "pluralize reason," as a serious reviewer suggested in a somewhat mistaken—I use this word with respect—reading of the project.[5] As my chapter on Marx will show, I argued not against the idea of universals as such but emphasized that the universal was a highly unstable figure, a necessary placeholder in our attempt to think through questions of modernity. We glimpsed its outlines only as and when a particular usurped its place. Yet nothing concrete and particular could ever be the universal itself, for intertwined with the sound-value of a word like "right" or "democracy" were concept-images that, while (roughly) translatable from one place to another, also contained elements that defied translation. Such defiance of translation was, of course, part of the everyday process of translation. Once put into prose, a universal concept carries within it traces of what Gadamer would call "prejudice"—not a conscious bias but a sign that we think out of particular accretion of histories that are not always transparent to us.[6] To provincialize Europe was then to know how universalistic thought was always and already modified by particular histories, whether or not we could excavate such pasts fully.

In undertaking this project, I was aware there were and still are many Europes, real, historical, and fantasized. Perhaps the boundaries between them are porous. My concern, however, was the Europe that has historically haunted debates on modernity in India. This Europe was made in the image of a colonizing power and, as I have said in the book, the making of such a Europe was not an act of Europeans alone. This Europe was, in the sense in which Lévi-Strauss once used the word, a founding "myth" for emancipatory thought and movements in India. Thinking about modernization, about liberalism, about socialism—that is to say, about various versions of modernity—assumed this Europe into existence. This was the Europe that was seen as the original home of the modern. We in India—and our political and intellectual leaders before us—used this Europe to resolve our debates about tensions arising from everyday inequalities and oppressions in India. For long many years, we waited in India for a return of this Europe in the shape of "democracy," "bourgeois civilization," "citizenship," "capital," and "socialism" in the same way as Gramsci once waited for the "first bourgeois revolution" of 1789 to reenact itself in his country.

The first part of *Provincializing Europe* (hereafter *PE*) sought to engage the form of thought that made it possible to postulate such a Europe. At issue, I argued, was a particular strand of developmentalist thought that I called "historicism." It was a mode of thinking about history in which one assumed that any object under investigation retained a unity of conception throughout its existence and attained full expression through a process of development in secular, historical time. Much of my thinking here was inspired by what Foucault had said, for instance, in criticizing historicism in his essay "Nietzsche, Genealogy, History."[7] Even earlier in my book on labor history, I had tried to think with Foucault's critique of any historical category that is "either transcendental in relation to the field of events or runs in its empty sameness throughout the course of history."[8] But poststructuralist thought was not the only ground on which I wanted to situate my critique. I could not but notice the fact that, long before Foucault, a radical aspect of anticolonial nationalist thought in India had in fact repudiated what I called "historicism" by first demanding and, on independence, actually granting full citizenship to unlettered masses at a time when all classical and Western theories of democracy advised a two-step program: first educate and thus develop them, and then grant them their citizenly rights. This critical relationship to developmental or stadial history was thus, I claimed, a part of the anticolonial heritage. It was not a coincidence that the *Subaltern Studies* historian (and our mentor) Ranajit Guha, in his book on peasant insurgency in colonial India, should reject Hobsbawm's characterization of modern peasants as "prepolitical."[9] The ground of anticolonial thought was clearly a fertile terrain for the cultivation of Foucault's poststructuralist critiques of "historicism."

Part I of the book joins this critique from several angles. The rest of the book demonstrates with historical examples how modernity was a historical process that involved not just transformation of institutions but categorial and practical translation as well.

II

There is, I hope, much history in *PE*. But I did not think of this history as representative of this or that group in particular societies. Because I have been associated with *Subaltern Studies*, which was indeed a project of writing into South Asian history the pasts of marginal and subaltern groups, some critics have seen in *PE* only further evidence of what the Indian historian Sumit Sarkar once called "the decline of the subaltern in *Subaltern Studies*," since the second part of *PE* draws all its illustrative material from the history of the Bengali middle classes, the so-called *bhadralok*.[10] This criticism has come from many quarters, but let me simply quote from one source, an anonymous and angry review that was posted on the Web on the site where Amazon.com first advertised this book. The review ended by saying:

> Finally, the fact that Chakrabarty's archive is the Bengali middle-class male and that he, along with his associates, is mired in theorizing to the neglect of substantive research of subaltern history speaks for itself. . . .[11]

The ellipsis points in the quotation above do not indicate matter that I have left out of the sentence; they are original to the sentence quoted, a dramatic gesture on the part of the critic about the obviousness of his point. What more could he or she have to say? My choice of material from the history of the social group I came from spoke for itself!

I do not select this review out of pique. *PE* has had worse reviews in the hands of some hostile Indian critics. After all, readers are free to make what they make of a book. Besides, one learns even from the most hostile of criticisms. I cite this particular review because, to my mind, what sustains the burden of this criticism is an inattentive reading of the book, especially the introduction, in which I had tried to explain my aims and methods. Even if a reader disagreed with my aims, the etiquette of criticism demands that my own explicit statement about the point at issue be acknowledged. I did say in the introduction that the histories I recounted here did not constitute any representative history of the *bhadralok*. Nor was it my aim to provide one. I said that the people whose writings and histories I drew on were themselves unrepresentative of the majority of the *bhadralok*, that these fragments of *bhadralok* history entered the book primarily as part of a methodological argument. But some critics simply did not pay heed to these statements. They accused me of leaving subaltern history for the more "elitist" pastures of *bhadralok* pasts. (I have too many indigent and semi-educated relatives not to know how unfortunate and unmeaning—if I may be permitted to coin a word—the expression "elite" is in this context, but will let that pass.) Their criticisms came from the absence of any attention to what I had said in explaining the shift between parts I and II of the book. "It is difficult to anticipate problems of readers who are inattentive," E. P. Thompson once said in frustration.[12] It is difficult indeed, but let me try once more.

One of the larger points of *PE* is that critical thought fights prejudice and yet carries prejudice at the same time, for critical thought, in my judgment, remains related to places (however tenuous such relation may seem). *PE* thus situated itself somewhat at odds with the various ways in which many theorists, mostly Marxist, criticize the idea of the local. Indeed, this position is common to so many Marxists that to single out a particular analyst could be a little unfair. Common to their thinking is the idea that any sense of the "local" is a surface phenomenon of social life; it is, in the ultimate analysis, some kind of an effect of capital. These scholars therefore emphasize the need to understand how one's sense of the local is actually produced. By looking on every sense of place in this particular way, these critics usually do not ask of themselves any questions about the place from where their own thinking comes. They presumably produce their criticisms from "nowhere" or—what is the same thing—the "everywhere" of a capitalism that always seems to be global in scope. In *PE*, I accepted this as one kind of universalistic thinking—it is reflective of what I have called History 1 in my chapter on Marx—but it is a mode of thinking that, in my judgment, evacuates all lived sense of place by assigning it to what is assumed to be a deeper and a more determining level, the level at which the capitalist mode of production creates abstract space. In the chapter on Marx, I try to produce a reading that resists this interpretation and sees the undertow of singular and unique histories, my History 2s, as always arresting the thrust of such universal histories and producing the concrete as a combination of the universal logic of History 1 and the heterotemporal horizons of innumerable History 2s. Space prevents me from developing this point further but I also risk repeating what I have already said in chapter 2.

Globalization theorists such as Michael Hardt and Antonio Negri, on the other hand, celebrate contemporary forms of placelessness as an expeditious tool to be used in the global struggle against capital. They also begin from the proposition that "localist positions" are both "false and damaging." False, because by "naturalizing" local differences, they put the "origin" of such differences "beyond question." And damaging, because one has to recognize that "local identities" actually "feed into and support the development of the capitalist imperial regime." It is globalization that "sets in play mobile and modulating circuits of differentiation and identification." "What needs to be addressed, instead," Hardt and Negri argue, "is precisely the *production of locality*."[13] The "place" that capital creates today through its own mobility and that of labor is, in their language, a "non-place."[14] Hence, labor must demand "global citizenship"—even more mobility than capital allows it at present—and make this "non-place" "limitless." Through such mobility will grow the revolutionary subject—"the multitude"—that will challenge what Hardt and Negri have called the Empire.[15] In their terms, then, the struggle against capital must at the same time be a struggle against all forms of attachment to particular places, for the desire for absolute mobility can only be based on the cultivation of a planetary sense of attachment.

I do not deny the insights that follow in particular contexts—especially at the level of the universal history of capital, my History 1—from such lines of thinking as I have elaborated above. But, overall, I find this argument to be oblivious of history itself. It is oblivious of the distinction between the mobility of colonizers that Europeans once enjoyed and the mobility of migrant labor today, skilled or unskilled. Wherever Europeans went in search of new homes, their imperial resources and their domination of the natives made it possible for them to reproduce—with local modifications no doubt—many of the important elements of the life-worlds they had left behind. Did European colonizers in any country ever lose any their own languages through migration? No. Often the natives did. Similarly, migrants in settler-colonial or European countries today live in fear of their children suffering this loss. Much of their local cultural activism is oriented to prevent this from happening. Only a critic blind to the question of how the unequal legacies of colonial rule actually inflect the contemporary processes of globalization can dismiss this activism as the malady of "nostalgia."[16]

Difference is not always a trick of capital. My sense of loss that ensues from my globalization is not always an effect of somebody else's marketing strategy. I am not always being duped into "mourning" by capital, for mourning does not always make a consumer of me. Often the loss in question relates to cultural practices that, so to speak, will no longer "sell." Not every aspect of our sense of the local can be commodified (I wish it could). *PE* mobilizes argument and evidence that are in tension with analyses that point to paths of salvation inevitably proceeding through the lure of the non-place.[17] Working through Heidegger and the hermeneutic tradition of thinking to which Gadamer belongs, *PE* attempts to bring into a productive tension gestures of thinking from nowhere and particular ways of being in the world. Whether or not my critique worked—I do not claim finality for my own critique—the proposition that thought is related to places is central to my project of provincializing Europe. It was thus incumbent on me to demonstrate from where—what kind of a place—my own critique issued, for this being-from-a-place is what gave the critique both its charge and its limitations. I said that in order carry out my critique, I needed to think through forms of life that I knew with some degree of intimacy, and hence resorted to material from aspects of the history of the *bhadralok* that have deeply molded my own relationship to the world. It was only in the case of that history that I claimed some competence that might enable me to demonstrate with examples the translational processes of modernity. This does not deny that there must be many different locations, even within Bengal or India, from which one could provincialize Europe with different results.[18] But the argument regarding place and non-place may still remain with us.

III

In summary, then, *PE* is a product of globalization. Globalization was its condition of possibility. But it is also, as Paul Stevens has remarked in an essay containing an astute reading of this book, an attempt to find a position from which to speak of the losses that globalization causes.[19] I am grateful for Stevens's reading, but it would only be fair to acknowledge how globalization, particularly in Europe and in European studies, has taken this book into exciting intellectual territories that I could not have foreseen. As European scholars and Europeanists have struggled to make sense of the changes happening in the continent and in their own spheres of studies, as they have engaged in discussions of European futures after globalization and addressed issues such as "Fortress Europe" versus "multicultural Europe," new avenues of inquiry have opened up. In their search for languages with which to understand the place of non-European immigrants and refugees in Europe, the question of Turkey's inclusion in the EU, and the place of postsocialist Eastern Europe, they have turned to models of postcolonial thinking to see if there are insights to be drawn from that branch of literature. Comparable developments appear to have taken place in (European) medieval and religious studies. Scholars have begun to question the very idea of the "medieval," the schema of periodization that underlies such an appellation.[20] Scholars of theology, on the other hand, are engaged in rethinking the question of divine agency in "religious historiography."[21] It has been a matter of gratification for me that *PE* has been drawn upon in several of these discussions, and I have found myself engaged, most profitably, with works of colleagues in areas far from those of my specialization.

I should like to end by expressing my gratitude to some particular individuals whose friendly but critical comments communicated personally to me in the years that have elapsed since the publication of the first edition have helped me to see both the limits and the possibilities of this work. But even here, I cannot be exhaustive. I can name only a few for obvious reasons of space and ask for the forgiveness of those I fail to mention: Bain Attwood, Ihar Babkov, Etienne Balibar, Teresa Berger, Ritu Birla, Marina Bollinger, Beppe Carlsson, Amit Chaudhuri, Kathleen Davis, Carola Dietze, Carolyn Dinshaw, Saurabh Dube, Constantin Fasolt, Dilip Gaonkar, Amitav Ghosh, Carlo Ginzburg, Catherine Halpern, Amy Hollywood, Lynn Hunt, John Kraniauskas, Claudio Lomnitz, Alf

Lüdtke, Rochona Majumdar, Ruth Mas, Achille Mbembe, Allan Megill, Cheryl McEwan, Hans and Doris Medik, Sandro Mezzadra, Donald Moore, Aamir Mufti, Almira Ousmanova, Anand Pandian, Luisa Passerini, Ken Pomeranz, Jorn Rüsen, Birgit Schaebler, Ajay Skaria, R. Srivatsan, Bo Strath, Charles Taylor, Susie Tharu, Peter Wagner, Milind Wakankar, and Kathleen Wilson. Dwaipayan Sen has provided much-appreciated research assistance: my thanks to him.

Chicago
1 February 2007

NOTES

1. Roland Barthes, "Myth Today," in his *Mythologies*, trans. Annette Lavers (New York: Hill and Wang, 1984), pp. 109–159.

2. Dipesh Chakrabarty, *Rethinking Working-Class History: Bengal 1890–1940* (Princeton: Princeton University Press, 2000).

3. For a history of this movement, see Sumanta Banerjee, *India's Simmering Revolution: The Naxalite Uprising* (London: Zed, 1984).

4. Ferdinand de Saussure, *Course in General Linguistics*, ed. Charles Bally and Albert Sechehaye, trans. Wade Baskin (New York: McGraw Hill, 1966), pp. 65–67.

5. See Jacques Pouchepadass's review of *PE*, published under the title "Pluralizing Reason," in *History and Theory* 41, no. 3 (2002): 381–391.

6. The "recognition," writes Gadamer, "that all understanding inevitably involves some prejudice gives the hermeneutic problem its real thrust." Hans-Georg Gadamer, *Truth and Method* (London: Sheed and Ward, 1979), p. 239. Gadamer generally sees prejudices as "conditions of understanding." See the discussion in pp. 235–258.

7. Michel Foucault, "Nietzsche, Genealogy, History" in his *Language, Counter-Memory, Practice*, ed. Donald F. Bouchard, trans. Donald F. Bouchard and Sherry Simon (Ithaca: Cornell University Press, 1977), pp. 139–164.

8. Michel Foucault, "Truth and Power" in his *Power/Knowledge: Selected Interviews and Other Writings, 1972–1977*, ed. Colin Gordon, trans. Colin Gordon et al. (Brighton: The Harvester Press, 1980), p. 117.

9. See the discussion in the introductory chapter of this book. See also the essay "A Small History of *Subaltern Studies*" in my *Habitations of Modernity: Essays in the Wake of Subaltern Studies* (Chicago: University of Chicago Press, 2002).

10. See Sumit Sarkar's essay by that name in his *Writing Social History* (Delhi: Oxford University Press, 1997).

11. See review by "Simicus" dated December 10, 2000, and entitled "Whither Subalternity?" at http://www.amazon.com/gp/product/customer-reviews/069104 9092/ref=cm_cr_dp_pt/102-6961987-3021759?ie=UTF8&n=283155&s=books.

12. E. P. Thompson, *Whigs and Hunters: The Origins of the Black Act* (Harmondsworth: Penguin, 1977), p. 302.

13. Michael Hardt and Antonio Negri, *Empire* (Cambridge, Mass.: Harvard University Press, 2000), pp. 44–45.

14. Ibid., pp. 208, 367.

15. Ibid., pp. 396–401.

16. For a fascinating account of French colonialists' struggle with their own sense of "nostalgia" in the nineteenth century, see Alice Bullard, *Exile to Paradise: Savagery and Civilization in Paris and the South Pacific* (Stanford: Stanford University Press, 2000).

17. The argument has since been taken up and expanded in Sanjay Seth, "Back to the Future?" *Third World Quarterly* 23, no. 3 (2002): 565–575; also published in a shorter version in G. Balakrishnan, ed., *Debating Empire* (London and New York: Verso, 2003), pp. 43–51. Saurabh Dube, "Presence of Europe: An Interview with Dipesh Chakrabarty," *South Atlantic Quarterly* (Fall 2002): 859–868.

18. See, for instance, Mark Thurner and Andrés Guerrero, eds., *After Spanish Rule: Postcolonial Predicaments of the Americas* (Durham: Duke University Press, 2003); Vicente L. Rafael, *White Love and Other Events in Filipino History* (Durham: Duke University Press, 2000); Frederick Cooper, *Colonialism in Question: Theory, Knowledge, History* (Berkeley: University of California Press, 2005); Achille Mbembe, *On the Postcolony* (Berkeley: University of California Press, 2001).

19. Paul Stevens, "Heterogenizing Imagination: Globalization, *The Merchant of Venice* and the Work of Literary Criticism," *New Literary History* 36, no. 3 (2005): 425–437.

20. See, for example, Kathleen Davis's forthcoming book, *Periods of Sovereignty* (2008).

21. Amy Hollywood, "Gender, Agency, and the Divine in Religious Historiography," *Journal of Religion* 84 (2004): 514–528.

Acknowledgments

Arjun Appadurai, Homi Bhabha, Gautam Bhadra, Carol Breckenridge, Faisal Devji, Simon During, Leela Gandhi, Anne Hardgrove, Pradeep Jeganathan, David Lloyd, Lisa Lowe, Uday Mehta, Meaghan Morris, Stephen Muecke, Rajyashree Pandey, Sheldon Pollock, Sanjay Seth, Ajay Skaria, and Kamala Visweswaran nurtured this book by providing me with an affectionate, critical, and constantly available conversational community. Ranajit Guha has been always there, a teacher, engaged critic, well-wisher, and friend at the same time. By his own example, Asok Sen demonstrated how to combine criticism, open-mindedness, and encouragement in the right doses. Tom Laqueur once read some of the chapters in draft and gave me characteristically friendly and honest criticism. Ron Inden, Steve Collins, C. M. Naim, Clinton Seely, Norman Cutler, James Chandler, Loren Kruger, Miriam Hansen, John Kelly—all colleagues at the University of Chicago—have helped by responding, critically or otherwise, to aspects of this project. And Philip Gossett has been a wonderfully supportive dean. My most grateful thanks go to them all.

Through correspondence and conversations, friends in different parts of the world have often helped me find my own perspectives. I am acutely aware of how much I owe to them individually but for reasons of space, I can only mention some of them by name. I am grateful to the scholars around the journals *Scrutiny 2* in South Africa (especially Leon de Cock), *Historia y Grafia* in Mexico, *Public Culture* in the United States, *Postcolonial Studies* in Australia, the "postcolonial geographies" group in the United Kingdom, and *Shiso* in Japan for the interest they have taken in this work. One privilege I have enjoyed over the years is that of being a member of the editorial collective of *Subaltern Studies*. The following pages will make obvious how much I owe to my colleagues in this group: Shahid Amin, David Arnold, Gautam Bhadra, Partha Chatterjee, David Hardiman, Shail Mayaram, Gyan Pandey, M.S.S. Pandian, Gyan Prakash, Susie Tharu, Ajay Skaria, and Gayatri Spivak. I thank them all.

I started this project while I was still teaching at the University of Melbourne in Australia. The Australian National University hosted me several times with short-term fellowships in the last one decade. I am grateful to the authorities of both of these institutions for the financial and moral support I have received from them. My friends in Australia have helped me to make the country my second home. For their intellectual, scholarly, and personal generosity, I remain deeply indebted to Ien Ang, David Bennett, Purushottom Bilimoria, John Cash, Charles Coppel, Phillip Darby, Greg Dening, Rashmi Desai, Michael Dutton, Mark Elvin, Antonia Finnane, John Fitzgerald, the late John Foster, Debjani Ganguly, Mary Gottschalk, Chris Healy, Barry Hindess, Jeanette Hoorn, Jane Jacobs, Robin Jeffrey, Miriam Lang, Jenny Lee, Ben Maddison, Vera Mackie, Brian Massumi, Lewis Mayo, Iain McCalman, Gavan McCormack, Jonathan Mee, Donna Merwick, Tony Milner, Tessa Morris-Suzuki, Klaus Neumann, Mary Quilty, Benjamin Penny, Peter Phipps, Christopher Pinney (when at ANU), Kalpana Ram, Anthony Reid, Craig Reynolds, Michael Roberts, John Rundell, Ken Ruthven, Renuka Sharma, Sanjay Srivastava, Julie Stephens, Helen Verran, Andrew Wells, and Patrick Wolfe. Anthony Low has been much more than a teacher. His support, encouragement, and good advice have always come to my aid when I needed them most.

The academic community in the United States has increasingly become my own over the last ten years or so. It is a pleasant task to acknowledge the gifts of ideas, criticisms, and friendship that have come my way. For all they have given and shared with me while I was engaged in thinking through this project, I thank Lila Abu-Lughod, Pranab and Kalpana Bardhan, Tani Barlow, Crystal Bartolovich, Dilip Basu, Sugata Bose, Alice Bullard, Sara Castro-Klaren, Dipankar Chakravarti, Choongmoo Choi, James Clifford, Lawrence Cohen, Rosemary Coombe, Fernando Coronil, Nicholas Dirks, Saurabh Dube and Ishita Banerjee-Dube, Sandria Freitag, Keya Ganguly, Dilip Gaonkar, Maitreesh Ghatak, Michael Hardt, Gail Hershatter, Lynn Hunt, Qadri Ismail, Vinay Lal, Patricia Limerick, George Lipsitz, Saba Mahmood, Lata Mani, Rob McCarthy, Allan Megill, Tom and Barbara Metcalf, Walter Mignolo, Tim Mitchell, Alberto Moreiras, Aamir Mufti, Mark Poster, Arvind Rajagopal, Sumathi Ramaswamy, Naoki Sakai, Ann Stoler, Julia Thomas, Lee Schlesinger, and Stephen Vlastos. Nicholas Dirks, Peter van der Veer, and Gauri Viswanathan read and commented helpfully on the whole manuscript. Alan Thomas, Timothy Brennan, and Ken Wissoker have long expressed interest in and enthusiasm for this project without, perhaps, knowing how much their encouragement meant to me.

It is also a pleasure to recall the kindness, appreciation, and intellectual support it has been my privilege to receive over many years in my own city, Calcutta. My thanks go to Anil Acharya, Pradyumna Bhattacharya, Gouri Chatterjee, Raghabendra Chattopadhyay, Ajit Chaudhuri, Subhendu and Keya Das Gupta, Arun and Manashi Das Gupta, Susanta Ghosh, Dhruba Gupta, Sushil Khanna, Indranath Majumdar, Bhaskar Mukhopadhayay, Rudrangshu Mukherjee, Tapan Raychaudhuri, Prodip Sett, friends associated with the journals *Naiya* and *Kathapat*, and colleagues in the History Department at Calcutta University and at the Centre for Studies in Social Sciences, Calcutta. I will always miss the affectionate criticisms that Hitesranjan Sanyal and Ranajit Das Gupta would probably have made of this work if they were still around. I thank Barun De for his intellectual generosity, from which I have always benefited. A visit to Jawaharlal Nehru University at Delhi in 1998 was made memorable by the warmth and comments I received from Sabyasachi Bhattacharya, Kunal and Shubhra Chakrabarti, Mushirul and Zoya Hasan, Majid Siddiqi, Muzaffar Alam, Neeladri Bhattacharya and Chitra Joshi, Prabhu Mohapatra, Dipankar Gupta, and Ania Loomba. I hope that they find their continuing interest in my work justified by this book. My dear friend Ahmed Kamal, a historian of the University of Dhaka, Bangladesh, has been my teacher of the social history of Bengali Muslims. Without his kind and critical interest in this work, I would have been even less aware of the inescapable Hinduness of my imagination.

I have had the good fortune of teaching some very talented students in Australia and the United States. Curious, critical, and intellectually adventurous, they provided me with the best sounding board one could ask for. Amanda Hamilton, Spencer Leonard, and Awadhendra Sharan helped additionally as research assistants for the project. My thanks and good wishes go to them all.

The circumstances of a "globalized" life spread thinly and precariously over three continents and some natural frailties of the body have made me ever more appreciative of the gifts of friendship and affection that I have been fortunate enough to receive in my personal life. I am, as always, grateful to my parents and my sister and her family for being there whenever I have needed them. Kaveri and Arko lovingly gave me a home during my visits to Australia in the last few years. This book, I hope, will explain to Arko what the "post-Marxist, postmodern gibberish" that he has often teased me for, has been all about. Sanjay Seth, Rajyashree Pandey, and Leela Gandhi in Melbourne, and Kamal and Thun in Dhaka have for long constituted my larger subcontinental family. My friends Shiloo and Rita Chattopadhyay, Debi and Tandra Basu, Gautam Bhadra and Narayani Banerjee—all of them in Calcutta—have allowed me to make claims on them that one would normally make only on one's siblings. Fiona Nicoll's friendship and her interest in Australian aboriginal studies enriched my life in more ways than I can tell. Robin Jeffrey has been unstinting in his friendship from the very first day of my arrival in Australia. And this book would have been impossible to write without Anne Hardgrove's love, friendship, and conversations in everyday life. To some of these people, this book is most gratefully and appreciatively dedicated.

I thank the staff of the National Library, Calcutta; the India Office Library and the British Library, London (in particular, Graham Shaw); the Baillieu Library at the University of Melbourne; the Menzies Library at the Australian National University; and the Regenstein Library at the University of Chicago (especially James Nye) for the courtesy and help they have extended me. Mary Murrell, my editor at the Princeton University Press, has been a model of intelligence, patience, and understanding in steering this manuscript to the stage of final publication. I can only confirm what others have already written in her praise. And my very grateful thanks to Margaret Case, whose careful and sensitive editing of the manuscript helped to bring more focus and clarity to the text than I could have ever achieved unaided.

Several of the chapters of this book are revised versions of essays published earlier. Chapter 1 was published originally in a longer version in *Representations*, no. 37, Winter 1992. Chapter 3 was published in Lisa Lowe and David Lloyd, eds., *The Politics of Culture in the Shadow of Capital* (Durham: Duke University Press, 1997). Chapter 4 was first published as a short statement in *Humanities Research*, Winter 1997, and *Perspectives* 35, no. 8 (November 1997), and subsequently revised for *Economic and Political Weekly* 33, no. 9 (1998); *Scrutiny* 2, 3, no. 1 (1998); and *Postcolonial Studies* 1, no. 1 (April 1998). An earlier version of chapter 5 was published in Timothy Mitchell and Lila Abu-Lughod, eds., *Contradictions of Modernity* (Minneapolis: University of Minnesota Press, 1999). Chapter 7 was published in *Public Culture* 11, no. 1 (1999). Chapter 8 draws on my essay "The Difference-Deferral of Colonial Modernity: Public Debates on Domesticity in British India," in *History Workshop Journal* 36 (1993). I am grateful to the editors of all these journals and volumes for making it possible for me to publish these essays now in their present form in this book. Thanks are also due to Communications and Media People, Calcutta, for permission to reproduce a sketch by Debabrata Mukhopadhyay.

Chicago
31 July 1999

PROVINCIALIZING EUROPE

INTRODUCTION

The Idea of Provincializing Europe

Europe . . . since 1914 has become provincialized, . . .
only the natural sciences are able to call forth a
quick international echo.
(*Hans-Georg Gadamer, 1977*)

The West is a name for a subject which gathers itself in
discourse but is also an object constituted discursively;
it is, evidently, a name always associating itself with
those regions, communities, and peoples that appear
politically or economically superior to other regions,
communities, and peoples. Basically, it is just like the
name "Japan," . . . it claims that it is capable of
sustaining, if not actually transcending, an impulse to
transcend all the particularizations.
(*Naoki Sakai, 1998*)

PROVINCIALIZING EUROPE is not a book about the region of the world we call "Europe." That Europe, one could say, has already been provincialized by history itself. Historians have long acknowledged that the so-called "European age" in modern history began to yield place to other regional and global configurations toward the middle of the twentieth century.[1] European history is no longer seen as embodying anything like a "universal human history."[2] No major Western thinker, for instance, has publicly shared Francis Fukuyama's "vulgarized Hegelian historicism" that saw in the fall of the Berlin wall a common end for the history of all human beings.[3] The contrast with the past seems sharp when one remembers the cautious but warm note of approval with which Kant once detected in the French Revolution a "moral disposition in the human race" or Hegel saw the imprimatur of the "world spirit" in the momentousness of that event.[4]

I am by training a historian of modern South Asia, which forms my archive and is my site of analysis. The Europe I seek to provincialize or decenter is an imaginary figure that remains deeply embedded in *clichéd and shorthand forms* in some everyday habits of thought that invariably subtend attempts in the social sciences to address questions of political modernity in South Asia.[5] The phenomenon of "political modernity"—namely, the rule by modern institutions of the state, bureaucracy, and capitalist enterprise—is impossible to *think* of anywhere in the world without invoking certain categories and concepts, the genealogies of which go deep into the intellectual and even theological traditions of Europe.[6] Concepts such as citizenship, the state, civil society, public sphere, human rights, equality before the law, the individual, distinctions between public and private, the idea of the subject, democracy, popular sovereignty, social justice, scientific rationality, and so on all bear the burden of European thought and history. One simply cannot think of political modernity without these and other related concepts that found a climactic form in the course of the European Enlightenment and the nineteenth century.

These concepts entail an unavoidable—and in a sense indispensable—universal and secular vision of the human. The European colonizer of the nineteenth century both preached this Enlightenment humanism at the colonized and at the same time denied it in practice. But the vision has been powerful in its effects. It has historically provided a strong foundation on which to erect—both in Europe and outside—critiques of socially unjust practices. Marxist and liberal thought are legatees of this intellectual heritage. This heritage is now global. The modern Bengali educated middle classes—to which I belong and fragments of whose history I recount later in the book—have been characterized by Tapan Raychaudhuri as the "the first Asian social group of any size whose mental world was transformed through its interactions with the West."[7] A long series of illustrious members of this social group—from Raja Rammohun Roy, sometimes called "the father of modern India," to Manabendranath Roy, who argued with Lenin in the Comintern—warmly embraced the themes of rationalism, science, equality, and human rights that the European Enlightenment promulgated.[8] Modern social critiques of caste, oppression of women, the lack of rights for laboring and subaltern classes in India, and so on—and, in fact, the very critique of colonialism itself—are unthinkable except as a legacy, partially, of how Enlightenment Europe was appropriated in the subcontinent. The Indian constitution tellingly begins by repeating certain universal Enlightenment themes celebrated, say, in the American constitution. And it is salutary to remember that the writings of the most trenchant critic of the institution of "untouchability" in British India refer us back to some originally European ideas about liberty and human equality.[9]

I too write from within this inheritance. Postcolonial scholarship is committed, almost by definition, to engaging the universals—such as the abstract figure of the human or that of Reason—that were forged in eighteenth-century Europe and that underlie the human sciences. This engagement marks, for instance, the writing of the Tunisian philosopher and historian Hichem Djait, who accuses imperialist Europe of "deny[ing] its own vision of man."[10] Fanon's struggle to hold on to the Enlightenment idea of the human—even when he knew that European imperialism had reduced that idea to the figure of the settler-colonial white man—is now itself a part of the global heritage of all postcolonial thinkers.[11] The struggle ensues because there is no easy way of dispensing with these universals in the condition of political modernity. Without them there would be no social science that addresses issues of modern social justice.

This engagement with European thought is also called forth by the fact that today the so-called European intellectual tradition is the only one alive in the social science departments of most, if not all, modern universities. I use the word "alive" in a particular sense. It is only within some very particular traditions of thinking that we treat fundamental thinkers who are long dead and gone not only as people belonging to their own times but also as though they were our own contemporaries. In the social sciences, these are invariably thinkers one encounters within the tradition that has come to call itself "European" or "Western." I am aware that an entity called "the European intellectual tradition" stretching back to the ancient Greeks is a fabrication of relatively recent European history. Martin Bernal, Samir Amin, and others have justly criticized the claim of European thinkers that such an unbroken tradition ever existed or that it could even properly be called "European."[12] The point, however, is that, fabrication or not, this is the genealogy of thought in which social scientists find themselves inserted. Faced with the task of analyzing developments or social practices in modern India, few if any Indian social scientists or social scientists of India would argue seriously with, say, the thirteenth-century logician Gangesa or with the grammarian and linguistic philosopher Bartrihari (fifth to sixth centuries), or with the tenth- or eleventh-century aesthetician Abhinavagupta. Sad though it is, one result of European colonial rule in South Asia is that the intellectual traditions once unbroken and alive in Sanskrit or Persian or Arabic are now only matters of historical research for most—perhaps all—modern social scientists in the region.[13] They treat these traditions as truly dead, as history. Although categories that were once subject to detailed theoretical contemplation and inquiry now exist as practical concepts, bereft of any theoretical lineage, embedded in quotidian practices in South Asia, contemporary social scientists of South Asia seldom have the training that would enable them to make these concepts into resources for critical thought for the present.[14] And yet past European thinkers and their categories are never quite dead for us in the same way. South Asian(ist) social scientists would argue passionately with a Marx or a Weber without feeling any need to historicize them or to place them in their European intellectual contexts. Sometimes—though this is rather rare—they would even argue with the ancient or medieval or early-modern predecessors of these European theorists.

Yet the very history of politicization of the population, or the coming of political modernity, in countries outside of the Western capitalist democracies of the world produces a deep irony in the history of the political. This history challenges us to rethink two conceptual gifts of nineteenth-century Europe, concepts integral to the idea of modernity. One is historicism—the idea that to understand anything it has to be seen both as a unity and in its historical development—and the other is the very idea of the political. What historically enables a project such as that of "provincializing Europe" is the experience of political modernity in a country like India. European thought has a contradictory relationship to such an instance of political modernity. It is both indispensable and inadequate in helping us to think through the various life practices that constitute the political and the historical in India. Exploring—on both theoretical and factual registers—this simultaneous indispensability and inadequacy of social science thought is the task this book has set itself.

THE POLITICS OF HISTORICISM

Writings by poststructuralist philosophers such as Michel Foucault have undoubtedly given a fillip to global critiques of historicism.[15] But it would be wrong to think of postcolonial critiques of historicism (or of the political) as simply deriving from critiques already elaborated by postmodern and poststructuralist thinkers of the West. In fact, to think this way would itself be to practice historicism, for such a thought would merely repeat the temporal structure of the statement, "first in the West, and then elsewhere." In saying this, I do not mean to take away from the recent discussions of historicism by critics who see its decline in the West as resulting from what Jameson has imaginatively named "the cultural logic of late-capitalism."[16] The cultural studies scholar Lawrence Grossberg has pointedly questioned whether history itself is not endangered by consumerist practices of contemporary capitalism. How do you produce historical observation and analysis, Grossberg asks, "when every event is potentially evidence, potentially determining, and at the same time, changing too quickly to allow the comfortable leisure of academic criticism?"[17] But these arguments, although valuable, still bypass the histories of political modernity in the third world. From Mandel to Jameson, nobody sees "late capitalism" as a system whose driving engine may be in the third world. The word "late" has very different connotations when applied to the developed countries and to those seen as still "developing." "Late capitalism" is properly the name of a phenomenon that is understood as belonging primarily to the developed capitalist world, though its impact on the rest of the globe is never denied.[18]

Western critiques of historicism that base themselves on some characterization of "late capitalism" overlook the deep ties that bind together historicism as a mode of thought and the formation of political modernity in the erstwhile European colonies. Historicism enabled European domination of the world in the nineteenth century.[19] Crudely, one might say that it was one important form that the ideology of progress or "development" took from the nineteenth century on. Historicism is what made modernity or capitalism look not simply global but rather as something that became global *over time*, by originating in one place (Europe) and then spreading outside it. This "first in Europe, then elsewhere" structure of global historical time was historicist; different non-Western nationalisms would later produce local versions of the same narrative, replacing "Europe" by some locally constructed center. It was historicism that allowed Marx to say that the "country that is more developed industrially only shows, to the less developed, the image of its own future."[20] It is also what leads prominent historians such as Phyllis Deane to describe the coming of industries in England as the *first* industrial revolution.[21] Historicism thus posited historical time as a measure of the cultural distance (at least in institutional development) that was assumed to exist between the West and the non-West.[22] In the colonies, it legitimated the idea of civilization.[23] In Europe itself, it made possible completely internalist histories of Europe in which Europe was described as the site of the first occurrence of capitalism, modernity, or Enlightenment.[24] These "events" in turn are all explained mainly with respect to "events" within the geographical confines of Europe (however fuzzy its exact boundaries may have been). The inhabitants of the colonies, on the other hand, were assigned a place "elsewhere" in the "first in Europe and then elsewhere" structure of time. This move of historicism is what Johannes Fabian has called "the denial of coevalness."[25]

Historicism—and even the modern, European idea of history—one might say, came to non-European peoples in the nineteenth century as somebody's way of saying "not yet" to somebody else.[26] Consider the classic liberal but historicist essays by John Stuart Mill, "On Liberty" and "On Representative Government," both of which proclaimed self-rule as the highest form of government and yet argued against giving Indians or Africans self-rule on grounds that were indeed historicist. According to Mill, Indians or Africans were *not yet* civilized enough to rule themselves. Some historical time of development and civilization (colonial rule and education, to be precise) had to elapse before they could be considered prepared for such a task.[27] Mill's historicist argument thus consigned Indians, Africans, and other "rude" nations to an imaginary waiting room of history. In doing so, it converted history itself into a version of this waiting room. We were all headed for the same destination, Mill averred, but some people were to arrive earlier than others. That was what historicist consciousness was: a recommendation to the colonized to wait. Acquiring a historical consciousness, acquiring the public spirit that Mill thought absolutely necessary for the art of self-government, was also to learn this art of waiting. This waiting was the realization of the "not yet" of historicism.

Twentieth-century anticolonial democratic demands for self-rule, on the contrary, harped insistently on a "now" as the temporal horizon of action. From about the time of First World War to the decolonization movements of the fifties and sixties, anticolonial nationalisms were predicated on this urgency of the "now." Historicism has not disappeared from the world, but its "not yet" exists today in tension with this global insistence on the "now" that marks all popular movements toward democracy. This had to be so, for in their search for a mass base, anticolonial nationalist movements introduced classes and groups into the sphere of the political that, by the standards of nineteenth-century European liberalism, could only look ever so unprepared to assume the political responsibility of self-government. These were the peasants, tribals, semi- or unskilled industrial workers in non-Western cities, men and women from the subordinate social groups—in short, the subaltern classes of the third world.

A critique of historicism therefore goes to the heart of the question of political modernity in non-Western societies. As I shall argue in more detail later, it was through recourse to some version of a stagist theory of history—ranging from simple evolutionary schemas to sophisticated understandings of "uneven development"—that European political and social thought made room for the political modernity of the subaltern classes. This was not, as such, an unreasonable theoretical claim. If "political modernity" was to be a bounded and definable phenomenon, it was not unreasonable to use its definition as a measuring rod for social progress. Within this thought, it could always be said with reason that some people were less modern than others, and that the former needed a period of preparation and waiting before they could be recognized as full participants in political modernity. But this was precisely the argument of the colonizer—the "not yet" to which the colonized nationalist opposed his or her "now." The achievement of political modernity in the third world could only take place through a contradictory relationship to European social and political thought. It is true that nationalist elites often rehearsed to their own subaltern classes—and still do if and when the political structures permit—the stagist theory of history on which European ideas of political modernity were based. However, there were two necessary developments in nationalist struggles that would produce at least a practical, if not theoretical, rejection of any stagist, historicist distinctions between the premodern or the nonmodern and the modern. One was the nationalist elite's own rejection of the "waiting-room" version of history when faced with the Europeans' use of it as a justification for denial of "self-government" to the colonized. The other was the twentieth-century phenomenon of the peasant as full participant in the political life of the nation (that is, first in the nationalist movement and then as a citizen of the independent nation), long before he or she could be formally educated into the doctrinal or conceptual aspects of citizenship.

A dramatic example of this nationalist rejection of historicist history is the Indian decision taken immediately after the attainment of independence to base Indian democracy on universal adult franchise. This was directly in violation of Mill's prescription. "Universal teaching," Mill said in the essay "On Representative Government," "must precede universal enfranchisement."[28] Even the Indian Franchise Committee of 1931, which had several Indian members, stuck to a position that was a modified version of Mill's argument. The members of the committee agreed that although universal adult franchise would be the ideal goal for India, the general lack of literacy in the country posed a very large obstacle to its implementation.[29] And yet in less than two decades, India opted for universal adult suffrage for a population that was still predominantly nonliterate. In defending the new constitution and the idea of "popular sovereignty" before the nation's Constituent Assembly on the eve of formal independence, Sarvepalli Radhakrishnan, later to be the first vice president of India, argued against the idea that Indians as a people were not yet ready to rule themselves. As far as he was concerned, Indians, literate or illiterate, were always suited for self-rule. He said: "We cannot say that the republican tradition is foreign to the genius of this country. We have had it from the beginning of our history."[30] What else was this position if not a national gesture of abolishing the imaginary waiting room in which Indians had been placed by European historicist thought? Needless to say, historicism remains alive and strong today in the all the developmentalist practices and imaginations of the Indian state.[31] Much of the institutional activity of governing in India is premised on a day-to-day practice of historicism; there is a strong sense in which the peasant is still being educated and developed into the citizen. But every time there is a populist/political mobilization of the people on the streets of the country and a version of "mass democracy" becomes visible in India, historicist time is put in temporary suspension. And once every five years—or more frequently, as seems to be the case these days—the nation produces a political performance of electoral democracy that sets aside all assumptions of the historicist imagination of time. On the day of the election, every Indian adult is treated practically and theoretically as someone already endowed with the skills of a making major citizenly choice, education or no education.

The history and nature of political modernity in an excolonial country such as India thus generates a tension between the two aspects of the subaltern or peasant as citizen. One is the peasant who has to be educated into the citizen and who therefore belongs to the time of historicism; the other is the peasant who, despite his or her lack of formal education, is already a citizen. This tension is akin to the tension between the two aspects of nationalism that Homi Bhabha has usefully identified as the pedagogic and the performative.[32] Nationalist historiography in the pedagogic mode portrays the peasant's world, with its emphasis on kinship, gods, and the so-called supernatural, as anachronistic. But the "nation" and the political are also *performed* in the carnivalesque aspects of democracy: in rebellions, protest marches, sporting events, and in universal adult franchise. The question is: How do we *think* the political at these moments when the peasant or the subaltern emerges in the modern sphere of politics, in his or her own right, as a member of the nationalist movement against British rule or as a full-fledged member of the body politic, without having had to do any "preparatory" work in order to qualify as the "bourgeois-citizen"?

I should clarify that in my usage the word "peasant" refers to more than the sociologist's figure of the peasant. I intend that particular meaning, but I load the word with an extended meaning as well. The "peasant" acts here as a shorthand for all the seemingly nonmodern, rural, nonsecular relationships and life practices that constantly leave their imprint on the lives of even the elites in India and on their institutions of government. The peasant stands for all that is not bourgeois (in a European sense) in Indian capitalism and modernity. The next section elaborates on this idea.

SUBALTERN STUDIES AND THE CRITIQUE OF HISTORICISM

This problem of how to conceptualize the historical and the political in a context where the peasant was already part of the political was indeed one of the key questions that drove the historiographic project of *Subaltern Studies*.[33] My extended interpretation of the word "peasant" follows from some of the founding statements Ranajit Guha made when he and his colleagues attempted to democratize the writing of Indian history by looking on subordinate social groups as the makers of their own destiny. I find it significant, for example, that *Subaltern Studies* should have begun its career by registering a deep sense of unease with the very idea of the "political" as it had been deployed in the received traditions of English-language Marxist historiography. Nowhere is this more visible than in Ranajit Guha's criticism of the British historian Eric Hobsbawm's category "prepolitical" in his 1983 book *Elementary Aspects of Peasant Insurgency in Colonial India*.[34]

Hobsbawm's category "prepolitical" revealed the limits of how far historicist Marxist thought could go in responding to the challenge posed to European political thought by the entry of the peasant into the modern sphere of politics. Hobsbawm recognized what was special to political modernity in the third world. He readily admitted that it was the "acquisition of political consciousness" by peasants that "made our century the most revolutionary in history." Yet he missed the implications of this observation for the historicism that already underlay his own analysis. Peasants' actions, organized—more often than not—along the axes of kinship, religion, and caste, and involving gods, spirits, and supernatural agents as actors alongside humans, remained for him symptomatic of a consciousness that had not quite come to terms with the secular-institutional logic of the political.[35] He called peasants "pre-political people who have not yet found, or only begun to find, a specific language in which to express themselves. [Capitalism] comes to them from outside, insidiously by the operation of economic forces which they do not understand." In Hobsbawm's historicist language, the social movements of the peasants of the twentieth century remained "archaic."[36]

The analytical impulse of Hobsbawm's study belongs to a variety of historicism that Western Marxism has cultivated since its inception. Marxist intellectuals of the West and their followers elsewhere have developed a diverse set of sophisticated strategies that allow them to acknowledge the evidence of "incompleteness" of capitalist transformation in Europe and other places while retaining the idea of a general historical movement from a premodern stage to that of modernity. These strategies include, first, the old and now discredited evolutionist paradigms of the nineteenth century—the language of "survivals" and "remnants"—sometimes found in Marx's own prose. But there are other strategies as well, and they are all variations on the theme of "uneven development"—itself derived, as Neil Smith shows, from Marx's use of the idea of "uneven rates of development" in his *Critique of Political Economy* (1859) and from Lenin's and Trotsky's later use of the concept.[37] The point is, whether they speak of "uneven development," or Ernst Bloch's "synchronicity of the non-synchronous," or Althusserian "structural causality," these strategies all retain elements of historicism in the direction of their thought (in spite of Althusser's explicit opposition to historicism). They all ascribe at least an underlying structural unity (if not an expressive totality) to historical process and time that makes it possible to identify certain elements in the present as "anachronistic."[38] The thesis of "uneven development," as James Chandler has perceptively observed in his recent study of Romanticism, goes "hand in hand" with the "dated grid of an homogenous empty time."[39]

By explicitly critiquing the idea of peasant consciousness as "prepolitical," Guha was prepared to suggest that the nature of collective action by peasants in modern India was such that it effectively stretched the category of the "political" far beyond the boundaries assigned to it in European political thought.[40] The political sphere in which the peasant and his masters participated was modern—for what else could nationalism be but a modern political movement for self-government?—and yet it did not follow the logic of secular-rational calculations inherent the modern conception of the political. This peasant-but-modern political sphere was not bereft of the agency of gods, spirits, and other supernatural beings.[41] Social scientists may classify such agencies under the rubric of "peasant beliefs," but the peasant-as-citizen did not partake of the ontological assumptions that the social sciences take for granted. Guha's statement recognized this subject as modern, however, and hence refused to call the peasants' political behavior or consciousness "prepolitical." He insisted that instead of being an anachronism in a modernizing colonial world, the peasant was a real contemporary of colonialism, a fundamental part of the modernity that colonial rule brought to in India. Theirs was not a "backward" consciousness—a mentality left over from the past, a consciousness baffled by modern political and economic institutions and yet resistant to them. Peasants' readings of the relations of power that they confronted in the world, Guha argued, were by no means unrealistic or backward-looking.

Of course, this was not all said at once and with anything like the clarity one can achieve with hindsight. There are, for example, passages in *Elementary Aspects of Peasant Insurgency in Colonial India* in which Guha follows the tendencies general to European Marxist or liberal scholarship. He sometimes reads undemocratic relationships—issues of direct "domination and subordination" that involve the so-called "religious" or the supernatural—as survivals of a precapitalist era, as not quite modern, and hence as indicative of problems of transition to capitalism.[42] Such narratives often make an appearance in the early volumes of *Subaltern Studies*, as well. But these statements, I submit, do not adequately represent the radical potential of Guha's critique of the category "prepolitical." For if they were a valid framework for analyzing Indian modernity, one could indeed argue in favor of Hobsbawm and his category "prepolitical." One could point out—in accordance with European political thought—that the category "political" was inappropriate for analyzing peasant protest, for the sphere of the political hardly ever abstracted itself from the spheres of religion and kinship in precapitalist relations of domination. The everyday relations of power that involve kinship, gods, and spirits that the peasant dramatically exemplified could then with justice be called "prepolitical." The persisting world of the peasant in India could be legitimately read as a mark of the incompleteness of India's transition to capitalism, and the peasant himself seen rightly as an "earlier type," active no doubt in nationalism but really working under world-historical notice of extinction.

What I build on here, however, is the opposite tendency of thought that is signaled by Guha's unease with the category "prepolitical." Peasant insurgency in modern India, Guha wrote, "was a *political* struggle."[43] I have emphasized the word "political" in this quote to highlight a creative tension between the Marxist lineage of *Subaltern Studies* and the more challenging questions it raised from the very beginning about the nature of the political in the colonial modernity of India. Examining, for instance, over a hundred known cases of peasant rebellions in British India between 1783 and 1900, Guha showed that practices which called upon gods, spirits, and other spectral and divine beings were part of the network of power and prestige within which both the subaltern and elite operated in South Asia. These presences were not merely symbolic of some of deeper and "more real" secular reality.[44]

South Asian political modernity, Guha argued, brings together two noncommensurable logics of power, both modern. One is the logic of the quasi-liberal legal and institutional frameworks that European rule introduced into the country, which in many ways were desired by both elite and subaltern classes. I do not mean to understate the importance of this development. Braided with this, however, is the logic of another set of relationships in which both the elites and the subalterns are also involved. These are relations that articulate hierarchy through practices of direct and explicit subordination of the less powerful by the more powerful. The first logic is secular. In other words, it derives from the secularized forms of Christianity that mark modernity in the West, and shows a similar tendency toward first making a "religion" out of a medley of Hindu practices and then secularizing forms of that religion in the life of modern institutions in India.[45] The second has no necessary secularism about it; it is what continually brings gods and spirits into the domain of the political. (This is to be distinguished from the secular-calculative use of "religion" that many contemporary political parties make in the subcontinent.) To read these practices as a survival of an earlier mode of production would inexorably lead us to stagist and elitist conceptions of history; it would take us back to a historicist framework. Within that framework, historiography has no other way of responding to the challenge presented to political thought and philosophy by involvement of the peasants in twentieth-century nationalisms, and by their emergence after independence as full-fledged citizens of a modern nation-state.

Guha's critique of the category "prepolitical," I suggest, fundamentally pluralizes the history of power in global modernity and separates it from any universalist narratives of capital. Subaltern historiography questions the assumption that capitalism necessarily brings bourgeois relations of power to a position of hegemony.[46] If Indian modernity places the bourgeois in juxtaposition with that which seems prebourgeois, if the nonsecular supernatural exists in proximity to the secular, and if both are to be found in the sphere of the political, it is not because capitalism or political modernity in India has remained "incomplete." Guha does not deny the connections of colonial India to the global forces of capitalism. His point is that what seemed "traditional" in this modernity were "traditional only in so far as [their] roots could be traced back to pre-colonial times, but [they were] by no means archaic in the sense of being outmoded."[47] This was a political modernity that would eventually give rise to a thriving electoral democracy, even when "vast areas in the life and consciousness of the people" escaped any kind of "[bourgeois] hegemony."[48]

The pressure of this observation introduces into the *Subaltern Studies* project a necessary—though sometimes incipient—critique of both historicism and the idea of the political. My argument for provincializing Europe follows directly from my involvement in this project. A history of political modernity in India could not be written as a simple application of the analytics of capital and nationalism available to Western Marxism. One could not, in the manner of some nationalist historians, pit the story of a regressive colonialism against an account of a robust nationalist movement seeking to establish a bourgeois outlook throughout society.[49] For, in Guha's terms, there was no class in South Asia comparable to the European bourgeoisie of Marxist metanarratives, a class able to fabricate a hegemonic ideology that made its own interests look and feel like the interests of all. The "Indian culture of the colonial era," Guha argued in a later essay, defied understanding "either as a replication of the liberal-bourgeois culture of nineteenth-century Britain or as the mere survival of an antecedent pre-capitalist culture."[50] This was capitalism indeed, but without bourgeois relations that attain a position of unchallenged hegemony; it was a capitalist dominance without a hegemonic bourgeois culture—or, in Guha's famous terms, "dominance without hegemony."

One cannot think of this plural history of power and provide accounts of the modern political subject in India without at the same time radically questioning the nature of historical time. Imaginations of socially just futures for humans usually take the idea of single, homogenous, and secular historical time for granted. Modern politics is often justified as a story of human sovereignty acted out in the context of a ceaseless unfolding of unitary historical time. I argue that this view is not an adequate intellectual resource for thinking about the conditions for political modernity in colonial and postcolonial India. We need to move away from two of the ontological assumptions entailed in secular conceptions of the political and the social. The first is that the human exists in a frame of a single and secular historical time that envelops other kinds of time. I argue that the task of conceptualizing practices of social and political modernity in South Asia often requires us to make the opposite assumption: that historical time is not integral, that it is out of joint with itself. The second assumption running through modern European political thought and the social sciences is that the human is ontologically singular, that gods and spirits are in the end "social facts," that the social somehow exists prior to them. I try, on the other hand, to think without the assumption of even a logical priority of the social. One empirically knows of no society in which humans have existed without gods and spirits accompanying them. Although the God of monotheism may have taken a few knocks—if not actually "died"—in the nineteenth-century European story of "the disenchantment of the world," the gods and other agents inhabiting practices of so-called "superstition" have never died anywhere. I take gods and spirits to be existentially coeval with the human, and think from the assumption that the question of being human involves the question of being with gods and spirits.[51] Being human means, as Ramachandra Gandhi puts it, discovering "the possibility of calling upon God [or gods] without being under an obligation to first establish his [or their] reality."[52] And this is one reason why I deliberately do not reproduce any sociology of religion in my analysis.

THE PLAN OF THIS BOOK

As should be clear by now, provincializing Europe is not a project of rejecting or discarding European thought. Relating to a body of thought to which one largely owes one's intellectual existence cannot be a matter of exacting what Leela Gandhi has aptly called "postcolonial revenge."[53] European thought is at once both indispensable and inadequate in helping us to think through the experiences of political modernity in non-Western nations, and provincializing Europe becomes the task of exploring how this thought—which is now everybody's heritage and which affect us all—may be renewed from and for the margins.

But, of course, the margins are as plural and diverse as the centers. Europe appears different when seen from within the experiences of colonization or inferiorization in specific parts of the world. Postcolonial scholars, speaking from their different geographies of colonialism, have spoken of different Europes. The recent critical scholarship of Latin Americanists or Afro-Caribbeanists and others points to the imperialism of Spain and Portugal—triumphant at the time of the Renaissance and in decline as political powers by the end of the Enlightenment.[54] The question of postcolonialism itself is given multiple and contested locations in the works of those studying Southeast Asia, East Asia, Africa, and the Pacific.[55] Yet, however multiple the loci of Europe and however varied colonialisms are, the problem of getting beyond Eurocentric histories remains a shared problem across geographical boundaries.[56]

A key question in the world of postcolonial scholarship will be the following. The problem of capitalist modernity cannot any longer be seen simply as a sociological problem of historical transition (as in the famous "transition debates" in European history) but as a problem of translation, as well. There was a time—before scholarship itself became globalized—when the process of translating diverse forms, practices, and understandings of life into universalist political-theoretical categories of deeply European origin seemed to most social scientists an unproblematic proposition. That which was considered an analytical category (such as capital) was understood to have transcended the fragment of European history in which it may have originated. At most we assumed that a translation acknowledged as "rough" was adequate for the task of comprehension.

The English-language monograph in area studies, for example, was a classic embodiment of this presupposition. A standard, mechanically put together and least-read feature of the monograph in Asian or area studies was a section called the "glossary," which came at the very end of the book. No reader was ever seriously expected to interrupt their pleasure of reading by having to turn pages frequently to consult the glossary. The glossary reproduced a series of "rough translations" of native terms, often borrowed from the colonialists themselves. These colonial translations were rough not only in being approximate (and thereby inaccurate) but also in that they were meant to fit the rough-and-ready methods of colonial rule. To challenge that model of "rough translation" is to pay critical and unrelenting attention to the very process of translation.

My project therefore turns toward the horizon that many gifted scholars working on the politics of translation have pointed to. They have demonstrated that what translation produces out of seeming "incommensurabilities" is neither an absence of relationship between dominant and dominating forms of knowledge nor equivalents that successfully mediate between differences, but precisely the partly opaque relationship we call "difference."[57] To write narratives and analyses that produce this translucence—and not transparency—in the relation between non-Western histories and European thought and its analytical categories is what I seek to both propose and illustrate in what follows.

This book necessarily turns around—and, if I may say so, seeks to take advantage of—a fault line central to modern European social thought. This is the divide between analytic and hermeneutic traditions in the social sciences. The division is somewhat artificial, no doubt (for most important thinkers belong to both traditions at once), but I underline it here for the purpose of clarifying my own position. Broadly speaking, one may explain the division thus. Analytic social science fundamentally attempts to "demystify" ideology in order to produce a critique that looks toward a more just social order. I take Marx to be a classic exemplar of this tradition. Hermeneutic tradition, on the other hand, produces a loving grasp of detail in search of an understanding of the diversity of human life-worlds. It produces what may be called "affective histories."[58] The first tradition tends to evacuate the local by assimilating it to some abstract universal; it does not affect my proposition in the least if this is done in an empirical idiom. The hermeneutic tradition, on the other hand, finds thought intimately tied to places and to particular forms of life. It is innately critical of the nihilism of that which is purely analytic. Heidegger is my icon for this second tradition.

The book tries to bring these two important representatives of European thought, Marx and Heidegger, into some kind of conversation with each other in the context of making sense of South Asian political modernity. Marx is critical for the enterprise, as his category "capital" gives us a way of thinking about both history and the secular figure of the human on a global scale, while it also makes history into a critical tool for understanding the globe that capitalism produces. Marx powerfully enables us to confront the ever-present tendency in the West to see European and capitalist expansion as, ultimately, a case of Western altruism. But I try to show in a pivotal chapter on Marx (Chapter 2) that addressing the problem of historicism through Marx actually pushes us toward a double position. On the one hand, we acknowledge the crucial importance of the figure of the abstract human in Marx's categories as precisely a legacy of Enlightenment thought. This figure is central to Marx's critique of capital. On the other hand, this abstract human occludes questions of belonging and diversity. I seek to destabilize this abstract figure of the universal human by bringing to bear on my reading of Marx some Heideggerian insights on human belonging and historical difference.

The first part of the book, comprising Chapters 1 to 4, is organized, as it were, under the sign of Marx. I call this part "Historicism and the

Narration of Modernity." Together, these chapters present certain critical reflections on historicist ideas of history and historical time, and their relationship to narratives of capitalist modernity in colonial India. They also attempt to explicate my critique of historicism by insisting that historical debates about transition to capitalism must also, if they are not to replicate structures of historicist logic, think of such transition as "translational" processes. Chapter 1 reproduces, in an abridged form, a programmatic statement about provincializing Europe that I published in 1992 in the journal *Representations*.[59] This statement has since received a substantial amount of circulation. *Provincializing Europe* departs from that statement in some important respects, but it also attempts to put into practice much of the program chalked out in that early statement. I have therefore included a version of the statement but added a short postscript to indicate how the present project uses it as a point of departure while deviating from it in significant ways. The other chapters (2–4) revolve around the question of how one might try to open up the Marxist narratives of capitalist modernity to issues of historical difference. Chapters 3 and 4 attempt this with concrete examples, whereas Chapter 2 ("The Two Histories of Capital") presents the theoretical pivot of the overall argument.

The second part of the book—I call it "Histories of Belonging"—I think of as organized under the sign of Heidegger. It presents some historical explorations of certain themes in the modernity of literate upper-caste Hindu Bengalis. The themes themselves could be considered "universal" to structures of political modernity: the idea of the citizen-subject, "imagination" as a category of analysis, ideas regarding civil society, patriarchal fraternities, public/private distinctions, secular reason, historical time, and so on. These chapters (5–8) work out in detail the historiographic agenda presented in the 1992 statement. I try to demonstrate concretely how the categories and strategies we have learned from European thought (including the strategy of historicizing) are both indispensable and inadequate in representing this particular case of a non-European modernity.

A word is in order about a particular switch of focus that happens in the book between Parts One and Two. The first part draws more from historical and ethnographic studies of peasants and tribals, groups one could call "subaltern" in a straightforward or sociological sense. The second part of the book concentrates on the history of educated Bengalis, a group which, in the context of Indian history, has often been described (sometimes inaccurately) as "elite." To critics who may ask why a project that arises initially from the histories of the subaltern classes in British India should turn to certain histories of the educated middle classes to make its points, I say this. This book elaborates some of the theoretical concerns that have arisen out of my involvement in *Subaltern Studies*, but it is not an attempt to represent the life practices of the subaltern classes. My purpose is to explore the capacities and limitations of certain European social and political categories in conceptualizing political modernity in the context of non-European life-worlds. In demonstrating this, I turn to historical details of particular life-worlds I have known with some degree of intimacy.

The chapters in Part Two are my attempts to begin a move away from what I have earlier described as the principle of "rough translation," and toward providing plural or conjoined genealogies for our analytical categories. Methodologically, these chapters constitute nothing more than a beginning. Bringing into contemporary relevance the existing archives of life practices in South Asia—to produce self-consciously and with the historian's methods anything like what Nietzsche called "history for life"—is an enormous task, well beyond the capacity of one individual.[60] It requires proficiency in several languages at once, and the relevant languages would vary according to the region of South Asia one is looking at. But it cannot be done without paying close and careful attention to languages, practices, and intellectual traditions present in South Asia, at the same time as we explore the genealogies of the guiding concepts of the modern human sciences. The point is not to reject social science categories but to release into the space occupied by particular European histories sedimented in them other normative and theoretical thought enshrined in other existing life practices and their archives. For it is only in this way that we can create plural normative horizons specific to our existence and relevant to the examination of our lives and their possibilities.

In pursuing this thought, I switch to Bengali middle-class material in the second part of the book. In order to provide in-depth historical examples for my propositions, I needed to look at a group of people who had been consciously influenced by the universalistic themes of the European Enlightenment: the ideas of rights, citizenship, fraternity, civil society, politics, nationalism, and so on. The task of attending carefully to the problems of cultural and linguistic translation inevitable in histories of political modernity in a non-European context required me to know, in some depth, a non-European language other than English, since English is the language that mediates my access to European thought. Bengali, my first language, has by default supplied that need. Because of the accidents and gaps of my own education, it is only in Bengali—and in a very particular kind of Bengali—that I operate with an everyday sense of the historical depth and diversity a language contains. Unfortunately, with no other language in the world (including English) can I do that. I have relied on my intimacy with Bengali to avoid the much-feared academic charges of essentialism, Orientalism, and "monolingualism." For one of the ironies of attempting to know any kind of language in depth is that the unity of the language is sundered in the process. One becomes aware of how plural a language invariably is, and how it cannot ever be its own rich self except as a hybrid formation of many "other" languages (including, in the case of modern Bengali, English).[61]

My use of specific historical material in this book from middle-class Bengali contexts is therefore primarily methodological. I have no exceptionalist or representational claims to make for India, or for that matter Bengal. I cannot even claim to have written the kind of "Bengali middle-class" histories that *Subaltern Studies* scholars are sometimes accused of doing these days. The stories I have retold in Part Two of the book relate to a microscopic minority of Hindu reformers and writers, mostly men, who pioneered political and literary (male) modernity in Bengal. These chapters do not represent the history of the Hindu Bengali middle classes today, for the modernity I discuss expressed the desires of only a minority even among the middle classes. If these desires are still to be found today in obscure niches of Bengali life, they are living well past their "expiration date." I speak from within what is increasingly—and perhaps inevitably—becoming a minor slice of Bengali middle-class history. I am also very sadly aware of the historical gap between Hindu and Muslim Bengalis, which this book cannot but reproduce. For more than a hundred years, Muslims have constituted for Hindu chroniclers what one historian once memorably called the "forgotten majority."[62] I have not been able to transcend that historical limitation, for this forgetting of the Muslim was deeply embedded in the education and upbringing I received in independent India. Indian-Bengali anticolonial nationalism implicitly normalized the "Hindu." Like many others in my situation, I look forward to the day when the default position in narratives of Bengali modernity will not sound exclusively or even primarily Hindu.

I conclude the book by trying to envisage new principles for thinking about history and futurity. Here my debt to Heidegger is most explicit. I discuss how it may be possible to hold together both secularist-historicist and nonsecularist and nonhistoricist takes on the world by engaging seriously the question of diverse ways of "being-in-the-world." This chapter seeks to bring to a culmination my overall attempt in the book to attend to a double task: acknowledge the "political" need to think in terms of totalities while all the time unsettling totalizing thought by putting into play nontotalizing categories. By drawing upon Heidegger's idea of "fragmentariness" and his interpretation of the expression "not yet" (in Division II of *Being and Time*), I seek to find a home for post-Enlightenment rationalism in the histories of Bengali belonging that I narrate. *Provincializing Europe* both begins and ends by acknowledging the indispensability of European political thought to representations of non-European political modernity, and yet struggles with the problems of representations that this indispensability invariably creates.

A NOTE ON THE TERM "HISTORICISM"

The term "historicism" has a long and complex history. Applied to the writings of a range of scholars who are often as mutually opposed and as different from each another as Hegel and Ranke, it not a term that lends itself to easy and precise definitions. Its current use has also been inflected by the recent revival it has enjoyed through the "new historicist" style of analysis pioneered by Stephen Greenblatt and others.[63] Particularly important is a tension between the Rankean insistence on attention to the uniqueness and the individuality of a historical identity or event and the discernment of a general historical trends that the Hegelian-Marxist tradition foregrounds.[64] This tension is now an inherited part of how we understand the craft and the function of the academic historian. Keeping in mind this complicated history of the term, I try to explicate below my own use of it.

Ian Hacking and Maurice Mandelbaum have provided these following, minimalist definitions for historicism:

> [historicism is] the theory that social and cultural phenomena are historically determined and that each period in history has its own values that are not directly applicable to other epochs.[65](Hacking)

> historicism is the belief that an adequate understanding of the nature of any phenomenon and an adequate assessment of its value are to be gained through considering it in terms of the place it occupied and the role which it played within a process of development.[66](Mandelbaum)

Sifting through these and other definitions, as well as some additional elements highlighted by scholars who have made the study of historicism their specialist concern, we may say that "historicism" is a mode of thinking with the following characteristics. It tells us that in order to understand the nature of anything in this world we must see it as an historically developing entity, that is, first, as an individual and unique whole—as some kind of unity at least in potentia—and, second, as something that develops over time. Historicism typically can allow for complexities and zigzags in this development; it seeks to find the general in the particular, and it does not entail any necessary assumptions of teleology. But the idea of development and the assumption that a certain amount of time elapses in the very process of development are critical to this understanding.[67] Needless to say, this passage of time that is constitutive of both the narrative and the concept of development is, in the famous words of Walter Benjamin, the secular, empty, and homogenous time of history.[68] Ideas, old and new, about discontinuities, ruptures, and shifts in the historical process have from time to time challenged the dominance of historicism, but much written history still remains deeply historicist. That is to say, it still takes its object of investigation to be internally unified, and sees it as something developing over time. This is particularly true—for all their differences with classical historicism—of historical narratives underpinned by Marxist or liberal views of the world, and is what underlies descriptions/explanations in the genre "history of"—capitalism, industrialization, nationalism, and so on.

Part One

HISTORICISM AND THE NARRATION OF MODERNITY

CHAPTER 1

Postcoloniality and the Artifice of History

Push thought to extremes.
(*Louis Althusser*)

IT HAS RECENTLY BEEN SAID in praise of the postcolonial project of *Subaltern Studies* that it demonstrates, "perhaps for the first time since colonisation," that "Indians are showing sustained signs of reappropriating the capacity to represent themselves [within the discipline of history]."[1] As a historian who is a member of the *Subaltern Studies* collective, I find the congratulation contained in this remark gratifying but premature. The purpose of this essay is to problematize the idea of "Indians" "representing themselves in history." Let us put aside for the moment the messy problems of identity inherent in a transnational enterprise such as *Subaltern Studies*, where passports and commitments blur the distinctions of ethnicity in a manner that some would regard as characteristically postmodern. I have a more perverse proposition to argue. It is that insofar as the academic discourse of history—that is, "history" as a discourse produced at the institutional site of the university—is concerned, "Europe" remains the sovereign, theoretical subject of all histories, including the ones we call "Indian," "Chinese," "Kenyan," and so on. There is a peculiar way in which all these other histories tend to become variations on a master narrative that could be called "the history of Europe." In this sense, "Indian" history itself is in a position of subalternity; one can only articulate subaltern subject positions in the name of this history.

Although the rest of this chapter will elaborate on this proposition, let me enter a few qualifications. "Europe" and "India" are treated here as hyperreal terms in that they refer to certain figures of imagination whose geographical referents remain somewhat indeterminate.[2] As figures of the imaginary they are, of course, subject to contestation, but for the moment I shall treat them as though they were given, reified categories, opposites paired in a structure of domination and subordination. I realize that in treating them thus I leave myself open to the charge of nativism, nationalism—or worse, the sin of sins, nostalgia. Liberal-minded scholars would immediately protest that any idea of a homogeneous, uncontested "Europe" dissolves under analysis. True, but just as the phenomenon of Orientalism does not disappear simply because some of us have now attained a critical awareness of it, similarly a certain version of "Europe," reified and celebrated in the phenomenal world of everyday relationships of power as the scene of the birth of the modern, continues to dominate the discourse of history. Analysis does not make it go away.

That Europe works as a silent referent in historical knowledge becomes obvious in a very ordinary way. There are at least two everyday symptoms of the subalternity of non-Western, third-world histories. Third-world historians feel a need to refer to works in European history; historians of Europe do not feel any need to reciprocate. Whether it is an Edward Thompson, a Le Roy Ladurie, a George Duby, a Carlo Ginzburg, a Lawrence Stone, a Robert Darnton, or a Natalie Davis—to take but a few names at random from our contemporary world—the "greats" and the models of the historian's enterprise are always at least culturally "European." "They" produce their work in relative ignorance of non-Western histories, and this does not seem to affect the quality of their work. This is a gesture, however, that "we" cannot return. We cannot even afford an equality or symmetry of ignorance at this level without taking the risk of appearing "old-fashioned" or "outdated."

The problem, I may add in parentheses, is not particular to historians. An unselfconscious but nevertheless blatant example of this "inequality of ignorance" in literary studies, for example, is the following sentence on Salman Rushdie from a recent text on postmodernism: "Though Saleem Sinai [of *Midnight's Children*] narrates in English . . . his intertexts for both writing history and writing fiction are doubled: they are, on the one hand, from Indian legends, films and literature and, on the other, from the West–*The Tin Drum*, *Tristram Shandy*, *One Hundred Years of Solitude* and so on."[3] It is interesting to note how this sentence teases out only those references that are from "the West." The author is under no obligation here to be able to name with any authority and specificity the Indian allusions that make Rushdie's intertextuality "doubled." This ignorance, shared and unstated, is part of the assumed compact that makes it "easy" to include Rushdie in English Department offerings on postcolonialism.

This problem of asymmetric ignorance is not simply a matter of "cultural cringe" (to let my Australian self speak) on our part or of cultural arrogance on the part of the European historian. These problems exist but can be relatively easily addressed. Nor do I mean to take anything away from the achievements of the historians I mentioned. Our footnotes bear rich testimony to the insights we have derived from their knowledge and creativity. The dominance of "Europe" as the subject of all histories is a part of a much more profound theoretical condition under which historical knowledge is produced in the third world. This condition ordinarily expresses itself in a paradoxical manner. It is this paradox that I shall describe as the second everyday symptom of our subalternity, and it refers to the very nature of social science pronouncements.

For generations now, philosophers and thinkers who shape the nature of social science have produced theories that embrace the entirety of humanity. As we well know, these statements have been produced in relative, and sometimes absolute, ignorance of the majority of humankind—that is, those living in non-Western cultures. This in itself is not paradoxical, for the more self-conscious of European philosophers have always sought theoretically to justify this stance. The everyday paradox of third-world social science is that *we* find these theories, in spite of their inherent ignorance of "us," eminently useful in understanding our societies. What allowed the modern European sages to develop such clairvoyance with regard to societies of which they were empirically ignorant? Why cannot we, once again, return the gaze?

There is an answer to this question in the writings of philosophers who have read into European history an entelechy of universal reason, if we regard such philosophy as the self-consciousness of social science. Only "Europe," the argument would appear to be, is *theoretically* (that is, at the level of the fundamental categories that shape historical thinking) knowable; all other histories are matters of empirical research that fleshes out a theoretical skeleton that is substantially "Europe." There is one version of this argument in Husserl's Vienna lecture of 1935, where he proposed that the fundamental difference between "oriental philosophies" (more specifically, Indian and Chinese) and "Greek-European science" (or as he added, "universally speaking: philosophy") was the capacity of the latter to produce "absolute theoretical insights," that is "*theoria* (universal science)," whereas the former retained a "practical-universal," and hence "mythical-religious," character. This "practical-universal" philosophy was directed to the world in a "naive" and "straightforward" manner, whereas the world presented itself as a "thematic" to *theoria*, making possible a praxis "whose aim is to elevate mankind through universal scientific reason."[4]

A similar epistemological proposition underlies Marx's use of categories such as "bourgeois" and "prebourgeois" or "capital" and "precapital." The prefix *pre* here signifies a relationship that is both chronological and theoretical. The coming of the bourgeois or capitalist society, Marx argues in the *Grundrisse* and elsewhere, gives rise for the first time to a history that can be apprehended through a philosophical and universal category, "capital." History becomes, for the first time, *theoretically* knowable. All past histories are now to be known (theoretically, that is) from the vantage point of this category, that is, in terms of their differences from it. Things reveal their categorical essence only when they reach their fullest development, or as Marx put it in that famous aphorism of the *Grundrisse*: "Human anatomy contains the key to the anatomy of the ape."[5] The category "capital," as I have discussed elsewhere, contains within itself the legal subject of Enlightenment thought.[6] Not surprisingly, Marx said in that very Hegelian first chapter of *Capital*, volume 1, that the secret of "capital," the category, "cannot be deciphered until the notion of human equality has acquired the fixity of a popular prejudice."[7] To continue with Marx's words:

> even the most abstract categories, despite their validity—precisely because of their abstractness—for all epochs, are nevertheless, . . . themselves . . . a product of historical relations. Bourgeois society is the most developed and the most complex historic organisation of production. The categories which express its relations, the comprehension of its structure, thereby also allow insights into the structure and the relations of production of all the vanished social formations out of whose ruins and elements it built itself up, whose partly still unconquered remnants are carried along within it, whose mere nuances have developed explicit significance within it, etc. . . . The intimations of higher development among the subordinate animal species . . . can be understood only after the higher development is already known. The bourgeois economy thus supplies the key to the ancient. . . .[8]

For capital or bourgeois, I submit, read "Europe" or "European."

HISTORICISM AS A TRANSITION NARRATIVE

Neither Marx nor Husserl spoke—at least in the words quoted above—in a historicist spirit. In parenthesis, we should recall that Marx's vision of emancipation entailed a journey beyond the rule of capital, in fact beyond the notion of juridical equality that liberalism holds so sacred. The maxim "from each according to his ability, to each according to his need" runs contrary to the principle of "equal pay for equal work," and this is why Marx remains—the Berlin wall notwithstanding (or not standing!)—a relevant and fundamental critic of both capitalism and liberalism and thus central to any postcolonial, postmodern project of writing history. Yet Marx's methodological/epistemological statements have not always successfully resisted historicist readings. There has always remained enough ambiguity in these statements to make possible the emergence of "Marxist" historical narratives. These narratives turn around the theme of historical transition. Most modern third-world histories are written within problematics posed by this transition narrative, of which the overriding (if often implicit) themes are those of development, modernization, and capitalism.

This tendency can be located in our own work in the *Subaltern Studies* project. My book on working-class history struggles with the problem.[9] *Modern India* by Sumit Sarkar (another colleague in the *Subaltern Studies* project), which is justifiably regarded as one of the best textbooks on Indian history written primarily for Indian universities, opens with the following sentences: "The sixty years or so that lie between the foundation of the Indian National Congress in 1885 and the achievement of independence in August 1947 witnessed perhaps the greatest transition in our country's long history. A transition, however, which in many ways remains grievously incomplete, and it is with this central ambiguity that it seems most convenient to begin our survey."[10] What kind of a transition was it that remained "grievously incomplete"? Sarkar hints at the possibility of there having been several by naming three: "So many of the aspirations aroused in the course of the national struggle remained unfulfilled—the Gandhian dream of the peasant coming into his own in *Ram-rajya* [the rule of the legendary and ideal god-king Ram], as much as the left ideals of social revolution. And as the history of independent India and Pakistan (and Bangladesh) was repeatedly to reveal, even the problems of a complete bourgeois transformation and successful capitalist development were not fully solved by the transfer of power of 1947."[11] Neither the peasant's dream of a mythical and just kingdom, nor the left's ideal of a social[ist] revolution, nor a "complete bourgeois transformation"—it is within these three absences, these "grievously incomplete" scenarios, that Sarkar locates the story of modern India.

It is also with a similar reference to "absences"—the "failure" of a history to keep an appointment with its destiny (once again an instance of the "lazy native," shall we say?)—that we announced our project of *Subaltern Studies*: "It is the study of this *historic failure of the nation to come to its own*, a failure due to the *inadequacy* of the bourgeoisie as well as of the working class to lead it into a decisive victory over colonialism and a bourgeois-democratic revolution of the classic nineteenth-century type . . . or [of the] 'new democracy' [type]—*it is the study of this failure which constitutes the central problematic of the historiography of colonial India.*"[12]

The tendency to read Indian history in terms of a lack, an absence, or an incompleteness that translates into "inadequacy" is obvious in these excerpts. As a trope it is ancient, going back to the beginnings of colonial rule in India. The British conquered and represented the diversity of Indian pasts through a homogenizing narrative of transition from a medieval period to modernity. The terms have changed with time. The medieval was once called "despotic" and the modern "the rule of law." "Feudal/capitalist" has been a later variant.

When it was first formulated in colonial histories of India, this transition narrative was an unashamed celebration of the imperialist's capacity for violence and conquest. In the nineteenth and twentieth centuries, generations of elite Indian nationalists found their subject positions as nationalists within this transition narrative that, at various times and depending on one's ideology, hung the tapestry of "Indian history" between the two poles of homologous sets of oppositions: despotic/constitutional, medieval/modern, feudal/capitalist. Within this narrative shared by imperialist and nationalist imaginations, the "Indian" was always a figure of lack. There was always, in other words, room in this story for characters who embodied, on behalf of the native, the theme of inadequacy or failure.

We do not need to be reminded that this would remain the cornerstone of imperial ideology for many years to come—subjecthood but not citizenship, as the native was never adequate to the latter—and would eventually become a strand of liberal theory itself.[13] This was, of course, where nationalists differed. For Rammohun Roy as for Bankimchandra Chattopadhyay, two of India's most prominent nationalist intellectuals of the nineteenth century, British rule was a necessary period of tutelage that Indians had to undergo in order to prepare precisely for what the British denied but extolled as the end of all history: citizenship and the nation-state. Years later, in 1951, an "unknown" Indian who successfully sold his "obscurity" dedicated the story of his life thus:

> To the memory of the
> British Empire in India
> Which conferred subjecthood on us
> But withheld citizenship;
> To which yet
> Everyone of us threw out the challenge

"Civis Britanicus Sum"
Because
All that was good and living
Within us
Was made, shaped, and quickened
By the same British Rule.[14]

In nationalist versions of this narrative, as Partha Chatterjee has shown, the peasants and the workers, the subaltern classes, were given the cross of "inadequacy" to bear for, according to this version, it was they who needed to be educated out of their ignorance, parochialism or, depending on your preference, false consciousness.[15] Even today the Anglo-Indian word "communalism" refers to those who allegedly fail to measure up to the secular ideals of citizenship.

That British rule put in place the practices, institutions, and discourse of bourgeois individualism in the Indian soil is undeniable. Early expressions of this desire to be a "legal subject"—that is, before the beginnings of nationalism—make it clear that to Indians in the 1830s and 1840s, to be a "modern individual" was become a European. *The Literary Gleaner*, a magazine in colonial Calcutta, ran the following poem in 1842, written in English by a Bengali school boy eighteen years of age. The poem was apparently inspired by the sight of ships leaving the coast of Bengal "for the glorious shores of England":

Oft like a sad bird I sigh
To leave this land, though mine own land it be;
Its green robed meads,—gay flowers and cloudless sky
Though passing fair, have but few charms for me.
For I have dreamed of climes more bright and free
Where virtue dwells and heaven-born liberty
Makes even the lowest happy;—where the eye
Doth sicken not to see man bend the knee
To sordid interest:—climes where science thrives,
And genius doth receive her guerdon meet;
Where man in his all his truest glory lives,
And nature's face is exquisitely sweet:
For those fair climes I heave the impatient sigh,
There let me live and there let me die.[16]

In its echoes of Milton and seventeenth-century English radicalism, this is obviously a piece of colonial pastiche.[17] Michael Madhusudan Dutt, the young Bengali author of this poem, eventually realized the impossibility of being European and returned to Bengali literature to become one of our finest poets. Later Indian nationalists abandoned such abject desire to be Europeans, since nationalist thought was premised precisely on the assumed universality of the project of becoming individuals, on the assumption that individual rights and abstract equality were universals that could find home anywhere in the world, that one could be both an "Indian" and a citizen at the same time. We shall soon explore some of the contradictions of this project.

Many of the public and private rituals of modern individualism became visible in India in the nineteenth century. One sees this, for instance, in the sudden flourishing in this period of the four basic genres that help express the modern self: the novel, the biography, the autobiography, and history.[18] Along with these came modern industry, technology, medicine, a quasi-bourgeois (though colonial) legal system supported by a state that nationalism was to take over and make its own. The transition narrative that I have been discussing underwrote, and was in turn underpinned by, these institutions. To think about this narrative was to think in terms of these institutions at the apex of which sat the modern state,[19] and to think about the modern or the nation-state was to think a history whose theoretical subject was Europe. Gandhi realized this as early as 1909. Referring to the Indian nationalists' demands for more railways, modern medicine, and bourgeois law, he cannily remarked in his book *Hind Swaraj* that this was to "make India English" or, as he put it, to have "English rule without the Englishman."[20] This Europe, as Michael Madhusudan Dutt's youthful and naive poetry shows, was of course nothing but a piece of fiction told to the colonized by the colonizer in the very process of fabricating colonial domination.[21] Gandhi's critique of this Europe is compromised on many points by his nationalism, and I do not intend to fetishize his text. But I find his gesture useful in developing the problematic of nonmetropolitan histories.

TO READ "LACK" OTHERWISE

I shall now return to the themes of "failure," "lack," and "inadequacy" that so ubiquitously characterize the speaking subject of "Indian" history. As in the practice of the insurgent peasants of colonial India, the first step in a critical effort must arise from a gesture of inversion.[22] Let us begin from where the transition narrative ends and read "plenitude" and "creativity" where this narrative has made us read "lack" and "inadequacy."

According to the fable of their constitution, Indians today are all "citizens." The constitution embraces almost a classically liberal definition of citizenship. If the modern state and the modern individual, the citizen, are but the two inseparable sides of the same phenomenon, as William Connolly argues in *Political Theory and Modernity*, it would appear that the end of history is in sight for us in India.[23] This modern individual, however, whose political/public life is lived in citizenship, is also supposed to have an interiorized "private" self that pours out incessantly in diaries, letters, autobiographies, novels, and, of course, in what we say to our analysts. The bourgeois individual is not born until one discovers the pleasures of privacy. But this is a very special kind of "private self"—it is, in fact, a deferred "public" self, for this bourgeois private self, as Jurgen Habermas has reminded us, is "always already oriented to an audience [*Publikum*]."[24]

Indian public life may mimic on paper the bourgeois legal fiction of citizenship—the fiction is usually performed as a farce in India—but what about the bourgeois private self and its history? Anyone who has tried to write "French" social history with Indian material would know how impossibly difficult the task is.[25] It is not that the form of the bourgeois private self did not come with European rule. There have been, since the middle of the nineteenth century, Indian novels, diaries, letters, and autobiographies, but they seldom yield pictures of an endlessly interiorized subject. Our autobiographies are remarkably "public" (with constructions of public life that are not necessarily modern) when written by men, and tell the story of the extended family when written by women.[26] In any case, autobiographies in the confessional mode are notable for their absence. The single paragraph (out of 963 pages) that Nirad Chaudhuri spends on describing his experience of his wedding night in the second volume of his celebrated and prize-winning autobiography is as good an example as any other and is worth quoting at length. I should explain that this was an arranged marriage (Bengal, 1932) and Chaudhuri was anxious lest his wife should not appreciate his newly acquired but unaffordably expensive hobby of buying records of Western classical music. Our reading of Chaudhuri is handicapped in part by our lack of knowledge of the intertextuality of his prose—there may have been at work, for instance, an imbibed puritanical revulsion against revealing "too much." Yet the passage remains a telling exercise in the construction of memory, for it is about what Chaudhuri "remembers' and "forgets" of his "first night's experience." He screens off intimacy with expressions like "I do not remember" or "I do not know how" (not to mention the very Freudian "making a clean breast of"), and this self-constructed veil is no doubt a part of the self that speaks:

> I was terribly uneasy at the prospect of meeting as wife a girl who was a complete stranger to me, and when she was brought in . . . and left standing before me I had nothing to say. I saw only a very shy smile on her face, and timidly she came and sat by my side on the edge of the bed. I do not know how after that both of us drifted to the pillows, to lie down side by side. [Chaudhuri adds in a footnote: "Of course, fully dressed. We Hindus . . . consider both extremes—fully clad and fully nude—to be modest, and everything in-between as grossly immodest. No decent man wants his wife to be an *allumeuse*."] Then the first words were exchanged. She took up one of my arms, felt it and said: "You are so thin. I shall take good care of you." I did not thank her, and I do not remember that beyond noting the words I even felt touched. The horrible suspense about European music had reawakened in my mind, and I decided to make a clean breast of it at once and look the sacrifice, if it was called for, straight in the face and begin romance on such terms as were offered to me. I asked her timidly after a while: "Have you listened to any European music?" She shook her head to say "No." Nonetheless, I took another chance and this time asked: "Have you heard the name of a man called Beethoven?" She nodded and signified "Yes." I was reassured, but not wholly satisfied. So I asked yet again: "Can you spell the name?" She said slowly: "B, E, E, T, H, O, V, E, N." I felt very encouraged . . . and [we] dozed off.[27]

The desire to be "modern" screams out of every sentence in the two volumes of Chaudhuri's autobiography. His legendary name now stands for the cultural history of Indo-British encounter. Yet in the 1,500-odd pages that he has written in English about his life, this is the only passage in which the narrative of Chaudhuri's participation in public life and literary circles is interrupted to make room for something approaching the intimate. How do we read this text, this self-making of an Indian male who was second to no one in his ardor for the public life of the citizen, yet who seldom, if ever, reproduced in writing the other side of the modern citizen, the interiorized private self unceasingly reaching out for an audience? Public without private? Yet another instance of the "incompleteness" of bourgeois transformation in India?

These questions are themselves prompted by the transition narrative that in turn situates the modern individual at the very end of history. I do not wish to confer on Chaudhuri's autobiography a representativeness it may not have. Women's writings, as I have already said, are different, and scholars have just begun to explore the world of autobiographies in Indian history. But if one result of European imperialism in India was to introduce the modern state and the idea of the nation with their attendant discourse of "citizenship," which, by the very idea of "the citizen's rights" (that is, "the rule of law"), splits the figure of the modern individual into public and private parts of the self (as the young Marx once pointed out in his "On the Jewish Question"), these themes have existed—in contestation, alliance, and miscegenation—with other narratives of the self and community that do not look to the state/citizen bind as the ultimate construction of sociality.[28] This as such will not be disputed, but my point goes further. It is that these other constructions of self and community, while documentable, will never enjoy the privilege of providing the metanarratives or teleologies (assuming that there cannot be a narrative without at least an implicit teleology) of our histories. This is partly because these narratives often themselves bespeak an antihistorical consciousness, that is, they entail subject positions and configurations of memory that challenge and undermine the subject that speaks in the name of history. "History" is precisely the site where the struggle goes on to appropriate, on behalf of the modern (my hyperreal Europe), these other collocations of memory.

HISTORY AND DIFFERENCE IN INDIAN MODERNITY

The cultural space the antihistorical invoked was by no means harmonious or nonconflictual, though nationalist thought of necessity tried to portray it as such. The antihistorical norms of the patriarchal extended family, for example, could only have had a contested existence, contested both by women's struggles and by those of the subaltern classes. But these struggles did not necessarily follow any lines that would allow us to construct emancipatory narratives by putting the "patriarchals" clearly on one side and the "liberals" on the other. The history of modern individuality in India is caught up in too many contradictions to lend itself to such a treatment.

I do not have the space here to develop the point, so I will make do with one example. It comes from the autobiography of Ramabai Ranade, the wife of the famous nineteenth-century social reformer from the Bombay Presidency, M. G. Ranade. Ramabai Ranade's struggle for self-respect was in part against the "old" patriarchal order of the extended family and for the "new" patriarchy of companionate marriage, which her reform-minded husband saw as the most civilized form of the conjugal bond. In pursuit of this ideal, Ramabai began to share her husband's commitment to public life and would often take part (in the 1880s) in public gatherings and deliberations of male and female social reformers. As she herself says: "It was at these meetings that I learnt what a meeting was and how one should conduct oneself at one."[29] Interestingly, however, one of the chief sources of opposition to Ramabai's efforts were (apart from men) the other women in the family. There is, of course, no doubt that they—her mother-in-law and her husband's sisters—spoke for the old patriarchal extended family. But it is instructive to listen to their voices (as they come across through Ramabai's text), for they also spoke for their own sense of self-respect and their own forms of struggle against men: "You should not really go to these meetings [they said to Ramabai]. . . . Even if the men want you to do these things, you should ignore them. You need not say no: but after all, you need not do it. They will then give up, out of sheer boredom. . . . You are outdoing even the European women." Or this:

> It is she [Ramabai] herself who loves this frivolousness of going to meetings. Dada [Mr. Ranade] is not at all so keen about it. But should she not have some sense of proportion of how much the women should actually do? If men tell you to do a hundred things, women should take up ten at the most. After all men do not understand these practical things!. . . The good woman [in the past] never turned frivolous like this. . . . That is why this large family . . . could live together in a respectable way. . . . But now it is all so different! If Dada suggests one thing, this woman is prepared to do three. How can we live with any sense of self-respect then and how can we endure all this?[30]

These voices, combining the contradictory themes of nationalism, patriarchal clan-based ideology, and women's struggles against men, and opposed at the same time to friendship between husbands and wives, remind us of the deep ambivalences that marked the trajectory of the modern private and bourgeois individuality in colonial India. Yet historians manage, by maneuvers reminiscent of the old "dialectical" card trick called "negation of negation," to deny a subject position to this voice of ambivalence. The evidence of what I have called "the denial of the bourgeois private and of the historical subject" is acknowledged in their accounts but subordinated to the supposedly higher purpose of making Indian history look like yet another episode in the universal and (in their view, the ultimately victorious) march of citizenship, of the nation-state, and of themes of human emancipation spelled out in the course of the European Enlightenment and after. It is the figure of the citizen that speaks through these histories. And so long as that happens, my hyperreal Europe will continually return to dominate the stories we tell. "The modern" will then continue to be understood, as Meaghan Morris has so aptly put it in discussing her own Australian context, "as a *known history*, something which has *already happened elsewhere*, and which is to be reproduced, mechanically or otherwise, with a local content." This can only leave us with a task of reproducing what Morris calls "the project of positive unoriginality."[31]

Yet the "originality"—I concede that this is a bad term—of the idioms through which struggles have been conducted in the Indian subcontinent has often been in the sphere of the nonmodern. One does not have to subscribe to the ideology of clannish patriarchy, for instance, to acknowledge that the metaphor of the sanctified and patriarchal extended family was one of the most important elements in the cultural politics of Indian nationalism. In the struggle against British rule, it was frequently the use of this idiom—in songs, poetry, and other forms of nationalist mobilization—that allowed Indians to fabricate a sense of community and to retrieve for themselves a subject position from which to address the British. I will illustrate this with an example from the life of Gandhi, "the father of the nation," to highlight the political importance of this cultural move on the part of the "Indian."

My example refers to the year 1946. There had been ghastly riots between Hindus and Muslims in Calcutta over the impending partition of the country into India and Pakistan. Gandhi was in the city, fasting in protest over the behavior of his own people. And here is how an Indian intellectual recalls the experience:

> Men would come back from their offices in the evening and find food prepared by the family [meaning the womenfolk] ready for them; but soon it would be revealed that the women of the home had not eaten the whole day. They [apparently] had not felt hungry. Pressed further, the wife or the mother would admit that they could not understand how they could go on [eating] when Gandhiji was dying for their own crimes. Restaurants and amusement centres did little business; some of them

> were voluntarily closed by the proprietors. . . . The nerve of feeling had been restored; the pain began to be felt. . . . Gandhiji knew when to start the redemptive process.[32]

We do not have to take this description literally, but the nature of the community imagined in these lines is clear. It blends, in Gayatri Spivak's words, "the feeling of community that belongs to national links and political organisations" with "that other feeling of community whose structural model is the [clan or the extended] family]."[33] Colonial Indian history is replete with instances in which Indians arrogated subjecthood to themselves precisely by mobilizing, within the context of modern institutions and sometimes on behalf of the modernizing project of nationalism, devices of collective memory that were both antihistorical and nonmodern.[34] This is not to deny the capacity of Indians to act as subjects endowed with what we in the universities would recognize as "a sense of history" (what Peter Burke calls "the renaissance of the past") but to insist that there were also contrary trends, that in the multifarious struggles that took place in colonial India, antihistorical constructions of the past often provided very powerful forms of collective memory.[35]

There is, then, this double bind through which the subject of "Indian" history articulates itself. On the one hand, it is both the subject and the object of modernity, because it stands for an assumed unity called the "Indian people" that is always split into two—a modernizing elite and a yet-to-be modernized peasantry. As a split subject, however, it speaks from within a metanarrative that celebrates the nation-state; and of this metanarrative the theoretical subject can only be a hyperreal "Europe," a Europe constructed by the tales that both imperialism and nationalism have told the colonized. The mode of self-representation that the "Indian" can adopt here is what Homi Bhabha has justly called "mimetic."[36] Indian history, even in the most dedicated socialist or nationalist hands, remains a mimicry of a certain "modern" subject of "European" history and is bound to represent a sad figure of lack and failure. The transition narrative will always remain "grievously incomplete."

On the other hand, maneuvers are made within the space of the mimetic—and therefore within the project called "Indian" history—to represent the "difference" and the "originality" of the "Indian," and it is in this cause that the antihistorical devices of memory and the antihistorical "histories" of the subaltern classes are appropriated. Thus peasant/worker constructions of "mythical" kingdoms and "mythical" pasts/futures find a place in texts that are designated "Indian" history precisely through a procedure that subordinates these narratives to the rules of evidence and to the secular, linear calendar that the writing of "history" must follow. The antihistorical, antimodern subject, therefore, cannot speak as "theory" within the knowledge procedures of the university even when these knowledge procedures acknowledge and "document" its existence. Much like Spivak's "subaltern" (or the anthropologist's peasant who can only have a quoted existence in a larger statement that belongs to the anthropologist alone), this subject can only be spoken for and spoken of by the transition narrative, which will always ultimately privilege the modern (that is, "Europe").[37]

So long as one operates within the discourse of "history" produced at the institutional site of the university, it is not possible simply to walk out of the deep collusion between "history" and the modernizing narrative(s) of citizenship, bourgeois public and private, and the nation-state. "History" as a knowledge system is firmly embedded in institutional practices that invoke the nation-state at every step—witness the organization and politics of teaching, recruitment, promotions, and publication in history departments, politics that survive the occasional brave and heroic attempts by individual historians to liberate "history" from the metanarrative of the nation state. One only has to ask, for instance: Why is history a compulsory part of education of the modern person in all countries today, including those that did quite comfortably without it until as late as the eighteenth century? Why should children all over the world today have to come to terms with a subject called "history" when we know that this compulsion is neither natural nor ancient?[38]

It does not take much imagination to see that the reason for this lies in what European imperialism and third-world nationalisms have achieved together: the universalization of the nation-state as the most desirable form of political community. Nation-states have the capacity to enforce their truth games, and universities, their critical distance notwithstanding, are part of the battery of institutions complicit in this process. "Economics" and "history" are the knowledge forms that correspond to the two major institutions that the rise (and later universalization) of the bourgeois order has given to the world—the capitalist mode of production and the nation-state ("history" speaking to the figure of the citizen).[39] A critical historian has no choice but to negotiate this knowledge. She or he therefore needs to understand the state on its own terms, that is, in terms of its self-justificatory narratives of citizenship and modernity. Because these themes will always take us back to the universalist propositions of "modern" (European) political philosophy—even the "practical" science of economics, which now seems "natural" to our constructions of world systems, is (theoretically) rooted in the ideas of ethics in eighteenth-century Europe[40]—a third-world historian is condemned to knowing "Europe" as the original home of the "modern," whereas the "European" historian does not share a comparable predicament with regard to the pasts of the majority of humankind. Thus the everyday subalternity of non-Western histories with which I began this paper.

Yet the understanding that "we" all do "European" history with our different and often non-European archive opens up the possibility of a politics and project of alliance between the dominant metropolitan histories and the subaltern peripheral pasts. Let us call this the project of provincializing "Europe," the Europe that modern imperialism and (third-world) nationalism have, by their collaborative venture and violence, made universal. Philosophically, this project must ground itself in a radical critique and transcendence of liberalism (that is, of the bureaucratic constructions of citizenship, the modern state, and bourgeois privacy that classical political philosophy has produced), a ground that late Marx shares with certain moments in both poststructuralist thought and feminist philosophy. In particular, I am emboldened by Carole Pateman's courageous declaration—in her remarkable book *The Sexual Contract*—that the very conception of the modern individual belongs to patriarchal categories of thought.[41]

PROVINCIALIZING EUROPE?

The project of provincializing "Europe" refers to a history that does not yet exist; I can therefore speak of it only in a programmatic manner. To forestall misunderstanding, however, I must spell out what it is *not*, while outlining what it could be.

To begin with, it does not call for a simplistic, out-of-hand rejection of modernity, liberal values, universals, science, reason, grand narratives, totalizing explanations, and so on. Jameson has recently reminded us that the easy equation often made between "a philosophical conception of totality" and "a political practice of totalitarianism" is "baleful."[42] What intervenes between the two is history—contradictory, plural, and heterogeneous struggles whose outcomes are never predictable, even retrospectively, in accordance with schemas that seek to naturalize and domesticate this heterogeneity. These struggles include coercion (both on behalf of and against modernity)—physical, institutional, and symbolic violence, often dispensed with dreamy-eyed idealism—and this violence plays a decisive role in the establishment of meaning, in the creation of truth regimes, in deciding, as it were, whose and which "universal" wins. As intellectuals operating in academia, we are not neutral to these struggles and cannot pretend to situate ourselves outside of the knowledge procedures of our institutions.

The project of provincializing Europe therefore cannot be a project of cultural relativism. It cannot originate from the stance that the reason/science/universals that help define Europe as the modern are simply "culture-specific" and therefore only belong to the European cultures. For the point is not that Enlightenment rationalism is always unreasonable in itself, but rather a matter of documenting how—through what historical process—its "reason," which was not always self-evident to everyone, has been made to look obvious far beyond the ground where it originated. If a language, as has been said, is but a dialect backed up by an army, the same could be said of the narratives of "modernity" that, almost universally today, point to a certain "Europe" as the primary habitus of the modern.

This Europe, like "the West," is demonstrably an imaginary entity, but the demonstration as such does not lessen its appeal or power. The project of provincializing Europe has to include certain additional moves: first, the recognition that Europe's acquisition of the adjective "modern" for itself is an integral part of the story of European imperialism within global history; and second, the understanding that this equating of a certain version of Europe with "modernity" is not the work of Europeans alone; third-world nationalisms, as modernizing ideologies par excellence, have been equal partners in the process. I do not mean to overlook the anti-imperial moments in the careers of these nationalisms; I only underscore the point that the project of provincializing Europe cannot be a nationalist, nativist, or atavistic project. In unraveling the necessary entanglement of history—a disciplined and institutionally regulated form of collective memory—with the grand narratives of rights, citizenship, the nation-state, and public and private spheres, one cannot but problematize "India" at the same time as one dismantles "Europe."

The idea is to write into the history of modernity the ambivalences, contradictions, the use of force, and the tragedies and ironies that attend it. That the rhetoric and the claims of (bourgeois) equality, citizen's rights, of self-determination through a sovereign nation-state have in many circumstances empowered marginal social groups in their struggles is undeniable—this recognition is indispensable to the project of *Subaltern Stud-*

ies. What is effectively played down, however, in histories that either implicitly or explicitly celebrate the advent of the modern state and the idea of citizenship is the repression and violence that are as instrumental in the victory of the modern as is the persuasive power of its rhetorical strategies. Nowhere is this irony—the undemocratic foundations of "democracy"—more visible than in the history of modern medicine, public health, and personal hygiene, the discourses of which have been central in locating the body of the modern individual at the intersection of the public and the private (as defined by, and subject to negotiations with, the state). The triumph of this discourse, however, has always been dependent on the mobilization, on its behalf, of effective means of physical coercion. I say "always" because this coercion is both originary/foundational (that is, historic) as well as pandemic and quotidian. Of foundational violence, David Arnold gives a good example in a recent essay on the history of the prison in India. The coercion of the colonial prison, Arnold shows, was integral to some of the earliest and pioneering research on the medical, dietary, and demographic statistics of India, for the prison was where Indian bodies were accessible to modernizing investigators.[43] Of the coercion that continues in the names of the nation and modernity, a recent example comes from the Indian campaign to eradicate smallpox in the 1970s. Two American doctors (one of them presumably of Indian origin) who participated in the process thus describe their operations in a village of the Ho tribe in the Indian state of Bihar:

> In the middle of gentle Indian night, an intruder burst through the bamboo door of the simple adobe hut. He was a government vaccinator, under orders to break resistance against smallpox vaccination. Lakshmi Singh awoke screaming and scrambled to hide herself. Her husband leaped out of bed, grabbed an axe, and chased the intruder into the courtyard. Outside a squad of doctors and policemen quickly overpowered Mohan Singh. The instant he was pinned to the ground, a second vaccinator jabbed smallpox vaccine into his arm. Mohan Singh, a wiry 40-year-old leader of the Ho tribe, squirmed away from the needle, causing the vaccination site to bleed. The government team held him until they had injected enough vaccine. . . . While the two policemen rebuffed him, the rest of the team overpowered the entire family and vaccinated each in turn. Lakshmi Singh bit deep into one doctor's hand, but to no avail.[44]

There is no escaping the idealism that accompanies this violence. The subtitle of the article in question unselfconsciously reproduces both the military and the do-gooding instincts of the enterprise. It reads: "How an army of samaritans drove smallpox from the earth."

Histories that aim to displace a hyperreal Europe from the center toward which all historical imagination currently gravitates will have to seek out relentlessly this connection between violence and idealism that lies at the heart of the process by which the narratives of citizenship and modernity come to find a natural home in "history." I register a fundamental disagreement here with a position taken by Richard Rorty in an exchange with Jurgen Habermas. Rorty criticizes Habermas for the latter's conviction "that the story of modern philosophy is an important part of the story of the democratic societies' attempts at self-reassurance."[45] Rorty's statement follows the practice of many Europeanists who speak of the histories of these "democratic societies" as if these were self-contained histories complete in themselves, as if the self-fashioning of the West was something that occurred only within its self-assigned geographical boundaries. At the very least, Rorty ignores the role that the "colonial theater" (both external and internal)—where the theme of "freedom" as defined by modern political philosophy was constantly invoked in aid of the ideas of "civilization," "progress," and latterly "development"—played in the process of engendering this "reassurance." The task, as I see it, will be to wrestle with ideas that legitimize the modern state and its attendant institutions, in order to return to political philosophy—in the same way as suspect coins are returned to their owners in an Indian bazaar—its categories whose global currency can no longer be taken for granted.[46]

And, finally—since "Europe" cannot after all be provincialized within the institutional site of the university whose knowledge protocols will always take us back to the terrain where all contours follow that of my hyperreal Europe—the project of provincializing Europe must realize within itself its own impossibility. It therefore looks to a history that embodies this politics of despair. It will have been clear by now that this is not a call for cultural relativism or for atavistic, nativist histories. Nor is this a program for a simple rejection of modernity, which would be, in many situations, politically suicidal. I ask for a history that deliberately makes visible, within the very structure of its narrative forms, its own repressive strategies and practices, the part it plays in collusion with the narratives of citizenships in assimilating to the projects of the modern state all other possibilities of human solidarity. The politics of despair will require of such history that it lay bare to its readers the reasons why such a predicament is necessarily inescapable. This is a history that will attempt the impossible: to look toward its own death by tracing that which resists and escapes the best human effort at translation across cultural and other semiotic systems, so that the world may once again be imagined as radically heterogeneous. This, as I have said, is impossible within the knowledge protocols of academic history, for the globality of academia is not independent of the globality that the European modern has created. To attempt to provincialize this "Europe" is to see the modern as inevitably contested, to write over the given and privileged narratives of citizenship other narratives of human connections that draw sustenance from dreamed-up pasts and futures where collectivities are defined neither by the rituals of citizenship nor by the nightmare of "tradition" that "modernity" creates. There are of course no (infra)structural sites where such dreams could lodge themselves. Yet they will recur so long as the themes of citizenship and the nation-state dominate our narratives of historical transition, for these dreams are what the modern represses in order to be.

A postscript (1999): This chapter reproduces in an abridged form my first attempt (in 1992) at articulating the problem of provincializing Europe. This original statement remains a point of departure for what follows. Several of the themes broached in it—the need to critique historicism and to find strategies for thinking about historical difference without abandoning one's commitment to theory—are fleshed out in the rest of the book. But the "politics of despair" I once proposed with some passion do not any longer drive the larger argument presented here.

CHAPTER 2

The Two Histories of Capital

THIS CHAPTER presents a selective but close reading of Marx. Marx's critique of "capital" builds into the category two aspects of nineteenth-century European thought that have been central to the history of intellectual modernity in South Asia: the abstract human of the Enlightenment and the idea of history.[1] Furthermore, Marx makes these two elements of thought into critical tools for understanding the capitalist mode of production and modern European imperialism. Debates of privilege and social justice in India are still animated by the rationalism, humanism, historicism, and anti-imperialism of this legacy. The project of *Subaltern Studies* would have been unthinkable without the vibrant tradition of Marxist historiography in India.[2] Marx's writings thus constitute one of the founding moments in the history of anti-imperial thought. To revisit them is to rework the relationship between postcolonial thinking and the intellectual legacies of post-Enlightenment rationalism, humanism, and historicism. A book such as this one cannot afford to ignore Marx.

There are various ways of thinking about the fact that global capitalism exhibits some common characteristics, even though every instance of capitalist development has a unique history. One can, for one, see these differences among histories as invariably overcome by capital in the long run. The thesis of uneven development, on the other hand, sees these differences as negotiated and contained—though not always overcome—*within* the structure of capital. And third, one can visualize capital itself as producing and proliferating differences. Historicism is present in all of these different modes of thought. They all share a tendency to think of capital in the image of a unity that arises in one part of the world at a particular period and then develops globally over historical time, encountering and negotiating historical differences in the process. Or even when "capital" is ascribed a "global," as distinct from a European, beginning, it is still seen in terms of the Hegelian idea of a totalizing unity—howsoever internally differentiated—that undergoes a process of development in historical time.

E. P. Thompson's deservedly celebrated essay on "Time, Work-Discipline and Industrial Capitalism" is a good example of historicist thought. Thompson's argument, fundamentally, is something like this: the worker in the history of advanced capitalism has no option but to shed precapitalist habits of work and "internalize" work-discipline. The same fate awaits the worker in the third world. The difference between these two figures of the worker is a matter of the secular historical time that elapses in the global career of capitalism. Thompson writes: "Without time-discipline we could not have the insistent energies of the industrial man; and whether this discipline comes in the form of Methodism, or of Stalinism, or of nationalism, it will come to the developing world."[3]

This statement sees capitalism as a force that encounters historical difference, but encounters it as something external to its own structure. A struggle ensues in this encounter, in the course of which capital eventually cancels out or neutralizes the contingent differences between specific histories. Through however tortuous a process, it converts those specificities into historically diverse vehicles for the spread of its own logic. This logic is ultimately seen not only as single and homogeneous but also as one that unfolds over (historical) time, so that one can indeed produce a narrative of a putatively single capitalism in the familiar "history-of" genre. Thompson's argument both recognizes and neutralizes difference, it is difficult for it to avoid a stagist view of history.

Even the liberal idea that capital works not so much by canceling out historical differences as by proliferating and converting differences into sets of preference, into taste, can harbor an implicit faith in historicism. A recent discussion on the Indian market in the financial press provides a good example of this view. "Repeat after me," the *Wall Street Journal* of 11 October 1996 has the Indian "marketing guru" Titoo Ahluwalia saying to potential American explorers of the Indian market: " 'India is different, India is different, India is different.' "[4] (Ahluwalia, a person from the business world, has clearly not had the academic fear of "Orientalism" instilled in him!) The aim of his statement is to help transnational capital appreciate and transform (Indian) historical and cultural differences so that such differences could be treated as measures of preference or taste. Making different life choices would then be like choosing between different brands of products.

Difference initially appears intractable in this discussion among capitalists. The same issue of the *Wall Street Journal* quotes Daralus Ardeshir, managing director of Nestle India Ltd., the local unit of the Swiss food company, as saying, " 'When I visit my father's house, I still kiss his feet.' " The journal's columnist remarks: "Indians who study in the US and Britain often return home to arranged marriages. Even many people who have chosen their own spouses opt to move in with their extended families. Such traditional family bonds inhibit Western marketeers' access. Yuppies, deferring to their elders, don't make household purchasing decisions." Indian social practices appear to have the effect of deferring—and thus making different—India's adoption of certain themes generally held to be canonical for both classical and late-capitalist modernity. India seems to resist these capitalist ideals: dissolution of the hierarchies of birth (Indians continue with paternal/parental authority); sovereignty of the individual (the norm of the extended family persists); and consumer choice (yuppies defer to their elders). The enduring quality of these features in Indian society so baffles the sensibility of the *Wall Street Journal* experts that they end up having recourse to a figure of paradox familiar in discussions of India. This is a trope that depicts the Indian capitalist/consumer subject as capable of doing the impossible: "Indians are capable of living in several centuries at once."[5]

These quotations show how obdurately and densely a certain idea of history and historical time as indicative of progress/development inhabit the everyday language with which an article in a leading American capitalist publication seeks to explain the nature of the Indian market. The "several centuries" in question above are identifiable as such precisely because the speaker has supposedly seen them separated and clearly laid out in some other (that is, European) history. This is what allows him to claim that in a place such as India, these different historical periods look as if they have been all telescoped into a confusing instant. This is merely an aesthetic variety of the thesis of "uneven development." Images of this kind are very popular in modernist descriptions of India. It is almost a cliché to describe India as precisely that state of contradiction in which an ancient temple can stand by the side of a modern factory, or a "nuclear scientist" can start the day "by offering *puja* (devotional offerings) to a clay god."[6]

These readings of the relationship between the logic of capital and historical difference appear to sustain historicism in different ways. In Thompson's position, historical time is the period of waiting that the third world has to go through for capital's logic to be fulfilled. One can modify the Thompsonian position by the thesis of "uneven development" and make distinctions between "formal" and "real" subsumption to capital.[7] But that still keeps in place the idea of empty and homogenous historical time, for it is over such time that the gap could ever close between the two kinds of subsumption. (In other words, one assumes that "real" capitalism means "real" subsumption.) Or one can also, it seems, speak through an image that collapses historical time into the aesthetic paradox of Indians "living in several centuries at once."

My analysis of the relationship between historical difference and the logic of capital aims to distance itself from this historicism. In what follows, I pursue Marx's philosophical concept "capital" in order to examine closely two of his ideas that are inseparable from his critique of capital: that of "abstract labor" and the relation between capital and history. Marx's philosophical category "capital" is global in its historical aspiration and universal in its constitution. Its categorial structure, at least in Marx's own argumentation, is predicated on the Enlightenment ideas of juridical equality and the abstract political rights of citizenship.[8] Labor that is juridically and politically free—and yet socially unfree—is a concept embedded in Marx's category of "abstract labor." The idea of "abstract labor" thus combines the Enlightenment themes of juridical freedom (rights, citizenship) and the concept of the universal and abstract human who bears this freedom. More importantly, it is also a concept central to Marx's explanation of why capital, in fulfilling itself in history, necessarily creates the ground for its own dissolution. Examining the idea of "abstract labor" then enables us to see what is politically and intellectually at stake—both for Marx and for the students of his legacy—in the humanist heritage of the European Enlightenment.

The idea of "abstract labor" also leads us to the question of how the logic of capital relates to the issue of historical difference. As is well known, the idea of "history" was central to Marx's philosophical understanding of "capital." "Abstract labor" gave Marx a way of explaining how the capitalist mode of production managed to extract from peoples and histories that were all different a homogenous and common unit for measuring human activity. "Abstract labor" may thus be read as part of an account of how the logic of capital sublates into itself the differences of history. In the second part of this chapter, however, I try to develop a distinction that Marx made between two kinds of histories: histories "posited by capital" and histories that do not belong to capital's "life process." I call them History 1 and History 2, and I explore the distinction between them to show how Marx's thoughts may be made to resist the idea that the logic of capital sublates differences into itself. I conclude this chapter by trying to open Marxian categories up to some Heideggerian ruminations on the politics of human diversity.

CAPITAL, ABSTRACT LABOR, AND THE SUBLATION OF DIFFERENCE

Fundamental to Marx's discussion of capital is the idea of the commodity, and fundamental to the conception of the commodity is the question of difference. Marx emphasizes the point that the process of generalized exchange through which things assume the commodity form is one that actually connects differences in the world. That is to say, commodity exchange is about exchanging things that are different in their histories, material properties, and use-value. Yet the commodity form, intrinsically, is supposed to make differences—however material they may be in their historical appearance—immaterial for the purpose of exchange. Commodity form does not negate difference, but it holds it in suspension so that we can exchange things as different from one another as beds and houses. But how could that happen? That is the question Marx begins with. How could things that apparently have nothing in common form items in a series of capitalist exchanges, a series that Marx would come to conceptualize as being, in principle, continuous and infinite?

Readers will remember Marx's argument with Aristotle on this point. Aristotle, in the course of his deliberations in *Nichomachean Ethics* on such issues as justice, equality, and proportionality, focused on the problem of exchange. Exchange, he argued, was central to the formation of a community. But a community was always made up of people who were "different and unequal." On the ground, there were only infinite incommensurabilities. Every individual was different. In order for exchange to act as the basis of community, there had to be a way of finding a common measure so as to equalize that which was not equal. Aristotle underscores this imperative: "they must be equalized [with respect to a measure]; and everything that enters into an exchange must somehow be comparable." Without this measure of equivalence that allowed for comparison, there could be no exchange and hence no community.[9]

Aristotle solved this problem by calling on the idea of "convention" or law. For him, money represented such a convention: "It is for this purpose [of exchanging dissimilar goods] that money has been introduced: it becomes, as it were, a middle term. . . . [I]t tells us how many shoes are equal to a house."[10] Money, according to Aristotle, represented a kind of a general agreement, a convention. A convention was ultimately arbitrary, held in place by the sheer force of law that simply reflected the will of the community. Aristotle would therefore introduce into his discussion the note of a radical political will that, as Castoriadis comments, is absent from the text of *Capital*. In Aristotle's words: "money has by general agreement come to represent need. That is why it has the name of 'currency': it exists by current convention and not by nature, and it is in our power to change and invalidate it."[11] The translator of Aristotle points out that "the Greek word for 'money,' 'coin,' 'currency' (nomisma) comes from the same root as nomos, 'law,' 'convention.' "[12]

Marx begins *Capital* by critiquing Aristotle. For Aristotle, what brought shoes and houses into a relationship of exchange was mere convention—"a makeshift for practical purposes," as Marx translated it. It was not satisfactory for Marx to think that the term that mediated between differences among commodities could be simply a convention, that is, an arbitrary expression of political will. Referring to Aristotle's argument that that there could not be a "homogeneous element i.e. the common substance" between the bed (Marx's copy of Aristotle seems to have used the example of the bed and not the shoe!) and the house, Marx asked: "But why not? Towards the bed the house represents something equal, in so far as it represents what is really equal, both in the bed and the house. And that is—human labour."[13]

This human labor, the common substance mediating differences, was Marx's conception of "abstract labor," which he described as "the secret of the expression of value." It was only in a society in which bourgeois values had acquired a hegemonic status that this "secret" could be unveiled. It "could not be deciphered," wrote Marx, "until the concept of human equality had already acquired the permanence of a fixed popular opinion." This in turn was possible "only in a society where the commodity-form [was] the universal form of the product of labour" and where, therefore, "the dominant social relation [was] the relation between men as the possessors of commodities." The slave-holding nature of the society of ancient Greece, according to Marx, occluded Aristotle's analytical vision. And by the same logic, the generalization of contractual equality under bourgeois hegemony created the historical conditions for the birth of Marx's insights.[14] The idea of abstract labor was thus a particular instance of the idea of the abstract human—the bearer of rights, for example—popularized by Enlightenment philosophers.

This common measure of human activity, abstract labor, is what Marx opposes to the idea of real or concrete labor (which is what any specific form of labor is). Simply put, "abstract labor" refers to an "indifference to any specific kind of labor." By itself, this does not make for capitalism.

A "barbarian" society—Marx's expression—may be marked by the absence of a developed division of labor such that its members "are fit by nature to do anything."[15] By Marx's argument, it was conceivable that such a society would have abstract labor even though its members would not be able to theorize it. Such theorizing would be possible only in the capitalist mode of production, in which the very activity of abstracting became the most common strand of all or most other kinds of labor.

What, indeed, was abstract labor? Sometimes Marx would write as though abstract labor was pure physiological expenditure of energy. For example: "If we leave aside the determinate quality of productive activity, and therefore the useful character of the labour, what remains is its quality of being an expenditure of human labour-power. Tailoring and weaving, although they are qualitatively different productive activities, are both a productive expenditure of human brains, muscles, nerves, hands etc."[16] Or this: "On the other hand, all labour is an expenditure of human labour-power, in the physiological sense, and it is in this quality of being equal, or abstract, human labour that it forms the value of commodities."[17] But students of Marx from different periods and as different from one another as I. I. Rubin, Cornelius Castoriadis, Jon Elster, and Moishe Postone have shown that to conceive of abstract labor as a substance, as a Cartesian *res extensa*, to reduce it to "nervous and muscular energy," is either to misread Marx (as Rubin and Postone argue) or to repeat a mistake of Marx's thoughts (as Castoriadis and Elster put it).[18] Marx does speak of "abstract labor" as a "social substance" possessing objectivity, but immediately qualifies this objectivity as spectral, "phantom-like" rather than thinglike: "Let us now look at the products of [abstract] labour. There is nothing left of them in each case but the same *phantom-like objectivity*: they are merely congealed quantities of homogenous human labour, i.e. of human labour-power expended without regard to the form of its expenditure. . . . As crystals of this social substance, which is common to them all, they are values—commodity values."[19] Or as he explains elsewhere in *Capital*: "Not an atom of matter enters into the objectivity of commodity as values; in this it is the direct opposite of the coarsely sensuous objectivity of commodities as physical objects. . . . [C]ommodities possess an objective character as values only in so far as they are all expressions of an identical social substance, human labour, that their objective character as value is purely social."[20]

How, then, is abstract labor to be conceptualized? If we do not share Marx's assumption that the exchange of commodities in capitalism necessarily forms a continuous and infinite series, then abstract labor is perhaps best understood as a performative, practical category. To organize life under the sign of capital is to act *as if* labor could indeed be abstracted from all the social tissues in which it is always embedded and which make any particular labor—even the labor of abstracting—concrete. Marx's "barbarians" had abstract labor: anybody in that society could take up any kind of activity. But their "indifference to specific labor" would not be as visible to an analyst as in a capitalist society because in the case of these hypothetical barbarians, this indifference itself would not be universally performed as a separate, specialized kind of labor. That is to say, the very concrete labor of abstracting would not be separately observable as a general feature of the many different kinds of specific labor that that society undertook. In a capitalist society, on the other hand, the particular work of abstracting would itself become an element of most or all other kinds of concrete labor, and would be thus be more visible to an observer. As Marx put it: "As a rule, most general abstractions arise only in the midst of the richest possible concrete development, where one thing appears as common to many, to all. Then it ceases to be thinkable in a particular form alone."[21] "Such a state of affairs," says Marx, "is at its most developed in the most modern form of existence of bourgeois society—in the United States. Here, then, for the first time, the point of departure of modern economics, namely the abstraction of the category 'labour,' 'labour as such,' labour pure and simple, becomes true in practice."[22] Notice Marx's expression: "The abstraction . . . becomes true in practice." Marx could not have written a clearer statement indicating that abstract labor was not a substantive entity, not physiological labor, not a calculable sum of muscular and nervous energy. It referred to a practice, an activity, a concrete performance of the work of abstraction, similar to what one does in the analytical strategies of economics when one speaks of an abstract category called "labor."

Sometimes Marx writes as if abstract labor was what one obtained after going through a conscious and intentional process—much as in certain procedures of mathematics—of mentally stripping commodities of their material properties:

> If . . . *we disregard* the use-value of commodities, only one property remains, that of products of labour. . . . If *we make abstraction* from its use-value, we also abstract from the material constituents and forms which make it a use-value. It is no longer a table, a house, a piece of yarn

> or any other useful thing. All its sensuous characteristics are extinguished. . . . With the disappearance of the useful character of the products of labour, the useful character of the kinds of labour embodied in them also disappears; this in turn entails the disappearance of the different concrete forms of labour. They can no longer *be distinguished*, but are all together reduced to the same kind of labour, human labour in the abstract.[23]

Expressions like "if we disregard" or "if we abstract," "they can no longer be distinguished," and so on, may give the impression that Marx is writing of a human subject who either "disregards," "abstracts," or "distinguishes." But Marx's discussion of factory discipline makes it clear that Marx does not visualize the abstraction of labor inherent in the process of exchange of commodities as a large-scale mental operation. Abstraction happens in and through practice. It precedes one's conscious recognition of its existence. As Marx put it: "Men do not . . . bring the products of their labour into relation with each other as values because they see these objects merely as the material integuments of homogeneous human labour. The reverse is true: by equating their different products to each other in exchange as values, they equate their different kinds of labour as human labour. They do this without being aware of it."[24] Marx's logic here, as in many other places in his writings, is retrospective.[25]

Marx agreed with Aristotle more than he acknowledged—abstract labor, one could indeed say, was a capitalist convention, so the middle term in commodity exchange remains a matter of convention, after all. But Marx's position that the convention was not the result of prior conscious decision to abstract would not have allowed Aristotle's voluntarism: "it is in our power to change and invalidate [this convention]." (Castoriadis erects a picture of voluntarist revolutionary politics by adopting this Aristotelian position into his Marxism.)[26] Marx decodes abstract labor as a key to the hermeneutic grid through which capital requires us to read the world.

Disciplinary processes are what make the performance of abstraction—the labor of abstracting—visible (to Marx) as a constitutive feature of the capitalist mode of production. The typical division of labor in a capitalist factory, the codes of factory regulation, the relationship between the machinery and men, state legislation guiding the organization of factory lives, the foreman's work—all these make up what Marx calls discipline.

The division of labor in the factory is such, he writes, that it "creates a continuity, a uniformity, a regularity, an order, and even an intensity of labour quite different from that found in an independent handicraft."[27] In sentences that anticipate a basic theme of Foucault's *Discipline and Punish* by about a hundred years, he describes how the "overseer's book of penalties replaces the slave-driver's lash [in capitalist management]." "All punishments," he writes, "naturally resolve themselves into fines and deductions from wages."[28]

Factory legislation also participates in this performance of disciplinary abstraction. First, says Marx, it "destroys both the ancient and transitional forms behind which the domination of capital is still partially hidden. . . . [I]n each individual workshop it enforces uniformity, regularity, order and economy" and thus contributes to sustaining the assumption that human activity is indeed measurable on a homogenous scale.[29] But it is in the way the law—and through the law, the state and the capitalist classes—imagine laborers through biological/physiological categories such as "adults," "adult males," "women," and "children" that the work of reductive abstraction of labor from all its attendant social integuments is performed. This mode of imagination, Marx further shows us, is also what structures from within the process of production. It is dyed into capital's own vision of the worker's relationship with the machine.

In the first volume of *Capital*, Marx uses the rhetorical ploy of staging what he calls the "voice" of the worker in order to bring out the character of his category "labor." This voice shows how abstracted the category "worker" or "labor" is from the social and the psychic processes that we common-sensically associate with "the everyday." Firstly, it reduces age, childhood, health, strength and so on to biological or physiological statements, separate from the diverse and historically specific experiences of aging, of being a child, of being healthy, and so on. "Apart from the natural deterioration through age etc.," Marx's category "worker" says to the capitalist in a voice that is introspective as well, "I must be able to work tomorrow with the same normal amount of strength, health, and freshness as today." This abstraction means that "sentiments" are no part of this imaginary dialogue between the abstracted laborer and the capitalist who is himself also a figure of abstraction. The voice of the worker says: "I . . . demand a working day of normal length . . . without any appeal to your heart, for in money matters sentiment is out of place. You may be a model citizen, perhaps a member of the R.S.P.C.A., and you may be in the odour of sanctity as well; but the thing you represent as you come face to face with me has no heart in its breast."[30] In this figure of a rational collective entity, the worker, Marx grounds the question of working-class unity, either potential or realized. The question of working-class unity is not a matter of emotional or psychic solidarity of empirical workers, as numerous humanist-Marxist labor historians, from E. P. Thompson on, have often imagined it to be. The "worker" is an abstract and collective subject by its very constitution.[31] It is within that collective and abstract subject that, as Gayatri Spivak has reminded us, the dialectic of class-in-itself and class-for-itself plays out.[32] The "collective worker," says Marx, "formed out of the combination of a number of individual specialized workers, is the item of machinery specifically characteristic of the manufacturing period."[33]

Marx constructs a fascinating and suggestive, though fragmentary, history of factory machinery in the early phase of industrialization in England. This history shows two simultaneous processes at work in capitalist production, both of them critical to Marx's understanding of the category "worker" as an abstract, reified category. The machine produces "the technical subordination of the worker to the uniform motions of the instruments of labour."[34] It transfers the motive force of production from the human or the animal to the machine, from living to dead labor. This can only happen on two conditions: that the worker be first reduced to his or her biological, and therefore, abstract body, and that the movements of this abstract body be then broken up and individually designed into the very shape and movement of the machine. "[C]apital absorbs labour into itself," Marx would write in his notebooks, quoting Goethe, " 'as though its body were by love possessed.' "[35] The body that the machine comes to possess is the abstract body it ascribed to the worker to begin with. Marx writes: "large-scale industry was crippled in its whole development as long as its characteristic instrument of production, the machine, owed its existence to personal strength and personal skill, [and] depended on the muscular development, the keenness of sight and the manual dexterity with which specialized workers . . . wielded their dwarf-like instruments."[36] Once the worker's capacity for labor could be translated into a series of practices that abstracted the personal from the social, the machine could appropriate the abstract body these practices posited. One tendency of the whole process was to make even the humanness of the capacity for labor redundant: "it is purely accidental that the motive power happens to be clothed in the form of human muscles; wind, water, steam could just as well take man's place."[37] At the same time, though, capital—in Marx's understanding of its logic—would not be able to do without living, human labor.

ABSTRACT LABOR AS CRITIQUE

The universal category "abstract labor" has a twofold function in Marx: it is both a description and a critique of capital. Whereas capital makes abstractions real in everyday life, Marx uses these very same abstractions to give us a sense of the everyday world that capitalist production creates—witness, for example, Marx's use of such reductively biological categories as "women," "children," "adult males," "childhood," "family functions," or the "expenditure of domestic labour."[38] The idea of abstract labor reproduces the central feature of the hermeneutic of capital—how capital reads human activity.

Yet "abstract labor" is also a critique of the same hermeneutic because it—the labor of abstracting—defines for Marx a certain kind of unfreedom. He calls it "despotism." This despotism is structural to capital; it is not simply historical. Thus Marx writes that "capital is constantly compelled to wrestle with the insubordination of the workers," and he says that discipline, "[the] highly detailed specifications, which regulate, with military uniformity, the times, the limits, the pauses of work by the stroke of the clock, . . . developed out of circumstances as natural laws of the modern mode of production. Their formulation, official recognition and proclamation by the state were the result of a long class struggle."[39] Here Marx is not speaking merely of a particular historical stage, the transition from handicrafts to manufactures in England, when "the full development of its [capital's] own peculiar tendencies comes up against obstacles from many directions . . . [including] the habits and the resistance of the male workers."[40] He is also writing about "resistance to capital" as something internal to capital itself. As Marx writes elsewhere, the self-reproduction of capital "moves in contradictions *which are constantly overcome but just as constantly posited.*" Just because, he adds, capital gets ideally beyond every limit posed to it by "national barriers and prejudices," "it does not by any means follow that it has *really* overcome it."[41]

From where does such resistance arise? Many labor historians think of resistance to factory work as the result of either a clash between the requirements of industrial discipline and preindustrial habits of workers in the early phase of industrialization or a heightened level of worker consciousness in a later phase. In other words, they see it as the result of a particular historical stage of capitalist production. Marx, in contrast, locates this resistance in the very logic of capital. That is to say, he locates it in the structural "being" of capital rather than in its historical "becoming." Central to this argument is what Marx sees as the "despotism of capital," which has nothing to do with either the historical stage of capitalism or the empirical worker's consciousness. It would not matter for Marx's argument whether the capitalist country in question were a developed one or not. Resistance is the Other of the despotism inherent in capital's logic. It is also a part of Marx's point about why, if capitalism were ever to realize itself fully, it would embody the conditions for its own dissolution.

Capital's power is autocratic, writes Marx. Resistance is rooted in a process through which capital appropriates the will of the worker. Marx writes: "In the factory code, the capitalist formulates his autocratic power over his workers like a private legislator, and purely as an emanation of his own will."[42] This will, embodied in capitalist discipline, Marx describes as "purely despotic," and he uses the analogy of the army to describe the coercion at its heart: "An industrial army of workers under the command of capital requires, like a real army, officers (managers) and N.C.O.s (foremen, overseers), who command during labour process in the name of capital. The work of supervision becomes their exclusive function."[43]

Why call capitalist discipline "despotic" if all it does is to act as though labor could be abstracted and homogenized? Marx's writings on this point underscore the importance of the concept of "abstract labor"—a version of the Enlightenment figure of the abstract human—as an instrument of critique. He thought of abstract labor as a compound category, spectrally objective and yet made up of human physiology and human consciousness, both abstracted from any empirical history. The consciousness in question was pure will. Marx writes: "Factory work exhausts the nervous system to the uttermost; at the same time, [through specialization and the consequent privileging of the machine] it does away with the many-sided play of the muscles, and *confiscates every atom of freedom*, both in bodily and intellectual activity. Even the lightening of labour becomes a torture."[44]

Why would freedom have to do with something as reductively physiological as "the nervous system . . . [and] the many-sided play of muscles"? Because, Marx explains, the labor that capital presupposes "as its contradiction and its contradictory being," and which in turn "presupposes capital," is a special kind of labor, "labour not as an object, but as activity, . . . as the living source of value."[45] "As against capital, labour is the merely abstract form, the mere possibility of value-positing activity, which exists only as a capacity, as a resource in the bodiliness of the worker."[46]

Science aids in this abstraction of living labor by capital: "In machinery, the appropriation of living labour by capital achieves a direct reality. . . . It is, firstly, the analysis and application of mechanical and chemical laws, arising directly out of science, which enables the machine to perform the same labour as that previously performed by the worker. However, the development of machinery along this path occurs only after . . . all the sciences have been pressed into the service of capital."[47]

The critical point is that the labor that is abstracted in the capitalist's search for a common measure of human activity is *living*. Marx would ground resistance to capital in this apparently mysterious factor called "life." The connections between the language of classical political economy and the traditions of European thought one could call "vitalist" are an underexplored area of research, particularly in the case of Marx. Marx's language and his biological metaphors often reveal a deep influence of nineteenth-century vitalism: "Labour is the yeast thrown into it [capital], which starts it fermenting." And labor power as "commodity exists in his [the laborer's] vitality. . . . In order to maintain this from one day to the next . . . he has to consume a certain quantity of food, to replace his used-up blood etc. . . . Capital has paid him the amount of objectified labour contained in his vital forces."[48] These vital forces are the ground of constant resistance to capital. They are the abstract living labor—a sum of muscles, nerves, and consciousness/will—which, according to Marx, capital posits as its contradictory starting point. In this vitalist understanding, life, in all its biological/conscious capacity for willful activity (the "many-sided play of muscles"), is the excess that capital, for all its disciplinary procedures, always needs but can never quite control or domesticate.

One is reminded here of Hegel's discussion, in his *Logic*, of the Aristotelian category "life." Hegel accepted Aristotle's argument that "life" was expressive of a totality or unity in a living individual. "The single members of the body," Hegel writes, "are what they are only by and in relation to their unity. A hand e.g. when hewn off from the body is, as Aristotle has observed, a hand in name only, not in fact."[49] It is only with death that this unity is dismembered and the body falls prey to the objective forces of nature. With death, as Charles Taylor puts it in explaining this section of Hegel's *Logic*, "mechanism and chemism" break out of the "subordination" in which they are held "as long as life continues."[50] Life, to use Hegel's expression, "is a standing fight" against the possibility of the dismemberment with which death threatens the unity of the living body.[51] Life, in Marx's analysis of capital, is similarly a "standing fight" against the process of abstraction that is constitutive of the category "labor." It is as if the process of abstraction and ongoing appropriation of the worker's body in the capitalist mode of production perpetually threatens to effect a dismemberment of the unity of the "living body."

This unity of the body that "life" expresses, however, is something more than the physical unity of the limbs. "Life" implies a consciousness that is purely human in its abstract and innate capacity for willing. This embodied and peculiarly human "will"—reflected in "the many-sided play of muscles"—refuses to bend to the "technical subordination" under which capital constantly seeks to place the worker. Marx writes: "The presupposition of the master-servant relation is the appropriation of an alien will." This will could not belong to animals, for animals could not be part of the politics of recognition that the Hegelian master-slave relation assumed. A dog might obey a man, but the man would never know for certain if the dog did not simply look on him as another, bigger, and more powerful "dog." As Marx writes: "the animal may well provide a service but does not thereby make its owner a master." The dialectic of mutual recognition on which the master-servant relationship turned could only take place between humans: "the master-servant relation likewise belongs in this formula of the appropriation of the instruments of production. . . . [I]t is reproduced—in mediated form—in capital, and thus . . . forms a ferment of its dissolution and is an emblem of its limitation."[52]

Marx's critique of capital begins at the same point where capital begins its own life process: the abstraction of labor. Yet this labor, although abstract, is always living labor to begin with. The "living" quality of the labor ensures that the capitalist has not bought a fixed quantum of labor but rather a variable "capacity for labor," and being "living" is what makes this labor a source of resistance to capitalist abstraction. The tendency on the part of capital would therefore be to replace, as much as possible, living labor with objectified, dead labor. Capital is thus faced with its own contradiction: it needs abstract but living labor as the starting point in its cycle of self-reproduction, but it also wants to reduce to a minimum the quantum of living labor it needs. Capital will therefore tend to develop technology in order to reduce this need to a minimum. This is exactly what will create the conditions necessary for the emancipation of labor and for the eventual abolition of the category "labor" altogether. But that would also be the condition for the dissolution of capital: "[C]apital . . . —quite unintentionally—reduces human labour, expenditure of energy, to a minimum. This will redound to the benefit of emancipated labour, and is the condition of its emancipation."[53]

The subsequent part of Marx's argument runs as follows. It is capital's tendency to replace living labor by science and technology—that is, by man's "understanding of nature and his mastery over it by virtue of his presence as a social body"—that will give rise to the development of the "social individual" whose greatest need will be that of the "free development of individualities." For the "reduction of the necessary labour of society to a minimum" would correspond "to the artistic, scientific etc. development of the individuals in the time set free, and with the means created, for all of them." Capital would then reveal itself as the "moving contradiction" it is: it both presses "to reduce labour time to a minimum" and at the same time posits labor time "as the sole measure and source of wealth." It would therefore work "towards its own dissolution as the form dominating production."[54]

Thus would Marx complete the loop of his critique of capital, which looks to a future beyond capital by attending closely to the contradictions in capital's own logic. He uses the vision of the abstract human embedded in the capitalist practice of "abstract labor" to generate a radical critique of capital itself. He recognizes that bourgeois societies in which the idea of "human equality" had acquired the "fixity of popular prejudice" allowed him to use the same idea to critique them. But historical difference would remain sublated and suspended in this particular form of the critique.

HISTORIES AND THE ANALYTIC OF CAPITAL

Yet Marx was always at pains to underline the importance of history to his critique of capital: "our method indicates the point where historical investigation must enter in." Or elsewhere: "bourgeois economy" always "point[s] towards a past lying beyond this system."[55] Marx writes of the past of capital in terms of a distinction between its "being" and "becoming." "Being" refers to the structural logic of capital, that is, the state when capital has fully come into its own. Marx would sometimes call it (using Hegel's vocabulary) "real capital," "capital as such," or capital's being-for-itself. "Becoming" refers to the historical process in and through which the logical presuppositions of capital's "being" are realized. "Becoming" is not simply the calendrical or chronological past that precedes capital but the past that the category retrospectively posits. Unless the connection between land/tool and laborers is somehow severed, for example, there would never be any workers available to capital. This would happen anywhere so long as there was capitalist production—this is the sense in which a historical process of this kind is indeed a process through which the logical presuppositions of capital are worked out. This is the past posited logically by the category "capital." While this past is still being acted out, capitalists and workers do not belong to the "being" of capital. In Marx's language, they would be called *not-capitalist* (Marx's term) or *not-worker.*[56] These "conditions and presuppositions of the *becoming*, of the *arising*, of capital," writes Marx, "presuppose precisely that it is not yet in being but merely in becoming; they therefore disappear as real capital arises, capital which itself, on the basis of its own reality, posits the condition for its realization."[57]

It goes without saying that it is not the actual process of history that does the "presupposing"; the logical presuppositions of capital can only be worked out by someone with a grasp of the logic of capital. In that sense, an intellectual comprehension of the structure of capital is the precondition of this historical knowledge. For history then exemplifies only for us—the investigators—the logical presuppositions of capital even though capital, Marx would argue, needs this real history to happen, even if the reading of this history is only retrospective. "Man comes into existence only when certain point is reached. But once man has emerged, he becomes the permanent pre-condition of human history, likewise its permanent product and result."[58] Marx therefore does not so much provide us with a teleology of history as with a perspectival point from which to read the archives.

In his notes on "revenue and its sources" in the posthumously collected and published volumes entitled *Theories of Surplus Value*, Marx gave this history a name: he called it capital's antecedent "posited by itself." Here free labor is both a precondition of capitalist production and "its invariable result."[59] This is the universal and necessary history we associate with capital. It forms the backbone of the usual narratives of transition to the capitalist mode of production. Let us call this history—a past posited by capital itself as its precondition—History 1.

Marx opposes to History 1 another kind of past that we will call History 2. Elements of History 2, Marx says, are also "antecedents" of capital, in that capital "encounters them as antecedents," but—and here follows the critical distinction I want to highlight—"not as antecedents established by itself, not as forms of its own life-process."[60] To say that something does not belong to capital's life process is to claim that it does not contribute to the self-reproduction of capital. I therefore understand Marx to be saying that "antecedent to capital" are not only the relationships that constitute History 1 but also other relationships that do not lend themselves to the reproduction of the logic of capital. Only History 1 is the past "established" by capital, because History 1 lends itself to the reproduction of capitalist relationships. Marx accepts, in other words, that the total universe of pasts that capital encounters is larger than the sum of those elements in which are worked out the logical presuppositions of capital.

Marx's own examples of History 2 take the reader by surprise. They are money and commodity, two elements without which capital cannot even be conceptualized. Marx once described the commodity form as something belonging to the "cellular" structure of capital. And without money there would be no generalized exchange of commodities.[61] Yet Marx appears to suggest that entities as close and necessary to the functioning of capital as money and commodity do not necessarily belong by any natural connection to either capital's own life process or to the past posited by capital. Marx recognizes the possibility that money and commodity, as relations, could have existed in history without necessarily giving rise to capital. Since they did not necessarily look forward to capital, they make up the kind of past I have called History 2. This example of the heterogeneity Marx reads into the history of money and commodity shows that the relations that do not contribute to the reproduction of the logic of capital can be intimately intertwined with the relations that do. Capital, says Marx, has to destroy this first set of relationships as independent forms and subjugate them to itself (using, if need be, violence, that is, the power of the state): "[Capital] originally finds the commodity already in existence, but not as its own product, and likewise finds money circulation, but not as an element in its own reproduction. . . . But both of them must first be destroyed as independent forms and subordinated to industrial capital. Violence (the State) is used against interest-bearing capital by means of compulsory reduction of interest rates."[62]

Marx thus writes into the intimate space of capital an element of deep uncertainty. Capital has to encounter in the reproduction of its own life process relationships that present it with double possibilities. These relations could be central to capital's self-reproduction, and yet it is also possible for them to be oriented to structures that do not contribute to such reproduction. History 2s are thus not pasts separate from capital; they inhere in capital and yet interrupt and punctuate the run of capital's own logic.

History 1, says Marx, has to subjugate or destroy the multiple possibilities that belong to History 2. There is nothing, however, to guarantee that the subordination of History 2s to the logic of capital would ever be complete. True, Marx wrote about bourgeois society as a "contradictory development"—"relations derived from earlier forms will often be found within it only in an entirely stunted form, or even travestied." But at the same time, he described some of these "remnants" of "vanished social formations" as "partly still unconquered," signaling by his metaphor of conquest that a site of "survival" of that which seemed pre- or noncapitalist could very well be the site of an ongoing battle.[63] There remains, of course, a degree of ambiguity of meaning and an equivocation about time in this fragment of a sentence from Marx. Does "partly *still* unconquered" refer to something that is "not yet conquered" or something that is in principle "unconquerable"?

We have to remain alert to—or even make good use of—certain ambiguities in Marx's prose. At first sight, Marx may appear to be offering a historicist reading, a version of what I called a "transition narrative" in the previous chapter. Marx's categories "not-capitalist" or "not-worker," for example, could appear to belong squarely to the process of capital's becoming, a phase in which capital "is not yet in being but merely in becoming."[64] But notice the ambiguity in this phrase; what kind of a temporal space is signaled by "not yet"? If one reads "not yet" as belonging to the historian's lexicon, a historicism follows. It refers us back to the idea of history as a waiting room, a period that is needed for the transition to capitalism at any particular time and place. This is the period to which, as I have said, the third world is often consigned.

But Marx himself warns us against understandings of capital that emphasize the historical at the expense of the structural or the philosophical. The limits to capital, he reminds us, are "constantly overcome but just as constantly posited."[65] It is as though the "not yet" is what keeps capital going. I will have more to say in the final chapter about nonhistoricist ways of thinking about the structure of "not yet." But for now let me note that Marx himself allows us to read the expression "not yet" deconstructively as referring to a process of deferral internal to the very being (that is, logic) of capital. "Becoming," the question of the past of capital, does not have to be thought of as a process outside of and prior to its "being." If we describe "becoming" as the past posited by the category "capital" itself, then we make "being" logically prior to "becoming." In other words, History 1 and History 2, considered together, destroy the usual topological distinction of the outside and the inside that marks debates about whether or not the whole world can be properly said to have fallen under the sway of capital. Difference, in this account, is not something external to capital. Nor is it something subsumed into capital. It lives in intimate and plural relationships to capital, ranging from opposition to neutrality.

This is the possibility that, I suggest, Marx's underdeveloped ideas about History 2 invite us to consider. History 2 does not spell out a program of writing histories that are alternatives to the narratives of capital. That is, History 2s do not constitute a dialectical Other of the necessary logic of History 1. To think thus would be to subsume History 2 to History 1. History 2 is better thought of as a category charged with the function of constantly interrupting the totalizing thrusts of History 1.

Let me illustrate this point further with the help of a logical fable to do with the category "labor power." Let us imagine the embodiment of labor power, the laborer, entering the factory gate every morning at 8 A.M. and leaving it in the evening at 5, having put in his/her usual eight-hour day in the service of the capitalist (allowing for an hour's lunch break). The contract of law—the wage contract—guides and defines these hours. Now, following my explanation of Histories 1 and 2 above, one may say that this laborer carries with himself or herself, every morning, practices embodying these two kinds of pasts, History 1 and History 2. History 1 is the past that is internal to the structure of being of capital. The fact is, that worker at the factory represents a historical separation between his/her capacity to labor and the necessary tools of production (which now belong to the capitalist) thereby showing that he or she embodies a history that has realized this logical precondition of capital. *This worker does not therefore represent any denial of the universal history of capital.* Everything I have said about "abstract labor" will apply to him or her.

While walking through the factory gate, however, my fictional person also embodies other kinds of pasts. These pasts, grouped together in my analysis as History 2, may be under the institutional domination of the logic of capital and exist in proximate relationship to it, but they also do not belong to the "life process" of capital. They enable the human bearer of labor power to enact other ways of being in the world—other than, that is, being the bearer of labor power. We cannot ever hope to write a complete or full account of these pasts. They are partly embodied in the person's bodily habits, in unselfconscious collective practices, in his or her reflexes about what it means to relate to objects in the world as a human being and together with other human beings in his given environment. Nothing in it is automatically aligned with the logic of capital.

The disciplinary process in the factory is in part meant to accomplish the subjugation/destruction of History 2. Capital, Marx's abstract category, says to the laborer: "I want you to be reduced to sheer living labor—muscular energy plus consciousness—for the eight hours for which I have bought your capacity to labor. I want to effect a separation between your personality (that is, the personal and collective histories you embody) and your will (which is a characteristic of sheer consciousness). My machinery and the system of discipline are there to ensure that this happens. When you work with the machinery that represents objectified labor, I want you to be living labor, a bundle of muscles and nerves and consciousness, but devoid of any memory except the memory of the skills the work needs." "Machinery requires," as Horkheimer put it in his famous critique of instrumental reason, "the kind of mentality that concentrates on the present and can dispense with memory and straying imagination."[66] To the extent that both the distant and the immediate pasts of the worker—including the work of unionization and citizenship—prepare him to be the figure posited by capital as its own condition and contradiction, those pasts do indeed constitute History 1. But the idea of History 2 suggests that even in the very abstract and abstracting space of the factory that capital creates, ways of being human will be acted out in manners that do not lend themselves to the reproduction of the logic of capital.

It would be wrong to think of History 2 (or History 2s) as necessarily precapitalist or feudal, or even inherently incompatible with capital. If that were the case, there would be no way humans could be at home—dwell—in the rule of capital, no room for enjoyment, no play of desires, no seduction of the commodity.[67] Capital, in that case, would truly be a case of unrelieved and absolute unfreedom. The idea of History 2 allows us to make room, in Marx's own analytic of capital, for the politics of human belonging and diversity. It gives us a ground on which to situate our thoughts about multiple ways of being human and their relationship to the global logic of capital. But Marx does not himself think through this problem, although his method, if my argument is right, allows us to acknowledge it. There is a blind spot, it seems to me, built into his method—this is the problem of the status of the category "use value" in Marx's thoughts on value.[68] Let me explain.

Consider, for instance, the passage in the *Grundrisse* where Marx discusses, albeit briefly, the difference between making a piano and playing it. Because of his commitment to the idea of "productive labor," Marx finds it necessary to theorize the piano maker's labor in terms of its contribution to the creation of value. But what about the labor of the piano player? For Marx, that will belong to the category of "unproductive labor" that he took over (and developed) from his predecessors in political economy.[69] Let us read closely the relevant passage:

> What is *productive labour* and what is not, a point very much disputed back and forth since Adam Smith made this distinction, has to emerge from the direction of the various aspects of capital itself. *Productive labour* is only that which produces capital. Is it not crazy, asks e.g. . . . Mr Senior, that the piano maker is a *productive worker*, but not the piano player, although obviously the piano would be absurd without the piano player? But this is exactly the case. The piano maker reproduces capital, the pianist only exchanges his labour for revenue. But doesn't the pianist produce music and satisfy our musical ear, does he not even to a certain extent produce the latter? He does indeed: his labour produces something; but that does not make it *productive labour* in the *economic sense*; no more than the labour of the mad man who produces delusions is productive.[70]

This is the closest that Marx would ever come to showing a Heideggerian intuition about human beings and their relation to tools. He acknowledges that our musical ear is satisfied by the music that the pianist produces. He even goes a step further in saying that the pianist's music actually—and "to a certain extent"—"produces" that ear as well. In other words, in the intimate and mutually productive relationship between one's very particular musical ear and particular forms of music is captured the issue of historical difference, of the ways in which History 1 is always modified by History 2s. We do not all have the same musical ear. This ear, in addition, often develops unbeknownst to ourselves. This historical but unintended relation between a music and the ear it has helped "produce"—I do not like the assumed priority of the music over the ear but let that be—is like the relationship between humans and tools that Heidegger calls "the ready to hand": the everyday, preanalytical, unobjectifying relationships we have to tools, relationships critical to the process of making a world out of this earth. This relationship would belong to History 2. Heidegger does not minimize the importance of objectifying relationships (History 1 would belong here)—in his translator's prose, they are called "present-at-hand"—but in a properly Heideggerian framework of understanding, both the present-at-hand and the ready-to-hand retain their importance; one does not gain epistemological primacy over the other.[71] History 2 cannot sublate itself into History 1.

But see what happens in the passage quoted. Marx both acknowledges and in the same breath casts aside as irrelevant the activity that produces music. For his purpose, it is "no more than the labour of the mad man who produces delusions." This equation, however, between music and a madman's delusion is baleful. It is what hides from view what Marx himself has helped us see: histories that capital anywhere—even in the West—encounters as its antecedents, which do not belong to its life process. Music could be a part of such histories in spite of its later commodification because it is part of the means by which we make our "worlds" out of this earth. The "mad" man, one may say in contrast, is world-poor. He powerfully brings to view the problem of human belonging. Do not the sad figures of the often mentally ill, homeless people on the streets of the cities of America, unkempt and lonely people pushing to nowhere shopping trolleys filled with random assortments of broken, unusable objects—do not they and their supposed possessions dramatically portray this crisis of ontic belonging to which the "mad" person of late capitalism is condemned? Marx's equation of the labor of the piano player with that of the production of a madman's delusions shows how the question of History 2 comes as but a fleeting glimpse in his analysis of capital. It withdraws from his thoughts almost as soon as it has revealed itself.

If my argument is right, then it is important to acknowledge in historical explanations a certain indeterminacy that we can now read back into Thompson's statement at the beginning of this chapter: "Without time-discipline we could not have the insistent energies of the industrial man; and whether this discipline comes in the form of Methodism, or of Stalinism, or of nationalism, it will come to the developing world." If any empirical history of the capitalist mode of production is History 1 modified—in numerous and not necessarily documentable ways—by History 2s, then a major question about capital will remain historically undecidable. Even if Thompson's prediction were to come true, and a place like India suddenly and unexpectedly boasted human beings as averse to "laziness" as the bearers of the Protestant ethic are supposed to be, we would still not be able to settle one question beyond all doubt. We would never know for sure whether this condition had come about because the time discipline that Thompson documented was a genuinely universal, functional characteristic of capital, or whether world capitalism represented a forced globalization of a particular fragment of European history in which the Protestant ethic became a value. A victory for the Protestant ethic, however global, would surely not be victory for any universal. The question of whether the seemingly general and functional requirements of capital represent specific compromises in Europe between History 1 and History 2s remains, beyond a point, an undecidable question. The topic of "efficiency" and "laziness" is a good case in point. We know, for instance, that even after years of Stalinist, nationalist, and free-market coercion, we have not been able to rid the capitalist world of the ever-present theme of "laziness." It has remained a charge that has always been leveled at some group or other, ever since the beginnings of the particular shape that capital took in Western Europe.[72]

No historical form of capital, however global its reach, can ever be a universal. No global (or even local, for that matter) capital can ever represent the universal logic of capital, for any historically available form of capital is a provisional compromise made up of History 1 modified by somebody's History 2s. The universal, in that case, can only exist as a place holder, its place always usurped by a historical particular seeking to present itself as the universal. This does not mean that one gives away the universals enshrined in post-Enlightenment rationalism or humanism. Marx's immanent critique of capital was enabled precisely by the universal characteristics he read into the category "capital" itself. Without that reading, there can only be particular critiques of capital. But a particular critique cannot by definition be a critique of "capital," for such a critique could not take "capital" as its object. Grasping the category "capital" entails grasping its universal constitution. My reading of Marx does not in any way obviate that need for engagement with the universal. What I have attempted to do is to produce a reading in which the very category "capital" becomes a site where both the universal history of capital and the politics of human belonging are allowed to interrupt each other's narrative.

Capital is a philosophical-historical category—that is, historical difference is not external to it but is rather constitutive of it. Its histories are History 1 constitutively but unevenly modified by more and less powerful History 2s. Histories of capital, in that sense, cannot escape the politics of the diverse ways of being human. Capital brings into every history some of the universal themes of the European Enlightenment, but on inspection the universal turns out to be an empty place holder whose unstable outlines become barely visible only when a proxy, a particular, usurps its position in a gesture of pretension and domination. And that, it seems to me, is the restless and inescapable politics of historical difference to which global capital consigns us. At the same time, the struggle to put in the ever-empty place of History 1 other histories with which we attempt to modify and domesticate that empty, universal history posited by the logic of capital in turn brings intimations of that universal history into our diverse life practices.

The resulting process is what historians usually describe as "transition to capitalism." This transition is also a process of translation of diverse life-worlds and conceptual horizons about being human into the categories of Enlightenment thought that inhere in the logic of capital. To think of Indian history in terms of Marxian categories is to translate into such categories the existing archives of thought and practices about human relations in the subcontinent; but it is also to modify these thoughts and practices with the help of these categories. The politics of translation involved in this process work in both ways. Translation makes possible the emergence of the universal language of the social sciences. But it must also, by the same token, enable a project of approaching social-science categories from both sides of the process of translation, in order to make room for two kinds of histories. One consists of *analytical* histories that, through the abstracting categories of capital, eventually tend to make all places exchangeable with one another. History 1 is just that, analytical history. But the idea of History 2 beckons us to more *affective* narratives of human belonging where life forms, although porous to one another, do not seem exchangeable through a third term of equivalence such as abstract labor. Translation/transition to capitalism in the mode of History 1 involves the play of three terms, the third term expressing the measure of equivalence that makes generalized exchange possible. But to explore such translation/transition on the register of History 2 is to think about translation as a transaction between two categories without any third category intervening. Translation here is more like barter than a process of generalized exchange. We need to think in terms of both modes of translation simultaneously, for together they constitute the condition of possibility for the globalization of capital across diverse, porous, and conflicting histories of human belonging. But globalization of capital is not the same as capital's universalization. Globalization does not mean that History 1, the universal and necessary logic of capital so essential to Marx's critique, has been realized. What interrupts and defers capital's self-realization are the various History 2s that always modify History 1 and thus act as our grounds for claiming historical difference.

CHAPTER 3

Translating Life-Worlds into Labor and History

In truth, the historian can never get away from the question of time in history: time sticks to his thinking like soil to a gardener's spade.
(*Fernand Braudel*)

The vulgar representation of time as a precise and homogeneous continuum has . . . diluted the Marxist concept of history.
(*Giorgio Agamben*)

A SECULAR SUBJECT like history faces certain problems in handling practices in which gods, spirits, or the supernatural have agency in the world. My central examples concern the history of work in South Asia. Labor, the activity of producing, is seldom a completely secular activity in India; it often entails, through rituals big and small, the invocation of divine or superhuman presence. Secular histories are usually produced by ignoring the signs of these presences. Such histories represent a meeting of two systems of thought, one in which the world is ultimately, that is, in the final analysis, disenchanted, and the other in which humans are not the only meaningful agents. For the purpose of writing history, the first system, the secular one, translates the second into itself. It is this translation—its methods and problems—that interests me here as part of a broader effort to situate the question of subaltern history within a postcolonial critique of modernity and of history itself.

This critique has to issue from within a dilemma: writing subaltern history, that is, documenting resistance to oppression and exploitation, must be part of a larger effort to make the world more socially just. To wrench subaltern studies away from the keen sense of social justice that gave rise to the project would violate the spirit that gives this project its sense of commitment and intellectual energy. Indeed, it may be said that it would violate the history of realist prose in India, for it may legitimately be argued that the administration of justice by modern institutions requires us to imagine the world through the languages of the social sciences, that is, as disenchanted.

THE TIME OF HISTORY

History's own time is godless, continuous and, to follow Benjamin, empty and homogeneous. By this I mean that in employing modern historical consciousness (whether in academic writing or outside of it), we think of a world that, in Weber's description, is already disenchanted. Gods, spirits, and other "supernatural" forces can claim no agency in our narratives. Further, this time is empty because it acts as a bottomless sack: any number of events can be put inside it; and it is homogeneous because it is not affected by any particular events; its existence is independent of such events and in a sense it exists prior to them. Events happen in time but time is not affected by them. The time of human history—as any popular book on the evolution of this universe will show—merges with the time of prehistory, of evolutionary and geological changes that go back to the beginning of the universe. It is part of nature. This is what allowed J.B.S. Haldane once to write a book with the title *Everything Has a History.*[1] Hence the time of Newtonian science is no different from the time historians automatically assume to provide the ontological justification of their work. Things may move faster or slower in this time; that is simply the problem of speed. And the time may be cyclical or linear—the weeks belong to cyclical time, the English years go in hundred-year cycles, while the procession of years is a line. And historians may with justification talk about different regions of time: domestic time, work time, the time of the state, and so on. But all these times, whether cyclical or linear, fast or slow, are normally treated not as parts of a system of conventions, a cultural code of representation, but as something more objective, something belonging to "nature" itself. This nature/culture division becomes clear when we look at nineteenth-century uses of archaeology, for instance, in dating histories that provided no easy arrangements of chronology.

It is not that historians and philosophers of history are unaware of such a commonplace as the claim that modern historical consciousness, or for that matter academic history, are genres of recent origin (as indeed are the imaginations of the modern sciences). Nor have they been slow to acknowledge the changes these genres have undergone since their inception.[2] The naturalism of historical time, however, lies in the belief that *everything* can be historicized. So although the non-naturalness of the discipline of history is granted, the assumed universal applicability of its method entails the further assumption that it is always possible to assign people, places, and objects to a naturally existing, continuous flow of historical time.[3] Thus, irrespective of a society's own understanding of temporality, a historian will always be able to produce a time line for the globe, in which for any given span of time, the events in areas X, Y, and Z can be named. It does not matter if any of these areas were inhabited by peoples such as the Hawaiians or the Hindus who, some would say, did not have a "sense of chronological history"—as distinct from other forms of memories and understandings of historicity—before European arrival. Contrary to whatever they themselves may have thought and however they may have organized their memories, the historian has the capacity to put them into a time we are all supposed to have shared, consciously or not. History as a code thus invokes a natural, homogeneous, secular, calendrical time without which the story of human evolution/civilization—a single human history, that is—cannot be told. In other words, the code of the secular calendar that frames historical explanations has this claim built into it: that independent of culture or consciousness, people exist in historical time. That is why it is always possible to discover "history" (say, after European contact) even if you were not aware of its existence in the past. History is supposed to exist in the same way as the earth.

I begin with the assumption that, to the contrary, this time, the basic code of history, does not belong to nature, that is, it is not completely independent of human systems of representation. It stands for a particular formation of the modern subject. This is not to say that this understanding of time is false or that it can be given up at will. But clearly the kind of correspondence that exists between our sensory worlds and the Newtonian imagination of the universe, between our experience of secular time and the time of physics, breaks down in many post-Einsteinian constructions. In the Newtonian universe, as in historical imagination, events are more or less separable from their descriptions: what is factual is seen as translatable from mathematics into prose or between different languages. Thus an elementary book on Newtonian physics can be written completely in the Bengali alphabet and numerals, using a minimum of mathematical signs. But not so with post-Einsteinian physics: language strains wildly when trying to convey in prose the mathematical imagination contained in an expression like "curved space" (for, thinking commonsensically, in what would such a space exist if not in space itself?). In this second case, one might say that the assumption of translatability does not quite hold, that really the imagination of Einsteinian physics is best learned through the language of its mathematics—for we are speaking of a universe of events in which the events cannot be separated from their descriptions. Modern physics, one might say, took the linguistic turn early in this century. Post-Einsteinian cosmology, as the physicist Paul Davis puts it, makes even mathematical sense only so long as we do not try to take "a God's-eye-view" of the universe (that is, so long as one does not try to totalize or to view a "whole.") "I have grown used to dealing with the weird and wonderful world of relativity," writes Davis. "The ideas of space-warps, distortions in time and space and multiple universes have become everyday tools in the strange trade of the theoretical physics. . . . I believe that the reality exposed by modern physics is fundamentally alien to the human mind, and defies all power of direct visualization."[4]

Historians writing after the so-called linguistic turn may not any longer think that events are completely accessible by language, but the more sober among them would strive to avoid lunacy by resorting to weaker versions of this position. As put in the recent book *Telling the Truth about History*, historians, writing in the aftermath of postmodernism, would work toward an ideal of "workable truths," approximations of facts that can be agreed to by all even after it is granted that language and representations always form a (thin?) film between us and the world (in the same way as we can mostly ignore the insights of Einsteinian or quantum physics in negotiating our everyday movements in practical life). The higher ideal of translatability between different languages—thus Vietnamese history into Bengali—remains worth striving for even if language always foils the effort. This ideal—a modified Newtonianism—is, in their view, the historian's protection against the sheer madness of postmodernist and cultural-relativist talk about "untranslatability," "incommensurability," and all that.[5]

Unlike the world of the physicist Paul Davis, then, in the discipline of history the imagination of reality is dependent on the capacities of "the human mind," its powers of visualization. The use of the definite article—"the human mind"—is critical here, for this reality aspires to achieve a status of transparency with regard to particular human languages, an ideal of objectivity entertained by Newtonian science in which translation between different languages is mediated by the higher language of science itself. Thus *pani* in Hindi and "water" in English can both be mediated by H_2O. Needless to say, it is only the higher language that is capable of appreciating, if not expressing, the capacities of "the human mind." I would suggest that the idea of a godless, continuous, empty, and homogeneous time, which history shares with the other social sciences and modern political philosophy as a basic building block, belongs to this model of a higher, overarching language. It represents a structure of generality, an aspiration toward the scientific, that is built into conversations that take the modern historical consciousness for granted.

A proposition of radical untranslatability therefore comes as a problem to the universal categories that sustain the historian's enterprise. But it is also a false problem created by the very nature of the universal itself, which aims to function as a supervening general construction mediating between all the particulars on the ground. The secular code of historical and humanist time—that is, a time bereft gods and spirits—is one such universal. Claims about agency on behalf of the religious, the supernatural, the divine, and the ghostly have to be mediated in terms of this universal. The social scientist-historian assumes that contexts explain particular gods: if we could all have the same context, then we would all have the same gods. But there is a problem. Although the sameness of our sciences can be guaranteed all the world over, the sameness of our gods and spirits could not be proved in the same objective manner (notwithstanding the protestations of the well-meaning that all religions speak of the same God). So it could be said that although the sciences signify some kind of sameness in our understanding of the world across cultures, the gods signify differences (bracketing for the moment the history of conversion, which I touch on very briefly in a later section). Writing about the presence of gods and spirits in the secular language of history or sociology would therefore be like translating into a universal language that which belongs to a field of differences.

The history of work in South Asia provides an interesting example of this problem. "Work" or "labor" are words deeply implicated in the production of universal sociologies. Labor is one of the key categories in the imagination of capitalism itself. In the same way that we think of capitalism as coming into being in all sorts of contexts, we also imagine the modern category "work" or "labor" as emerging in all kinds of histories. This is what makes possible studies in the familiar genre of "history of work in . . .". In this sense, labor or work has the same status in my posing of the problem as does H_2O in the relation between "water" and *pani*. Yet the fact is that the modern word "labor," as every historian of labor in India would know, translates into a general category a whole host of words and practices with divergent and different associations. What complicates the story further is the fact that in a society such as the Indian, human activity (including what one would, sociologically speaking, regard as labor) is often associated with the presence and agency of gods or spirits in the very process of labor. *Hathiyar puja* or the "worship of tools," for example, is a common and familiar festival in many north

Indian factories. How do we—and I mean narrators of the pasts of the subaltern classes in India—handle this problem of the presence of the divine or the supernatural in the history of labor as we render this enchanted world into our disenchanted prose—a rendering required, let us say, in the interest of social justice? And how do we, in doing this, retain the subaltern (in whose activity gods or spirits present themselves) as the subjects of their histories? I shall go over this question by examining the work of three *Subaltern Studies* historians who have produced fragments of histories of work in the context of "capitalist transition" in India: Gyan Prakash, Gyan Pandey, and myself. I hope that my discussion will have something to say about the historian's enterprise in general.

RENDERING ACTIVITY INTO "LABOR"

Let me begin with an example from my own research in labor history. Consider the following description from the 1930s of a particular festival (still quite common in India) that entails the worshiping of machinery by workers: "In some of the jute mills near Calcutta the mechanics often sacrifice goats at this time [autumn]. A separate alter is erected by the mechanics. . . . Various tools and other emblems are placed upon it. . . . Incense is burnt. . . . Towards evening a male goat is thoroughly washed . . . and prepared for a . . . final sacrifice. . . . The animal is decapitated at one stroke . . . [and] the head is deposited in the . . . sacred Ganges."[6] This particular festival is celebrated in many parts of north India as a public holiday for the working class, on a day named after the engineer god Vishvakarma.[7] How do we read it? To the extent that this day has now become a public holiday in India, it has obviously been subjected to a process of bargaining between employers, workers, and the state. One could also argue that insofar as the ideas of recreation and leisure belong to a discourse of what makes labor efficient and productive, this "religious" holiday itself belongs to the process through which labor is managed and disciplined, and is hence a part of the history of emergence of abstract labor in commodity form. The very public nature of the holiday shows that it has been written into an emergent national, secular calendar of production. We could thus produce a secular narrative that would apply to any working-class religious holiday anywhere. Christmas or the Muslim festival Id could be seen in the same light. The difference between Vishvakarma *puja* (worship) and Christmas or Id would then be explained anthropologically, that is, by holding another master code—"culture" or "religion"—constant and universal. The differences between religions are by definition incapable of bringing the master category "culture" or "religion" into any kind of crisis. We know that these categories are problematic, that not all people have what is called "culture" or "religion" in the English senses of these words, but we have to operate as though this limitation was not of any great moment. This was exactly how I treated this episode in my own book. The eruption of Vishvakarma *puja* interrupting the rhythm of production, was no threat to my Marxism or secularism. Like many of my colleagues in labor history, I interpreted worshiping machinery—an everyday fact of life in India, from taxis to scooter-rickshaws, minibuses and lathe machines—as "insurance policy" against accidents and contingencies. That in the so-called religious imagination (as in language), redundancy—the huge and, from a strictly functionalist point of view, unnecessarily elaborate panoply of iconography and rituals—proved the poverty of a purely functionalist approach never deterred my secular narrative. The question of whether or not the workers had a conscious or doctrinal belief in gods and spirits was also wide of the mark; after all, gods are as real as ideology is—that is to say, they are embedded in practices.[8] More often than not, their presence is collectively invoked by rituals rather than by conscious belief.

The history of weaving in colonial Uttar Pradesh that Gyanendra Pandey examines in his book *The Construction of Communalism in Colonial North India* offers us another example of this tension between the general secular time of history and the singular times of gods and spirits.[9] Pandey's work deals with the history of a group of north Indian Muslim weavers called the Julahas, and constitutes an imaginative and radical reexamination of the stereotype of religious fanatics through which the British colonial officials saw them. The Julahas, Pandey shows, faced increasing displacement from their craft as a consequence of colonial economic policies in the late nineteenth and early twentieth centuries, and this had much to do with the history of their cultural practices in this period. Pandey's text, however, reveals problems of translation of specific life-worlds into universal sociological categories similar to those implicit in my work on labor. On the one hand, he has recourse to a general figure, that of the weaver-in-general during early industrialization. This figure underlies his comparativist gestures toward European history. The sentence that opens the chapter on "The Weavers" in *The Making of the English Working Class*—"The history of the weavers in the nineteenth century is haunted by the legend of better days"—and a generalizing quote from Marx act as the framing devices for Pandey's chapter. "[B]ecause of the nature of their occupation," writes Pandey, "weavers *everywhere* [emphasis added] have been commonly dependent on money lenders and other middlemen and vulnerable to the play of the market forces, all the more so in the era of the advance of industrial capitalism." He adds a few pages later, "The history of the north Indian weavers in the nineteenth century is, in E. P. Thompson's phrase from another context, 'haunted by the legend of better days.' "[10] Further on, he writes in a Thompsonian vein of the weavers' "fight to preserve . . . their economic and social status" and of "their memories and pride" that fueled this fight.[11]

Pandey's own sensitivity and his acute sense of responsibility to the evidence, on the other hand, present the question of historical difference—already hinted at in his gesture of assigning the Thompson quote to a "different context"—in such a forceful manner that the comparativist stance is rendered problematic. The "legend of better days" in Thompson's account is entirely secular. It refers to a "golden age" made up of stories about "personal and . . . close" relations between "small masters and their men," about "strongly organized trade societies," relative material prosperity, and the weavers' "deep attachment to the values of independence."[12] A Wesleyan church in the village community marked, if anything, the physical and existential distance between the loom and God, and the weavers, as Thompson says, were often critical of the "parish-church pa'son's."[13] God, on the other hand, is ever present in the phenomenology of weaving in north India as Pandey explains it, and it is a god quite different from Thompson's. Indeed, as Pandey makes clear, work and worship were two inseparable activities to the Julahas, so inseparable, in fact, that one could ask whether it makes sense to ascribe to them the identity that only in the secular and overlapping languages of the census, administration, and sociology becomes the name of their "occupation": weaving.

As Pandey explains, his weavers called themselves *nurbaf* or "weavers of light." Drawing on Deepak Mehta's study of "Muslim weavers in two villages of Bara Banki district," Pandey notes "the intimate connection between work and worship in the lives of the weavers, and the centrality of the weavers' major religious text (or *kitab*), the *Mufid-ul-Mominin* in the practice of both." The *Mufid-ul-Mominin*, Pandey adds, "relates how the practice of weaving came into the world at its very beginning" (by a version of the Adam, Hawwa [Eve], and Jabril [Gabriel] story), and "lists nineteen supplicatory prayers to be uttered in the different stages of weaving."[14] During the initiation of novices, notes Pandey, "all the prayers associated with the loom are recited. . . . The male head-weaver, in whose household this initiation takes place, reads out all of Adam's questions and Jabril's answers from the *kitab* during the first six days of the month when both the loom and the *karkhana* [workshop or work loom] are ritually cleaned." When the loom is passed on from father to son, again, "the entire conversation between Adam and Jabril is read out once by a holy man."[15] This was nothing like an enactment of some memory of times past, nor a nostalgia, as Thompson puts it, haunted by the "legend of better days." The *Mufid-ul-Mominin* is not a book that has come down to present-day Julahas from a hoary antiquity. Deepak Mehta expressed the view to Pandey that it "may well date from the post-Independence period." Pandey himself is of the opinion that "it is more than likely that the *Mufid-ul-Mominin* came to occupy this place as *the* "book" of the weavers fairly recently—not before the late nineteenth or the early twentieth century, in any case—for it is only from that time that the name "Momin" (the faithful) was claimed as their own by the weavers.[16]

So Pandey's Julahas are actually both like and unlike Thompson's weavers, and it is their difference that allows us to raise the question of how one may narrate the specificity of their life-world as it was increasingly being subordinated to the globalizing urges of capital. Was their god the same as the god of Thompson's Wesleyans? How would one translate into the other? Can we take this translation through some idea of a universal and freely exchangeable God, an icon of our humanism? I cannot answer the question because of my ignorance—I have no intimate knowledge of the Julahas' god—but Richard Eaton's study of Islamic mysticism in the Deccan in India gives us some further insights into what I might crudely call nonsecular and phenomenological histories of labor.[17]

Eaton quotes from seventeenth-, eighteenth-, and early nineteenth-century Sufi manuscripts songs that Muslim women in the Deccan sang while engaged in such tasks as spinning, grinding millet, and rocking children to sleep. They all reveal, as Eaton puts it, "the ontological link between God, the Prophet, the *pir* [the Sufi teacher], and [work]."[18] "As the *chakki* [grindstone] turns, so we find God," Eaton quotes an early eighteenth-century song: "it shows its life in turning as we do in breathing." Divinity is sometimes brought to presence through analogy, as in:

> The *chakki's* handle resembles *alif*, which means Allah;
> And the axle is Muhammad . . .

and sometimes in ways that make the bodily labor of work and worship absolutely inseparable experiences, as is suggested by this song sung at the spinning wheel:

As you take the cotton, you should do *zikr-i jali* [*zikr*: mention of God].
As you separate the cotton, you should do *zikr-i qalbi*,
And as you spool the thread you should do *zikr-i ʿaini*.
Zikr should be uttered from the stomach through the chest,
And threaded through the throat.
The threads of breath should be counted one by one, oh sister,
Up to twenty-four thousand.
Do this day and night,
And offer it to your *pir* as a gift.[19]

Straining further toward the imaginative richness of this phenomenology of turning the *chakki* would require us to explore the differences between the different kinds of *zikrs* mentioned in this song and to enter imaginatively the "mysticism" (once again, a generalizing name!) that envelops them. But on what grounds do we assume, ahead of any investigation, that this divine presence invoked at every turn of the *chakki* will translate neatly into a secular history of labor so that—transferring the argument back to the context of the tool-worshiping factory workers—the human beings collected in modern industries may indeed appear as the subjects of a metanarrative of Marxism, socialism, or even democracy?

Gyan Prakash's monograph on the history of "bonded" labor in Bihar in colonial India contains an imaginative discussion of *bhuts* (spirits) that are thought to have supernatural power over humans, although they do not belong to the pantheon of divinity. Prakash documents how these *bhuts* intercede in the relations of agrarian production in Gaya, particularly a special category of *bhut* called *malik devata* (spirits of dead landlords). But Prakash's monograph, at the same time, is part of a conversation in academia, as all good historical work has to be, for that is the condition of its production. This conversation is an inherent part of the process through which books and ideas express their own commodified character; they all participate in a general economy of exchange made possible through the emergence of abstract, generalizing categories. It is instructive, therefore, to see how the protocols of that conversation necessarily structure Prakash's explanatory framework and thereby obliterate from view some of the tensions of irreducible plurality I am trying to visualize in the history of labor itself. Prakash writes: "In such fantastic images, the malik's [landlord's] power was reconstructed. Like Tio, the devil worshipped by the miners in Bolivia, the malik represented subordination of the Bhuinyas [laborers] by landlords. But whereas Tio expressed the alienation of miners from capitalist production, as Michael Taussig so eloquently argues, the malik devata of colonial Gaya echoed the power of the landlords over kamiyas, based on land control."[20]

Now, Prakash is not wrong in any simple sense; his sensitivity to the "logic of ritual practice" is, in fact, exemplary. It is just that I am reading this passage to understand the conditions for intertextuality that govern its structure and allow a conversation to emerge between Prakash's study, located in colonial Bihar in India, and Taussig's study of labor in the Bolivian tin mines. How do the specific and the general come together in this play of intertextuality, as we try to think our way to the art of "holding apart" that which coalesces *within* the process of this "coming together" of disparate histories?

The intertextuality of the passage from Prakash is based on the simultaneous assertion of likeness and dissimilarity between *malik devata* and Tio: witness the contradictory moves made by the two phrases, "like Tio" and "whereas Tio." They are similar in that they have similar relationship to "power": they both "express" and "echo" it. Their difference, however, is absorbed in a larger theoretic-universal difference between two different kinds of power, capitalist production and "land control." Pressed to the extreme, "power" itself must emerge as a last-ditch universal-sociological category (as indeed happens in texts that look for sociology in Foucault). But this "difference" already belongs to the sphere of the general.

Normally, the condition for conversation between historians and social scientists working on disparate sites is a structure of generality within which specificities and differences are contained. Paul Veyne's distinction between "specificity" and "singularity" is relevant here. As Veyne puts it: "History is interested in individualized events . . . but it is not interested in their individuality; it seeks to understand them—that is, to find among them a kind of generality or, more precisely, of specificity. It is the same with natural history; its curiosity is inexhaustible, all the species matter to it and none is superfluous, but it does not propose the enjoyment of their singularity in the manner of the beastiary of the Middle Ages, in which one could read descriptions of noble, beautiful, strange or cruel animals."[21]

The very conception of the "specific" as it obtains in the discipline of history, in other words, belongs to the structure of a general that necessarily occludes our view of the singular. Of course, nothing exists out there as a "singular-in-itself." Singularity is a matter of viewing. It comes into being as that which resists our attempt to see something as a particular instance of a general idea or category. Philosophically, it is a limiting concept, since language itself mostly speaks of the general. Facing the singular might be a question of straining against language itself; it could, for example, involve the consideration of the manner in which the world, after all, remains opaque to the generalities inherent in language. Here, however, I am using a slightly weaker version of the idea. By "singular" I mean that which defies the generalizing impulse of the sociological imagination. To indicate what the struggle to view the singular might entail in the case of writing history, let us begin from a seemingly absurd position and see what happens to our intertextual conversation if we reverse the propositions of Prakash (and Taussig) to claim first, that the "alienation of [Bolivian] miners from capitalist production" expressed the spirit of Tio, and second, that "the power of the landlord over [Bihari] kamiyas" "echoed" the power of the *malik devata*. The conversation stalls. Why? Because we do not know what the relationship is between *malik devata* and Tio. They do not belong to structures of generalities, nor is there any guarantee that a relationship could exist between the two without the mediation of the language of social science. Between "capitalist production" and the "power of the landlord," however, the relationship is known—or at least we think we know it—thanks to all the grand narratives of transition from precapital to capital. The relationship is always at least implicit in our sociologies that permeate the very language of social-science writing.

TWO MODELS OF TRANSLATION

Let me make it clear that the raging Medusa of cultural relativism is not rearing her ugly head in my discussion at this point. To allow for plurality, signified by the plurality of gods, is to think in terms of singularities. To think in terms of singularities, however—and this I must make clear since so many scholars these days are prone to see parochialism, essentialism, or cultural relativism in every claim of non-Western difference—is *not* to make a claim against the demonstrable and documentable permeability of cultures and languages. It is, in fact, to appeal to models of cross-cultural and cross-categorical translations that do not take a universal middle term for granted. The Hindi *pani* may be translated into the English "water" without having to go through the superior positivity of H_2O. In this, at least in India but perhaps elsewhere as well, we have something to learn from nonmodern instances of cross-categorial translation.

I give an example here of the translation of Hindu gods into expressions of Islamic divinity that was performed in an eighteenth-century Bengali religious text called *Shunya-puran.* (The evidence belongs to the "history of conversion" to Islam in Bengal.) This text has a description, well known to students of Bengali literature, of Islamic wrath falling upon a group of oppressive Brahmins. As part of this description, it gives the following account of an exchange of identities between individual Hindu deities and their Islamic counterparts. What is of interest here is the way this translation of divinities works:

> Dharma who resided in Baikuntha was grieved to see all this [Brahminic misconduct]. He came to the world as a Muhammadan . . . [and] was called Khoda. . . . Brahma incarnated himself as Muhammad, Visnu as Paigambar and Civa became Adamfa (Adam). Ganesa came as a Gazi, Kartika as a Kazi, Narada became a Sekha and Indra a Moulana. The Risis of heaven became Fakirs. . . . The goddess Chandi incarnated herself as Haya Bibi [the wife of the original man] and Padmavati became Bibi Nur [Nur = light].[22]

Eaton's recent study of Islam in Bengal gives many more such instances of translation of gods. Consider the case of an Arabic-Sankrit bilingual inscription from a thirteenth-century mosque in coastal Gujarat that Eaton cites in his discussion. The Arabic part of this inscription, dated 1264, "refers to the deity worshiped in the mosque as Allah" while, as Eaton puts it, "the Sanskrit text of the same inscription addresses the supreme god by the names Visvanatha ('lord of the universe'), Sunyarupa ('one whose form is of the void'), and Visvarupa ('having various forms')."[23] Further on, Eaton gives another example: "The sixteenth-century poet Haji Muhammad identified the Arabic Allah with Gosai (Skt. 'Master'), Saiyid Murtaza identified the Prophet's daughter Fatima with Jagat-janani (Skt. 'Mother of the World'), and Saiyid Sultan identified the God of Adam, Abraham, and Moses with Prabhu (Skt. 'Lord')."[24]

In a similar vein, Carl W. Ernst's study of South Asian Sufism mentions a coin issued by Sultan Mahmud of Ghazna (c. 1018 C.E.) that contained "a Sanskrit translation of the Islamic profession of faith." One side of the coin had an Arabic inscription whereas the other side said, in Sanskrit: *avyaktam ekam muhamadah avatarah nrpati mahamuda* (which Ernst translates as, "There is One unlimited [unmanifest?], Muhammad is the *avatar,* the king is Mahmud"). Ernst comments, expressing a sensibility that is no doubt modern: "The selection of the term *avatar* to translate the Arabic *rasul,* 'messenger,' is striking, since *avatar* is a term reserved in Indian thought for the descent of the god Vishnu into earthly form. . . . It is hard to do more than wonder at the theological originality of equating the Prophet with the *avatar* of Vishnu."[25]

The interesting point, for our purpose and in our language, is how the translations in these passages take for their model of exchange barter rather than the generalized exchange of commodities, which always needs the mediation of a universal, homogenizing middle term (such as, in Marxism, abstract labor). The translations here are based on very local, particular, one-for-one exchanges, guided in part, no doubt—at least in the case of *Shunya-puran*—by the poetic requirements of alliterations, meter, rhetorical conventions, and so on. There are surely rules in these exchanges, but the point is that even if I cannot decipher them all—and even if they are not all decipherable, that is to say, even if the processes of translation contain a degree of opacity—it can be safely asserted that these rules cannot and would not claim to have the "universal" character of the rules that sustain conversations between social scientists working on disparate sites of the world. As Gautam Bhadra has written: "One of the major features of these types of cultural interaction [between Hindus and Muslims] is to be seen at the linguistic level. Here, recourse is often had to the consonance of sounds or images to transform one god into another, a procedure that appeals more . . . to popular responses to alliteration, rhyming and other rhetorical devices—rather than to any elaborate structure of reason and argument."[26]

One critical aspect of this mode of translation is that it makes no appeal to any of the implicit universals that inhere in the sociological imagination. When it is claimed, for instance, by persons belonging to devotional traditions (*bhakti*) that "the Hindu's Ram is the same as the Muslim's Rahim," the contention is not that some third category expresses the attributes of Ram or Rahim better than either of these two terms and thus mediates in the relationship between the two. Yet such claim is precisely what would mark an act of translation modeled on Newtonian science. The claim there would be that not only do H_2O, water, and *pani* refer to the same entity or substance but that H_2O best expresses or captures the attributes, the constitutional properties, of this substance. "God" became such an item of universal equivalence in the nineteenth century, but this is not characteristic of the kind of cross-categorial translations we are dealing with here.

Consider the additional example Ernst provides of such nonmodern translation of gods. He mentions "a fifteenth century Sanskrit text written in Gujarati for guidance of Indian architects employed to build mosques.

In it, the god Visvakarma says of the mosque, 'There is no image and there they worship, through *dhyana*, . . . the formless, attributeless, all-pervading Supreme God whom they call Rahamana.' "[27] The expression "supreme God" does not function in the manner of a scientific third term, for it has no higher claims of descriptive ability, it does not stand for a truer reality. For, after all, if the supreme One was without attributes, how could one human language claim to have captured the attributes of this divinity better than a word in another language that is also human? These instances of translation do not necessarily suggest peace and harmony between Hindus and Muslims, but they are translations in which codes are switched locally, without going through a universal set of rules. There are no overarching censoring/limiting/defining systems of thought that neutralize and relegate differences to the margins, nothing like an overarching category of "religion" that is supposed to remain unaffected by differences between the entities it seeks to name and thereby contain. The very obscurity of the translation process allows the incorporation of that which remains untranslatable.

HISTORICAL TIME AND THE POLITICS OF TRANSLATION

It is obvious that this nonsociological mode of translation lends itself more easily to fiction, particularly of the nonrealist or magic-realist variety practiced today, than to the secular and realist prose of sociology or history. In these fictive narratives, gods and spirits can indeed be agents. But then what of history? What of its abiding allegiance to secular, continuous, empty, homogenous time? And what of the project of Marxist-subaltern history in which this work participates? Mine is not a postmodern argument announcing the death of history and recommending fiction writing as a career for all historians. For, the question of personal talents apart, there is a good reason why the training of the mind in modern historical consciousness is justified even from the point of view of the subaltern, and this has to do with the intermeshing of the logic of secular human sciences with that of bureaucracies. One cannot argue with modern bureaucracies and other instruments of governmentality without recourse to the secular time and narratives of history and sociology. The subaltern classes need this knowledge in order to fight their battles for social justice. It would therefore be unethical not to make historical consciousness available to everybody, in particular the subaltern classes.

Yet historicism carries with it, precisely because of its association with the logic of bureaucratic decision making, an inherent modernist elitism that silently lodges itself in our everyday consciousness.[28] Eaton begins the last chapter of his meticulously researched book on Bengali Islam with a historicist sentence that aims to appeal to the trained aesthetic sensibility of all historians: "Like the strata of a geologic fossil record, place names covering the surface of a map silently testify to past historical processes."[29] However, the point at issue is not how individual historians think about historical time, for it is not the self-regarding attitude of historians that make history, the subject, important in the world outside academia. History is important as a form of consciousness in modernity (historians may want to see themselves as its arbiters and custodians, but that is a different question). Let me explain, therefore, with the help of an ordinary, casual example, how a certain sense of historical time works in the everyday speech of public life in modern societies.

Consider the following statement in a newspaper article by the cultural-studies specialist Simon During in an issue of the Melbourne daily *Age* (19 June 1993): "thinking about movies like *Of Mice and Men* and *The Last of the Mohicans* allows us to see more clearly where contemporary culture is going."[30] During is not the target of my comments. My remarks pertain to a certain habit of thought that the statement illustrates: the imagination of historical time that is built into this use of the word "contemporary." Clearly, the word involves the double gesture of both inclusion and exclusion, and an implicit acceptance of this gesture is the condition that enables the sentence to communicate its point. On the one hand, "contemporary" refers to all that belongs to a culture at a particular point on the (secular) calendar that the author and the intended reader of this statement inhabit. In that sense, everybody is part of the "contemporary." Yet, surely, it is not being claimed that every element in the culture is moving toward the destination that the author has identified in the films mentioned. What about, for instance, the peasants of Greece, if we could imagine them migrating to the "now" of the speaker? (I mention the Greeks because they constitute one of the largest groups of European immigrants into Australia.) They may inhabit the speaker's "now" and yet may not be going in the direction that *The Last of the Mohicans* suggests.[31] The implicit claim of the speaker is not that these people are not moving but that whatever futures these others may be building for themselves will soon be swamped and overwhelmed by the future the author divines on the basis of his evidence. That is the gesture of exclusion built into this use of the word "contemporary."

If this sounds like too strong a claim, try the following thought experiment. Suppose we argue that the contemporary is actually plural, so radically plural that it is not possible for any particular aspect or element to claim to represent the whole in any way (even as a possible future). Under these conditions, a statement such as During's would be impossible to make. We would instead have to say that "contemporary culture," being plural and there being equality within plurality, was going many different places at the same time (I have problems with "at the same time," but let's stay with it for the present). Then there would be no way of talking about the "cutting edge," the avant-garde, the latest that represents the future, the most modern, and so on. Without such a rhetoric and a vocabulary and the sentiments that go with them, however, many of our everyday political strategies in the scramble for material resources would be impossible to pursue. How would you get government backing, research funding, institutional approval for an idea if you could not claim on its behalf that it represents the "dynamic" part of the contemporary, which thus is pictured as always split into two, one part rushing headlong into the future, and another passing away into the past, something like the living dead in our midst?

A certain kind of historicism, the metanarrative of progress, is thus deeply embedded in our institutional lives however much we may develop, as individual intellectuals, an attitude of incredulity toward such metanarratives. (Lyotard in *The Postmodern Condition* actually concedes this point.)[32] This we need to develop critiques of institutions on their own terms, secular critiques for secular institutions of government. Marx's thoughts, still the most effective secular critique of "capital," remain indispensable to our engagement with the question of social justice in capitalist societies. But my point is that what is indispensable remains inadequate, for we still have to translate into the time of history and the universal and secular narrative of "labor" stories about being human that incorporate agency on the part of gods and spirits.

At this point I want to acknowledge and learn from the modes of translation that I have called nonmodern, the barterlike term-for-term exchanges that bypass all the implicit sociologies of our narratives of capitalism. This mode of translation is antisociology and for that reason has no obligation to be secular. The past is pure narration, no matter who has agency in it. Fiction and films, as I have said, are the best modern media for handling this mode. But this option is not open to the historian writing in search of social justice and equity. Criticism in the historical mode, even when it does not institute a human subject at the center of history, seeks to dispel and demystify gods and spirits as so many ploys of secular relationships of power. The moment we think of the world as disenchanted, however, we set limits to the ways the past can be narrated. As a practicing historian, one has to take these limits seriously. For instance, there are cases of peasant revolts in India in which the peasants claimed to have been inspired to rebellion by the exhortations of their gods. For a historian, this statement would never do as an explanation, and one would feel obliged to translate the peasants' claim into some kind of context of understandable (that is, secular) causes animating the rebellion. I assume that such translation is both inevitable and unavoidable (for we do not write for the peasants). The question is: How do we conduct these translations in such a manner as to make visible all the problems of translating diverse and enchanted worlds into the universal and disenchanted language of sociology?

Here I have learned from Vincente Raphael's and Gayatri Spivak's discussions of the politics of translation.[33] We know that given the plurality of gods, the translation from godly time into the time of secular labor could proceed along a variety of paths. But whatever the nature of the path, this translation, to borrow from Spivak's and Rafael's handling of the question, must possess something of the "uncanny" about it. An ambiguity must mark the translation of the tool-worshiping jute worker's labor into the universal category "labor": it must be enough like the secular category "labor" to make sense, yet the presence and plurality of gods and spirits in it must also make it "enough unlike to shock."[34] There remains something of a "scandal"—of the shocking—in every translation, and it is only through a relationship of intimacy to both languages that we are aware of the degree of this scandal.

This property of translation—that we become more aware of the scandalous aspects of a translation process only if we know both of the languages intimately—has been well expressed by Michael Gelven:

> If an English-speaking student . . . sets out to learn German, he first looks up in a lexicon or vocabulary list a few basic German words. At this point, however, these German words are not German at all. They are merely sounds substituted for English meanings. They are, in a very real sense, English words. This means that they take their contextual significance from the . . . totality of the English language. . . . If a novice in German language picked up a copy of Schopenhauer's book and wondered what *Vorstellung* meant in the title, he would probably look the term up in the lexicon, and find such suggestions as "placing before."

> And although he might think it strange to title a book "The World as Will and Placing Before," he would nevertheless have some idea of the meaning of that remarkable work. But as this novice worked himself through the language, and became familiar with the many uses of the term *Vorstellung* and actually used it himself . . . [h]e might, to his own surprise, realize that although he knew what the term meant, he could not translate the German term back into his own language—an obvious indication that the reference of meaning was no longer English as in his first encounter with it.[35]

Usually, or at least in South Asian studies, the Marxist or secular scholar who is translating the divine is in the place of the student who knows well only one of the two languages he is working with. It is all the more imperative, therefore, that we read our secular universals in such a way as to keep them open to their own finitude, so that the scandalous aspects of our unavoidable translations, instead of being made inaudible, actually reverberate through what we write in subaltern studies. To recognize the existence of this "scandal" in the very formation of our sociological categories is the first step we can take toward working the universalist and global archives of capital in such a way as to "blast . . . out of the homogeneous course of history" times that produce cracks in the structure of that homogeneity.[36]

LABOR AS A HISTORY OF DIFFERENCE IN THE TRANSLATION INTO CAPITALISM

In this concluding section I will try to show, by reading Marx with the help of the Derridean notion of the trace, how one may hold one's categories open in translating and producing, out of the pasts of the subaltern classes, what is undeniably a universal history of labor in the capitalist mode of production.[37]

Looking back at my own work on Indian "working-class" history a few years ago, I seem to have only half thought through the problem. I documented a history whose narrative(s) produced several points of friction with the teleologies of "capital." In my study of the jute-mill workers of colonial Bengal, I tried to show how the production relations in these mills were structured from the inside, as it were, by a whole series of relations that could only be considered precapitalist. The coming of capital and commodity did not appear to lead to the politics of equal rights that Marx saw as internal to these categories. I refer here in particular to the critical distinction Marx draws between "real" and "abstract" labor in explaining the production and the form of the commodity. These distinctions refer to a question in Marx's thought that we may now recognize as the question of the politics of difference. The question for Marx was: If human beings are individually different from one another in their capacity to labor, how does capital produce out of this field of difference an abstract, homogeneous measure of labor that makes the generalized production of commodities possible?

This is how I then read the distinction between real and abstract labor (with enormous debt to Michel Henry and I. I. Rubin):[38]

> Marx places the question of subjectivity right at the heart of his category "capital" when he posits the conflict between "real labour" and "abstract labour" as one of its central contradictions. "Real labour" refers to the labor power of the actual individual, labor power "as it exists in the personality of the labourer"—that is, as it exists in the "immediate exclusive individuality" of the individual. Just as personalities differ, similarly the labor power of one individual is different from that of another. "Real labour" refers to the essential heterogeneity of individual capacities. "Abstract" or general labor, on the other hand, refers to the idea of uniform, homogeneous labor that capitalism imposes on this heterogeneity, the notion of a general labor that underlies "exchange value." It is what makes labor measurable and makes possible the generalized exchange of commodities. It expresses itself . . . in capitalist discipline, which has the sole objective of making every individual's concrete labor—by nature heterogeneous—"uniform and homogeneous" through supervision and technology employed in the labor process. . . . Politically, . . . the concept of "abstract labour" is an extension of the bourgeois notion of the "equal rights" of "abstract individuals," whose political life is reflected in the ideals and practice of "citizenship." The politics of "equal rights" is thus precisely the "politics" one can read into the category "capital."[39]

It now seems to me that Marx's category of commodity has a certain built-in openness to difference that I did not fully exploit in my exposition. My reading of the term "precapital" remained, in spite of my efforts, hopelessly historicist, and my narrative never quite escaped the (false) question, Why did the Indian working class fail to sustain a long-term sense of class consciousness? The metaproblem of "failure" arises from the well-known Marxist tradition of positing the working class as a transcultural subject. It is also clear from the above quote that my reading took the ideas of the "individual" and "personality" as unproblematically given, and read the word "real" (in "real labour") to mean something primordially natural (and therefore not social).

But my larger failure lay in my inability to see that if one reads the word "real" not as something that refers to a Rousseauian "natural," that is, the naturally different endowments of different, and ahistorical, individuals but rather as something that questions the nature-culture distinction itself, other possibilities open up, among them that of writing "difference" back into Marx. For the "real" then (in this reading) must refer to different kinds of "social," which could include gods and spirits—and hence to different orders of temporality, as well. It should in principle even allow for the possibility that these temporal horizons are mutually incommensurable. The transition from "real" to "abstract" is thus also a question of transition/translation from many and possibly incommensurable temporalities to the homogeneous time of abstract labor, the transition from nonhistory to history. "Real" labor, the category, itself a universal, must nevertheless have the capacity to refer to that which cannot be enclosed by the sign "commodity" even though what remains unenclosed constantly inheres in the sign itself. In other words, by thinking of the category "commodity" as constituted by a permanent tension between "real" and "abstract" labor, Marx, as it were, builds a memory into this analytical category of that which it can never completely capture. The gap between real and abstract labor and the force ("factory discipline," in Marx's description) constantly needed to close it, are what then introduce the movement of difference into the very constitution of the commodity, and thereby eternally defer the achievement of its true/ideal character.

The sign "commodity," as Marx explains, will always carry as part of its internal structure certain universal emancipatory narratives. If one overlooked the tension Marx situated at the heart of this category, these narratives could indeed produce the standard teleologies one normally encounters in Marxist historicism: that of citizenship, the juridical subject of Enlightenment thought, the subject of political theory of rights, and so on. I have not sought to deny the practical utility of these narratives in modern political structures. The more interesting problem for the Marxist historian, it seems to me, is the problem of temporality that the category "commodity," constituted through the tension and possible noncommensurability between real and abstract labor, invites us to think. If real labor, as we have said, belongs to a world of heterogeneity whose various temporalities cannot be enclosed in the sign "history,"—Michael Taussig's work on Bolivian tin miners has shown that they are not even all "secular" (that is, bereft of gods and spirits)— then it can find a place in a historical narrative of commodity production only as a Derridean trace of that which cannot be enclosed, an element that constantly challenges from within capital's and commodity's—and by implication, history's—claims to unity and universality.[40]

The prefix *pre* in "precapital," it could be said similarly, is not a reference to what is simply chronologically prior on an ordinal, homogeneous scale of time. "Precapitalist" speaks of a particular relationship to capital marked by the tension of difference in the horizons of time. The "precapitalist," on the basis of this argument, can only be imagined as something that exists within the temporal horizon of capital and that at the same time disrupts the continuity of this time by suggesting another time that is not on the same, secular, homogeneous calendar (which is why what is precapital is not chronologically prior to capital, that is to say, one cannot assign it to a point on the same continuous time line). This is another time that, theoretically, could be entirely immeasurable in terms of the units of the godless, spiritless time of what we call "history," an idea already assumed in the secular concepts of "capital" and "abstract labor."

Subaltern histories, thus conceived in relationship to the question of difference, will have a split running through them. One the one hand, they are "histories" in that they are constructed within the master code of secular history and use the accepted academic codes of history writing (and thereby perforce subordinate to themselves all other forms of memory). On the other hand, they cannot ever afford to grant this master code its claim of being a mode of thought that comes to all human beings naturally, or even to be treated as something that exists in nature itself. Subaltern histories are therefore constructed within a particular kind of historicized memory, one that remembers history itself as an imperious code that accompanied the civilizing process that the European Enlightenment inaugurated in the eighteenth century as a world-historical task. It is not enough to historicize "history," the discipline, for that only uncritically keeps in place the very understanding of time that enables us to historicize in the first place. The point is to ask how this seemingly imperious, all-pervasive code might be deployed or thought about so that we have at least a glimpse of its own finitude, a glimpse of what might constitute an outside to it. To hold history, the discipline, and other forms of memory together so that they can help in the interrogation of each other, to work out the ways these immiscible forms of recalling the past are juxtaposed in our negotiations of modern institutions, to question the narrative strategies in academic history that allow its secular temporality the appearance of successfully assimilating to itself memories that are, strictly speaking, unassimilable—these are the tasks that subaltern histories are suited to accomplish in a country such as India. For to talk about the violent jolt the imagination has to suffer to be transported from a temporality cohabited by nonhumans and humans to one from which the gods are banished is not to express an incurable nostalgia for a long-lost world. Even for the members of the Indian upper classes, in no sense can this experience of traveling across temporalities be described as merely historical.

Of course, the empirical historians who write these histories are not peasants or tribals themselves. They produce history, as distinct from other forms of memory, precisely because they have been transposed and inserted—in our case, by England's work in India—into the global narratives of citizenship and socialism. They write history, that is, only after the social existence from their own labor has entered the process of being made abstract in the world market for ideational commodities. The subaltern, then, is not the empirical peasant or tribal in any straightforward sense that a populist program of history writing may want to imagine. The figure of the subaltern is necessarily mediated by problems of representation. In terms of the analysis that I have been trying to develop here, one may say that the subaltern fractures from within the very signs that tell of the emergence of abstract labor; the subaltern is that which constantly, from within the narrative of capital, reminds us of other ways of being human than as bearers of the capacity to labor. It is what is gathered under "real labor" in Marx's critique of capital, the figure of difference that governmentality (that is, in Foucault's terms, the pursuit of the goals of modern governments) all over the world has to subjugate and civilize.[41]

There are implications that follow. Subaltern histories written with an eye to difference cannot constitute yet another attempt, in the long and universalistic tradition of "socialist" histories, to help erect the subaltern as the subject of modern democracies, that is, to expand the history of the modern in such a way as to make it more representative of society as a whole. This is a laudable objective on its own terms and has undoubted global relevance. But thought does not have to stop at political democracy or the concept of egalitarian distribution of wealth (though the aim of achieving these ends will legitimately fuel many immediate political struggles). Subaltern histories will engage philosophically with questions of difference that are elided in the dominant traditions of Marxism. At the same time, however, just as real labor cannot be thought of outside of the problematic of abstract labor, subaltern history cannot be thought of outside of the global narrative of capital—including the narrative of transition to capitalism—though it is not grounded in this narrative. Stories about how this or that group in Asia, Africa, or Latin America resisted the "penetration" of capitalism do not, in this sense, constitute "subaltern" history, for these narratives are predicated on imagining a space that is external to capital—the chronologically "before" of capital—but that is at the same time a part of the historicist, unitary time frame within which both the "before" and the "after" of capitalist production can unfold. The "outside" I am thinking of is different from what is simply imagined as "before or after capital" in historicist prose. This "outside" I think of, following Derrida, as something attached to the category "capital" itself, something that straddles a border zone of temporality, that conforms to the temporal code within which capital comes into being even as it violates that code, something we are able to see only because we can think/theorize capital, but that also always reminds us that other temporalities, other forms of worlding, coexist and are possible. In this sense, subaltern histories do not refer to a resistance prior and exterior to the narrative space created by capital; they cannot therefore be defined without reference to the category "capital." Subaltern studies, as I think of it, can only situate itself theoretically at the juncture where we give up neither Marx nor "difference," for, as I have said, the resistance it speaks of is something that can happen only *within* the time horizon of capital, and yet it has to be thought of as something that disrupts the unity of that time. Unconcealing the tension between real and abstract labor ensures that capital/commodity has heterogeneities and incommensurabilities inscribed in its core.

The real labor of my mill workers, then—let us say their relationship to their own labor on the day of Vishvakarma *puja*—is obviously a part of the world in which both they and the god Vishvakarma exist in some sense (it would be silly to reduce this coexistence to a question of conscious belief or of psychology). History cannot represent, except through a process of translation and consequent loss of status and signification for the translated, the heterotemporality of that world. History as a code comes into play as this real labor is transformed into the homogeneous, disciplined world of abstract labor, of the generalized world of exchange in which every exchange will be mediated by the sign "commodity." Yet, as the story of the Vishvakarma *puja* in the Calcutta mills shows, "real" labor inheres in the commodity and its secularized biography; its presence, never direct, leaves its effect in the breach that the stories of godly or ghostly intervention make in history's system of representation. As I have already said, the breach cannot be mended by anthropological cobbling, for that only shifts the methodological problems of secular narratives on to another, cognate territory. In developing Marxist histories after the demise of Communist party Marxisms, our task is to write and think in terms of this breach as we write history (for we cannot avoid writing history). If history is to become a site where pluralities will contend, we need to develop ethics and politics of writing that will show history, this gift of modernity to many peoples, to be constitutionally marked by this breach.

Or, to put it differently, the practice of subaltern history would aim to take history, the code, to its limits in order to make its unworking visible.

CHAPTER 4

Minority Histories, Subaltern Pasts

RECENT STRUGGLES and debates around the rather tentative concept of multiculturalism in Western democracies have often fueled discussions of minority histories. As the writing of history has increasingly become entangled with the so-called "politics and production of identity" after the Second World War, the question has arisen in all democracies of whether to include in the history of the nation histories of previously excluded groups. In the 1960s, this list usually contained names of subaltern social groups and classes, such as, former slaves, working classes, convicts, and women. This mode of writing history came to be known in the seventies as history from below. Under pressure from growing demands for democratizing further the discipline of history, this list was expanded in the seventies and eighties to include the so-called ethnic groups, the indigenous peoples, children and the old, and gays, lesbians, and other minorities. The expression "minority histories" has come to refer to all those pasts on whose behalf democratically minded historians have fought the exclusions and omissions of mainstream narratives of the nation. Official or officially blessed accounts of the nation's past have been challenged in many countries by the champions of minority histories. Postmodern critiques of "grand narratives" have been used to question single narratives of the nation. Minority histories, one may say, in part express the struggle for inclusion and representation that are characteristic of liberal and representative democracies.

Minority histories as such do not have to raise any fundamental questions about the discipline of history. Practicing academic historians are often more concerned with the distinction between good and bad histories than with the question of who might own a particular piece of the past. Bad histories, it is assumed sometimes, give rise to bad politics. As Eric Hobsbawm says in a recent article, "bad history is not harmless history. It is dangerous."[1] "Good histories," on the other hand, are supposed to enrich the subject matter of history and make it more representative of society as a whole. Begun in an oppositional mode, "minority histories" can indeed end up as additional instances of "good history." The transformation of once-oppositional, minority histories into "good histories" illustrate how the mechanism of incorporation works in the discipline of history.

MINORITY HISTORIES: ASSIMILATION AND RESISTANCE

The process through which texts acquire canonical status in the academic discipline of history in Anglo-American universities is different from the corresponding process in literature/English departments. History is a subject primarily concerned with the crafting of narratives. Any account of the past can be absorbed into, and thus made to enrich, the mainstream of historical discourse so long two questions are answered in the affirmative: Can the story be told/crafted? And does it allow for a rationally defensible point of view or position from which to tell the story? The first question, that of crafting a story, enriched the discipline for a long time by challenging historians to be imaginative and creative both in their research and narrative strategies. How do you write the histories of suppressed groups? How do you construct a narrative of a group or class that has not left its own sources? Questions of this kind often stimulate innovation in historians' practices. The point that the authorial position should be rationally defensible is also of critical importance. The author's position may reflect an ideology, a moral choice, or a political philosophy, but the choices are not unlimited. A madman's narrative is not history. Nor can a preference that is arbitrary or just personal—based on sheer taste, say—give us rationally defensible principles for narration (at best it will count as fiction and not history). The investment in a certain kind of rationality and in a particular understanding of the "real" means that history's—the discipline's—exclusions are ultimately epistemological.

Consider for a moment the results of incorporating into the discourse of history the pasts of major groups such as the working classes and women. History has not been the same since Thompson and Hobsbawm took up their pens to make the working classes look like major actors in society. Feminist interventions of the last two decades have also had an unquestionable impact on contemporary historical imagination. Does the incorporation of these radical moves into the mainstream of the discipline change the nature of historical discourse? Of course it does. But the answer to the question, Did such incorporation call the discipline into any kind of crisis? is more complicated. In mastering the problems of telling the stories of groups hitherto overlooked—particularly under circumstances in which the usual archives do not exist—the discipline of history renews and maintains itself. This inclusion appeals to the sense of democracy that impels the discipline ever outward from its core.

The point that historical narratives require a certain minimum investment in rationality has recently been made in the book *Telling the Truth about History.*[2] The question of the relationship between postmodernism, minority histories, and postwar democracies is at the heart of this book authored jointly by three leading feminist historians of the United States. To the extent that the authors see in postmodernism the possibility of multiple narratives and multiple ways of crafting these narratives, they welcome its influence. However, the book registers a strong degree of discomfiture when the authors encounter arguments that in effect use the idea of multiplicity of narratives to question any idea of truth or facts. If minority histories go to the extent of questioning the very idea of fact or evidence, then, the authors ask, how would one find ways of adjudicating between competing claims in public life? Would not the absence of a certain minimum agreement about what constitutes fact and evidence seriously fragment the body politic in the United States of America, and would not that in turn impair the capacity of the nation to function as a whole? Hence the authors recommend a pragmatic idea of "workable truths," which would be based on a shared, rational understanding of historical facts and evidence. For a nation to function effectively even while eschewing any claims to a superior, overarching grand narrative, these truths must be maintained in order for institutions and groups to be able to adjudicate between conflicting stories and interpretations.

Historians, regardless of their ideological moorings, display a remarkable consensus when it comes to defending history's methodological ties to a certain understanding of rationality. Georg Iggers's recent textbook on twentieth-century historiography emphasizes this connection between facticity and rationality in determining what may or may not constitute historical evidence: "Peter Novick has in my opinion rightly maintained that objectivity is unattainable in history; the historian can hope for nothing more than plausibility. But plausibility obviously rests not on the arbitrary invention of an historical account but involves *rational* strategies of determining what in fact is plausible."[3] Hobsbawm echoes sentiments not dissimilar to those expressed by others in the profession: "The fashion for what (at least in Anglo-Saxon academic discourse) is known by the vague term 'postmodernism' has fortunately not gained as much ground among historians as among literary and cultural theorists and social anthropologists, even in the USA. . . . [I]t ['postmodernism'] throws doubt on the distinction between fact and fiction, objective reality and conceptual discourse. It is profoundly relativist."[4]

What these historians oppose in postmodernism is the latter's failure, at least in their eyes, to meet the condition of rationality for incorporating narratives into the discipline of history. *Telling the Truth about History* thus demonstrates the continuing relevance of the two conditions that sustain history's connection to public life: democracy requires hitherto neglected groups to tell their histories, and these different histories come together in accepting shared rational and evidentiary rules. Successfully incorporated "minority histories" may then be likened to yesterday's revolutionaries who become today's gentlemen. Their success helps routinize innovation.

FROM MINORITY HISTORIES TO SUBALTERN PASTS

But this is not the only fate possible. The debate about minority histories allows for alternative understandings of the expression "minority" itself. Minority and majority are, as we know, not natural entities; they are constructions. The popular meanings of the words "majority" and "minority" are statistical. But the semantic fields of the words contain another idea: of being a "minor" or a "major" figure in a given context. For example, the Europeans, numerically speaking, are a minority in the total pool of humanity today and have been so for a long while; yet their colonialism in the nineteenth century was based on certain ideas about major and minor. For example, they often assumed that their histories contained the majority instances of norms that every other human society should aspire to; compared to them, others were still the "minors" for whom they, the "adults" of the world, had to take charge, and so on. So numerical advantage by itself is no guarantor of a major/majority status. Sometimes, you can be a larger group than the dominant one, but your history would still qualify as "minor/minority history."

The problem of minority histories thus leads us to the question of what may be called the "minority" of some particular pasts. Some constructions and experiences of the past stay "minor" in the sense that their very incorporation into historical narratives converts them into pasts "of lesser importance" vis-à-vis dominant understandings of what constitutes fact and evidence (and hence vis-à-vis the underlying principle of rationality) in the practices of professional history. Such "minor" pasts are those experiences of the past that always have to be assigned to an "inferior" or "marginal" position as they are translated into the academic historian's language. These are pasts that are treated, to use an expression of Kant's, as instances of human "immaturity," pasts that do not prepare us for either democracy or citizenly practices because they are not based on the deployment of reason in public life.[5]

My use of the word "minor" then does not quite reproduce the nuances of the way the word has been used in literary theory following Deleuze and Guattari's interpretation of Kafka, but there is some similarity between the two uses. Just as the "minor" in literature implies "a critique of narratives of identity" and refuses "to represent the attainment of autonomous subjectivity that is the ultimate aim of the major narrative," the "minor" in my use similarly functions to cast doubt on the "major."[6] For me, it describes relationships to the past that the "rationality" of the historian's methods necessarily makes "minor" or "inferior," as something "nonrational" in the course of, and as a result of, its own operation. And yet these relations return, I argue, as an implicit element of the conditions that make it possible for us to historicize. To anticipate my conclusion, I will try to show how the capacity (of the modern person) to historicize actually depends on his or her ability to participate in nonmodern relationships to the past that are made subordinate in the moment of historicization. History writing assumes plural ways of being in the world.

Let me call these subordinated relations to the past "subaltern" pasts. They are marginalized not because of any conscious intentions but because they represent moments or points at which the archive that the historian mines develops a degree of intractability with respect to the aims of professional history. In other words, these are pasts that resist historicization, just as there may be moments in ethnographic research that resist the doing of ethnography.[7] Subaltern pasts, in my sense of the term, do not belong exclusively to socially subordinate or subaltern groups, nor to minority identities alone. Elite and dominant groups can also have subaltern pasts to the extent that they participate in life-worlds subordinated by the "major" narratives of the dominant institutions. I illustrate my proposition with a particular instance of subaltern pasts, which comes from an essay by the founder of the Subaltern Studies group, Ranajit Guha. Since Guha and the group have been my teachers in many ways, I offer my remarks not in a hostile spirit of criticism but in a spirit of self-examination, for my aim is to understand what historicizing the past does and does not do. With that caveat, let me proceed.

SUBALTERN PASTS: AN EXAMPLE

As is well known, an explicit aim of *Subaltern Studies* was to write the subaltern classes into the history of nationalism and the nation, and to combat all elitist biases in the writing of history. To make the subaltern the sovereign subject of history, to listen to their voices, to take their experiences and thought (and not just their material circumstances) seriously—these were goals we had deliberately and publicly set ourselves. These original intellectual ambitions and the desire to enact them were political in that they were connected to modern understandings of democratic public life. They did not necessarily come from the lives of the subaltern classes themselves, though one of our objectives, as in the British tradition of history from below, was to ground the struggle for democracy in India in the facts of subaltern history. Looking back, however, I see the problem of subaltern pasts dogging the enterprise of *Subaltern Studies* from the very outset. Indeed, it is arguable that what differentiates the *Subaltern Studies* project from the older tradition of history from below is the self-critical awareness of this problem in the writings of the historians associated with this group.

Ranajit Guha's celebrated and brilliant essay, "The Prose of Counter-Insurgency," was published in an early volume of *Subaltern Studies* and is now justly considered a classic of the genre. A certain paradox that results precisely from the historian's attempt to bring the histories of the subaltern classes into the mainstream of the discourse of history, it seems to me, haunts the exercise Guha undertakes in this essay. A principal aim of Guha's essay was to use the 1855 rebellion of the Santals to demonstrate a cardinal principle of subaltern history: making the insurgent's consciousness the mainstay of a narrative about rebellion. (The Santals were a tribal group in Bengal and Bihar who rebelled against both the British and nonlocal Indians in 1855.) As Guha put it in words that capture the spirit of early *Subaltern Studies*: "Yet this consciousness [the consciousness of the rebellious peasant] seems to have received little notice in the literature on the subject. Historiography has been content to deal with the peasant rebel merely as an empirical person or a member of a class, but not as an entity whose will and reason constituted the praxis called rebellion. . . . [I]nsurgency is regarded as *external* to the peasant's consciousness and Cause is made to stand in as a phantom surrogate for Reason, the logic of that consciousness."[8]

The critical phrase here is "the logic of that consciousness," which marks the analytical distance Guha, the historian, has to take from the object of his research, which is this consciousness itself. For in pursuing the history of the Santal rebellion of 1855, Guha unsurprisingly came across a phenomenon common in the lives of the peasants: the agency of supernatural beings. Santal leaders explained the rebellion in supernatural terms, as an act carried out at the behest of the Santal god Thakur. Guha draws our attention to the evidence and underscores how important this understanding was to the rebels themselves. The leaders of the rebellion, Sidhu and Kanu, said that Thakur had assured them that British bullets would not harm the devotee-rebels. Guha takes care to avoid any instrumental or elitist reading of these statements. He writes: "These were not public pronouncements meant to impress their followers. . . . [T]hese were words of captives facing execution. Addressed to hostile interrogators in military encampments they could have little use as propaganda. Uttered by men of a tribe which, according to all accounts had not yet learnt to lie, these represented the truth and nothing but the truth for their speakers."[9]

A tension inherent in the project of *Subaltern Studies* becomes perceptible here in Guha's analysis. His phrase "logic of consciousness" or his idea of a truth that was only "truth for their speakers" are all acts of assuming a critical distance from that which he is trying to understand. Taken literally, the rebel peasants' statement shows the subaltern himself as refusing agency or subjecthood. "I rebelled," he says, "because Thakur made an appearance and told me to rebel." In their own words, as reported by the colonial scribe: "Kanoo and Sedoo Manjee are not fighting. The Thacoor himself will fight." In his own telling, then, the subaltern is not necessarily the subject of his or her history, but in the history of *Subaltern Studies* or in any democratically minded history, he or she is. What does it mean, then, when we both take the subaltern's views seriously—the subaltern ascribes the agency for their rebellion to some god—and want to confer on the subaltern agency or subjecthood in their own history, a status the subaltern's statement denies?

Guha's strategy for negotiating this dilemma unfolds in the following manner. His first move, against practices common in secular or Marxist historiography, is to resist analyses that see religion simply as a displaced manifestation of human relationships that are in themselves secular and worldly (class, power, economy, and so on). Guha was conscious that his was not a simple exercise in demystification:

> Religiosity was, by all accounts, central to the *hool* (rebellion). The notion of power which inspired it . . . [was] explicitly religious in character. It was not that power was a content wrapped up in a form external to it called religion. . . . Hence the attribution of the rising to a divine command rather than to any particular grievance; the enactment of rituals both before (eg. propitiatory ceremonies to ward off the apocalypse of the Primeval Serpents . . .) and during the uprising (worshipping the goddess Durga, bathing in the Ganges, etc.); the generation and circulation of myth is its characteristic vehicle—rumour.[10]

But in spite of Guha's desire to listen to the rebel voice seriously, his analysis cannot offer the Thakur the same place of agency in the story of the rebellion that the Santals' statements had given him. A narrative strategy that is rationally defensible in the modern understanding of what constitutes public life—and the historians speak in the public sphere—cannot be based on a relationship that allows the divine or the supernatural a direct hand in the affairs of the world. The Santal leaders' own understanding of the rebellion does not directly serve the historical cause of democracy or citizenship or socialism. It needs to be reinterpreted. Historians will grant the supernatural a place in somebody's belief system or ritual practices, but to ascribe to it any real agency in historical events will be go against the rules of evidence that gives historical discourse procedures for settling disputes about the past.

The Protestant theologian-hermeneutist Rudolf Bultmann has written illuminatingly on this problem. "The historical method," says Bultmann, "includes the presupposition that history is a unity in the sense of a closed continuum of effects in which individual events are connected by the succession of cause and effect." By this, Bultmann does not reduce the historical sciences to a mechanical understanding of the world. He qualifies his statement by adding:

> This does not mean that the process of history is determined by the causal law and that there are no free decisions of men whose actions determine the course of historical happenings. But even a free decision does not happen without a cause, without a motive; and the task of the historian is to come to know the motives of actions. All decisions and all deeds have their causes and consequences; and the historical method presupposes that it is possible in principle to exhibit these and their connection and thus to understand the whole historical process as a as closed unity.

Here Bultmann draws a conclusion that allows us to see the gap that must separate the set of explanatory principles that the historian employs to explain the Santal rebellion from the set that the Santals themselves might use (even after assuming some principles might be shared between them). I find Bultmann's conclusion entirely relevant to our discussion of subaltern pasts:

> This closedness [the presupposed, "closed unity" of the historical process] means that the continuum of historical happenings cannot be rent by the interference of supernatural, transcendent powers and that therefore there is no "miracle" in this sense of the word. Such a miracle would be an event whose cause did not lie within history. While, for example, the Old Testament narrative speaks of an interference by God in history, historical science cannot demonstrate such an act of God, but merely perceives that there are those who believe in it. To be sure, as historical science, it may not assert that such a faith is an illusion and that God has not acted in history. But it itself as science cannot perceive such an act and reckon on the basis of it; it can only leave every man free to determine whether he wants to see an act of God in a historical event that it itself understands in terms of that event's immanent historical causes.[11]

Fundamentally, then, the Santal's statement that God was the main instigator of the rebellion has to be anthropologized (that is, converted into somebody's belief or made into an object of anthropological analysis) before it finds a place in the historian's narrative. Guha's position with respect to the Santal's own understanding of the event becomes a combination of the anthropologist's politeness—"I respect your beliefs but they are not mine"—and a Marxist (or modern) tendency to see "religion" in modern public life as a form of alienated or displaced consciousness. "[I]n sum," he writes, "it is not possible to speak of insurgency in this case except as a religious consciousness," and yet hastens to add: "except that is, as a massive demonstration of self-estrangement (to borrow Marx's term for the very essence of religiosity) which made the rebel look upon their project as predicated on a will other than their own."[12]

Here is a case of what I have called subaltern pasts, pasts that cannot ever enter academic history as belonging to the historian's own position. These days one can devise strategies of multivocal histories in which we hear subaltern voices more clearly than we did in the early phase of *Subaltern Studies*. One may even refrain from assimilating these different voices to any one voice and deliberately leave loose ends in one's narrative (as does Shahid Amin in his *Events, Memory, Metaphor*).[13] But the point is that the historian, as historian and unlike the Santal, cannot invoke the supernatural in explaining/describing an event.

THE POLITICS OF SUBALTERN PASTS

The act of championing minority histories has resulted in discoveries of subaltern pasts, constructions of historicity that help us see the limits to modes of viewing enshrined in the practices of the discipline of history. Why? Because the discipline of history—as has been argued by many (from Greg Dening to David Cohen in recent times)—is only one among ways of remembering the past.[14] In Guha's essay, the resistance that the "historical evidence" offers to the historian's reading of the past—a Santal god, Thakur, stands between the democratic-Marxist historian and the Santals in the matter of deciding who is the subject of history—produces minor or subaltern pasts in the very process of weaving modern historical narratives. Subaltern pasts are like stubborn knots that stand out and break up the otherwise evenly woven surface of the fabric. When we do minority histories within the democratic project of including all groups and peoples within mainstream history, we both hear and anthropologize the Santal at the same time. We cannot write history from within what we regard as their beliefs. We thus produce "good," not subversive, histories, which conform to the protocols of the discipline.

An appreciation of this problem has led to a series of attempts to craft histories differently, to allow for a certain measure of equality between historians' histories and other constructions of the past. Some scholars now *perform* the limits of history in various ways: by fictionalizing the past, experimenting to see how films and history might intersect in the new discipline of cultural studies, studying memory rather than just history, playing around with forms of writing, and other similar means.[15] The kind of disciplinary consensus around the historian's methods that was once—say, in the sixties—represented (in Anglo-American universities at least) by "theory" or "methods" courses that routinely dished out Collingwood or Carr or Bloch as staple for historians has now begun to be questioned, at least by those involved in writing histories of marginalized groups or non-Western peoples. This does not necessarily mean methodological anarchy (though some feel insecure enough to fear this), or that Collingwood et al. have become irrelevant, but it does mean that E. H.

Carr's question "What is History?" needs to be asked again for our own times. The pressure of pluralism inherent in the languages and moves of minority histories has resulted in methodological and epistemological questioning of what the very business of writing history is all about.

Only the future will tell how these questions will resolve themselves, but one thing is clear: the question of including minorities in the history of the nation has turned out to be a much more complex problem than a simple operation of applying some already settled methods to a new set of archives and adding the results to the existing collective wisdom of historiography. The additive, "building-block" approach to knowledge has broken down. What has become an open question is: Are there experiences of the past that cannot be captured by the methods of the discipline, or which at least show the limits of the discipline? Fears that such questioning will lead to an outbreak of irrationalism, that some kind of postmodern madness will spread through Historyland, seem extreme, for the discipline is still securely tied to the positivist impulses of modern bureaucracies, the judiciary, and to the instruments of governmentality. Hobsbawm, for instance, provides some unwitting evidence of history's close ties to law and other instruments of government. He writes: "the procedures of the law court, which insist on the supremacy of evidence as much as historical researchers, and often in much the same manner, demonstrate that difference between historical fact and falsehood is not ideological. . . . When an innocent person is tried for murder, and wishes to prove his or [her] innocence, what is required is the techniques not of the 'postmodern' theorist, but of the old-fashioned historian."[16] This is why Hobsbawm would argue that minority histories must also conform to the protocols of "good history," for history speaks to forms of representative democracy and social justice that liberalism or Marxism—in their significantly different ways—have already made familiar.

But minority histories can do more than that. The task of producing "minority" histories has, under the pressure precisely of a deepening demand for democracy, become a double task. I may put it thus: "good" minority history is about expanding the scope of social justice and representative democracy, but the talk about the "limits of history," on the other hand, is about struggling, or even groping, for nonstatist forms of democracy that we cannot not yet either understand or envisage completely. This is so because in the mode of being attentive to the "minority" of subaltern pasts, we stay with heterogeneities without seeking to reduce them to any overarching principle that speaks for an already given whole.

There is no third voice that can assimilate the two different voices of Guha and the Santal leader; we have to stay with both, and with the gap between them that signals an irreducible plurality in our own experiences of historicity.

PASTS DEAD AND ALIVE

Let me explore a bit more the question of heterogeneity as I see it. We can—and we do usually in writing history—treat the Santal of the nineteenth century to doses of historicism and anthropology. We can, in other words, treat him as a signifier of other times and societies. This gesture maintains a subject-object relationship between the historian and the evidence. In this gesture, the past remains genuinely dead; the historian brings it "alive" by telling the story.[17] But the Santal with his statement "I did as my god told me to do" also faces us as a way of being in this world, and we could ask ourselves: Is that way of being a possibility for our own lives and for what we define as our present? Does the Santal help us to understand a principle by which we also live in certain instances? This question does not historicize or anthropologize the Santal, for the illustrative power of the Santal as an example of a present possibility does not depend on his otherness. Here the Santal stands as our contemporary, and the subject-object relationship that normally defines the historian's relationship to his or her archives is dissolved in this gesture. This gesture is akin to the one Kierkegaard developed in critiquing explanations that looked on the Biblical story of Abraham's sacrifice of his son Isaac either as deserving an historical or psychological explanation or as a metaphor or allegory, but never as a possibility for life open today to one who had faith. "[W]hy bother to remember a past," asked Kierkegaard, "that cannot be made into a present?"[18]

To stay with the heterogeneity of the moment when the historian meets with the peasant is, then, to stay with the difference between these two gestures. One is that of historicizing the Santal in the interest of a history of social justice and democracy; and the other, that of refusing to historicize and of seeing the Santal as a figure illuminating a life possibility for the present. Taken together, the two gestures put us in touch with the plural ways of being that make up our own present. The archives thus help bring to view the disjointed nature of any particular "now" one may inhabit; that is the function of subaltern pasts.

A plurality of one's own being is a basic assumption in any hermeneutic of understanding that which seems different. Wilhelm von Humboldt put the point well in his 1821 address "On the Task of the Historian" delivered to the Berlin Academy of Sciences: "Where two beings are separated by a total gap, no bridge of understanding extends from one to the other; in order to understand one another, they must have in another sense, already understood each other."[19] We are not the same as the nineteenth-century Santal, and that the Santal is not completely understood in the few statements quoted here. Empirical and historical Santals would also have had other relationships to modernity and capitalism that I have not considered. One could easily assume that the Santal today would be very different from what they were in the nineteenth century, that they would inhabit a very different set of social circumstances. They might even produce professional historians; no one would deny these historical changes. But the nineteenth-century Santal—and indeed, if my argument is right, humans from any other period and region—are always in some sense our contemporaries: that would have to be the condition under which we can even begin to treat them as intelligible to us. Thus the writing of history must implicitly assume a plurality of times existing together, a disjuncture of the present with itself. Making visible this disjuncture is what subaltern pasts allow us to do.

An argument such as this is actually at the heart of modern historiography. One could argue, for instance, that the writing of medieval history for Europe depends on this assumed contemporaneity of the medieval, or what is the same thing, the noncontemporaneity of the present with itself. The medieval in Europe is often strongly associated with the supernatural and the magical. But what makes the historicizing of it possible is the fact that its basic characteristics are not completely foreign to us as moderns (which is not to deny the historical changes that separate the two). Historians of medieval Europe do not always consciously or explicitly make this point, but it is not difficult to see this operating as an assumption in their method. In the writings of Aron Gurevich, for example, the modern makes its pact with the medieval through the use of anthropology—that is, in the use of contemporary anthropological evidence from outside of Europe to make sense of the past of Europe. The strict temporal separation of the medieval from the modern is here belied by global contemporaneity. Peter Burke comments on this intellectual traffic between medieval Europe and contemporary anthropological evidence in introducing Gurevich's work. Gurevich, writes Burke, "could already have been described in the 1960s as a historical anthropologist, and he did indeed draw inspiration from anthropology, most obviously from the economic anthropology of Bronislaw Malinowski and Marcel Mauss, who had begun his famous essay on the gift with a quotation from a medieval Scandinavian poem, the *Edda*."[20]

Similar double moves—both of historicizing the medieval and of seeing it as contemporary with the present—can be seen at work in the following lines from Jacques Le Goff. Le Goff is seeking to explain here an aspect of the European medieval sensibility: "People today, even those who consult seers and fortune-tellers, call spirits to floating tables, or participate in black masses, recognize a frontier between the visible and the invisible, the natural and the supernatural. This was not true of medieval man. Not only was the visible for him merely the trace of the invisible; the supernatural overflowed into daily life at every turn."[21] This is a complex passage. On the surface, it is about what separates the medieval from the modern. Yet this difference is what makes the medieval an ever-present possibility that haunts the practices of the modern—if only we, the moderns, could forget the "frontier" between the visible and the invisible in Le Goff's description, we would be on the other side of that frontier. The people who consult seers today are modern in spite of themselves, for they engage in "medieval" practices but are not able to overcome the habits of the modern. Yet the opening expression "even today" contains a reference to the sense of surprise one feels at their anachronism, as if the very existence of these practices today opens up a hiatus in the continuity of the present by inserting into it something that is medieval-like and yet not quite so. Le Goff rescues the present by saying that even in the practice of these people, something irreducibly modern lingers—their distinction between the visible and the invisible. But it lingers only as a border, as something that defines the difference between the medieval and the modern. And since difference is always the name of a relationship, for it separates just as much as it connects (as, indeed, does a border), one could argue that alongside the present or the modern the medieval must linger as well, if only as that which exists as the limit or the border to the practices and discourses that define the modern.

Subaltern pasts are signposts of this border. With them we reach the limits of the discourse of history. The reason for this, as I have said, is that subaltern pasts do not give the historian any principle of narration that can be rationally defended in modern public life. Going a step further, one can see that this requirement for a rational principle, in turn, marks the deep connections that exist between modern constructions of public life and projects of social justice. It is not surprising that the Marxist scholar Fredric Jameson should begin his book *The Political Unconscious* with the injunction: "Always historicize!" Jameson describes "this slogan" as "the one absolute and we may even say 'transhistorical' imperative of all dialectical thought."[22] If my point is right, then historicizing is not the problematic part of the injunction, the troubling term is "always." For the assumption of a continuous, homogeneous, infinitely stretched out time that makes possible the imagination of an "always" is put to question by subaltern pasts that makes the present, as Derrida says, "out of joint."[23]

ON TIME-KNOTS AND THE WRITING OF HISTORY

One historicizes only insofar as one belongs to a mode of being in the world that is aligned with the principle of "disenchantment of the universe," which underlies knowledge in the social sciences (and I distinguish knowledge from practice).[24] But "disenchantment" is not the only principle by which we world the earth. The supernatural can inhabit the world in these other modes of worlding, and not always as a problem or result of conscious belief or ideas. The point is made in an anecdote about the poet W. B. Yeats, whose interest in fairies and other nonhuman beings of Irish folk tales is well known. I tell the story as it has been told to me by my friend David Lloyd:

> One day, in the period of his extensive researches on Irish folklore in rural Connemara, William Butler Yeats discovered a treasure. The treasure was a certain Mrs. Connolly who had the most magnificent repertoire of fairy stories that W.B. had ever come across. He sat with her in her little cottage from morning to dusk, listening and recording her stories, her proverbs and her lore. As twilight drew on, he had to leave and he stood up, still dazed by all that he had heard. Mrs. Connolly stood at the door as he left, and just as he reached the gate he turned back to her and said quietly, "One more question Mrs. Connolly, if I may. Do you believe in the fairies?" Mrs. Connolly threw her head back and laughed. "Oh, not at all Mr. Yeats, not at all." W.B. paused, turned away and slouched off down the lane. Then he heard Mrs. Connolly's voice coming after him down the lane: "But they're there, Mr. Yeats, they're there."[25]

As old Mrs Connolly knew, and as we social scientists often forget, gods and spirits are not dependent on human beliefs for their own existence; what brings them to presence are our practices.[26] They are parts of the different ways of being through which we make the present manifold; it is precisely the disjunctures in the present that allow us to be with them. These other ways of being are not without questions of power or justice, but these questions are raised—to the extent that modern public institutions allow them space, for they do cut across one another—on terms other than those of the political-modern.

However—and I want to conclude by pointing this out—the relation between what I have called subaltern pasts and the practice of historicizing is not one of mutual exclusion. It is because we already have experience of that which makes the present noncontemporaneous with itself that we can actually historicize. Thus what allows historians to historicize the medieval or the ancient is the very fact these worlds are never completely lost. We inhabit their fragments even when we classify ourselves as modern and secular. It is because we live in time-knots that we can undertake the exercise of straightening out, as it were, some part of the knot (which is how we might think of chronology).[27]

Time, as the expression goes in my language, situates us within the structure of a *granthi*; hence the Bengali word *shomoy-granthi*, *shomoy* meaning "time" and *granthi* referring to joints of various kinds, from the complex formation of knuckles on our fingers to the joints on a bamboo-stick. That is why one may have two relationships with the Santal. First, we can situate ourselves as a modern subject for whom the Santal's life-world is an object of historical study and explanation. But we can also look on the Santal as someone illuminating possibilities for our own life-worlds. If my argument is right, then the second relationship is prior to the first one. It is what makes the first relationship possible.

Subaltern pasts thus act as a supplement to the historian's pasts. They are supplementary in a Derridean sense—they enable history, the discipline, to be what it is and yet at the same time help to show what its limits are. In calling attention to the limits of historicizing, they help us distance ourselves from the imperious instincts of the discipline—the idea that *everything* can be historicized or that one should *always* historicize. Subaltern pasts return us to a sense of the limited good that modern historical consciousness is. Gadamer once put the point well in the course of discussing Heidegger's philosophy. He said: "The experience of history, which we ourselves have, is . . . covered only to a small degree by that which we would name *historical consciousness*."[28] Subaltern pasts remind us that a relation of contemporaneity between the nonmodern and the modern, a shared and constant "now," which expresses itself on the historical plane but the character of which is ontological, is what allows historical time to unfold. This ontological "now" precedes the historical gap that the historian's methods both assume and posit between the "there-and-then" and the "here-and-now." Thus what underlies our capacity to historicize is our capacity not to. What gives us a point of entry into the times of gods and spirits—times that are seemingly very different from the empty, secular, and homogeneous time of history—is that they are never completely alien; we inhabit them to begin with.

The historian's hermeneutic, as Humboldt suggested in 1821, proceeds from an unstated and assumed premise of identification that is later disavowed in the subject-object relationship. What I have called subaltern pasts may be thought of as intimations we receive—while engaged in the specific activity of historicizing—of a shared, unhistoricizable, and ontological now. This now is, I have tried to suggest, what fundamentally rends the seriality of historical time and makes any particular moment of the historical present out of joint with itself.

Part Two

HISTORIES OF BELONGING

CHAPTER 5

Domestic Cruelty and the Birth of the Subject

EKSHAN, a Calcutta-based literary magazine, published an essay in one of its issues in 1991 called "Baidhabya kahini" or "Tales of Widowhood."[1] The author was Kalyani Datta, a Bengali woman who, since the 1950s, had been collecting from older Bengali widows she knew stories about the oppression and marginalization they had suffered as widows. Datta's article reproduced these widows' stories in their own telling, based on notes she had taken from informal interviews. Unfunded and unprompted by any academic institutions, Datta's research showed how deeply a certain will to witness and document suffering—in this case, the plight of the widow—for the interest of a general reading public has embedded itself in modern Bengali life. Both this will and the archive it has built up over the last hundred years are part of a modernity that British colonial rule inaugurated in nineteenth-century India.

What underlay this will to document was an image of the Bengali widow of upper-caste Hindu families as a general figure of suffering. This figure itself is an abstraction of relatively recent times. There have been widows, of course, in Bengali upper-caste families for as long as such families have existed. It is also true that that there have been, from time immemorial, pernicious little customs in place for regulating and dominating the lives of widows. It is not that that every Bengali upper-caste widow has suffered in the same way or to the same extent throughout history, or that there have been no historical changes in widows' conditions. Many widows earned unquestionable familial authority by willingly subjecting themselves to the prescribed regimes and rituals of widowhood. Many have also resisted the social injunctions meant to control their lives. Besides, factors such as women's education, their entry into public life, the subsequent decline in the number of child brides, and the overall increase in life expectancies have helped reduce the widows' vulnerability. Kalyani Datta's private act of (public) recording of some widows' own voices is itself a testimony to these undeniable historical changes.

Yet there is no question that widowhood exposes women to some real problems in the patrilineal, patrilocal system of kinship of upper-caste Bengali society. The prescribed rituals of widowhood suggest that it is regarded as a state of inauspiciousness (for the supposed inauspiciousness of the woman is traditionally blamed for bringing death to a male member of the household). The rituals take the form of extreme and lifelong atonement on the part of the widow: celibacy, a ban on meat eating, avoidance of certain kinds of food, and frequent fasting. Unadorned bodies that carry certain marks (such as the lack of jewelry, shaved head or cropped hair, and white saris with no—or black—borders) aim to make widows unattractive and set them aside from others. Stories recounted since the nineteenth century reveal the element of torture, oppression, and cruelty that often, if not always, accompanied the experience of widowhood.

Until the coming of colonial rule, however, widowhood was not thematized as a problem in Bengali society. Pre-British Bengali literature and writing concerned itself with many aspects of women's lives: the daughter-in-law's suffering at the hands of the mother-in-law and sisters-in-law, the question of chastity of women, jealousy and quarrel between cowives, but seldom, if ever, did the problems of widowhood receive attention.[2] Colonial rule changed all that. From the question of *sati* (widow burning) that raged in the 1820s and 1830s through the Widow Remarriage Act (1856), and to the early Bengali novels written between the 1870s and 1920s, the widow and her plight remained a subject of central importance in Bengali writing. In addition, in the last hundred and thirty years or so, many Bengali Hindu widows—both in life and in fiction—have told their own stories in the different genres of fiction, memoirs, and autobiographies. Ever since the nineteenth century, the question of the widow's oppression has remained an important aspect of modern critiques of Bengali kinship. Kalyani Datta's short essay in *Ekshan* was part of this continuing and collective act of documentation of the suffering that widowhood has traditionally inflicted on women.

The history of modern widowhood has interested many students of Bengali colonial society. They have demonstrated a connection between "colonial discourse"—in particular the British use of "conditions of women" as an index for measuring the quality of a civilization—and the beginnings of a modern form of social criticism in Bengal that focused on such issues as *sati* and widow remarriage.[3] The questions I want to ask here are somewhat different from those pursued by these scholars. It is obvious that the general figure of the suffering widow was produced in Bengali history by creating a collective, "public" past out of many individual and familial memories of the experience of widowhood. This collective past was needed for the pursuit of justice under conditions of a modern public life. What kind of a subject is produced at the intersection of these two kinds of memories, public and familial? What does this subject have to be like in order to be interested in documenting suffering? How would one write a history of a modern and collective Bengali subject who is marked by this will to witness and document oppression and injury?

COMPASSION AND THE SUBJECT OF ENLIGHTENMENT

The capacity to notice and document suffering (even if it be one's own suffering) from the position of a generalized and necessarily disembodied observer is what marks the beginnings of the modern self. This self has to be generalizable in principle; in other words, it should be such that it signifies a position available for occupation by anybody with proper training. If it were said, for instance, that only a particular type of person—such as a Budhha or a Christ—was capable of noticing suffering and of being moved by it, one would not be talking of a generalized subject position. To be a Budhha or Christ is not within the reach of everybody through simple education and training. So the capacity for sympathy must be seen as a potential inherent in the nature of man in general and not in the uniqueness of a particular person. Such a "natural theory of sentiments," as we shall see, was indeed argued by Enlightenment philosophers such as David Hume and Adam Smith.

A critical distinction also has to be made between the act of displaying suffering and that of observing or facing the sufferer. To display suffering in order to elicit sympathy and assistance is a very old—and perhaps universal and still current—practice. The deformed beggars of medieval Europe or of contemporary Indian or U.S. cities are subjects of suffering, but they are not disembodied subjects. The sufferer here is an embodied self, which is always a particular self, grounded in this or that body. Nor would the sympathy felt for only a particular sufferer (such as a kin or a friend) be "modern" in my sense. The person who is not an immediate sufferer but who has the capacity to become a secondary sufferer through sympathy for a generalized picture of suffering, and who documents this suffering in the interest of eventual social intervention—such a person occupies the position of the modern subject. In other words, the moment of the modern observation of suffering is a certain moment of self-recognition on the part of an abstract, general human being. It is as though a person who is able to see in himself or herself the general human also recognizes the same figure in the particular sufferer, so that the moment of recognition is a moment when the general human spilts into the two mutually recognizing and mutually constitutive figures of the sufferer and the observer of suffering. It was argued, however, in the early part of the nineteenth century that this could not happen without the aid of reason, for habit and custom—unopposed by reason—could blunt the natural human capacity for sympathy. Reason, that is, education in rational argumentation, was seen as a critical factor in helping to realize in the modern person this capacity for seeing the general.

Something like such a natural theory of sentiments was argued, in effect, by the two most important nineteenth-century Bengali social reformers who exerted themselves on questions concerning the plight of widows: Rammohun Roy (1772/4–1833) and Iswarchandra Vidyasagar (1820–1901). Roy was instrumental in the passing of the act that made *sati* illegal in 1829, and Vidyasagar successfully agitated for widows to have the legal right to remarry, a right enshrined in the Act for the Remarriage of Hindu Widows, 1856. These legal interventions also allow us to make a further distinction between suffering as viewed by religions such as Budhhism and suffering as a subject of modern social thought. In religious thought, suffering is existential. It shadows man in his life. In social thought, however, suffering is not an existential category. It is specific and hence open to secular interventions.

Rammohun Roy's well-known tract entitled *Brief Remarks Regarding Modern Encroachments on the Ancient Right of Females*, was one of the first written arguments in modern India in favor of women's right to property. This document on property rights also discusses the place of sentiments such as cruelty, distress, wounding feelings, misery, and so on, in human relations. Both strands—rights and sentiments—were intertwined in Roy's argument connecting the question of property with the issue of sentiments, and both saw suffering as an historical and eradicable problem in society:

> In short a widow, according to the [current] exposition of the law, can receive nothing . . . . [unless her husband dies] leaving two or more sons, and all of them survive and be inclined to allot a share to their mother. . . . The consequence is, that a woman who is looked upon as the sole mistress of a family one day, on the next becomes dependent on her sons, and subject to the slights of her daughters-in-law. . . . Cruel sons often wound the feelings of their dependent mothers. . . . Step-

mothers, who are often numerous on account of polygamy, are still more shamefully neglected in general by their step-sons, and sometimes dreadfully treated by their sisters-in-law. . . . [The] restraints on female inheritance encourage, in a great degree, polygamy, a frequent source of the greatest misery in native families.[4]

There are two interesting features of this document that make it the work of a modern observer of suffering. First, in observing this cruelty to widows and women, Roy put himself in the transcendental position of the modern subject. This becomes clear if we look closely at the following sentence of his text: "How distressing it must be to the female community and to those who interest themselves in their behalf, to observe daily that several daughters in a rich family can prefer no claim to any portion of the property . . . left by their deceased father . . . ; while they . . . are exposed to be given in marriage to individuals who already have several wives and have no means of maintaining them."[5] Roy presents himself here both as a subject experiencing affect—"distress"—as well as a representative subject, one who "interests [himself] in their [women's] behalf." The capacity for sympathy is what unites the representative person with those who are represented; they share the same "distress." The second clause in the sentence refers to a new type of representation: people who took an interest in women's condition on behalf of women. But who were these women? They were not particular, specific women marked by their belonging to particular families or particular networks of kinship. Women here are a collective subject; the expression "female community" connotes a general community. It is this "general community" that shares the distress of a Rammohun Roy, the observer who observes on behalf of this collective community. And therefore the feeling of "distress" that Rammohun Roy speaks of refers to a new kind of compassion, something one could feel for suffering beyond one's immediate family. Compassion in general, we could call it.

But from where would such compassion or sympathy spring? What made it possible for a Rammohun or Vidyasagar to feel this "compassion in general" that most members of their community (presumably) did not yet feel? How would society train itself to make this compassion a part of the comportment of every person, so that compassion became a generally present sentiment in society? It is on this point that both Rammohun and Vidyasagar gave an answer remarkable for its affiliation to the European Enlightenment. Reason, they argued in effect, was what could release the flow of the compassion that was naturally present in all human beings, for only reason could dispel the blindness induced by custom and habit. Reasonable human beings would see suffering and that would put to work the natural human capacity for sympathy, compassion, and pity.

Rammohun raised the question of compassion in a pointed manner in his 1819 answer to Kashinath Tarkabagish's polemical tract *Bidhayak nishedhak shombad* directed against his own position on *sati*. "What is a matter of regret," he said, "is that the fact of witnessing with your own eyes women who have thus suffered much sadness and domination, does not arouse even a small amount of compassion in you so that the forcible burning [of widows] may be stopped."[6] Why was this so? Why did the act of seeing not result in sympathy? Rammohun's answer is clearly given in his 1818 tract called *Views on Burning Widows Alive*, which targeted the advocates of the practice. Here Rammohun refers to the forcible way in which widows were "fastened" to the funeral pyre in the course of the performance of *sati*, and directly raises the question of mercy or compassion (*daya*): "you are unmercifully resolved to commit the sin of female murder." His opponent, the "advocate" of *sati*, replies: "You have repeatedly asserted that from want of feeling we promote female destruction. This is incorrect. For it is declared in our Veda and codes of law, that mercy is the root of virtue, and from our practice of hospitality, &c., our compassionate dispositions are well known."[7]

Rammohun's response to this introduces an argument for which he presents no scriptural authority and which went largely unanswered in the debates of the time. This is the argument about "habits of insensibility." Much like the Enlightenment thinkers of Europe, and perhaps influenced by them, Rammohun argued that it was because the practice of *sati* had become a custom—a matter of blind repetition—that people were prevented from experiencing sympathy even when they watched somebody being forced to become a *sati*. The natural connection between their vision and feelings of pity was blocked by habit. If this habit could be corrected or removed, the sheer act of seeing a woman being forced to die would evoke compassion. Roy said:

> That in other cases you show charitable dispositions is acknowledged. But by witnessing from your youth the voluntary burning of women amongst your elder relatives, your neighbours and the inhabitants of the surrounding villages, and by observing the indifference at the time when the women are writhing under the torture of the flames, habits of insensibility are produced. For the same reason, when men or women are suffer-

> ing the pains of death, you feel for them no sense of compassion, like worshippers of female deities who, witnessing from their infancy the slaughter of kids and buffaloes, feel no compassion for them in the time of their suffering death.[8]

We encounter the same argument about the relationship between sight and compassion in the writings of Iswarchandra Vidyasagar, the Bengali reformer responsible for the act that in 1856 permitted Hindu widows to remarry. Vidyasagar's fundamental reasoning as to the solution of widows' problems had some critical differences from the position of Rammohun Roy but like the latter, he too argued that it was custom and habit that stymied the otherwise natural relationship between the sight and compassion:[9]

> People of India! . . . Habit has so darkened and overwhelmed your intellect and good sense that it is hard for the juice of compassion to flow in the ever-dry hearts of yours even when you see the plight of hapless widows. . . . Let no woman be born in a country where men have no compassion, no feelings of duty and justice, no sense of good and bad, no consideration, where only the preservation of custom is the main and supreme religion—let the ill-fated women not take birth in such a country.
>
> Women! I cannot tell what sins [of past lives] cause you to be born in India![10]

Both Rammohun and Vidyasagar thus espoused a natural theory of compassion, the idea that compassion was a sentiment universally present in something called "human nature," however blocked its expression might be in a particular situation. This recalls Adam Smith, explaining his theory of sympathy: "How selfish soever man may be supposed, there are some principles in his nature which interest him in the fortune of others. . . . Of this kind is pity or compassion, the emotion we feel for the misery of others."[11] Hume also defined "pity" as a general sentiment, as "a concern for . . . the misery of others, without any friendship . . . to occasion this concern," and connected it to the general human capacity for sympathy. He wrote: "No quality of human nature is more remarkable . . . than that propensity we have to sympathize with others."[12] It is only on the basis of this kind of an understanding that Roy and Vidyasagar assigned to reason a critical role in fighting the effects of custom. Reason did not produce the sentiment of compassion; it simply helped in letting sentiments take their natural course by removing the obstacle of mindless custom. Needless to say, the underlying vision of the human being was truly a universal one.

SUPPLEMENTING THE SUBJECT OF ENLIGHTENMENT: A TRANSLATION OF DIFFERENCE

There were two problems with the Bengali adaptation of a natural theory of compassion in dealing with the question of domestic cruelty toward widows. One was inherent in the theory: by making truly human sentiments natural and universal, it filled up what would later be regarded as the space of human subjectivity with reason alone. But reason, being universal and public, could never delineate the private side of the modern individual. To this problem, I will turn in the next section.

The second problem was that Bengali history was not a clean slate on which Enlightenment questions and answers could be written at will. It was not that the question of compassion had never been discussed in Bengali history before the arrival of the British. There were alternative understandings of the problem that also determined Bengali responses to the Enlightenment question, "From where does compassion come?" Most interesting, in this context, is the fact that Bengali biographies of Rammohun Roy or Vidyasagar often present us with an answer to this question that is very different from the answer that Roy and Vidyasagar themselves proposed. One of the central questions that the biographers found themselves obliged to address in writing the life stories of Rammohun and Vidyasagar was: What made it possible for these two Bengali men to see the suffering of women, which sometimes even the women's parents did not see? What made them compassionate? The biographers typically gave two different answers. One was the Enlightenment answer: the role of reason in freeing vision from the blindfold of custom. But they also had another answer, which was *hriday* (heart). They argued, in effect, that it was the "heart" that Rammohun and Vidyasagar were born with that made them compassionate.

Nagendranath Chattopadhyay's biography of Rammohun Roy, *Mahatma Raja Rammohon rayer jibancharit* (first published 1881/2), sees "sympathy and compassion" (*shahanubhuti o daya*) as part of Roy's inborn character: "Rammohun Roy was full of sympathy (*shahanubhuti*) and compassion (*daya*) for the suffering poor. Their misery always made his heart cry."[13] Chandicharan Bandyopadhyay's biography of Vidyasagar, *Vidyasagar* (first published c. 1895), describes several anecdotes to document the compassion that Vidyasagar felt for the suffering sections of humanity. Indeed, one of the most remarkable things about the biographies of this legendary Bengali public man of the nineteenth century is that they all, without exception, describe with approval and in detail his propensity to cry in public—not an admirable trait, as we shall see, by Adam Smith's standards. Crying stands as proof of his tenderheartedness. Incident after incident is recounted to document how plentiful was the compassion (*daya* or *karuna*) in Vidyasagar's heart. Sentences such as the following were typical: "We have already seen that, while a scholar in the Sanskrit College[,] he showed his kindness of heart by giving food and clothing to the needy."[14] Or consider this anecdote, said to be representative of Vidyasagar's life. When Vidyasagar was still a student in Calcutta, a respected teacher of his, Shambhuchandra Bachaspati, who taught Vidyasagar Vedantic philosophy and who was by then an old, physically decrepit man, married a very young girl. Vidyasagar, it is said, was opposed to this marriage and advised his teacher against it. His biographers are unanimous in describing how on meeting this girl, Vidyasagar "could not hold back his tears" thinking of the widowhood she seemed destined to suffer.[15] "Isvar Chandra only cast a glance at the beautiful girl's face, and immediately left the place. The sight move[d] his tender heart, and drew tears from his eyes. He foresaw the miserable, wretched life which the unfortunate little girl must have in a very short time, and he sobbed and wept like a child."[16] Chandicharan writes of this event: "This one single incident helps us to understand how tender was Ishvarchandra's heart and how easily it was stricken by other people's suffering."[17]

The biographies thus explain Rammohun's or Vidyasagar's capacity to generalize their compassion by reference to the special quality of their *hriday* or heart. They could generalize their sympathies from the particular instance to the general because the supply of sympathy in their hearts was plentiful. In this they were different from, say, people such as the eighteenth-century king Raja Rajballabh of Vikrampur, Dhaka, who, it is said, once attempted unsuccessfully to get his widowed daughter married again; or somebody like "one Syama Charan Das" of Calcutta in the early 1850s, who tried to do the same and was foiled by the local pundits.[18] These people had compassion, but did not have it in measure ample enough to move them to see their daughters' problem as a problem afflicting, potentially, all upper-caste women. Rammohun and Vidyasagar, however, were capable of moving to the general case from the particular because they were born with plentiful measures of *karuna* (compassion).

Vidyasagar, in fact, was dubbed *karunasagar* ("ocean of compassion" as distinct from *vidyasagar,* "ocean of learning") by the Bengali poet Michael Madhusudan Dutt.[19] Their biographers cite some critical evidence from childhood stories to establish this *karuna* as an inborn trait in their character. Rammohun's revulsion toward the idea of *sati,* we are told, arose first when he learned of a close female relative being forced to this fate by the men of the household.[20] Similarly, Vidyasagar's determination to fight for the amelioration of widows' conditions is traced back to a childhood experience when he discovered that a young girl who was once a playmate of his had become widowed and was now subject to all the prohibitions of widowhood. "He felt so much commiseration for the little girl that he, there and then, resolved that he would give his life to relieve the sufferings of widows. He was at the time only 13 or 14 years old."[21]

Generalized sympathy here is seen as a gift on the part of Vidyasagar: "he would give his life to relieve the sufferings of the widows." It is a gift of his heart. This understanding of compassion as a person's inborn capacity for *shahanubhuti* (*shaha* = equal, *anubhuti* = feelings) was different from the Smithian or Humean position that it was a part of the general nature in every man. The Sanskrit-derived Bengali word *shahanubhuti* is usually translated as "sympathy" in English, but there are some profound differences. The idea of "sympathy" entails the practice and faculty of (another very European word) "imagination." We sympathize with someone's misery because we can through the faculty of imagination place ourselves in the position of the person suffering; that is sympathy. As Adam Smith writes: "We sometimes feel for another . . . because, when we put ourselves in his case, that passion arises in our breast from the imagination."[22] This capacity to imagine was part of human nature, in Smith's discussion: "nature teaches the spectators to assume the circumstances of the person principally concerned."[23] The Bengali authors, however, in explaining Rammohun or Vidyasagar's inborn character as *shahriday* (with *hriday* or heart), and therefore marked by the capacity for *shahanubhuti,* were drawing practically but implicitly on Sanskritic aesthetic theories of the *rasa shastra* (aesthetics: the science of *rasa* or "moods"), according to which it was not given to everybody to appreciate the different *rasas* of life (including that of *karuna* or compassion). The capacity for *shahanubhuti* was, unlike in European theory of sympathy, not dependent on a naturally given mental faculty like "imagination"; it was seen rather as a characteristic of the person with *hriday,* the word "hriday" being assimilated in the nineteenth century to the English word "heart." The quality of being "with *hriday*" was called *shahridayata.* A *rasika* person—who could appreciate the different *rasas* or moods—had this mysterious entity called *hriday.* And it was in that sense that a Rammohun or a Vidyasagar could be called a *shahriday vyakti* (person with *hriday*).[24] Whatever the exact status of the category *hriday* in the complex theories of Sanskrit aesthetics, there is no theory of a general human nature in the *rasa shastra* to explain its occurrence. For the biographers of the nineteenth-century reformers, possessing *hriday* was a matter of exception rather than the rule. A Rammohun or a Vidyasagar was born that way. That is what made them rare and godlike, and placed them above ordinary humans. There could not be, therefore, a natural theory of compassion from this point of view.

There were thus two separate and unconnected theoretical ways of looking at compassion and personhood that jostled together in the Bengali biographies of Vidyasagar and Rammohun Roy. One was the European-derived natural theory of sentiments. The other, derived from Indian aesthetics, was inscribed in the Bengali or Sanskrit words used to describe the capacity for sympathy or compassion. Words derived from Sanskrit texts of *rasa-shastra* circulated in Bengali writing as a form of practical consciousness, as words belonging to the vocabulary of everyday relationships. They represented a different hermeneutic of the social that supplemented the one represented by European Enlightenment thought. After all, Adam Smith's or David Hume's theories—in their conscious appeal to experience as the ground for generalization—often offered as universally applicable hypotheses that were clearly derived from very particular and specific cultural practices of the societies they themselves knew. Smith, for instance, would blithely assume it to be a universal proposition that "the man who, under the greatest calamities, could command his sorrow, seems worthy of the highest admiration," or that "nothing is so mortifying as to be obliged to express our distress to the view of the public." This position could never explain, for instance, why Bengalis valued the fact that a man of Vidysagar's stature would cry in public.[25] European thinkers' statements were as much theories as they were matters of prejudice (in the Gadamerian sense), in that they were interpretations as well.[26] Between them and the already existing interpretations structuring Bengali lives was created a field in which was played out the politics of translating difference.

This politics may be seen in a duality of attitudes that authors of biographies often express. Nineteenth-century biographical writing in Bengal was inspired by the Victorian idea that biographies contributed to social improvement by providing models of character that members of a society could emulate. A natural theory of compassion was helpful in this regard, for modern education (that is, training in rational argumentation) could then be seen as the prescribed weapon for fighting the effects of custom. Biographies were tools of such education. But if, on the other hand, compassion-in-general was a function of such a contingent and rare factor such as the *hriday* one was born with, and was therefore a quality that was by definition in short supply, how would one train people in the art of this sentiment? How could every person cultivate that which, by its nature, could only be acquired as a special gift worthy of veneration? Biographers of compassionate Bengali social reformers were often caught in this contradiction.

A biographer such as Bandyopadhyay would have to make two contradictory claims at once. He would convey the impression that Vidyasagar's greatness lay in the natural rarity of his kind of people—not everybody was born with a heart as full of *shahanubhuti* as Vidyasagar's. And yet he would want his biography to provide an example of Vidyasagar's life that others, less gifted, could follow. "The lord of our destiny willing," he says toward the end of his book, "may the reading of [Vidya]sagar's life . . . spread the desire to imitate [his] . . . qualities."[27] Sometimes his text would directly address the reader, exhorting him to exercise his "imagination" and emulate Vidyasagar's noble example.[28] Yet on other occasions he would emphasize the inborn nature of Vidyasagar's compassion and sentiments, leaving a degree of ambiguity as to whether compassion for all was something that followed from natural human capacity for sympathy triggered by sight and reason, or whether it was a feeling that only the very exceptional were capable of experiencing.

Unable to resolve this contradiction between a view of *hriday* as a quasi-divine gift and their commitment to a Victorian understanding of social "improvement" through the remolding of individual characters by disseminating stories of good examples, Bengali biographies of "great men" often fell somewhere between biographies and hagiographies. They remained, for all their secular humanism, expressions of *bhakti* (devotion), an act of worship, on the part of the biographer toward his or her subject. Bandyopadhyay indicates clearly in his preface that writing the life of Vidyasagar was for him an action of the same category as offering *puja* (worship) to a deity. He adopts the gesture of the religious devotee (*bhakta*), whose language of humility was necessarily a language of self-deprecation as well: "Vidyasagar deserves veneration from the community of learned people; unfortunately, his present biographer, in comparison, would only count amongst the leaders of fools. . . . He was extremely affectionate toward me . . . and I will also do *puja* to him for that reason all my life. This biography began as part of that . . . *puja* and this is the only right I have to narrate the story of his very sacred life."[29]

This was in keeping with the understanding that an excess of compassion in one's character was a rare gift from the world of the gods. This understanding had its historical genealogies in aesthetic theories and devotional practices unconnected to Enlightenment thought, but it shadowed and supplemented what came from Europe. There were thus at least two answers given to the question: For whom did sight generate sympathy or compassion? The answer could be the Enlightenment subject, or the subject who, as a rare gift, possessed the quality called *hriday.* The fact that we come across these two different answers in the same body of texts suggests that they did not displace each other but existed in a relationship of mutual supplementation to constitute an intertwined strand in Bengali modernity.

THE WIDOW AS THE MODERN SUBJECT: INTERIORITY AND THE PROBLEM OF PURITY

Rammohun or Vidyasagar saw the widow from outside herself. The archive of accounts of the widows' suffering they helped to build did not include the widow's own experience of it. Her subjectivity was not in question. By the time Kalyani Datta's published her essay in 1991, however, recording the widow's voice was the chief aim of her exercise. It was not only Kalyani Datta, the observer, who was documenting suffering; the sufferer herself spoke of her conditions. She was her own observer of herself. One of the archival values of Datta's essay is created by the different older women who address the reader directly from within it. Thus the archives of the history of the widow-as-sufferer eventually came to include the subjectivity of the widow herself. The widow became both the object and the subject of the gaze that bore witness to oppression and suffering.

This was in keeping with what a standard account of the modern subject in European political thought—a history of the figure of the citizen, say—would lead us to expect. Smith's or Hume's theories of sentiments did not provide for individual subjectivities. Human nature for them was as universal as the biological human body. Subjectivity itself, or what many commentators would call the "interiority" of the subject, comes to be constituted by a tension between the individual's private experiences and desires (feelings, emotions, sentiments) and a universal or public reason. One could say that it is this opposition that manifests itself in the split between the private and the public in modernity.

C. B. Macpherson's *The Political Theory of Possessive Individualism* traces one source of the modern subject to the rise in the seventeenth century of the idea of right of private ownership in one's own person. The subject who enjoyed this right, however, could only be a disembodied, private subject—for the object over which his right extended was his own body.[30] Grounded in the idea of natural rights, it was not imperative in the seventeenth century that this subject be endowed with a deep interiority. The "private" self of such a subject would indeed have been empty. But from late eighteenth century on, this private self was filled up to create what eventually became the domain of subjectivity. The young Marx writing on the "Jewish question"—polemicizing against Bruno Bauer and building on Hegel's *Philosophy of Right*—drew attention to this public/private split in the very conception of the citizen as spelled out in the 1791–1793 French Declaration of the Rights of Man and of the Citizen. The citizen was the public-universal and political side of the human who retained "natural rights" to private interests as a member of civil society. Religion could only be part of his private, egoistic sphere of self-interest.[31] William Connolly's recent genealogy of the subject of European political thought tracks a process whereby accounts of "strife and conflict in civil society" are gradually shifted to a "site within the individual itself" until the individual becomes, by the end of the nineteenth century, the more familiar figure whose private self, now regarded as constituted through a history of psychological repression, can be pried open only by the techniques of psychoanalysis. In Connolly's words: "The modern theory of the stratified subject, with its levels of unconscious, preconscious, conscious and self-conscious activity, and its convoluted relays among passions, interests, wishes, responsibility and guilt, locates within the self conflicts which Hobbes and Rousseau distributed across regimes."[32]

The birth of the modern subject in nineteenth-century European theory required a conflicted interiority where reason struggled to bring under its guidance and control something that distinguished one subject from another and that at the same time was different from reason. This was the (initially) conscious and (later) subconscious world of passions, desires, and sentiments that make up human subjectivity. Without this move, it would have been difficult to develop in individuals their sense of being human but at the same time uniquely individual subjects. Although reason is a human faculty, it cannot constitute individual subjectivity because it is by definition universal and public. For the modern subject to emerge, passions, sentiments, and like have to be located within the mind and within a very particular understanding of the relationship between them and reason. This relationship is pedagogic. Passions and sentiments, in order for their bearer to be modern, require the guiding hand of reason. At the same time, this is a relationship of struggle between the two because they are of opposed and contradictory character. This struggle is what marks the interiority of the subject. This is how Connolly describes this transition in the writings of Rousseau: "Rousseau . . . shifts strife and conflict from civil society to a site within the individual itself. Demanding more from the self than Hobbes did, he must identify the struggle within it which Hobbes identified, and he must seek a more complete victory for the interior voice of virtue. Politics become interiorized. . . . Rousseau withdraws politics from the general will and relocates it quietly inside the selves which will these general laws."[33]

Why was it important that the modern individual be conceptualized in terms of this internal struggle between passion/sentiments and reason? Timothy Mitchell's discussion of Durkheim in *Colonising Egypt* offers a suggestive answer. The very conception of modern individual, Mitchell says in discussing Durkheim's texts, poses a threat to the conception of the social and the general, for if individuals are endowed with infinite individuality (which is what the drama of passions is supposed to reveal—each person his or her own novelist and analysand at the same time), what is there to guarantee the unity of the social? What would prevent the social realm, made up of such individuals (that is, people not simply subject to social practice, as they were supposed to be in primitive societies), from collapsing into the nightmare of anomie?[34] The answer, at the level of the individual, would be: reason. Reason, by focusing the mind on the general and the universal, would guide the individual's passion into its rightful place in the social realm. This thought, taken by itself, was not necessarily modern, but its generalization through society, one could argue, marks the coming of modernity.

Archiving and observing the Bengali widow as the subject of modernity, then, meant documenting not just the external conditions of the widow's life but her internal suffering as well, the way passion struggled with reason within her to mark her as modern. This indeed was missing from the framework of the early reformers. Consider, once again, the following statement by Vidyasagar, which I have quoted in part before:

> People of India! . . . Open your eyes for once and see how India, once a land of virtue, [is now] awash with the sins of adultery and foeticide. . . . You are prepared to consign your daughters . . . to the intolerable fire and torture of widowhood. You agree to connive at their conduct when, under the influence of irresistible passions, they become the victims of *adultery.* You are prepared to help them commit *foeticide* throwing aside all fears of immoral conduct and only out of the fear of being exposed to the public eye, and yet—the wonder of wonders!—you are not ready to follow the injunctions of the *shastras*, get them remarried, and free them from the insufferable pain of widowhood and free yourselves from the risk of all kinds of danger. You perhaps imagine that *with the loss of their husbands, women's bodies turn into stone, that they do lose all feelings of pain and sadness, that their passions are eradicated once for all.* . . . Let no woman be born in a country where the men have no compassion.[35]

I should explain that the reason why feticide and adultery assume such a prominent place in Vidyasagar's text was because the addressees of this text—those whom Vidyasagar in a generalizing and inflationary manner addressed as "people of India"—were the middle-class Bengali male householders of Calcutta of the mid-nineteenth century. The text was about their newfound sense of respectable forms of domesticity and addressed their fear of unwanted and illegitimate pregnancies caused by sexual liaisons between young widows and men in or outside the family. The scandals of adultery and feticide—the Bengali word is *kelenkari* (disgrace) derived from the word *kalanka* meaning, literally, a spot or a stain (the moon's dark spots are called in Bengali the moon's *kalanka*)—were the "danger" that Vidyasagar alluded to. With a young widow in their midst, a middle-class family ran the risk of such *kelenkari* and the widow of acquiring the stigma (*kalanka)* of an illicit relationship that could destroy the respectability of her family. Where is the subjecthood/agency of the young widow located in this text? Vidyasagar's answer was unambiguous: the real problems were in the widow's body, in the drives and passions of youth that were too strong to be regulated by the purificatory and self-renunciatory rituals of the celibacy customarily recommended for widows. What made young women vulnerable to the danger of illegitimate pregnancy was the very nature of the passion that physical youth engendered in their bodies. Recall Vidyasagar's words: "You perhaps imagine that . . . women's bodies turn into stone, that they do lose all feelings of pain and sadness, that their passions are eradicated once for all." Vidyasagar was not alone in thinking of the widow's passions as something arising from the youth of her body. Bengali plays written at this time on the question of widow remarriage suggest that this understanding was a common one.[36]

To build an archive of the widow's interiority, to see her self as deep and stratified, to hear her own voice, as it were, required the development of a set of observational techniques for studying and describing human psychology. This was a role performed primarily by the novel. All three stalwarts of early Bengali fiction—Bankimchandra Chattopadhyay (1838–1894), Rabindranath Tagore (1861–1941), and Saratchandra Chattopadhyay (1876–1938)—made the forbidden love of the widow a subject of their novels. The issue of romantic love was itself a problem in the history of democracy. The idea of choosing one's life partner—or of love as an act of self-expression of the subject—came up against the norms of social regulation enshrined in the custom of arranged marriages. Indeed, one reason why the figure of the widow may have held a special fascination for the early Bengali novelists is the fact that the unrecognized desires of the widow represented a case of complete subordination of the individual to society. In the widow one could see the expressivist subject clamoring for (self-) recognition. To delve into the interior world of the widow, whose innermost feelings were denied recognition by society, was to write the desire for freedom and self-expression into the very structure of the new Bengali subject. In doing this, however, the Bengali novelists also brought the question of the widow's interiority into general view. Thus, long before there were disciplines like history and sociology that expressed the familiar modern will to document oppression, there was humanist literature experimenting with and perfecting the tools of modern description of "experience."[37]

The terrain of this literary development is complex. For reasons of space, I will have to simplify issues that have more twists and turns in them than I can accommodate here. In Rabindranath Tagore's novel *Chokher bali* (1903), which focused on the problem of a young widow's unrequited love, we see a self-conscious step taken in the depiction of human interiority as an absolute and autonomous inside of the subject. *Chokher bali* is the story of the passion of a young man, Mahendra, who was married to Asha and who fell violently in love with a young widow, Binodini, who came from a village to stay with Mahendra, Asha, and Mahendra's mother in Calcutta. It is also a story about Binodini's own feelings of love, her initial attraction to Mahendra eventually replaced by her love for Mahendra's best friend, Bihari. Unlike the widow characters in Bankim's novels, Binodini was literate; she was, in fact, depicted as an avid reader of Bankim's *Bishabriksha* (discussed below). In a preface written for a later edition of the book, Tagore described how, for Bengali literature, the appearance of *Chokher bali* had heralded a sudden change. Its novelty lay in its emphasis on the interior space of human beings. True, there was still a role for the the body and its sense organs, for the idea of *ripu* (the traditional Hindu view of six particular embodied passions that destroy man), but all this was now subordinated in Tagore's novels to the work of psychological forces. As he himself put it: "What drives the story of *Chokher bali* from inside and gives it its intensity is the jealousy of the mother. It is this jealousy that provided Mahendra's *ripu* with an opportunity to bare itself, all tooth and claw, which would not have happened under normal circumstances. . . . The method of new literature no longer simply delineates events in the right order, it analyzes them in order to extract stories about the inside of human beings [Tagore uses the expression *aanter katha*]. This new method made an appearance in *Chokher bali*".[38]

One may read this statement as installing in Bengali fiction the modern subject endowed with interiority. In Vidyasagar, the widow's desire was understood as lust, a purely physical passion of youth regulated by the laws of nature and hence powerful beyond human control. With Bankimchandra, Rabindranath, and Saratchandra, there began a new and self-conscious discussion of romantic (heterosexual) love (*prem*), as distinct from the problem of lust. There is, however, a twist to this story of the birth of the modern subject in Bengali literature. That twist and its history are now condensed in a word that came into wide circulation in the period 1870 to 1920: *pabitra*, used as a qualifier of secular, human love. Usually glossed in English as "pure" but connoting a combination of "sacred," "auspicious," and "unstained" or "untainted"—untainted, that is, by physical passion—this word has been used by many Bengali writers to signify love that transcends physical passion. The *prem* (love) that was *pabitra* was the highest kind of love that could happen between men and women. Bankimchandra defined *pabitra* as that which has conquered or transcended the senses (*jitendriya*). The thought as such was ancient. It reached back to certain strands of Vedantic philosophy, but it became central to nineteenth-century nationalist discussions of conduct and the self, where the ideal of self was posited as that of being *jitendriya*, literally someone who had conquered his or her physical senses.[39] The Bengali discussion of love at the end of the nineteenth century, however, was more immediately indebted to medieval Vaishnava poetry (followers of the preserver-god Vishnu and his incarnations are called Vaishnava), which modern Bengali writers increasingly rediscovered from the 1870s onward.[40]

Much Vaishnava poetry was structured around the theme of the illicit love that Radha, the married heroine of this poetry, bore for Krishna, an incarnation of the god Vishnu in a human form. This extramarital love had brought on Radha the opprobrium of *kalanka*, which many Vaishnava poets exonerated by portraying Radha's love as symbolic of the devotee's spiritual longing for union with god and therefore as actually having very little to do with narrowly construed physical passion or self-indulgence. It was in this ideal of love as a spiritual sentiment, as devoid of any hint of lust, that Bengali writers found an elaboration of desire between the sexes. In an essay comparing the two medieval Vaishnava poets Jayadeva (12th century) and Vidyapati (15th century), Bankimchandra made a distinction between two kinds of nature (*prakriti*): external (*bahihprakriti*) and internal (*antahprakriti*). The body and its passions belonged to external nature, to the realm of the senses. Interiority was the nature internal to humans, and it was in that sphere that one could get away from the rule of the senses and make love spiritual or *pabitra*. Bankimchandra wrote:

> The writers of lyrical poetry in Bengali may be divided into two groups: those who look at man setting him in the context of natural beauty and those attend solely to the human heart, keeping external nature at a distance. . . . It is external nature (*bahihprakriti*) that is predominant in Jayadeva and his likes, while in the likes of Vidyapati we find the domain of nature that is internal (*antahprakriti*). Jayadeva and Vidyapati both sing of the love between Radha and Krishna. But the love that Jayadeva sings of obeys the external sense organs. The poems of Vidyapati, and especially those of Chandidasa, transcend our external senses . . . and become *pabitra*, that is to say, devoid of any association with the senses or with self-indulgence.[41]

Vaishnava doctrines were mixed with European romanticism in these discussions. Bankim, for instance, refers to Wordsworth as the poet of the spiritual *antahprakriti* (internal nature) in the same essay.

The story, apparently popular since the seventeenth century, of the socially scandalous love between the famous fifteenth-century Bengali poet Chandidasa, a Vaishnavite Brahman, and a low-caste washerwoman called Rami was recycled time and again in modern Bengali writing to illustrate the ideal of romantic love.[42] Chandidasa himself compared

Rami's love to something as pure as "gold without dross," without, he said, even the scent of (physical) desire in it. When he was about twenty, Tagore wrote a highly influential essay in which he upheld these lines of Chandidasa as the ideal of love between men and women: "How pure was Chandidasa's love! He could separate love from self-indulgence. That is why he said of his lover's beauty that there was not even a scent of [physical] desire in it. . . . I will be with her but not touch her body. . . . This is not a love of the external world, a love of seeing and touching. This is the treasure of dreams. It is wrapped up in dreams and has no relationship to the world which is awake. It is love in its absolute purity and nothing else. Chandidasa's statement does not belong [only] to the time when he wrote it."[43]

Historians of Bengali literature from Dines Chandra Sen at the beginning of this century to the more recent Asit Bandyopadhayay have followed Tagore in this opinion.[44] Thus while the documentary gaze of Bengali novelists created and opened up the interior space of the widow, modern secular and romantic love emerged washed in the light Vaishnava doctrines of "purity." Novels allowed the widow to experience love, but not before love had been theorized as a spiritual struggle to free desire from any suggestion of physicality. Reason was pressed into service on the side of the spiritual. This marginalization of the physical determined to a large degree the specific nature of the subject in Bengali literary modernity.

In Bankimchandra, Rabindranath, and Saratchandra, the body is what threatens the domain of interiority; it threatens the subject's capacity to be pure or *pabitra*. There are differences, however. In Bankim, although reason struggles with passion, and this struggle is the central fact of human interiority, the body still enjoys an autonomous existence—autonomous of the mind that is—through Bankim's category of beauty or external appearance (*rup*), which belongs to his understanding of external nature (*prakriti*). According to Bankim, it is in the nature of man to be attracted to *rup*. In his novel *Bishabriksha* (the Poison-Tree), published in 1873, the *rup* of a young and beautiful widow called Kunda plays a critical role in drawing a happily married man Nagendra to itself like a moth to fire. Nagendra leaves his wife and marries Kunda. This fire-moth relationship was, for Bankim, a perfect image of the way external nature or *bahihprakriti* tempts humans to their destiny. As he himself wrote in his ironic, witty, and humorous series of essays in the book *Kamalakanter daptar*:

> From now on it seemed to me that every man was but an insect. Each one of them had his own kind of fire [lamp] in which he desired to die . . . some do and some are stopped by glass. Knowledge is one such fire, wealth another, status, beauty, religion, sense organs are of other kinds—this world is full of fires. The world is also full of glass. The light that attracts us, the light into which we want to tumble down, drawn by that attraction—well, we do not reach it, do we? We buzz back and forth only to return again and again. If it had not been for the existence of [this] glass, the world would have been burned down by now.[45]

The interiority of someone like Nagendra, the tragic hero of *Bishabriksha*, is described by a story in which his reason/will struggles, unsuccessfully, with *bahihprakriti* or external nature. Human freedom, suggests Bankim, lies in being able to distinguish—with the help of moral reasoning—between that which belongs to the interior space of the subject, the *prakriti* or nature of the interior (*antahprakriti*), and that which belongs to external nature or *bahihprakriti*. Humans are apt to feel an attraction for physical beauty. Nagendra, the hero of Bankim's novel, calls it *chokher bhalobasha* (lit., love of the eyes).[46] To this "love of the eyes" Bankim opposed something one might call "love of the mind." The theory is elaborated by another character in the novel, Haradev Ghosal, Nagendra's brother-in-law, who says to Nagendra the following—the reader will see how the ideal of *pabitra prem* (pure love) provided a framework through which Bengali authors consumed European literature as well: "There are many sensations in the mind which people call love. . . . The desire to enjoy the beauty of a beautiful woman is not love. . . . This propensity . . . is sent by God; it is by means of it, too, that the world's desires are realized, and it fascinates all creatures. Kalidasa, Byron, Jayadeva are its poets. . . . But it is not love. Love is born of the faculties of the mind. [Its] result is sympathy, and in the end, self-forgetfulness and self-renunciation. This is truly love. Shakespeare, Valmiki, and the author of the Bhagavat Purana are its poets."[47]

We would miss the complexity of Bankim's thought if we read him as simply reinventing the nature/culture distinction of European sociology and locating woman in nature. Bankim, it is true, makes a distinction between external and internal nature, *bahihprakriti* and *antarprakriti*. But the word *prakriti*, in Bankim, always resonates on two separate registers, symptomatic of the processes of cultural translation that modernity involved in colonial Bengal. Bankim's category *prakriti* mediates between the modern scientific understanding of nature as a collection of inert bodies driven by blind, unconscious physical laws, and the older Tantric understanding of *prakriti* (nature) as a form of consciousness, a feminine power animating the world, creating it in collaboration with *purush*, man or the masculine power, and tempting the latter both to live and to die.[48]

The problem of *rup* (external beauty) dies out in the hands of Tagore and Saratchandra; there is no "love of the eye" in *Chokher bali*. Physical beauty, as we have seen, remains a part of Bankim's cosmology; he warns against its impact on the mind precisely because he considers it genuinely powerful. Tagore, however, leaves us in no doubt that his heroine Binodini is the new woman endowed with interiority and subjectivity. However physically attractive she may be, Binodini is a product of new education and enlightenment. Unlike the novels of Bankim, *Chokher bali* does not portray reason struggling to distinguish between love born of *rup* and love born of a "faculty of the mind." It was as if in response to Bankim's idea that love or attraction could be caused by the fact that human sight, could not help being influenced by physical beauty (*rup*), Tagore would quip (through the voice of Binodini): "Has God given men only sight and no insight at all?"[49] By thus subordinating sight to insight, Tagore shifted the drama of sentiments from the external space of physicality to the space of interiority in the subject.

Purity or *pabitrata* emerges in Bengali fiction as a set of techniques of interiority, the use of which could make one's innermost emotions (such as love) "pure" and thus help them transcend anything that was external to the subject's interior space—the body, interests, social conventions, and prejudices. There is no denying the contribution it has made in spiritualizing the experience of individuality. It created an extreme autonomy in the status of affect and a strong sense of resolve in the subject. For this acquisition of the quality of *pabitrata* did not come without a determined struggle against the senses that connected one to the exterior world. It made the struggle to be an individual a spiritual struggle. Tagore could thus create in his fiction extremely powerful characters of widows whose struggle against social injustice took on the aura of a spiritual vigilance. In *Chokher bali*, for instance, a character called Annapurna, Asha's aunt who, much like a "traditional" widow, decides to live in the holy city of Banaras, illustrates this point. An elderly person, she stays well outside the circuit of youthful romantic love in the novel. But her conversations with Asha leave us in no doubt that this widowed aunt was nothing but her own person. Her resolution to keep her innermost self in a state of purity or *pabitrata* was at the same time her quiet but proud defiance of social conventions:

> Asha one day asked her, "Tell me Auntie, do you remember our uncle?" Annapurna said, "I became a widow at eleven. My husband's image I can only recall as a shadow." Asha asked, "Then who do you think about, auntie?" Annapurna smiled a little and said, "I think of Him in whom my husband lives now, I think of that god." Asha said, "Does that make you happy?" Annapurna ran her fingers through Asha's hair affectionately, and said, "What would you understand, my child, of what happens inside me? Only my mind knows it. And it is known to Him, he who resides in my thoughts. . . . There was a time when this aunt of yours, when she was your age, entered the commerce of give and take with the world, just as you are doing now. Like you, I also used to think, Why wouldn't my service and my nurturing give rise to contentment in the man I served? Why would I not receive grace from the person whom I worshiped?. . . But at every step I saw that this did not happen. One day I left the world out of the feeling that everything in this world had failed me. But today I see that nothing had failed. . . . If only I knew it then. If I had done my duties in the world as though they were my duties to Him, if I had offered my heart to this world only as a ruse for offering it to Him, then who could have made me suffer?. . . This is my advice: whatever the suffering you receive, keep your faith and devotion intact. And may your sense of *dharma* [proper action] be unflinching."[50]

The later writer Saratchandra Chatterjee espoused a view similar to Tagore's. In a move reminiscent of the way Tagore converted the problem of (male) "sight" into that of "insight," Saratchandra effected a displacement of Bankim's problematic of *rup* (beauty) in order introduce the idea of *prakrito rup* (true or real beauty). This referred to a human interior that now seemed more beautiful than mere external beauty or outward appearance. Speaking in anger at the treatment of a young widow whom he had known from his childhood and who one day lost all her social standing overnight simply because a man was found in her bedroom, Saratchandra said in 1932:

> Perhaps she has nothing called chastity left any more. Suppose I accept that. But what about her femininity? Will her nursing of the sick for days and nights on end . . . and her unstinting giving to the poor receive no . . . consideration? Is the woman's body everything that matters, does

> her inside (*antar*) count for nothing? Even if this woman, widowed in her childhood and driven by the unbearable urgings of youth, failed to preserve the purity (*pabitrata*) of her body, will that make all the qualities of her inside false?. . . Where do we get to see the true beauty (*prakrito rup*) of the human being? In the covering of his or her body or in the covering of his or her interiority?—You tell me.[51]

The details of Saratchandra's argument here are worth some attention, for they help us see the working of the aesthetic marginalization of the body in early modern fiction in Bengal. Saratchandra does not argue against the idea of chastity as such; more typically and primarily, he sees it as a practice of the mind and not of the body. The young widow might have been with another man but that destroyed, if anything, only the purity of her body. The more valuable purity was the purity of her mind, which was reflected in her acts of compassion and self-sacrifice, and that—and not her body—was what gave her real beauty (*prakrito rup*). The argument about *pabitrata* or purity was about the interior self. Its cultivation made the woman her own person. Saratchandra saw this inner purity of the good woman as a sign of her individuality. He would use it as ground for opposing men's unquestioned rights over women. He wrote to a woman correspondent about the idea "that she who became a widow at the age of sixteen or seventeen would have no right to love or marry anybody else." "Why not?" he asked and added, "It takes only a little thought to see that there is but one prejudice hidden in this [proposition], that the wife is a possession of the husband."[52]

The novels thus established the idea of a disembodied, private, but communicable sphere of interiority—something critical to the category of the modern subject in European thought.[53] Bengali literary thought acknowledged lust as animal passion residing in the body. To this it opposed the idea of *prem* or love. *Prem* came to mark the autonomy of the individual in the widow by seeing the achievement of purity or *pabitrata* in love as the act of separating the self from the body. Society could indeed oppress the individual—in this case, the widow—but it could not take away her individuality. Fiction thus shone a light by which to see (and archive) the widow as an individual subject endowed with interiority. The widow, qua widow, could now both write about herself and be written about.

The body remains an unresolved problem in these novels. It is either completely marginalized as the seat of the lust that *pabitra prem* (true/pure love) conquers, or it comes back (as in Bankim) in the problem of *rup* (form, appearance), as fate that teases and tempts the human's internal nature (*antahprakriti*). In either case, there is nothing like the Freudian category of "sexuality" mediating between the body and the interior space of the subject. In *Chokher bali*, Tagore gives a name to the form of reason that struggles with physical passion to produce the practices of purity: *kartabyabudhhi* (*kartabya* = duty; *budhhi* = intellect). This, in other words, was the mode of reasoning that kept one tied to one's worldly duties, a kind of common sense about the householder's life in a context where the extended family, even if unworkable in practice, ideally constituted the horizon of well-being. As Tagore himself interjected in an authorial intervention in the novel: "If love is ever plucked out and isolated—as one plucks a flower—from the difficult duties that make up the householder's world, it cannot sustain itself by [feeding] only on its own sap. It gradually wilts and becomes distorted."[54]

The struggle that constitutes the interiority of the subject as imagined in this Bengali modernity is played out between passions on one side and familial or kinship obligations on the other, and it is in this struggle that sentiments need the guiding hand of (a moral) reason. It was the respectability of the extended family—and not just of the loving couple—that was at issue. Vidyasagar's problematic of "respectable domesticity" had thus indeed survived into the writings of Tagore. The pursuit of *pabitrata* gave the modern subject an interior space of struggle, created an autonomy vis-à-vis the body, but it also sustained a particularly Bengali family romance. This was nothing like the European psychological triangle of the mother, father, and the child that Freud both technicalized and popularized in early twentieth century. The Bengali modern self was not quite the bourgeois modern self of Europe. The category of *pabitrata*, tied to an idealization of kinship and the patriarchal extended family, obviated the emergence of a category such as "sexuality" that could have mediated between the physical and psychological aspects of sexual attraction.

Bengali modernity thus reflects some of the fundamental themes of European modernity—for instance, the idea that the modern subject is propertied (as in Rammohun Roy's call for property rights for women); that the subject was an autonomous agent (as depicted in Bengali novels); or that suffering could be documented from the position of the citizen (see Kalyani Datta's efforts to do so). Yet the family romance speaks of a significantly different subject. In a later chapter, where we examine this romance in more detail, we shall see how it leads to ideas of personhood and fraternity fundamentally different from those propounded by, say, Locke. For now, we will focus on how the presence of these other themes of family and personhood brought a sense of plurality into the history of the modern observer of suffering. It would be rash to assimilate Kalyani Datta's essay of 1991 into a straightforward narrative of rights and citizenship.

WHO GETS CALLED TO WITNESS SUFFERING?

Modern Bengali literature, then, played a crucial role in generalizing a will to document the suffering of the widow and in enabling certain ways of seeing. As a genre, the novel was particularly suited to aiding in the reproduction of a general and generalizing sentiment while preserving and nurturing the idea of the individual and private. Its techniques of verisimilitude promoted a sense of the particular, while at the same time creating a vision of the general. The growing and close connection forged between literature, middle-class reading practices, and new forms of personhood is a history still unexplored in the case of Bengal. It would seem, for example, that by the 1930s readers of Bengali novels actually compared the many widow characters created in fiction, and mentally placed them in a series signifying the progressive evolution of the modern individual. The following lines from Suresh Samajpati, the editor of the Bengali literary journal *Sahitya*, addressed to Saratchandra, illustrates this comparative and historicist mode of reading on the part of a reader:

> There is a substantial difference between the character of Rohini that Bankimchandra created and that of your Sabitri. First, Rohini was the niece of Brahmananda, she had no lack of status in society. Her only crime was that in spite of being a widow, she loved Gobindalal. Your . . . Sabitri enjoys no such social standing. Second, it required a lot of arranging [of events] for the love affair between Gobindalal and Rohini to look inevitable [in Bankim's novel]. . . . At least in the eyes of society there is an excuse for the love between Rohini and Gobindalal. But there can be no such excuse possible for the love between Sabitri and Satish. One depends on the contingency of events, the other on desire alone.[55]

Individuals, including female readers of this humanist fiction, came to see their lives in the light of literature. In her autobiographical book, *Kom boyosher ami* (The Me of Younger Years), the contemporary writer Manashi Dasgupta describes an older, widowed aunt, "Itupishi" (father's sister/cousin called Itu) as being "somebody straight out of the pages of Bengali fiction." Dasgupta writes of this aunt: "she became a widow at a young age, now she worked for the government's education department having put herself through school. . . . With ease she would converse with my father on the subjects such as the failure of the United Nations while helping my mother cook *nimki* [popular savories]."[56] Kalyani Datta's researches into the condition of Bengali widows in the 1950s and the 1960s were themselves inspired by fiction: "Widowhood has featured endlessly in Bengali literature over the last hundred and fifty years. . . . My interest in the lives of widows was aroused in my childhood as a result of meeting at close quarters characters in real life who resembled those encountered in stories and novels."[57]

If we assume that the different practices of writing about widows—fiction, autobiographies, diaries, reminiscences, and investigative reporting of the widow's suffering—created in Bengal something like the European bourgeois public sphere inhabited by a discursive and collective subject of modernity, an interesting problem follows. How would we understand this collective subject? Was this subject the same as the citizen-subject of European political thought? There is no doubt that colonial law itself molded aspects of both action and subjectivity on the part of the widows. The Bengali poet Prasannamayi Devi (1857–1939), who had become a widow at the age of twelve, tells the story, for example, of a brave nineteenth-century village woman called Kashiswari who, on becoming a widow at a young age, successfully sought legal intervention against possible oppression and harassment by men.[58] Widows' own accounts of domestic cruelty, however, bridge two kinds of memory that together form the modern archive of familial oppression in Hindu middle-class Bengal. These are the social-public memory addressed by the citizen-historian who documents suffering and social injury in the interest of justice in public life, and familial memories articulated within specific locations of kinship.[59] Kalyani Datta's essay itself is an example of this, for she puts into print—and thus makes into public memory—memories she could sometimes access only as a member of a particular network of kinship.

In standard narratives of European-bourgeois modernity, these two kinds of memories—the familial and the public—would eventually be aligned with each other. First, families based on modern romantic love would replace the extended kin structure with the Freudian oedipal triangle. And the unitary-expressive and rights-bearing bourgeois subject would be split into private and public selves. Anything that could not align itself with the laws of public life would eventually be assimilated into a structure of private repression. So the history of repression and sexuality would come to constitute the private history of the subject of public life. As Foucault's *History of Sexuality* shows, such a repressive hypothesis and a consequent incitement to speech were critical to the birth of the modern subject and the documentation of bourgeois interiority.[60] In the Bengali case, the addressees of these two memories—the social-public and the familial-private one, the citizen-subject and the subject of kinship—remain much less aligned or streamlined with each other. The collective subject whom we could call the Bengali modern subject can perhaps be conceptualized as a mobile point on something like a relay network in which many different subject positions and even nonbourgeois, nonindividualistic practices of subjectivity intersect. Kalyani Datta's text murmurs with multiple, heterogeneous voices she can collect only in a general gesture of seeking justice. The discursive collective Bengali subject of modernity was made up of multiple and noncommensurable practices, some of them distinctly nonmodern by the standards of modern political thought.

First, there was voice of the subject whose cry of pain was addressed to the exceptional subject (not the normalized citizen) who could both receive and appreciate the *rasa* of *karuna* (compassion). Whoever hears this cry is called to the position of somebody with *hriday*—a Rammohun, a Vidyasagar, a Jesus, a Chaitanya, or a Budhha. Consider, for example, this statement from a Bengali widow: "a woman who has lost her father, mother, husband and son, has nobody else left in the world. It is *only if* others in the household are of a kind disposition that a widow's life can be happy. Otherwise, it is like being consigned to a hell-pit."[61] The conditional clause in this statement—only if—makes it clear that compassion was not a part of the normal order of life for this speaker. Its existence was unpredictable. This is the widow speaking indeed, but not as a citizen-subject seeking the promise and protection of law.

Then there is the voice that addresses itself to gods in search of strength and support. Listen to the voice of Gyanadasundari speaking to Kalyani Datta sometime in 1965. A child widow who in fact had never met her husband, she was sent to her in-laws to spend the rest of her life as a widow. Here she recounts an experience of deprivation in which the Hindu goddess Kali plays a critical role helping her to survive:

> I entered the kitchen [she said, speaking of her daily round of activities] immediately after my morning bath [to cook for] this large family. By the time I was finished, it would be late afternoon. A room full of cooked

> food—I cannot describe how hungry the smell of rice and curry made me feel. Sometimes I felt tempted to put some in my mouth. But my [deceased] husband's aunt had told me the story of the wife of certain [deceased] person—this woman had been struck down with blindness on account eating stealthily in the kitchen. Stories of this kind helped me control my hunger. Everyday I would pray to [the goddess] Kali: Mother, please take away my greed. Perhaps it was through the grace of the goddess that I gradually lost any appetite I used to have.[62]

What is the nature of the human subject here? In what way do we recognize ourselves in Gyanadasundari Devi? How is Kalyani Datta—and indeed, the reader—positioned by this text? In more ways than one, it would seem. Datta (or the reader) may have been there to document the subject of suffering in the interest of eventual social intervention. Her intended position may have been that of the modern, secular, historicizing human being. She may have indeed heard the religious reference to the goddess in light of the spirit of toleration with which the secular subject approaches religion: "it is the sigh of the oppressed, the soul of a soulless world."[63] But does not Gyanadasundari's voice also place us alongside another human, one who acts as though she or he implicitly knew that being human meant one could address gods without having first to prove their reality?[64] This positioning takes us beyond the logic of the social sciences.

Cruelty toward widows in the context of extended kinship constantly proliferated the positions and voices of both its agents and victims, and sometimes blurred the distinctions between the two. Kalyani Datta reports the story of both the victimhood and the agency that a mother took on herself when her daughter, a six- or seven-year-old child, lost her husband. To the mother fell the duty of ensuring that the girl, who did not even understand the change in her status, observed all the self-renunciatory rites of widowhood. The incident relates to fish, not allowed to widows but considered a delicacy in the cuisine of riverine Bengal. We have the story in Kalyani Datta's telling:

> [The young girl's] mother used to feed her widows' food. The boys of the household would sit on another side of the room and be served fish. They said to her one day, "How come you haven't got any fish?" Her mother pointed to fried lentil balls and said to her: "This is your fish." The mischievous boys would suck on fish-bones and ask the girl: "How

come your piece of fish does not have any bones?" The girl would ask her mother, "Mother, why doesn't my fish have any bones?". . . The mother later used to break off bamboo slips from baskets and stick them into the lentil balls and the girl would proudly show them off to the boys. . . . It was a long time before she even realized the deception.[65]

The mother who administered the cruelty of deceiving her own child suffered—we assume—no less than her child. One can also read this story as a tribute to a loving mother's ingenuity—faced with the cruelty of both custom and callous boys—in preserving her little child's dignity. However we read it, clearly the actions of the boys (not necessarily the mother's sons), the mother, and the child widow in this anecdote create a dynamic network of relationships that cannot be contained within the figure of a single victim.[66]

Indeed, one of the most interesting aspects of widows' own critiques—in the nineteenth and twentieth centuries—of the cruelty they received at the hands of their relatives was an appeal to an ideal subject of the extended family. How should a brother behave toward a widowed sister, or a brother-in-law toward a widowed sister-in-law? Or a nephew toward a widowed aunt? Putting widows' complaints into print and reading them were often part of a larger discussion about sentiments proper to the ideal Bengali family, which was seldom seen as nuclear. A telling case in this regard is that of Indumati, an aunt of Kalyani Datta. Indumati (born c. 1872), a young widow of a *zamindar* (landlord) family, decided to live in the holy city of Banaras—a traditional refuge for many a hapless widow—on a monthly allowance from her inheritance of the deceased husband's estate. She was subsequently cheated out of her inheritance. Her allowance dwindled from Rs 250 a month to Rs 10, reducing her to the status of a beggar. Kalyani Datta last saw Indumati in Banaras in 1955 (and we hear her in print in 1991). She had by then reached the depth of her penury and was living in an institution. "I did not recognize her," says Datta:

> Our aunt, the wife of a *zamindar* (landlord) family with 50 percent share in the estate, sat naked in a dark room without windows, cursing God in a muttering voice. She could not see very well. Feeling helpless, I started yelling out my name and that of my father. She recognized me then and immediately started crying. . . . After a while, she asked me how long I had been in Kashi [Banaras]. When she realized that I had been there for twenty days and had come to see her only a day before my day of departure, her tears returned. "Here I am," she said, "hoping that I

would [now] be able to shed some tears and spend some days in the comfort of your company, and all you offer me is this *fake [perfunctory] sense of kinship*. I don't even want to see your face." So saying, she turned her back on me.[67]

This entire passage, one could say, is a modern discussion of what Bengalis call *atmiyata* (kinship, the quality of being one's own people), a much-valued category in Tagore and other modern writers.[68] Notice how in Kalyani Datta's telling of the story a subject-voice emerges that absolutizes a modern and relational subject of kinship, and does so by placing the very sentiment of obligation in kinship above considerations of either interest or perfunctory social form. Indumati/Kalyani Datta—for the two voices are actually indistinguishable here—obviously make a distinction between a fake show of kinship sentiment and a "real" one. But they do not require such a sentiment to be an expression of the personality of the individual expressing it, for the sentiment would be demanded of any member of the kin group without reference to the differences between their individual personalities. And yet the language allows certain claims to be made on another person's affection in a way that, strictly speaking, would not be possible in the context of typically expressivist individualism, where feelings, once dead to the individual concerned, are seen as inauthentic and hypocritical if expressed. The subject of this emotional transaction is modern and yet, as I have said, not like the bourgeois individual of Europe inscribed in the family romance of the typical triangle of the nuclear family.[69] I am not claiming that this idealized subject of kinship was necessarily a modern construction. What is modern is the way the coming of a public sphere opened up a space in public life for the modern subject of extended kinship alongside, say, the sphere of intervention made possible by law and the idea of the rights-bearing individual.

The subject of Bengali modernity who demonstrates a will to witness and document oppression is thus inherently a multiple subject, whose history produces significant points of resistance and intractability when approached with a secular analysis that has its origins in the self-understanding of the subject of European modernity. Thus we may read the author Kalyani Datta in two different ways. As an author and a person, it is indeed possible that in writing her essay she acts as a citizen-subject engaged in a struggle for democracy and social justice in the realm of the family. One could, in the same mode, read her essay as a chapter in the biography/history of some larger collective entity such as "middle-class Bengali women" or "the Bengali *bhadramahila*" (as women of the respectable classes are called). But what is also documented in her essay and elsewhere, thanks to the resolute will to witness suffering that marks modern attempts at social justice, are practices of the self that call us to other ways of being civil and humane. These are practices of the self that always leave an intellectually unmanageable excess when translated into the politics and language of political philosophies we owe to European intellectual traditions. The very colonial crucible in which Bengali modernity originated ensured that that it would not be possible to fashion a historical account of the birth of this modernity without reproducing some aspect of European narratives of the modern subject—for European modernity was present at this birth. Colonialism guarantees a certain Europe of the mind—the Europe of liberalism or Marxism—this precedence. What a historian of a colonial modernity can do today—taught as he or she is in the (European) art of historicizing—is to re-energize the word "birth" with all the motor power of Nietzschean thought that Michel Foucault revived for us in recent times.[70] To see birth as genealogy and not as a clear-cut point of origin, to make visible—as Nietzsche said—the otherness of the ape that always gets in the way of any attempt to trace human descent directly from God, is to open up the question of the relationship between diversity of life practices or life-worlds and universalizing political philosophies, which remain the global heritage of the Enlightenment.[71] Kalyani Datta's essay *Baidhabya kahini* may then be seen as belonging to an archive of the birth of the citizen-subject in Bengal. The site of the birth is where accounts of the oppression of widows, lodged in the crevices of familial memories, are recovered for discussion and dissemination in the public sphere. But this single subject breaks up, on examination, into multiple ways of being human, which make it impossible for us to reduce this moment to any summary narrative of transition from a premodern stage to modernity.

CHAPTER 6

Nation and Imagination

THIS CHAPTER moves out into three concentric circles. The innermost circle tells the story of a certain literary debate in Bengal in the early part of the twentieth century. This was a debate about distinctions between prose, poetry, and the status of the real in either, and it centered on the writings of Rabindranath Tagore. Into these debates—and here is my second circle—I read a global history of the word "imagination." Benedict Anderson's book *Imagined Communities* has made us all aware of how crucial the category "imagination" is to the analysis of nationalism.[1] Yet, compared to the idea of community, imagination remains a curiously undiscussed category in social science writings on nationalism. Anderson warns that the word should not be taken to mean "false."[2] Beyond that, however, its meaning is taken to be self-evident. One aim of this chapter is to open up the word for further interrogation and to make visible the heterogenous practices of seeing we often bring under the jurisdiction of this one European word, "imagination." My third and last move in the chapter is to build on this critique of the idea of imagination an argument regarding a nontotalizing conception of the political. To breathe heterogeneity into the word "imagination," I suggest, is to allow for the possibility that the field of the political is constitutively not singular. I begin, then, with the story of a literary debate.

NATIONALISM AS WAYS OF SEEING

It does not take much effort to see that a photographic realism or a dedicated naturalism could never answer all the needs of vision that modern nationalisms create. For the problem, from a nationalist point of view, is this: If the nation, the people, or the country were not just to be observed, described, and critiqued but loved as well, what would guarantee that they were indeed worth loving unless one also saw in them something that was already lovable? What if the real, the natural, and the historically accurate did not generate the feeling of devotion or adoration? An objectivist, realist view might lead only to disidentification. Nationalism, one may then say, presents the question of vision and imagination in ways more complicated than a straightforward identification of the realist or the factual with the political might suggest.

This problem of how one sees the nation was once raised in a pointed manner by Rabindranath Tagore, speaking at a meeting organized in Calcutta on the occasion of Sister Nivedita's death in 1911. Sister Nivedita, an Irish nationalist whose original name was Margaret Noble and who came to India as a disciple of the nineteenth-century Indian saint Swami Vivekananda, dedicated her life to serving the colonized Indians. She had been able to love Indians, said Tagore, because she was able to "pierce the veil" of that which was objectively real: "We hear about Europeans who came to India with feelings of devotion toward her, having been attracted by our scriptures or by the character or the words of some of our holy men . . . but they returned empty-handed, their sense of devotion waning over time and discarded in the end. They could not pierce the veil of poverty and incompleteness in the country as a whole to see what they had read about in the scriptures or what they had seen in the characters of holy men."[3]

It was not Tagore's contention that Europeans who were repelled by what they saw in India simply misread the country or its people. Realistically seen, India could indeed be disappointing, and this European reaction was therefore quite justified. Tagore went on to say, "It is beyond our comprehension as to how our manners, conversations, and everyday practices could be insufferably offensive to a European, and thus we think of their rudeness toward us as completely unreasonable." His point was precisely that a view that was merely realist might not present an India that was lovable. To be able to love India was to go beyond realism, to pierce the veil of the real, as Tagore put it. It was this barrier of the objective or the real that, Tagore thought, Nivedita would have had to overcome to find in herself a true love for India: "We have to remember that every moment of the days and nights that Sister Nivedita spent in a dark Bengali home in a lane in a Bengali neighborhood of Calcutta, contained a hidden history of pain. . . . There is no doubt that she would have been acutely troubled by our inertia, slothfulness, uncleanliness, mismanagement, and a general want of effort on our part, things that at every step speak of the dark side of our nature." But "this was not able to defeat" Nivedita because she could see beyond the real, she could pierce the veil of poverty and incompleteness at which a realist gaze stopped.[4]

What did it mean to pierce the veil of the real or to see beyond it? Blending, as we will see, idioms of European romanticism with those of

Hindu metaphysics, Tagore sometimes explained such sight as a matter of seeing the eternal that lay beyond the "veil" of the everyday. Of Nivedita's love for the country, he said, using a language inflected by religion and referring to the Hindu goddess Sati's devotion to her husband Shiva: "Her affection for the good [Tagore actually uses a more resonant word, *mangal*, which also connotes auspiciousness] of India was true, it was not an infatuation; this Sati had dedicated herself completely to the Shiva who resides in all men."[5] In parenthesis, we should also note that this use of the "eternal" had already made Tagore's proposition exceed the problematic of nationalist vision, for the Irish woman Nivedita's love for India or Indians surely could not be called "nationalist" in any simple sense.[6]

PROSE, POETRY, AND THE QUESTION OF REALITY

How could one reconcile the need for these two different and contradictory ways of seeing the nation: the critical eye that sought out the defects in the nation for the purpose of reform and improvement, and the adoring eye that saw the nation as already beautiful or sublime? Tagore developed a "romantic" strategy quite early on his literary career for dealing with this problem. His initial solution—I say "initial" because he later destabilized it—was to create a division of labor between prose and poetry or, more accurately, between the prosaic and the poetic. The strategy is illustrated in what he wrote in a nationalist vein in the period 1890 to about 1910, when he helped create two completely contradictory images, for example, of the typical "Bengali" village.

On the one side were his prose pieces, in particular the short stories about Bengali rural life in the collection *Galpaguchha*, in which a trenchant critique of society and a clear political will for reform were visible. Bengali literary critics have often noted how *Galpaguchha* "contained [stories of] the evils of dowry, the domination of wives by husbands, of oppression of women, of selfishness between families marrying into each other, . . . of quarrels among brothers over property." Critics also note the variety of characters and classes represented in this collection: "Ramsundar, the father burdened with the responsibility of having to get his daughter married (*Denapaona*), the religious-minded Ramkanai (*Ramkanaier nirbudhbhita*), . . . the shy writer Taraprasanna (*Taraprasannar kirti*), . . . the loyal servant Raicharan (*Khokababur protyaborton*). . . ."[7]

Tagore himself took considerable pride in the realism of these stories. "People say of me," he complained in his old age, "he comes from a rich family . . . what would he know of villages?"[8] His answer was unambiguously stated in an essay he wrote in 1940/41:

> Let me have my final word here. The time has come for me to give an explanation to those who complain that they do not find any traces of the middle class (*moddhobitto* = middle-propertied) in my writings. . . . There was a time when month after month I wrote stories about life in the countryside. It is my belief that never before had such pictures been serialized in Bengali literature. There was no dearth of writers from the middle-propertied classes then [but] they were almost all absorbed in contemplating [romantic historical] figures such as Pratapsingha or Pratapaditya. My fear is that one day *Galpaguchha* will become untouchable "non-literature" for having kept the company of a "bourgeois writer." Already [I notice that] they are not even mentioned—as if they did not even exist—when assessments are made of the class character of my writings.[9]

Tagore, in fact, never lacked in realist criticisms of village life and contributed substantially to what became a realist, and negative, stereotype of the Bengali village. Later in life in the 1920s and the 1930s, when involved in rural reconstruction work around his educational institution at Santiniketan, he made several references to his realistic knowledge of village life: "I have spent a long time in villages, I do not want to say anything simply to please. The image I have seen of villages is extremely ugly. Jealousy, rivalry, fraudulence, and trickery between people find a variety of manifestations. . . . I have seen with my own eyes how deep the roots of corruption have gone there."[10] Or here is another critical passage from later essay (c. 1938): "I had the opportunity . . . [as a landlord in East Bengal] to get to know close-up the villages of Bengal. I have seen . . . the scarcity of drinking water in the houses of the villagers, and noticed the . . . manifestations in their bodies of the influence of diseases and of the want of appropriate food. Many a time I have received proof of how they remain oppressed and cheated at every step, their minds afflicted by ignorance and inertia."[11] These negative images of village life were to be the stock in trade of the realist prose of socially engaged nationalist writers in the twentieth century, one of the most famous examples of this genre being the novel *Pallisamaj* (1916) by Saratchandra Chattopadhyay.[12]

At the same time, however, as he employed his prosaic writings to document social problems, Tagore put his poetic compositions (not always in verse), and songs to a completely different use. These created and deployed images of the same generic category—the Bengali village—but this time as the as a land of arcadian and pastoral beauty overflowing with the sentiments that defined what Tagore would increasingly—from the 1880s on—call "the Bengali heart."[13] This was the "golden Bengal" of his famous 1905 song later adopted as the national anthem of Bangladesh:

> My golden Bengal, I love you.
> Your sky, your breezes ever play through the flute of my heart.
> O Mother, the fragrance of your spring mango
> groves drives me wild,
> Ah me—
> O Mother, what honeyed smiles I have seen upon
> your fields of late autumn.[14]

Or there were the famous lines of his poem *Dui bigha jami* that Tagore wrote around 1895 while traveling in East Bengal as a landlord. Upen, the central character in the poem, is a villager who is evicted from his land by a greedy and grabbing landlord. In sorrow and grief, Upen leaves the village until he returns to it one day and, on sighting it from a distance, recites to himself in a state of rapture lines that have become a schooltext staple for Bengali children ever since:

> I salute you Bengal, my beautiful mother,
> The soothing breeze on the banks of the Ganga comforts me.
> The open fields—the forehead of the sky—kiss the dust of your feet
> Little abodes of peace are your villages
> Nestling in dark and intimate shadows.[15]

The prosaic and the poetic thus came to share a division of labor in Tagore's writings. The prosaic element spoke of poverty, ill health, factionalism, ignorance, casteism, "feudal" oppression, and so on, and the poetic pictured the Bengali home/village as a place blessed with divine grace and beauty, a peaceful home for the tender Bengali heart, the golden Bengal of nationalist sentiments. The former was amenable to historicist and objectivist treatment; it stood for the familiar political desire of the modern to align the world with that which was real and rational. The poetic, argued Tagore, took us outside of historical time. Together, prose and poetry posed and answered the question of the two ways of seeing in Bengali nationalism.

Several scholars have commented on the connection between political and social reform in nineteenth-century Bengal and the rise of descriptive realism in Bengali prose. Srikumar Bandyopadhyay's comprehensive and masterful survey of the history of the Bengali novel, *Bangla shahitye upanyasher dhara*—first serialized in a Bengali magazine around 1923/24—made much the same connection between the realism of prose fiction and the coming of a new, modern politics of democratic sensibility.[16] "The main characteristic of a novel," said Bandyopadhyay, was that "it was a completely modern object." It signaled the transition from the middle ages to modernity.

> Of all the different branches of literature, the novel is the one most influenced by democracy. Democracy is its foundation . . . the emancipation of man from the social shackles of the middle ages and the inauguration of individualism are indispensable elements of the novel. The novel appears at the same time as this sense of individualism. Second, the awakening of a sense of self-respect in the minds of the lower classes which accompanies the development of individuality [in them], and which the other classes have to acknowledge sooner or later, is also a main ingredient of the novel.[17]

Yet another characteristic of the novel, Bandyopadhyay goes on to explain, is its commitment to naturalism and realism—the Bengali word *bastabata* (*bastab* = real) works to signify both. Realism meant the avoidance of both the supernatural and the divine as well as the unnaturalism of ancient Indian tales (of the *Panchatantra*, for instance) in which animals were made to speak wisely and in human voice, giving the reader no idea of their "true form/nature" (*prokrito rup*).[18] Thus the ultimate ingredient of the novel, in Bandyopadhyay's reckoning, is a rational outlook on life. It is true, he admits, that the biographies of the medieval Bengali religious reformer Chaitanya written by his followers of the sixteenth and seventeenth centuries contain much realistic detail. They may even arouse in us a sense of history. But they are marred by an excess of devotionalism: "the rush of devotional sentiments [in them] has swept away the cautious carefulness of scientific discussion."[19]

Bandyopadhyay's points were repeated by Humayun Kabir, once India's minister of education, in his Tagore centennial lectures at the University of Wisconsin, Madison, in 1961. "Social life in India," said Kabir, borrowing heavily from Bandyopadhyay, "was essentially traditional and conservative. . . . This fact and the segregation of the sexes are two major reasons why the novel is a late comer in Indian literature. . . . There were of course the Jataka stories which have a certain democratic feeling, but realism and supernaturalism are so intermingled in them that they cannot be regarded as the precursor of the novel."[20] Echoing Bandyopadhyay, he added: "The novel is essentially a modern form of art and could not emerge till a more democratic spirit had pervaded society in Europe." Novels needed "democratic temper," "individuality," and "the development of the scientific temper."[21] The new prose of fiction—novels and short stories—was thus seen as intimately connected to questions of political modernity. It was tied to the emergence of the real and signified a realistic, objectivist engagement with the world.

By the 1940s, this distinction between prose and poetry had become naturalized. It did not seem to matter that the Sanskrit word *gadya*, used in modern Bengali to designate prose, was once considered a branch of *kavya*, the word designating verse and poetry.[22] The young and gifted poet Sukanta Bhattacharya used the distinction between them to produce political poetry in the context of the famine of 1943. "In the kingdom of hunger the world is only prosaic," declared an immortal line of Bhattacharya. His short but powerful poem plays on a distinction between prose and poetry that by the forties was obviously ready at hand for Bengali poets and writers to use:

> O Great Life, no more of this poetic fancy (*kabya*) now,
> Bring in prose (*gadya*), hard and harsh,
> Let the jingling charm of verse be silenced,
> Strike with the severe hammer of prose!
> There is no need for the soothing touch of poetry—
> Verse, I grant you leave today,
> In the kingdom of hunger the world is only prosaic—
> The moon, when full, is like a browned chapati.[23]

Prose in this poem aligned itself with reality, hunger, and the struggle for justice, and thus with the time of history making and politics. Poetry, on the other hand, bespoke an absence of realism, of a sense of distance from the political, though the irony of Bhattacharya writing these lines in verse was not lost on his contemporaries.[24]

PROSE, POETRY AND MODERNISM IN CALCUTTA

The distinction between the functions of prose and poetry that Tagore had helped to found and elaborate at the turn of the century and that addressed the nationalist politics of vision in early twentieth century eventually created a lively debate in the history of Bengali literary modernism. My use of the word "modernism" follows that of Marshall Berman in designating the aesthetic means by which an urban and literate class subject to the invasive forces of modernization seeks to create, however falteringly, a sense of being at home in the modern city.[25] Tagore's poetry, complained many of the poets of the 1920s and later, provided few means for doing for Calcutta what Baudelaire had done for nineteenth-century Paris.[26] Tagore's writings, and in particular his poetry, it was said, lacked in realism.

This charge had always been there, ever since Tagore made a name for himself in the nineteenth century. At its crudest, it came in the form of a jealous accusation that their ancestral wealth had enabled Tagore and his relatives to pursue the fine arts by sparing them the usual struggles of middle-class lives in Calcutta. In not too veiled a reference to the talented Tagore family, a short story published in the magazine *Sahitya* in 1898 said the following in a tone of sarcasm, using a mock autobiographical voice: "It was because we did not have to worry about feeding our stomachs that we could afford an intense degree of opposition to the school and the university. Just as people keep pigeons or go fishing or ride horses . . . in pursuit of a hobby, it was to satisfy our whims in a similar manner that someone among us became a painter, someone else a poet, or some other person a philosopher.[27]

The accusation that increasingly made itself heard in the twentieth century, around the time that Tagore was awarded the Nobel prize (1913), was that his writings lacked a sense of *bastab*, the Bengali word for the real. One of the first to make this accusation was the nationalist leader Bipin Chandra Pal, who in the 1910s was moving toward the idea of socialism. Writing in the journal *Bangadarshan* in the year 1912, Pal wrote: "Much of Rabindranath's creation is illusory. His poetry has seldom been materialistic (*bostutantrik*); one can also observe this want of materialism in the characters he has created. Rabindranath has written many short stories and a few large novels, yet very rarely does one come across in reality (*bastab*) resemblances to any of the characters he has drawn."[28]

Pal's explanation for this emphasized once again the wealth of the Tagore family: "The modern aristocracy of Calcutta live inside a small circle. The common people cannot enter the inner quarters of their lives, nor they into the lives of the common people."[29] The complaint was repeated in a series of essays by the Bengali sociologist Radhakamal Mukherjee, who also argued that "Tagore's writings are without any quality of materialism." "What he has painted in *Achalayatan* and *Gora* has no relationship to real life (*bastab jiban*)."[30] His novel *Char Adhyay* was subject to the criticism that it had not done justice to the major political movements of the day, "the Harijan movement, labor movement, khaddar movement, or to other aspects of mass movements." Binoy Ghosh, who wrote this in his youth and who was later to become a noted Bengali social historian, made the searing critique that Tagore's "abstract world-humanism" was nothing but the identification of "love for the world with love for God": "But we say, this is simple day dreaming, spiritualism has become its refuge because of its disassociation from reality. This is impossible, absurd, and opposed to human history."[31] Realism and historicism came together in this debate as the twin pillars supporting the ideas of democracy and historical materialism.

Some of these were extreme views and many of them not a little hurtful to Tagore. He often did not respond directly to these charges, but he had to take notice when a younger generation of writers—associated with new and avant-garde magazines such as *Kallol* (1923), *Kalikalam* (1926), *Pragati* (1927), *Parichay* (1931), and *Kabita* (1935)—began to talk, often respectfully but strongly, about the relative absence of poverty and sexuality in Tagore's aesthetics. As Achintyakumar Sengupta, one of the founders of *Kallol*, put it later in his reminiscences: "*Kallol* had moved away from Rabindranath . . . into the worlds of the lower middle classes, the coal mines, . . . slums, pavements, into the neighborhoods of those who were rejected and deceived."[32] The poet Buddhadev Bose thus described the development: "The main symptom of the so-called Kallol era was rebellion, and the main target of that rebellion was Rabindranath. . . . It was felt that his poems had no intimate connection to reality (*bastab*), no intensity of passion, no signs of the agony of existence, that his philosophy of life had unfairly ignored the undeniable corporeality of human beings."[33] Jibanananda Das, one of the most important poets of the post-Tagore age, addressed a letter to Tagore that spoke of the same sense of distance: "I am a young Bengali man who sometimes writes poetry. I have seen you many times, and then lost myself in the crowds. Your enormous luminosity and my insignificant life have [together] always created a gap between [us] that I have never been able to cross."[34]

From here it was only one step to argue that Tagore was not of the Bengali middle classes, that he was altogether exotic and, curiously, much too Western. The complaint could be harsh, as in a letter from a Bengali man quoted in Edward Thompson's book on Tagore. Thompson does not reveal the name of his correspondents, we are only told that the writer of the following lines was a "distinguished scholar":

> His [Tagore's] mode of thinking is so essentially English that I appreciate his English translation of the Gitanjali far better than the original Bengali. . . . Among us those only who have lost all touch with the old vernacular literature and with the life of the people, reading only European books, are his admirers. . . . If our country loses herself headlong in the sea of foreign culture, he will no doubt be the harbinger of a new literary age. But if otherwise, I am sure his fame will fade. . . . European appreciation does not weigh much with us, it only shows that he has acquired the political knack of saying things in such a way as will readily appeal to the European mind. . . .
>
> Bengal has not given Rabindranath to Europe—rather Europe has given him to the Bengalis. By praising him, European scholars praise their own gift. I would feel more proud if our own poets had received such fame in foreign countries.[35]

We now know from E. P. Thompson's researches on his father's book on Tagore that the author of this letter written in 1922 was none other than the famous literary scholar Dinesh Chandra Sen, himself often a beneficiary of Tagore's generosity and patronage.[36]

The burden of the observations of Dinesh Chandra, if not the antipathy of his exact words, was to linger on into the 1960s, when both Budhhadev Bose and Sudhindranath Datta, important poets of the post-1930s period, made the following statements:

> Rabindranath's works are European literature written in Bengali language and they are the first of its kind.

> In the hands of [Rabindranath] Bengali literature turned occidental in all but speech.[37]

The issue of personal tastes and animosities apart, at the heart of these debates around Tagore's alleged lack of realism was the question of modernism in Bengali literature. The Bengali middle class in Calcutta was born and raised within the miserable governmental institutions of a colonial capitalism. The experience of school and university, of examinations that led to degrees rather than education, of being a petty clerk in some office, of having to cope with crowded streets and derelict modes of transport, of the grime, heat, dust, dirt, and diseases bred in the unsanitary conditions of the city—these were critical to the everyday sense of being a middle-class Bengali person. Yet the greatest Bengali poet experienced few or none of these institutions deeply in his personal life, having been saved from them by the good fortune of being born in a wealthy landed aristocratic family of the city.

More than that, the similes and metaphors Tagore used in a series of articles from the 1920s on, to defend his understanding of the relationship between the poetic and the real (*bastab*), make it clear that he did not see anything aesthetic in these experiences of middle-class urban life. Not for him, to borrow an expression Benjamin uses with regard to Baudelaire's poetry, any "botanizing on [Calcutta's] asphalt."[38] Tagore's writings expressed clearly his sense of distance from the world of the Bengali office clerk or the schoolteacher. He saw very little in salaried work or in the institutions of civil society that was worthy of poetry. Notice, for instance, how words signifying *chakuri* (salaried employment), or those for the office, examinations, committees and meetings, trams, factories, public life and influenza, and so on, are all used by Tagore in the following extracts from his writings. They serve invariably as the inferior term in pairs of opposition in which words like *griha* (home), *grihalakshmi* (the figure of the housewife imagined as an auspicious embodiment of the goddess Lakshmi), the sky (standing in for nature), and so on, have the higher valency:

> The identity of a man as the head clerk of an office is made obvious by his office papers and files, but the markers that make a woman a *grihalakshmi* are the vermilion mark on the parting of her hair and the bangle on her hand. In other words, the latter needs metaphors and *alamkar* (meaning both jewelry and rhetoric) because she is more than mere information, [our] encounter with her happens not only in knowledge but also in the heart. That we can call the *grihalakshmi* Lakshmi [the goddess of well-being] signifies something by the mere hint of a word. But we never feel any desire to call the head clerk *kerani-narayan* (kerani = writer, clerk; the god Narayan is also the husband of Lakshmi), even though religious theory says that Narayan is present in every man. So it is clear that the head clerk of the office has nothing ineffable about him.[39]

> One cannot compare the lack of beauty of the office room with the simple grace of the *antahpur* [traditionally, the inner quarters of a household where women resided; lit., the internal city].[40]

Why does the flute play on the day of a festival?. . . It is as though the ugly chariots [tramcars] are no longer moving along the iron rails for the sake of the offices, as if all this bargaining and buying and selling amounted to nothing. It [the sound of the flute] hid it all.[41]

There is no other people as devoid of faith as the Bengalis. . . . They cannot even imagine that there could be any other destination in this big world if one ever gave up the paths marked out by the wheels of the office-bound car.[42]

A piece of the sky circumscribed by the wall lies completely trapped in my office room. It can be sold and bought at the same rate as for measures of land, it is even possible to rent it out. But it is an unbroken sky outside spread all over the stars and the planets—the joy of its infinitude exists only in my realization.[43]

The problem about all this was put to Tagore very mildly, and with affection and respect, by Amiya Chakravarty, once a close personal secretary to Tagore, and himself a renowned poet of the thirties and later. In a letter to Tagore written in March 1925, Chakravarty referred to a conversation he had had with Havelock Ellis. Ellis admitted that he found Tagore's "vehement denunciation" of modern civilization "inspiring." But he wondered why the poet had written nothing about the "high romance" of technology, the thrills, "the external beauty" of the aeroplane, for instance.[44] Budhhadev Bose put it more directly in an essay in *Pragati* in 1929: "Our kitchens, our tea stalls, our streets crowded with trams and buses and motor cars, [our] trains—why would not they find places in our poetry? . . . if you happen to believe that they are not good subjects for poetry, just read the two poems of Robert Brooks, 'The Great Lover' and 'Dining Room Tea.' "[45] The poets of the thirties turned to Baudelaire, Eliot, Pound, Hopkins, and other European poets to define their sense of the city and its possibilities for poetry. Budhhadev Bose announced in 1931 that "the age of Tagore was gone."[46] And a few years later, in 1941, Jibanananda admitted that Tagore was no longer satisfactory for the modern Bengali poets.[47]

Some of the younger poets tried the new and ironic technique of including fragments of poems by Tagore in deliberately "unromantic" descriptions of the city. Bishnu Dey, a noted poet and a lecturer in English literature, thus worked a line from Tagore (O Bird, etc.) into the following description of rush-hour traffic in crowded Calcutta:

What horn-locking obstinacy of the bus!
What whimsicality of the machine!
Yet only twenty-five minutes are left—
O bird, O my bird.[48]

Samar Sen's poem *Shvarga hote biday* ironically uses a line from Tagore with a mythical reference to the heavens to speak of the weary urban sexuality of debauched men who every evening crossed the Kalighat bridge to visit prostitutes:

On the Kalighat bridge
Do you hear
The footsteps of the debauched,
Do you hear the sound of the march of time,
O city, O grey city?

Sen's poem echoes the famous lines of a poem "Do you hear the sound of the march of time?" with which Tagore ended his novel *Shesher kabita*.[49]

If the story of literary modernism in Calcutta had ended here, I could have produced a relatively unproblematic narrative about a realist consciousness finally coming into its own in Bengali literature after going through an excusable if not inevitable early phase of idealism/romanticism influenced by English poetry and represented by Tagore. In that case, poetry would have finally aligned itself with the historical and the real—maybe even with democracy—as the novel was said to do. And the poetic/prosaic distinction that Sukanta Bhattacharya put to such memorable use in the 1940s would have been too outdated for him to use with any great effect.

Some of this indeed happened. In his old age, Tagore himself sometimes accepted in his writings the historicist distinctions between the "modern" and that which was not modern, that which represented a bygone era, an age passed, an era living on borrowed time, and saw himself as the embodiment of such a passing. While writing a poem on Africa in 1937 for a global audience at the request of Amiya Chakravarty, Tagore expressed his extreme sense of isolation in a letter: "You requested me to write a poem on Africa, I have obliged. But I don't understand to what end. I am unused to the stance of the modern. The tongue of the foreigner will not reach there where the *rasa* [lit., juice] of my own language flows."[50]

But the fact that the Tagorean distinction between the prosaic and the poetic survives so powerfully in Bhattacharya's poem of the 1940s suggests that the problems of nationalist vision that Tagore addressed early in his career continued to linger in the anticolonial nationalism of Bengali literature. Indeed, the complex relationship between Tagore and his younger contemporaries points to a far deeper problem in Bengali modernity than suggested by a stage theory of development, which posits that Tagore's lack of politics was superseded by a more heightened political consciousness. Most if not all of his younger detractors also remained his secret and not-so-secret devotees. Budhhadev Bose later wrote of his own youthful hostility to Tagore: "I know at least of one young man who every night in bed recited [the poems] of 'Purabi' like crazy, and spent the daytime denouncing Tagore in writing."[51] Sudhindranath Datta, the editor of *Parichay* who had earlier argued why Tagore was unacceptable after the war and why his idealism was unattractive, later retracted in a mode of confession. He wrote: "Having failed in my youth to create poetry according to the Tagorean ideals and under the influence of unconscious jealousy, I did not spare any opportunity to spread the word that not only was Rabindranath inferior to Western poets but that he was also an unsuccessful imitation of them."[52]

Most interesting, in this context, is the fact that even the younger poets who wanted poetry to grapple with the reality of the city and modern life never gave up the bountiful and rural vision of Bengal that Tagore had inaugurated in his nationalist poetry. The same Jibanananda Das who looked to European poets for modernist accents wrote a collection of sonnets posthumously published as *Rupashi Bangla* (Bengal the Beautiful) in the 1950s. They enjoyed a revival at the time of the Bangladesh freedom war in 1970–1971. These sonnets were written in the mid-1930s when, to be realist and historical, Bengal had been ravaged by the agricultural depression of 1930–1934.[53] Yet Das wrote of the plenitude of the Bengal countryside, of birds, trees, and goddesses that marked an eternal Bengal of purely nationalist construction:

> I have looked upon the face of Bengal—the world's beauty
> I need to no longer seek: in the darkness I awake and glimpse
> In a fig tree, sitting beneath umbrella-like foliage,
> The early morning magpie—I see all around piles of leaves
> Of *jam*, banyan, jackfruit, cashew, *aswattha*, lying still;
> Shade falls upon the cactus clump, upon the *sati* grove.
> I know not when Chand from Champa, from his boat the Honeybee,
> Had seen Bengal's exquisite beauties, the same blue shadows.[54]

Or consider these following lines (written in 1962) from the pen of the otherwise historicist and Communist poet Shubhash Mukhopadhyay seeing, as if through a camera, the snapshot of a Bengali mud hut as the perennial Bengali home, blessed with the presence of the goddess of domestic well being, Lakshmi:

> However far I go—
> Attached
> To my eyelids
> Remain
> Rows of footprints of Lakshmi
> Painted
> On a courtyard
> Mopped clean with cowdung and water.[55]

PIERCING THE VEIL, SEEING BEYOND

Stung by the charge that his conception of the poetic lacked ways of handling the miserable realities of everyday life in Calcutta and Bengal, Tagore invented a new prose form called *gadyakabita* or prose-poetry. This is usually dated to the period when he wrote the poems of *Lipika* (1918–1922), though most of his books using this form came out in the years between 1932 and 1936 (*Punascha*, *Shesh Shaptak*, *Patraput*, and *Shyamali*).[56] Tagore's own reasons for inventing this form had to do with literary experimentation. He said that while translating his *Gitanjali* into English, he had become aware of the possibility of writing "rhythmic prose" and wanted to carry that out in Bengali itself. Without in any way belittling the importance of the justification he gave, it is easy to see—as indeed a few Bengali literary critics have pointed out—that this formal innovation carried a polemical charge. It helped Tagore to make his point about the specific relationship between the poetic and the real (*bastab*). The fact that these poems were written in prose allowed him to incorporate into individual poems precisely the kind of topics that his critics said were too prosaic for him to touch: the grime and dirt of Calcutta, lower-middle-class lives, and their everyday frustrations. As Ujjval Majumdar puts it: "Everyday realities and the aesthetic world are inextricably intertwined in *gadyakabita*."[57] Yet, by keeping within the realm of poetry, Tagore could demonstrate his view of what the function of the poetic was in the world of the modern. One has to remember that these were years when

Tagore had made angry remarks about the "curry powder of realism" and the "boasts of poverty and lust" that he thought were being used to spice up literary offerings in Bengali.[58]

To make my point, I shall only discuss one poem, *Bansi* (The Flute), included in the book *Punshcha*. The poem is about the realities of lower-middle-class existence.[59] The poem begins with a prosaic, precise, almost clinical description of the miserable life and living conditions of a petty clerk who lives in an obscure lane of Calcutta. The name of the street still bears witness to its unglorifiable origins—it is called the lane of Kinu goala, Kinu the milkman, who must have made a fortune in the history of the city but whose humble origins the city fathers never erased from public memory. Our narrator, the clerk, Haripada, is so poor that there is really no home for him. He rents a small room in a house in this lane. His life is made up simply of the lane and his office in the city. Haripada ran away from his own wedding because he could not afford the responsibility. Yet the woman he never married and his original home in the riverine countryside of eastern Bengal continue to haunt him in his life in the city.

Tagore begins in a descriptive, realistic vein:

> Kinu Goala's Lane.
> Rising from the very edge of the road
> is a ground-floor room
> which belongs to a two-story building.
> The damp walls have lost their plaster here and there,
> with moist patches in between.
> On the door is pasted
> a printed paper image of the God Ganesh,
> The Remover of Obstacles,
> taken from a piece of machine-stamped cloth.
> There is another creature who lives here
> in addition to myself—
> on the same rent—
> a household lizard.
> The only difference between us
> is that he is not short of food.
>
> My salary is twenty-five rupees.
> A junior clerk in a merchant's office,
> I manage to get some food

giving tuition to a son of the Dattas.
The evenings I spend
at the Sealdah [railway] Station,
saving on electricity.
The engine's *dhash dhash* sound,
the sound of the whistle,
the rush of passengers,
the clamor of coolies—
the clock turns to ten thirty
by the time I return home to a lonely, silent darkness.

My aunt's village is on the banks of the river Dhaleswari.
Firm arrangements had been made
for the daughter of her brother-in-law
to be married to this unfortunate soul.
The hour must have been auspicious—
the proof was sure—
for I escaped when the hour came.
At least the girl was saved,
and so was I.
She who did not come into my home
comes and goes in my mind all the time—
dressed in a *dhakai* sari,
vermilion mark on her forehead.

The rains become heavy.
My expenses on trams go up.
Sometimes I am fined as well.
On the corners of this lane
collect and rot in heaps
mango seeds and skin,
cores of jackfruit,
gills of fish,
dead kittens
mixed with ashes and other assorted rubbish.
The condition of my umbrella
resembles that of my salary after fines—
it has numerous holes.
. . .

The dark shadow of monsoon
lies unconscious and inert
in this damp room
like an animal trapped.
. . .
On the corner of the lane lives
Kantababu.
His long hair is carefully parted.
Has large eyes.
Likes to live it up.
He plays the cornet as a hobby.

This is where the poem changes its mood and register. Tagore, having taken advantage of the prose-poem form to incorporate a piece of realist and almost prosaic description, executes something like what the language of film might call a dissolving shot, one that replaces one frame with another and challenges our vision. The poem mounts nothing short of a full-scale attack on the historical and the objective. This lane, Tagore says, is both a fact and not. And that, he would go on to argue, was the function of the poetic, to help us see beyond and pierce the veil of the real. Tagore returns here to the distinction he had made between prose and poetry in the 1890s. The function of the poetic was to create a caesura in historical time and transport us to a realm that transcended the historical. This other realm was what Tagore would call the eternal. The cornet effects the shift in the mood of the poem. Tagore uses the full force of the historical irony of the assimilation of this European instrument into the lower-middle-class lives of Calcutta Bengalis—the cornet player in the poem has no majesty about him, and the title of the poem *Bansi* translates the cornet into the pastoral *bansi*, usually glossed as "flute." Yet Tagore makes this European instrument play an Indian raga that both transcends and captures the pathos of the life that flows in this obscure part of Calcutta. Let us read the poem to its end:

Sometimes
a tune rises in the grotesque air of this lane—
sometimes in the depth of night,
or at dawn,
or in the play of light and shade of the late afternoon.
Suddenly some evening
the raga *Sindhu-baroan* would be played,
and the whole sky would resonate

with the pain of separation
of all times.
And then in an instant
it becomes clear
that this lane is a terrible lie
like the insufferable delirium of a drunkard.
Suddenly
the message would come
that there is no difference at all
between Akbar the emperor and
Haripada the clerk.
Flowing along with the plaintive song of the flute
the imperial parasol and the broken umbrella
go together
toward the same Vaikuntha.[60]

There, where this song is true,
the Dhaleswari flows
in the eternal auspicious hour of the twilight.
On her banks the *tamal* trees cast their deep shadows,
and she who waits in the courtyard
is dressed in a *dhakai* sari
with the vermilion mark on her forehead.[61]

Tagore mobilized an eclectic series of propositions to defend, theoretically, his position on the poetic. He appealed to European romanticism, in particular to Keats's 1819 poem "Ode on a Grecian Urn." He also appealed to the Upanishads and to Sanskrit aesthetics in drawing a distinction between *bostu* (things of utility) and *rasa*, the disinterested, generalized emotions that are meant to be produced by aesthetic performance, according to the theories of Sanskrit poetics.[62] There was, in addition, his own philosophy, based on the Upanishads, about the existence of a transcendental or cosmic sense of *leela* or play, which functions as an ultimate critique of reason and which thus interrupts—without making it irrelevant—the specifically political.[63] He once explained his preference for the expression *jiban leela* (life-play) over the Western expression "struggle for existence (or survival)" by pointing out that in his understanding, "struggle" was a more partial description of the business of existence than *leela* was. *Leela*, ultimately, was about the limits of reason. As Tagore once said, playfully, and as if to himself:

> why, my dear, what is this unnecessary struggle about?
> About survival.
> But why do I have to survive at any cost?
> You die otherwise.
> So what if I die?
> But I do not want to.
> Why don't you want to?
> I don't want to because I don't want to.
> If we were to summarize this reply in one word,
> it would be called *leela*.[64]

In the main, Tagore made a distinction between the *pratyahik* (the everyday) and the *nitya* or the *chirantan*, or the eternal. The former was *anitya*, impermanent, subject to the changes of history.[65] The realm of the poetic laced the everyday but had to be revealed by the operation of the poetic eye. As he explained it once to Dhurjatiprasad Mukherjee, using his favorite example of the housewife or the *grihini* (in whose figure, as distinct from the figure of the officegoer, he always saw the possibility of the poetic):

> The question will be asked, Through what rule then will the prosaic be raised to the level of the poetic? The answer is easy. If you imagine prose to be like the *grihini* [the mistress of the *griha*, home], then you will know that she is somebody who argues, keeps accounts of the clothes sent to the washerman's house, suffers from bouts of cough, cold, and fever and so on, and reads the monthly *Basumati*—these belong to the story of the everyday, to the category of "information." In the middle of all this, a current of sweetness spills over like a spring jumping over stones. What does not make the subject of news, makes the subject of poetry. You can select and use it in prose-poetry.[66]

The poetic then was that which, in the middle of the everyday, helped to transport one to the level of the transcendental. The prosaic, in contrast, pertained to the realm of needs and utility. The things that inhabited such a realm were mere *bostu*s, things. The *bostu* was a purely utilitarian view of an object; or an object that was exhausted in its utilitarian use could be called a *bostu*. Tagore left his readers in no doubt as to the hierarchy between the poetic and the prosaic. "Through what rule then," he asked, "will the prosaic be *raised* to the level of the poetic?" In an essay entitled "Tathya o satya" (Fact and Truth) written around 1925, he referred to Keats's "Ode on a Grecian Urn" and said:

The English poet Keats wrote a poem addressed to a Greek urn. The artist who made the urn did not simply make a container. This urn was not made simply to present an opportunity for taking offerings to the temple. That is to say, it was not made merely to reveal a human need. Of course, some need would have been served by it, but the serving of the need did not exhaust it. . . . Keats lets us know through his poem the identity that this urn shares with the unity of the universe. He wrote:

Thou, silent form! dost tease
us out of thought
As doth eternity.[67]

Students of European romanticism will not be surprised at this critique of "utility" articulated through Tagore's discussion of the utilitarian thing or *bostu*.[68] In this, Tagore perhaps expressed a criticism of (Benthamite) utilitarianism that was fundamental to the romantic aspects of Bengali nationalism. Bakimchandra Chattopadhyay had made the same criticism in the nineteenth century. Whereas John Stuart Mill's brand of utilitarianism, with its talk of women's emancipation and representative government, found many adherents in Bengal, Bentham's doctrines, as Eric Stokes showed some years ago, formed the ideological justification for the authoritarianism of the empire after the 1830s, and it was this brand of the idea of "utility" that was ridiculed by Bengali intellectuals.[69] Whereas Mill had a specific theory of poetry, Bentham's calculus—"By utility is meant that property in an object, whereby it tends to produce benefit, advantage, pleasure, good or happiness . . . etc."—was considered by some prominent Bengalis too crude even to be called *darshan* (outlook/philosophy).[70] In effect, they asked, What was so beautiful or uplifting about utility? Bankimchandra called it *udar-darshan* or "stomach-outlook," and quipped thus in his humorous and satirical collection of essays *Kamalakanter daptar*:

> What is the meaning of the word "utility"? Does it have a Bengali equivalent? I do not know English myself and Kamalakanta has said nothing—so I asked my son. He consulted the dictionary and explained it thus: "U" means "you," "till" is to cultivate, "it" is to "eat," and he could not say what the meaning of "y" was. But perhaps Kamalakanta has meant precisely this by "utility," that "you all live by cultivating and eating." What a scoundrel! He called everybody a peasant! . . . My son has turned out to be good in English studies, otherwise we would not have been able to make sense of such a difficult word.[71]

There is an echo of this anti-Benthamite position in Tagore's aesthetic theories. He would often take the Bengali word for realism, *bastabata*, and work with its root word *bostu* (thing). For him, *bastab* or the naturalist/realist real referred to the world of things, which in turn only referred back to the prosaic world of utilities (the Bengali word Tagore uses is *proyojon* or needs).[72] The poetic helped transcend the mere thingness of things by letting us see beyond the real or *bastab*. It is true that Tagore did not give middle-class Bengalis the literary wherewithal with which to aestheticize directly their salaried labor, rickety institutions of civic life, and other life possibilities in the urban landscape of Calcutta. Bengali literary modernism could not be itself without somehow moving beyond Tagore. But—and this is my point—Tagore's idealist romanticism remained an indispensable aspect of the literary strategies that made life in the city pleasurable for the literate.

Tagore made a place for himself in middle-class lives by making language this medium of pleasure, by making it an instrument for transfiguring reality. Language was the one material dimension of Bengali modernity that he, more than anybody else, helped libidinize. There was no aspect of the language that Tagore did not research and work on: grammar, folklore, meter, pronunciation, spelling, and so on.[73] He deliberately imported Sanskrit words and diction into Bengali poetry to overcome the problem that the long and short vowels were often not distinguished in Bengali speech, and to get around the fact that Bengali words normally had an even accent on all the syllables.[74] He collected folk songs and proverbs to find in Bengali rural life the sentiments that urban Bengalis needed to fabricate a modern sense of domesticity.[75] He wrote songs in which music had the express purpose of helping the words reach out to that which was ineffable yet everyday.[76] His songs and poems made their way into middle-class Bengali hearts and homes, even though they never spoke to middle-class realities.[77]

It was as if to the question, "How would a Bengali poet develop poetry into a way of coping with the city, with examinations, offices, salaries, the relentless noise of ramshackle trams and buses, with the garbage that piled up in the melancholy, sun-starved lanes of Calcutta?" Tagore in practice gave one answer. His response was to libidinize the very materiality of language in such a way that every time one made the language poetic it acquired the power to transport. Poetry could create the moment of epiphany and execute the dissolving shot that Tagore himself exemplified so beautifully in the poem *Bansi*. He also thus confounded any historicist expectations one might have of modernism as following and replacing romanticism in the history of modern cities. Tagore's writings presented the poetic and its powers of transport as precisely a resource for living in the city, as a powerful means of transfiguring the real and historical Calcutta. In that, it was contemporaneous with realist and political modernism, and was as much a resource for living in the city as any modernism could be.

Such compensatory use of the poetic may be seen in several Bengali reminiscences that involved Tagore and/or his writings. I cite two incidents to illustrate the point. In his book, *Kabitar muhurta* (The Moment of Poetry), the poet Shankha Ghosh tells a story about his father's use of Tagore. Ghosh's father was a teacher in an undergraduate institution. Once, when told by doctors that a son of his faced death within a few hours, the grief-stricken father went to his class and just read out one poem after another from Tagore's book *Naibedya*.[78] Tagore had obviously helped make the very materiality of the language into a source of deep and profound solace for the devastated father.

My second example comes from the reminiscences of the painter Benodbehari Mukhopadhyay, once an art student at Tagore's school at Santiniketan and later a teacher to the film maker Satyajit Ray. Mukhopadhyay writes thus of the early days of Tagore's school:

> On rainy days the student residences at Santiniketan would almost go under water. Often the rainwater would gush in through leaky roofs and broken windows and drench the beds. Once, feeling extremely irritated after spending a whole night sleepless, some of us students told him [Tagore] of our difficulties. Rabindranath said in a calm voice, "Take a seat. It rained through my thatched roof too last night. So I sat up and wrote a song. Listen to it and see how you find it." So saying, Rabindranath started singing
>
> *Ogo dukho jagania tomay gan shonabo*
> *Taito amay jagiye rakho*
> [You, who awaken sadness in me,
> keep me up so that I can sing for you]
>
> When he finished singing, Rabindranath said, "Artists and poets—we suffer the same plight. There is nobody to care for us." It is true that it rained a little in Rabindranath's room. [But] we all emerged from his room feeling exhilarated and said to ourselves, "we would not have been able to do this." Today I will definitely admit that Rabindranath made no arrangements to have our rooms repaired. [Or] I do not remember

now if he made any such arrangements. But his song did make us forget all the suffering that that night had caused.[79]

Both Tagore and Mukhopadhyay—and the intended reader of this story—use the poetic here as a compensatory move; they use the materiality of a language, its sounds, rhythms, and melodies, to reconstitute (not deny) a reality that contained material and other forms of deprivation.

IMAGINATION AS A PROBLEM IN THE HISTORY OF NATIONALISM

Was "piercing the veil of the real"—the phrase Tagore used to describe the mode of viewing in which India appeared as already lovable, was this mode of viewing the same as what is conveyed by "imagining" in Benedict Anderson's book on nationalism?

Let us go back to some of Tagore's nationalist poetry that employed this mode of viewing, the act of seeing that transcended the objective and historical vision. Almost as a matter of rule, in these writings Bengal comes across as the image of an affectionate, protective, all-giving, powerful mother goddess of the Hindus, either Durga or Lakshmi. Many of the songs that Tagore wrote for the movement against the first partition of Bengal, the Swadeshi movement (1905–1908), made the country/nation vivid in the shape of these two goddesses. Thus we have a description of Bengal as Durga in the following lines:

> The message of courage glows in your right hand,
> Your left hand removes all fear
> Loves smiles in your two eyes
> And the eye in your forehead assumes the color of fire.
> O Mother, however much I look
> I cannot take my eyes away from you.
> Your doors have opened on to a golden temple today.[80]

Bengal is molded in the image of Lakshmi, the goddess and protector of domestic well-being, in the poem *Bangalakshmi* (Bengal the Lakshmi):

> In your fields, by your rivers, in your thousand homes set deep in the mango groves, in your pastures whence the sound of milking rises, in the shadow of the banyan, in the twelve temples besides the Ganges, O ever-gracious Lakshmi, O Bengal my mother, you go about your endless chores day and night with a smile on your face.[81]

Or consider these lines that were recited in Calcutta as late as the 1960s—and perhaps even later—by schoolchildren to mark the onset of autumn, when the goddess Durga is worshiped all over Bengal:

> Today, in the autumn dawn,
> Did I see your lovely form
> O my mother Bengal, your green limbs glowing
> In stainless beauty?
> The brimming river cannot flow,
> The fields can hold no more grain,
> The *doel* calls, the *koel* sings,
> In your woodland court.
> In the midst of all, you are standing, Mother,
> In the autumn dawn.[82]

There is a family of terms in north Indian languages for this activity of seeing beyond the real, of being in the presence of the deity. One of them is *darshan* (to see) and refers to the exchange of human sight with the divine that supposedly happens inside a temple or in the presence of an image in which the deity has become manifest (*murati*).[83] Tagore, personally, was not either a believer in or a practitioner of idol worship. His family were Brahmos, a religious group that had rejected the idolatrous side of Hinduism early in the nineteenth century. Yet the word he used in Bengali for the "form" of the Mother he claims to have seen on an autumn morning was *murati*, which Thompson mistranslated as "form." *Murati*, literally meaning a material form of embodiment or manifestation, refers typically to the image of a deity (though in secular prose it has also come to stand in for the English word "statue"). When Tagore saw the *murati* of Mother Bengal, he practiced *darshan*. This was not because he was a believer in Hindu practices of idolatry or that he wanted to practice *darshan*, but because in this nationalist "seeing beyond," the real, shared practices sedimented in the language itself—more than his own personal and doctrinal beliefs—spoke through the figures of speech Tagore employed. *Darshan* as such was not an aesthetic practice, but Tagore aestheticized it in the interest of displacing one frame of the real by another. Indeed, as some of the ancient Indian theorists of aesthetic practice held, such sudden change of frames and a "cessation of the ordinary historical world" were essential to the enjoyment of *rasa* (aesthetic mood). The tenth-century theoretician Abhinavagupta's theory of the production of aesthetic experience is thus explained by one of his European translators:

"The general idea underlying these words [*chamatkara* and *vismaya*, words used to explain the work of *rasa*] . . . is that both the mystical and the aesthetic experience imply the cessation of the world—the ordinary historical world, the *samsara*—and its sudden replacement by a new dimension of reality."[84] The enjoyment of the *rasa* of nationalism required the animation of such ancient practices.

I do not intend to reduce Tagore's point about "seeing beyond the real" to practices that preceded British rule in India and thus present Indian nationalism as a site of an unbridgeable difference between the West and the East. Tagore (and nationalism in general) obviously derived much from European romanticism. His idea of the transcendental was unmistakably idealist. My point is that the moment of vision that effected a "cessation of the historical world" included plural and heterogenous ways of seeing that raise some questions about the analytical reach of the European category "imagination."

Benedict Anderson has made an enormously suggestive use of the word "imagination" to describe roles the novel, the newspaper, the map, the museum, and the census play in creating the empty, homogenous time of history that allows the different parts of a nation to exist all at once in some nationalist imaginary of simultaneity. Anderson, as I said at the outset, takes the meaning of imagination to be self-evident but cautions that it should not be read to mean false.[85] Yet imagination is a word with a long and complex history in European thought. In addition, its status as a criterion for judging literary merit has been questioned in discussions of Sanskrit aesthetics.[86] Matilal's discussions of theories of perception in Hindu and Budhhist logic uses Sanskrit equivalents to imagination that approximate what Coleridge in his *Biographia Literaria* (1815–1817) called "fancy," the associative connections formed through memory but not entirely determined by it.[87] In European thought, as many observers have pointed out, the word comes out of seventeenth-century theories of psychology and makes its way through many debates and through Hume, Kant, Schelling, and others into Coleridge's theories of "primary" and "secondary imagination" in *Biographia Literaria*.[88] In its use in European romanticism, the word has deep connections to Christian conceptions of the divine, and even its later secular form cannot quite overcome an older distinction between the mind and the senses. As Thomas McFarland pithily points out, at the core of the word (in its applications by Coleridge) remains the distinction and a tension between "I am" and "it is," for the word designates a relationship between an observing mind and its surrounding objects. It goes back to an old question that was rehearsed in

Coleridge's arguments against the Spinozian tradition: Was God a subject endowed with a (mental) faculty called "imagination," or did God exist simply in the ways of the world without being gathered into anything in the nature of a subject?[89] Imagination, I submit, remains a mentalist, subject-centered category in Anderson's thought-provoking account of nationalism.

But *darshan* or *divyadrishti* (divine sight)—I am using these names for a family of viewing practices—as they occur in modern Bengali nationalist writing are not necessarily subject-centered, mentalist categories. One does not have to be a believer to have *darshan*. As I have already said, when Tagore sees the "lovely *murati*" of Mother Bengal, his language refers to *darshan* almost as an unconscious habit. *Darshan* belongs here to the history of practice and habitus. To understand it we do not have to erect a category called "the mind." Coleridge captures something like this moment of practice when he writes about "language itself . . . as it were think[ing] for us," a process he likens to the activity of "the sliding rule which is the mechanics safe substitute for arithmetical knowledge."[90] Or, to follow the more contemporary Deleuzian instincts of analysis, one could say that the moment of practice is a moment that bypasses—and not just dissolves—the subject-object distinction.[91]

The practice of *darshan* or *divyadrishti* (divine sight) can enter the self-consciousness of the modern subject by producing—as Freud pointed out a long time ago—the shock of the uncanny, something that gives one's self-recognition a jolt.[92] Consider this example that comes from an essay called "Bharatbarsha" by the Bengali writer S. Wajed Ali, written sometime in the 1930s. A quintessential product of secular nationalism—by a Muslim writer writing on Hindu epics who deployed categories of thought associated with Hinduism—this essay remained compulsory reading for high school students from the 1930s to the mid-1960s. A historicist and political reading today would perhaps see nothing but a crude nationalist essentialism at work in this essay, which even used the English word "tradition" to describe its own subject. That would not necessarily be wrong. What is interesting, however, is the way "tradition" here is itself posed as a question of "divine sight," of a sight, as Wajed Ali explains, that dissolves the historical point of view. The essay recounts two episodes in the author's life. Wajed Ali made a trip to Calcutta about 1900/1 as a boy of ten or eleven, when he found an old man in a grocery shop in his neighborhood reading the Hindu epic *Ramayana* to a few children. He came back to the city twenty-five years later and duly noticed all the signs of historical change in the neighborhood; motorcars, man-sions, and electricity had replaced the quiet streets, the gas lights, and the huts. Yet Wajed Ali's sense of the historical was powerfully challenged when he came across exactly the same scene in the same grocery shop—in fact, the very same section of the *Ramayana* being read aloud to a few children—as he had witnessed twenty-five years previously. On his inquiring about this strange experience, the old man reading the *Ramayana* explained that the person in the first scene was his father reading the book to his children, and he was now reading it to his grandchildren. The book itself belonged to his grandfather. Wajed Ali felt the historical dissolve around him. He writes: "I saluted the old man and left the shop. It was as if I had gained divine sight. A perfect picture of the true/real Bharatvarsha [India] appeared before my eyes! That old *tradition* [in English] has continued unbroken, nowhere has it changed!"[93]

Wajed Ali clearly experienced the shock of the uncanny: "It was *as if* I had gained divine sight." By using "as if," he leaves open the possibility that this seeing could have been all in his mind, the work of *kalpana* or imagination. But there is also the possibility that Ali's *kalpana* had nothing to do with the practice of seeing that he experienced as the uncanny. In writing histories of seeing that made romantic nationalism possible in the subcontinent, we have to stay with this moment of undecidability in Wajed Ali's text between "imagination" in its mentalist sense and "divine sight," *divyadrishti*, as something belonging to the history of practice. There is no doubt that the Tagorean move of transcending the historical in order to be able to see an India already worthy of adoration owes a debt to European romanticism and to its mentalist categories. His reference to Keats and his critique of "utility," as well as his spiritual/material distinctions, mix Vedantic thought with European romanticism. My point, however, is this. If the moment of "seeing beyond" includes phenomena such as *darshan* or *divyadrishti* that do not necessarily require the assumption of a subject, then there are interesting implications for how the category "imagination" may be addressed in postcolonial histories.

There is in the record a well-known experience of Jawaharlal Nehru's youth when he used to travel the Indian countryside speaking to peasants about national issues. Nehru describes incidents in which peasants would greet him with shouts of "Bharat Mata ki jay—Victory to Mother India [Bharat = India; Mata = Mother]."[94] On at least one occasion, Nehru's pedagogic instincts and his modernist opposition to superstitions were immediately aroused by this battle cry of the peasant. Like a schoolteacher wanting to test his students' conceptual skills, he asked the assembled peasants who this Bharat Mata was "whose victory they wanted." The question flummoxed the peasants, who could not articulate a clear answer. Nehru writes with the glee of a teacher who has just been able to catch the attention of a class: "My question would surprise them, and not knowing exactly what to answer, they would look at each other and at me. At last a vigorous Jat, wedded to the soil from immemorial generations, would say that it was the *dharti*, the good earth of India they meant." Nehru, by his own account, then proceeded to explain to them the proper meaning of the expression. His triumphant words will bear repetition:

> What earth? Their particular village patch, or all the patches in the district or province, or in the whole of India? . . . I would endeavour to . . . explain that India was all this that they had thought, but it was so much more. The mountains and the rivers of India, and the forests and the broad fields, which gave us food, were all dear to us, but what counted ultimately were the people of India, people like them and me who were spread all over this vast land. *Bharat Mata*, Mother India, was essentially these millions of people. . . . [A]s this idea soaked into their brains, their eyes would light up as if they had made a great discovery.[95]

Nehru thought of the whole question of "being with" Bharat Mata, being in her presence, as it were, as a conceptual problem, a problem of thought. He overlooked the fact that the word *dharti*, meaning the earth, could not be reduced to the specific geographical boundaries of British India, and found the concept empty of content. He proceeded to fill it up with material proper to nationalist thought. This was, in Bhabha's terms, a pedagogic moment of nationalism.[96] But if we think of the peasants' use of the expression "Bharat Mata" as referring to practices sedimented into language itself and not necessarily to concepts either that the mind elaborates or that contain experiential truths, we see the legitimacy of peasant or subaltern nationalism. Their practice of being in the presence of Bharat Mata was not based on the training of the mind that print capitalism could administer to the formally educated nationalist subject. Nor were they making a claim about having experienced the land as a mother figure. "India" or Bharat could indeed be the mother because, long before there were the newspaper and the novel, there was the age-old practice of *darshan* that came to constitute a critical element in the "performative" aspect of peasants' nationalism. As a practice, it bypassed the question of the experiencing subject.

Literate members of the elite such as Tagore or Wajed Ali were not peasants. For them, nationalism was inseparable from their aesthetic experience of the phenomenon. But the aesthetic moment, which resists the realism of history, creates a certain irreducible heterogeneity in the constitution of the political. This heterogeneity appears in references to practices such as *darshan* or *divyadrishti* (divine sight), which occur on two registers in the writings of Tagore or Wajed Ali. Insofar as these authors wrote as experiencing, imagining subjects of nationalism, these practices constituted for them experiences of the uncanny. Wajed Ali's essay exemplifies this. But the practice of *darshan* also entered their vocabulary in a mode that did not necessarily connote experience—as in the poem in which Tagore spoke of seeing the divine image of mother Bengal ("Today in this lovely dawn," etc.). Here Tagore used the idolatrous word for image, *murati*, simply through linguistic association, as indicative of a habit of speech, as merely an element that belonged to his habitus. Together, these modes of perception suggest that "imagination" can be both a subject-centered and a subjectless practice. It is, in that sense, an inherently heterogeneous category in which the antagonistic spirits of both Spinoza and Coleridge survive and struggle.

This inherent plurality of the category "imagination" is also what in the end makes it impossible to see the political as something that constitutes a "one" or a whole. Consider, once again, the poem of Sukanta Bhattacharya's. On the surface, the poem railed against poetry: "In the kingdom of hunger, the world is only prosaic." Poesy was to be banished, exiled in the interest of aligning literature, now only prose, with the struggle to rid the world of the injustice and exploitation symbolized by hunger. Bhattacharya's anxiety about the dangers of poetry was historicist. It belonged to a familiar body of complaint: that romanticism gave rise to apathy, lethargy—or much worse, to fascism—and that it was dangerous to aestheticize the political. The world had to be approached at right angles through a prose that admitted of no optical errors of parallax. Yet just imagine how banal and weak Bhattacharya's critique would have been if he had said it in prose, if he had not embraced in the very practice of writing all those qualities of verse that he so boldly denounced. In other words, the poem achieved its full political effect precisely because it did not carry out to the full any one understanding of the political. Instead, it interrupted one definition of the political—the one that aligned the political with the realist and the prosaic—to introduce unannounced the political charge that only poetry could deliver. It thus made the political effective by making it not-one. This, it seems to me, is the heterogeneity in the very constitution of the political that the nationalist in Tagore articulated in proposing to his compatriots that the nationalist eye needed to possess two radically contradictory modes of vision. One was charged with the responsibility to locate the political in historical time; the other created a political that resisted historicization. This constitutional heterogeneity of the political mirrors the irreducible pluralities that contend in the history of the word "imagination."

CHAPTER 7

Adda: A History of Sociality

And it is a good sign that I still enjoy *adda*,
for *adda* and youth are inseparable.
(*Manashi Das Gupta, 1957*)

NOW THAT IT IS CLEAR at the end of this millennium that there is no escaping the rule of capital anywhere in the world, a question that Marshall Berman asked a while ago becomes even more insistent in the lives of many. In his celebrated book *All That Is Solid Melts into Air*, Berman was interested in exploring how "modern men and women may become subjects as well as objects of modernization," how they might "get a grip on the modern world and make themselves at home in it."[1] I am not confident that this can be achieved by or for all in a programmatic manner, for the control that different groups can exercise on capitalism is at best uneven and subject to global distribution of institutional power. But the struggle to make a capitalist modernity comfortable for oneself, to find a sense of community in it, to be—as Berman puts it—at home in modernity, is an ongoing, ceaseless process for all. We do not have a choice in the matter, even when the problem does not admit of any permanent resolutions. Whatever our philosophical critiques of metaphysics today, the process of producing metaphysical identities for oneself—both collectively and individually—marks this struggle. Yet the struggle is by no means simple. As the philosopher J. L. Mehta reminds us: "the appropriation of what is our very own occurs only as a homecoming, as a return from a journey into the alien and the other; this is the law of being at home as a making oneself at home."[2] The return, one assumes, is ever incomplete.

The history I present here of a social practice, *adda*, from the city of Calcutta in the first half of the twentieth century, is a specific historical study of that struggle to be at home in modernity. The word *adda* (pronounced "uddah") is translated by the Bengali linguist Sunitikumar Chattopadhyay as "a place" for "careless talk with boon companions" or "the chats of intimate friends" (I will have more to say later on this interchangeability of talk and place).[3] Roughly speaking, it is the practice of friends getting together for long, informal, and unrigorous conversations.

This history of *adda* should be more properly described as a history of the desire for—or against—*adda*. By many standards of judgment in modernity, *adda* is a flawed social practice: it is predominantly male in its modern form in public life; it is oblivious of the materiality of labor in capitalism; and middle-class *addas* are usually forgetful of the working classes. Some Bengalis even see it as a practice that promotes sheer laziness in the population. Yet its perceived gradual disappearance from the urban life of Calcutta over the last three or four decades—related no doubt to changes in the political economy of the city—has now produced an impressive amount of mourning and nostalgia. It is as if with the slow death of *adda* will die the identity of being a Bengali.

Because *adda* is now perceived to be a dying practice, Calcutta has seen a series of self-conscious efforts in recent times to collect and preserve memories and descriptions of Bengali *addas* of the last hundred years or so. The internet carries several chat networks for Bengalis of both West Bengal and Bangladesh which are designated *addas*.[4] A book of essays, *Kolkatar adda* (The Addas of Calcutta), published for Calcutta's tricentenary, is a response to this market. It begins by pointing to the "horrendous possibility" that Bengalis might soon forget to enjoy *adda*, that a busy and all-consuming ethic of work might overtake their lives.[5] Saiyad Mujtaba Ali, a distinguished Bengali writer of humor, touched a note of mourning over the alleged disappearance of *adda* as early as the 1970s. "It is incontrovertible," he wrote, "that genuinely distinguished *addas* are now as good as dead even if they seem alive. How many of the five-story, ten-story buildings going up in Calcutta today have [room] for *adda*?"[6] Even a catalogue of Bengali books in print brought out by the Publishers' Guild in Calcutta on the occasion of the Calcutta Book Fair in 1997 began by mourning the loss of the spirit of *adda* from the trade itself. The introductory essay, surveying the history of the last fifty years of publishing in Calcutta, ended on a nostalgic and melancholy note: "The cover-designs of [Bengali] books have changed, as has changed the artistry of publication. There is a larger variety of topics now. Along with new writers will come new publishers. . . . But will we ever get back that which has now disappeared forever from the world of Bengali literature—literary *addas*? Perhaps some will be struck by pain at this. But what other path is there to follow except to press forward even as our hearts ache?"[7]

I am not interested in reading this nostalgia as an error of some kind. As a first-generation migrant with my homing instincts permanently damaged, I have no easy way of determining in what proportions the archives of the nostalgia for *adda* that this essay documents are mixed with my own desire—as an immigrant in Australia or the United States—to be at home in a Calcutta of a once-upon-a-time. Such nostalgia can only be oriented toward a future. It helps me to be at home somewhere else. I therefore have no easy critique of nostalgia.[8] The apparent nostalgia in Calcutta today for *adda* must occupy the place of another—and unarticulated—anxiety: How does one sing to the ever-changing tunes of capitalist modernization and retain at the same time a comfortable sense of being at home in it? Many Indian cities now display the symptoms of what Arjun Appadurai has evocatively called "urban exhaustion."[9] The individually distinct ambiences of modernism that the metropolitan cities of India built up in the first half of the twentieth century are now faced with serious challenges in the context of demographic changes and—compared to the past—greater globalization of the media and the economy. A history of *adda* that is also a desire for *adda* may indeed be a requiem for a practice of urban modernism now overtaken by other pleasures and dangers of the city.

It is not surprising, therefore, that Bengali intellectuals should have produced a lot of unintended metaphysics in their discussions of *adda* over the last few decades. *Adda* is often seen as something quintessentially Bengali, as an indispensable part of the Bengali character, or as an integral part of such metaphysical notions as "life" and "vitality" for the Bengalis. Benoy Sarkar, a sociologist of the 1940s, many of whose writings were published in dialogue form as though they were fragments of conversations from an *adda*, spoke in 1942 of the "vitality" of *adda* that had helped Bengalis "sustain and enrich" their natural instincts as a people. "What we need is *adda*," he declaimed in one of his conversations.[10] In his preface to the book *Kolkatar adda*, the historian Nisithranjan Ray describes Bengalis as "an *adda*-loving people."[11] The Bengali writer Nripendrakrishna Chattopadhyay wrote in the 1970s in praise of the institution: "Bengalis enjoy a tremendous reputation in the world as the people best at practicing *adda*. No other race has been able to build up such an institution as *adda* that stands above all ideas of need or utility. To enjoy *adda* is a primordial and perennial principle of life—no other people have succeeded in acknowledging this in life as Bengalis have." And a page later he adds: "so deep is the spiritual connection between *adda* and the water and atmosphere of Bengal that *adda* . . . has now spread to the

[Calcutta] Corporation, offices, state-meetings, *rawk* [verandah, the raised terrace of a building], tea-shops, sports pavilions, the district organizations of political parties, and to schools and colleges—everywhere. Everywhere, in the pores of all activity, it is *adda* that exists in many different guises."[12] In the reckoning of Saiyad Mujtaba Ali, the men of Calcutta come second only to the men of Cairo in being devoted to *adda*. The men of Cairo, in Ali's adoring description, are to be found at home only for a reluctant six hours every day (midnight to six in the morning), and prefer instead to spend the rest of their time at work and cafeterias, enjoying conversations with their male friends.[13]

It is not my aim to defend the Bengali metaphysical claim that the practice of *adda* is peculiarly Bengali. The tradition of men and women gathering in social spaces to enjoy company and conviviality is surely no monopoly of any particular people. Nor is the word only a Bengali word; it exists in Hindi and Urdu, and means a "place of gathering" (bus terminals in north India are called *bus-addas*). What is peculiar, if anything, in twentieth-century Bengali discussions of the practice of *adda* is the claim that the practice is peculiarly Bengali and that it marks a primary national characteristic of the Bengali people to such a degree that the "Bengali character," it is said, could not be thought of without it. It is this claim and its history that I study here in terms of Berman's question: How does one manage to feel at home in the context of capitalist cities?

My concern with the history of the practice of *adda* is restricted here to the world and culture of twentieth-century Bengali literary modernism. It was within that world, as we shall see, that the practice was given a self-consciously nationalist home. This is one reason why I focus on developments in the city of Calcutta. Calcutta was once the leading center of Bengali literary production.

THE BENGALI DEBATE ON *ADDA*

The widespread acceptance of the status of *adda* as a marker of Bengali character did not mean that Bengali intellectuals were all of the same opinion as to the value of this practice. Let me begin, therefore, by giving the reader some sense of the kind of debate in which the practice was and is still embroiled. A good starting point is provided by the contradictory opinions of two well-known cultural commentators in modern Bengali history, the critic Nirad C. Chaudhuri and the writer Buddhadev Bose, who also founded the discipline of comparative literature in India.

Chaudhuri's famous book, *The Autobiography of an Unknown Indian*, sees *adda* as symptomatic of a deep and continuing malaise in the Bengali character. He uses the word "gregariousness" both to describe the institution of *adda* and to explain what, in his view, is wrong with Calcutta's men. He begins by noting how old and ubiquitous the Bengali cultural practice of *adda* is. Bhabanicharan Bandyopadhyay's *Kalikata kamalalaya*—a text published in 1823 that contains vignettes of Bengali social life in the early history of the colonial city of Calcutta—provides him with convincing evidence that the common Bengali practices of "the morning gossip, the midday spell of business or siesta, the afternoon relaxation, and the evening court, had all come down unmodified" from the 1820s to the Calcutta of the 1930s.[14] Chaudhuri's description of this Bengali penchant for company is evocative, through its tone betrays the moral disapproval with which he regarded this cultivation of gregariousness:

> What the native of the city lacked in sociability he made up in gregariousness. No better connoisseur of company was to be found anywhere in the world, and no one else was more dependent on the contiguity of his fellows with the same incomprehension of his obligation towards them. The man of Calcutta found the company he needed so badly and continuously readily assembled, without any effort on his part, in his office, or in his bar-library, or in his college, which were no less places for endless gossip than for work.
>
> . . . Perhaps gregariousness was the only disinterested thing in Calcutta society. Outside working hours the true native would always be roving in search of company, and his very striving for it often defeated its purpose. Every able-bodied person after his return from office and a hurried wash and tea rushed out of his house with the intention of meeting his friends, and these friends being on the same errand it occasionally happened that everybody missed everybody else. The more usual practice, however, was to avoid these misadventures by having fixed rendezvous or, as they were called in Bengali, *addas*. Each *adda* had its fixed adherents. . . . These gathering places were most often in the outer parlour of one of the wealthier members of the group, but at times also an office after office hours, and more rarely, a tea-shop. . . . As a general rule, these meeting places were located in the quarter in which the greater majority of the frequenters lived. But it was not at all unusual to find a man travelling five or six miles by tram in order to join his company. . . . A man was far less ready to join a new *adda* than he was to shift to a new house in a new quarter.

The colonial-Victorian prejudices lurking behind Chaudhuri's disapproval of *adda* are not hard to discern. In Chaudhuri's description, *adda* is, first of all, idleness itselfs, it denotes a lethargy of spirit. "In sharp contrast to the demoniac energy shown in rushing to the rendezvous," he writes, "the languor of the actual proceedings was startling." Second, the practice of *adda* revealed to him a lack of individuality, the presence of a "herd instinct." He writes: "I did not understand this behaviour until in 1922 I read for the first time McDougall's *Social Psychology*, in which I found the distinction between the social and the gregarious instinct clearly drawn and properly emphasised. Reinforcing my critical armoury from the book, I began to call the gregarious natives of Calcutta Galton's Oxen, that is to say, the oxen of Damaraland in Africa. Individually these animals hardly appear even to be conscious of one another, but if separated from the herd they display extreme signs of distress."[15]

Third, *adda* signified for Chaudhuri the absence of a controlled sociality which, according to him, only individuals with a developed sense of individuality were capable of achieving. The people of Calcutta had *adda* because "there was very little" of what Chaudhuri understood by "social life": "No afternoon or evening parties, no dinners, no at-homes, and, of course, no dances, enlivened their existence." And finally, for Chaudhuri, *adda* was inimical to bourgeois domesticity. As he puts it: "The strong herd-instinct of the natives of Calcutta has virtually killed family life. There is no custom among them of a man sitting with his wife and children in the evening. It is hardly possible even to find them at home at any hour of the day suitable for calls, because their days are divided into three major outings—the morning wandering in search of casual gossip, the midday stay in office, and the systematised cultivation of company in the evenings." Clearly, what Chaudhuri's critique both values and finds missing from the lives of his contemporaries in Calcutta is the familiar trichotomous bourgeois grid of home-work-leisure by which many textbooks in the discipline of sociology attempt to explain modernity. Chaudhuri's writings remind us that the grid was clearly there at least as an object of desire, if not as a practice, in the lives of modern Bengalis. Chaudhuri's was not an exogenous critique.

Yet at the same time as Chaudhuri published his denunciation of *adda*, Buddhadev Bose wrote an essay in the 1950s on the subject of *adda*, the mood of which could not be more opposed to that of Chaudhuri's reflections. The opening two paragraphs of Bose are worth quoting at length if only to document the elaborate nature of the affection that many Bengali intellectuals have felt for the institution of *adda*:

I am not a pundit [writes Bose], I do not know the etymology of the word. It sounds non-Sanskritic [and] Muslim. If we Hinduize it and call it *sabha*, it loses everything. If we Anglicize it and call it "party," we kill its spirit. The [appropriate] dress for meetings is khaki or *khadi* [coarse hand-spun cotton], while the clothes one wears at a party are light but firmly pressed, and the *sabha* is white, decorous, [and yet] uncomfortable. I don't know if the French salon still exits, but their descriptions suggest a degree of elaborateness which may not be good. Does *adda* have an exact synonym in any other language of the world? Even without being a linguist, I can say, no. Because in no other country would there be the spirit of *adda* or the right environment. People of other countries make speeches, crack jokes, offer arguments, have fun all night, but they do not do [the Bengali verb is "give"] *adda*. . . . What would they do with the club, those who have the *adda*?

Bose was quite clear that the "they" of his description could only be the Bengalis. Not only that—much like Nripendrakrishna Chattopadhyay, whom I have already quoted, he literally naturalized this practice, seeing in *adda* a reflection of the soft, alluvial soil of Bengal:

Adda is an all-India thing, but it is only in the moist, tender soil of Bengal that it can achieve its fullest expression. Just as our seasons give rise to poetry, in the same way do they help make *addas* intense. Our Chaitra [mid-March to mid-April, the last month of the Bengali year] evenings, the rain-patter-filled afternoons of Sravan [the rainy fourth month of the Bengali calendar], the moon-washed nights of autumn, the sweet and the bright mornings of winter—they all go ringing the silent bell of *adda*; some hear it and some don't. It is inevitable that [the spirit of] *adda* will wither in countries of extreme heat and cold. . . . My heart trembles if I have to go to a *sabha*, I run away at the mention of a party, but *adda*? I cannot live without it. . . . That is why I cannot be satisfied simply being its worshiper, I also have to be its [high] priest and preach its glory.[16]

Formed at the opposite pole of Chaudhuri's sensibility, such self-consciously lyrical panegyric to the spirit of *adda* is relatively rare. There are, after all, Bengali words like *gultani*, *gyajano*, and so on, that generally refer to "useless talk." They suggest the existence of a critical attitude to *adda* that may not be indebted to the modern capitalist-colonial theme of "the lazy native." It is possible that the middle-class emphasis on discipline prevalent since the colonial times built not only on Victorian conceptions of laziness but also on preexisting understandings of what constituted "work" and "idleness." In any case, even confirmed votaries of *adda* such as Sunitikumar Chattopadhyay and Buddhadev Bose mention how the word *adda* was never popular with "guardians and parents," who presumably associated it at least with neglect of duties when they did not see it as a complete waste of time.[17] At the same time, there is enough evidence to suggest that in Bengali modernity, *adda* provided for many a site for self-presentation, of cultivating a certain style of being in the eyes of others. To be good at *adda* was also a cultural value. The famous Bengali physicist Satyen Bose (of Bose-Einstein statistics fame) was often fondly described by others of his time as *addar raja*, the king of *adda*. And the writer Saiyad Mujtaba Ali, whose speech and writing both displayed the raconteur style popular in *addas*, was decorated by his admirers with the mock royal title *adda chakrabarti* (emperor of *Adda*).[18]

The many different tensions that constitute the modern Bengali understanding of *adda* are encapsulated in the semantic range that a contemporary Bengali-to-English dictionary ascribes to the word. Here is a dictionary entry from 1968:

> *Adda* – n. a dwelling-place; a haunt; a (fixed or permanent) meeting-place, a rendezvous; a place or institution for practising anything (*ganer adda*: [*adda* for musicians]); a club; a company of idle talkers, their meeting-place or talk; a place for assemblage, a station or stand (*garir adda* [*adda* for vehicles]). *Adda gara* – v. to take up abode (usu[ally]. permanently), to settle. *adda deoya*, *adda mara* – v. to join in an assembly of idle talkers; to indulge in idle talk with others. *addadhari* – n. the keeper or the chief person of a club; a regular club-goer. *addabaj* – a. fond of indulging in idle talk with others or of haunting clubs where such talk is indulged in.[19]

The reader will note that something of Nirad Chaudhuri's sensibility survives in this extract in the moralistic description of *adda* as "idle talk"; the aspiration to "modernity," on the other hand, survives in the comparison suggested to the English "club"; the Sanskritized word *addadhari* and the Persianized expression *addabaj(z)* point to the ways of being, a certain temperament or character, that the word connotes, while the word also carries the older sense of "dwelling," a "gathering place," a settlement, suggesting perhaps a dialectic of settlement and nomadology whose full sense is now beyond our grasp.

The very different meanings of the word obviously bear witness to the heterogeneous pasts that are invoked by the practice of *adda*, a simultaneously celebrated and condemned—but in any case ubiquitous—institution of Calcutta's urban life. It would be simplistic to see *adda* simply as a hangover of an older feudal lifestyle, as a vestige of a rural, preurban past surviving as an obstacle to Bengali modernity. Similarly, we would be mistaken to read Bose's praise of *adda* as defending a precapitalist sense of time and sociality. And it would be equally wrong to hear the ghosts of Luther and Weber speak through the prose of Chaudhuri. The institution of *adda* resists being seen within such a stark story of transition from feudalism to capitalism. After all, the votaries of the practice were often people who helped form a modern Bengali literary public in Calcutta and who contributed to a distinctly modern sense of nationality.

ADDA AND THE BIRTH OF DEMOCRATIC SPEECH: A GENEALOGY

In contemporary Bengali language, *adda*, *majlish* (from the Arabic *majlis*, meaning a gathering, meeting, or a party), *baithak* (an assembly; *baithak-khana*: drawing room) and other similar words are used as practical synonyms. One could now use both *majlishi* and *addabaj* to refer to a person who truly enjoys being part of an *adda* or *majlish*. This equivalence—at least in Bengali usage of these words—is of recent origin, however. In nineteenth-century writings, the word *adda* does not appear to replace the word *majlish* as frequently as it does now. In fact, I have not come across any use of the word *adda* in the nineteenth century that confers respectability on the practice. What made the word *adda* respectable in the twentieth century was its association with the spaces for the production of a modern Bengali reading public.

The custom of men gathering together—and women, too, gathering in separate social spaces—to talk informally about all kinds of things affecting their lives is an old tradition in rural Bengal. The word *chandimandap*—a permanent place for the worship of the goddess Chandi but used by village elders at other times as a meeting place—attests to that, and it is interesting that self-conscious discussions of the institution of *adda* often remind Bengali authors of this older feature of Bengali village life.[20] One of the spaces in Calcutta most associated with *adda* was that of the *rawk* or *rowak*, the elevated verandas attached to older Calcutta houses, where young men of the neighbourhood often assembled to have their noisy *addas*. This was much to the annoyance of middle-class householders, who saw these raucous *addas* of the *rawk* as a threat to their respectability, especially if there were young women resident in the house. The external veranda or *rawk*, an architectural feature of Bengali houses until rising land prices made it obsolete, may indeed have been a structural remnant of the *daoa* (veranda) that went around a traditional mud hut in the villages of Bengal. Similarly, the practice of men collecting in such a space may have had something to do with earlier practices. But the *addas* of the *rawk* in the city mainly involved young men, and were not usually associated with modern literary production. In the nineteenth century, some of these *addas* were dominated by men who were the social leaders in a neighbourhood.[21] The Bengali writer Premankur Atarthi has left us pen-pictures of *addas* of young men gathering on the *rawks* of Calcutta neighborhoods around the middle of the twentieth century:

> One house in the neighborhood had a wide *rowak*. The boys would have their *adda* there on every Sunday and on other holidays. . . . Conversation ran across all different kinds of topics: patriotism, wrestling, sports, England, Germany, Switzerland. . . .
>
> Often arguments that began in a friendly way in these *addas* would turn so acrimonious and abusive that the people living inside the house would get worried, fearing an outbreak of physical violence. But people those days were so devoted to *adda* that they would dutifully turn up at their *addas* in spite of all their fights.[22]

In Lal Behari Dey's *Recollections of My School-Days*—written in the 1870s but reminiscing about the 1830s—the word *adda* is used to mean a resting place and occurs in the following way in his discussion of his first trip to Calcutta from his native village of Talpur (Sonapalashi): "We travelled only eight miles. We put up in an *adda*, or inn, bathed, cooked our food, ate and drank (Adam's ale only), lounged about, again cooked and ate at night, washed our feet in hot water, and laid ourselves on the ground—a thin piece of date-matting being interposed between our flesh and the mud floor."[23]

In the well-known satirical social sketches of *Hutom pyanchar naksha* (hereafter *Hutom*) written by Kaliprasanna Sinha and first published 1861/2 with the English title "Sketches by Hootom [Nightowl] Illustrative of Every Day Life and Every Day," the word *adda* is clearly distinguished from the word *majlish*. *Adda* in *Hutom* refers a place of gathering, but its use is at least as irreverent as when he uses it to make fun of the congregational form of worship, modeled on Christian practices and introduced into Calcutta by the Hindu reformist sect of the Brahmo Samaj: "It is almost impossible to understand the ways of Brahmo dharma [religion] these days. . . . Is the Almighty an upcountry immigrant or a

Maharashtrian brahman that He wouldn't be able to hear unless addressed [in the collective voice of] an *adda*?"[24] The other uses of *adda* in *Hutom* associate the word with lowly lives, "dens" where opium or ganja were consumed: *charaser adda*, *ganjar adda*. Pyarimohan Mukhopadhyay's memories of Calcutta in the early part of the twentieth century confirm this usage. He refers to places near the "burning ghats" (where the Hindu dead were cremated, the word *ghat* literally referring to steps on the banks of river leading to the water) and underneath the Howrah Bridge on northern side of the city as harboring *addas* for those addicted to opium and marijuana.[25] This use is in consonance with the way older Bengali dictionaries suggest a connection between *adda* and marginalized existence: a gathering place of "bad" people or people of bad occupations (*kulok*, *durbritta*).[26]

Majlish, on the other hand—whether in *Hutom* or elsewhere—suggests forms of social gathering that invariably involve wealth and patronage, and often conjure up the picture of men gathered in a rich man's parlor (*baithak* or *baithakkhana*). In *Hutom*, for instance, *majlish* goes with wine, dancing girls, chandeliers, expensive apparel, and drunken brawls that involve the newly rich of early-nineteenth-century Calcutta and their "spoiled" descendants.[27] Many of these associations weaken in the twentieth century but, structurally, *majlish* as a place retains the ideas of a patron, the wealthier person without whose parlor or *baithakkhana* the gathering cannot take place. And, usually, the word is also associated with a place where some kind of performance takes place—singing, dancing, recitation of poetry, and so on. Conversation here, even when it was not directly sycophantic, could never be totally democratic, for the very presence of a patron would influence the speech pattern of such a group in all kinds of ways. It is not surprising that Subal Mitra's dictionary, first published in 1906, explains *majlish* as *kartabhaja daler sabha* or literally "a meeting of those who worship their master" (the Kartabhaja, incidentally, were also a religious sect in Bengal).[28]

In contrast, whatever the later overlapping between the semantic fields of the two words *adda* and *majlish*, the *adda* that Buddhadev Bose celebrates in the 1950s has an unmistakably middle-class, democratic, ring to it. "Everybody must enjoy equal status in an *adda*," Bose writes, and adds:

> It is inevitable that there will be distinctions made between human beings in that part of life which is concerned with the earning of one's livelihood. But those who cannot shed that sense of division just as one sheds

> one's office clothes will never know the taste of *adda*. If there happens to be somebody around whose status is so exalted that we can never forget his glory, then we will sit at his feet as devotees, but he will have no invitation to [share in] our pleasure, for the very spring of *adda* will freeze to ice the moment his eyes fall on it. But similarly, if there are people whose mental level [*maner star*] is much below that of others, they need to be kept out too, and that is comfortable for them, as well.[29]

Of course, no *adda* was ever just this, a pure practice of democracy. Many *addas* were dominated by important people who often acted as patrons by providing the venue for the gathering—their living rooms. *Adda* in the twentieth century remained a hybrid form that combined elements of the *majlish* with that of coffee-house conversation. Yet the emergence of a democratic sensibility is what separates the speech pattern of an *adda* in someone's *baithakkhana* from that of an *adda* in a public place.

Parashuram [Rajshekhar Bosu]'s humorous and witty short stories "Lambakarna" and "Dakshinray"—the first published around 1915/16 and the second around 1928/29, both written during the period of the anti-British nationalist movement—give us interesting examples of conversations in a fictional *adda* that meets regularly in somebody's *baithakkhana*. The patron in these two stories is a well-to-do Bengali landlord introduced in the story as "Roy Bangshalochan Banerjee Bahadur, Zamindar and Honorary Magistrate, Beleghata Bench." The first story, "Lambakarna," introduces the cast of characters of the *adda* that regularly meets at Bangshalochan's place:

> The evening *adda* that gathers at the *baithakkhana* of Bangshalochanbabu hears many tall claims every night. The governor, Suren[dranath] Banrujje [a leading nationalist politician], Mohunbagan [a soccer club], spiritual truths, the funeral ceremony of the old man Adhar in the neighbourhood, the new crocodile at the Alipore [zoo]—no subject is left undiscussed. Recently, for the last seven days, the subject of discussion has been the tiger. Nagen, Bangshalochan's brother-in-law, and Uday, a distantly related "nephew" of his, almost came to blows last night over this [topic]. With great difficulty, the other members persuaded them to desist.[30]

This description captures the spirit of a Bengali *adda*. "A pure *adda*," writes Radhaprasad Gupta, who was a member of an well-known *adda* in the 1940s, "has no . . . hard and fast *agenda* [the italicized English words are in English in the original]. . . . There is no certainty as to what topic an *adda* will start with one day, what will cause argumentation and fights, and where it will all end. Suppose this moment the conversation is about [a] *supernova* beyond the solar system, the next moment the discussion could be about *Plekhanov's 'The Role of the Individual in History.'* "[31]

By the very catholicity of their interests—ranging from the nationalist movement to the Royal Bengal tiger—the members of Bangshalochanbabu's parlor establish the fact that the nature of their gathering is indeed that of an *adda*. Yet the second story, set in the same living room with the same characters but now placed somewhere in the 1920s, illustrates how the patron of a *majlish/adda* could intervene at critical points to direct the conversation, making it fall significantly short of the democratic speech Budhhadev Bose idealized in his praise of the modern *adda*. Here is the beginning of the second story, "Dakshinray"; the subject is once again that of the tiger. Notice how Bangshalochan's participation is minimal but critical:

> Mr. Chatterjee said, "Talking about tigers, those at Rudraprayag [a pilgrimage spot] are [the best]. Huge, gigantic things. . . . But such is the [sacred] power/glory of the place that they do not attack anybody. After all, [the people there] are all pilgrims. They only catch and eat *sahibs* [Europeans, white people]." . . . Binod, the lawyer, said, "What wonderful tigers! Couldn't a few be imported here? *Swaraj* [self-rule, independence, a word associated with Gandhi] would come quickly. *Swadeshi* [economic nationalism], bombs, the spinning wheel, splitting the legislative councils [referring to particular nationalist tactics]—none of these would be needed."
>
> The conversation was being conducted one evening in the *baithakkhana* of Bangshalochanbabu. He was engrossed in reading an English book, *How to Be Happy though Married*. His brother-in-law, Nagen, and his nephew, Uday, were also present.
>
> Chatterjee took a drag on the hookah for one full minute and said, "Why do you presume that that [method] has not been tried?"
>
> "Really? But the Rowlatt Report [on sedition] doesn't mention it."
>
> "So what if you have read the report? Look, does the government know everything? There are more things—or however the saying goes."
>
> "Why don't you tell us about it?"
>
> Chatterjee remained silent for a while and then said, "Hmm."
>
> Nagen pleaded, "Why don't you, Mr. Chatterjee?"

Chatterjee got up and looked out through the door and the window and, resuming his seat, repeated, "Hmm."

Binod: "What were you looking for?"

Chatterjee: "Just making sure that Haren Ghosal didn't turn up all of a sudden. He is a spy of the police, it is better to be careful from the beginning."

Bangshalochan put the book aside and said, "You'd better not discuss these matters here. It is better that these stories not be told in a magistrate's house."

Eventually, Chatterjee proceeds to narrate the story, only after agreeing to Bangshalochan's condition that he would leave out the "overly seditious" elements.[32] There are two things I want to highlight here. First, the editorial/censorial role of the patron, which becomes clear only at the end of the sequence, when the patron of the gathering, Bangshalochan, speaks minimally and yet effectively decides the rules of speaking at this *adda*. This marks the space of this gathering as more of a *majlish* than a democratic, modern *adda*. My second point relates to the subtle way—through the title of an English book that Bangshalochan is reading—the author of the story draws our attention to the gendered nature of this space, a theme I will return to in a later part of the essay

If the patron's hospitality gave him the subtle (or sometimes not so subtle) power to edit the conversations of a *majlish*, at the other extreme was the coffeehouse or tea-shop *adda* where the absence of a patron was signaled by the acceptance of the ritual of "going Dutch" (with Bengali apologies to the Dutch!).[33] There is, however, an interesting twist to this Bengali adaptation of democracy and individualism to the culture of *adda*. The Bengali expression for "going Dutch" is actually a string of English words that do not make any sense in English: "his his, whose whose." It is a literal and (reversed) translation of *jar jar tar tar* (whose whose, his his). The expression was already in use in the 1960s. I do not know when it originated, but Sagarmay Ghosh, the editor of the well-known Bengali literary magazine *Desh*, mentions this expression in his reminiscences of an *adda* that seems to have met in the 1950s and 1960s.[34]

Why was "going Dutch" given a funny, English-sounding name? A deep analysis of this phenomenon would no doubt have to engage with the question of the use of language and the production of linguistically based humor by Bengalis. But I also think that the humorous use of English words here is meant to cover up a sense of embarrassment felt precisely over the absence of hospitality that "going Dutch" signifies. The Bengali expression *jar jar tar tar* is a disapproving description of what is, in effect, seen as an attitude of selfishness. The deep association between food and munificence in Bengali culture meant a certain unease in middle-class consciousness over acknowledging the individualism entailed when everybody paid separately for his or her own food. The deliberately absurd grammar of the expression "his his whose whose" probably helped a tea-shop *adda* to overcome its sense of embarrassment when faced precisely with the moment that spoke of the death of the patron. It was as though the democratic *adda* carried within its structure a nostalgia for the *majlish*. No wonder, then, that the aesthetics of the twentieth-century *adda* should always relate to a hybrid form that would never be able to tear itself away completely from the form of the *majlish*.

ADDA AND THE PRODUCTION OF URBAN SPACE

Between the *majlish* and the *adda*, then, there is the history of modernity, the process of emergence of a Bengali middle class whose public life was marked by its literary and political endeavors. The word *adda*, as I have said, attained respectability by its associations with the literary and political groups that flourished in the city in the 1920s, 1930s, and later. But this in turn was mediated by the development of certain institutions and spaces characteristic of modernity anywhere.

The first of these was the (high) school and the space it made for literary intimacy among young men, a space surely homosocial and sometimes bordering perhaps on the homoerotic as well. An early instance of such friendship may be seen in the letters the young Michael Madhusudan Dutt, eighteen in 1842, wrote to his school friend Gourdas Bysack (Basak), both students at Hindu College in that year. They were written in English and the emphases are Dutt's own; the influence of English Romantic literature is clear:

> My heart beats when the thought that *you* are my friend, comes into my mind! You say you will honour my place . . . with your "Royal presence." Your presence, Gour Dass, is something more than Royal. Oh! it is *angelic*! oh! no! it is something *more exquisite* still!
>
> Wednesday last I did go to the Mechanics—not to learn Drawing, "Oh! no! 'twas for something more exquisite still!" that is to see you. . . . Shall I see you at the Mechanics tomorrow? O! come for my sake![35]

Later in the century, Bipinchandra Pal would form a similarly intense friendship with Sundarimohan Das, and Dinesh Chandra Sen with somebody called Ramdayal.[36] For the twentieth century, a similar friendship is recorded between Achintyakumar Sengupta and Premendra Mitra in their youth, a sense of attachment in which one experienced feelings not altogether dissimilar from those of romantic love.[37] Similar friendships blossomed between young women, too, with the establishment of girls' schools, but their histories, for understandable reasons, are harder to recover. My point is that the history of the modern Bengali *adda* has some roots in the way literature came into the space of friendship and fashioned new sentiments of intimacy.

The Tagores were pioneers and patrons of many forms of literary gathering that combined more formal setups—and were usually given Sanskritized names like *ashar* or *sammilani*—with some of the more spontaneous elements of *adda*.[38] In this family, the pleasures of kinship were garnished with those of literature. Sarala Devi, a niece of the poet Rabindranath Tagore, later wrote about the period 1887–1888 when, on a holiday with the family at Darjeeling, the poet would read out English literature to his family at a gathering (*ashar*) that met every evening. Sarala Devī writes: "My literary tastes were formed by Rabimama [*mama* = maternal uncle]. He was the person who opened my heart to the aesthetic treasure in Matthew Arnold, Browning, Keats, Shelley, and others. I remember how when we were at the Castleton House in Darjeeling for a month or so . . . every evening [he] would read aloud from and explain [to us] Browning's 'Blot in the Scutcheon.' That was my first introduction to Browning."[39]

Anecdotes from the life of the nationalist writer Bankimchandra Chattopadhyay also provide evidence of this process of percolation of literature into the space of intimacy and sociality. The Bengali essayist Akshoychandra Sarkar mentions once spending a few hours in a waiting room at a railway station in the company of Bankimchandra discussing the literary genre of "mysteries": "Out of that sharing of aesthetic pleasure (*rasa*) [in 1870]," he writes, "was born a feeling of mutual appreciation between us. Over time that grew into . . . a special friendship. He was my superior in age, caste, education, and accomplishment, but this never interfered with our friendship."[40] Bankimchandra's nephew and biographer Sachishchandra Chattopadhyay relates the story of a stormy argument one day between Bankimchandra and a literary friend of his that continued uninterrupted from nine in the evening to after midnight, and comments: "The mention of Hugo, Balzac, Goethe, Dante, Chaucer, and

Figure 1.

others still reminds me of that night." Sachishchandra also mentions how Bankimchandra's *baithakkhana* was sometimes transformed into a space for literary *adda* (he in fact uses both of these words writing in 1911/12) where writers met.[41]

Two other institutions helped move the discussion of a *baithak* toward cosmopolitan concerns. One of these was the newspaper. *Hutom* mentions how the "Anglicized" people of the 1860s were always excited about the "best news of the day," but in those years the newspaper was something that distinguished the Anglicized.[42] A sketch (Figure 1, c. 1920s) by the Bengali artist Charu Ray, which depicts a typical scene of a *baithak*, suggests the newspaper and books as permanent, defining, everyday features of the new, twentieth-century *baithakkhana*.[43] Compare this, however, with the drawing (Figure 2) of Suniti Chattopadhyay that illustrates an *adda* in a students' hostel in Calcutta in 1913, along with Chattopadhyay's description of the usual proceedings of a typical *adda*; the process of democratization and indigenization of literary tastes in the lives of the young of the middle classes will become clear.[44] Unlike in the sedate and aristocratic *baithak*, the atmosphere here is animated, and the furnishing more sparse and much less comfortable than in the picture of the *baithak*. The scene gathers most of its energy from the extended arms, pointed fingers, and focused eyes in the foreground, suggesting intense argumentation. As Chattopadhyay explains, the arguments themselves showed an emerging new association between literature and and the production of Bengali selves:

> The evening is one of the liveliest hours of the day in the hostel. . . . There is no end to talk and discussion on all manners of topics, and joking and singing. . . . Some of the favourite literary topics are Mr Rabindra Nath Tagore and the late Mr D. L. Roy as poets, the places of Hem Chandra Banerji and Michael Madhusudan Datta in Bengali poetry, the dramatic genius of the late Girish Chandra Ghosh. . . . The first subject is by far

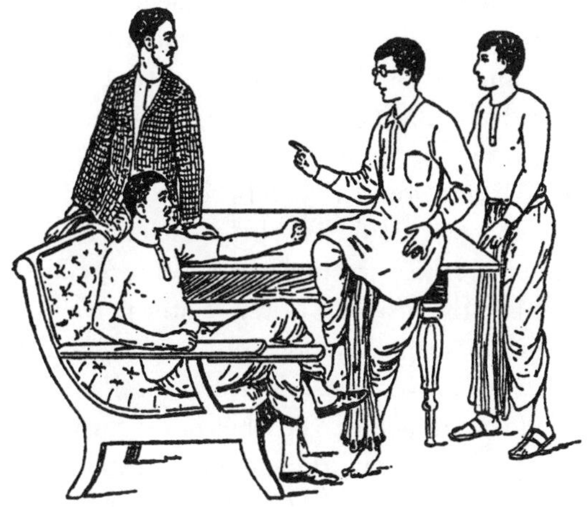

Figure 2.

> the most popular one: and there are "Rabi-ites" and "Dijoo-ites" in every hostel, as hostile to each other's opinions as were the Whigs and Tories of the past."[45]

It is important to note that the literary references in the quotation above are all Bengali, marking a further step in the popularization of literature into Bengali lives, a development that was soon to be aided by the fact that Bengali literature was introduced as a formal subject of study by Calcutta University in 1919.[46] Debates in *addas* among young men were critical to this propagation of literature into middle-class lives. And this in turn brought respectability to *adda* as a form of social activity. As Suniti Chattopadhyay wrote of his student days: "The student has a large stock of hybrid words [mixing Bengali with English], which he can invent whenever he likes. *Addify* and *addification* have got nothing to do with mathematical addition; they simply mean *to enjoy a chat* . . . and come from the Bengali word *adda*."[47]

One begins to see in the early part of the twentieth century the tendency on the part of literate Bengali men to form something like clubs where arts and literature (and later politics) could be discussed. One such club that has recently had a certain amount of writing devoted to it was the Monday Club, so called from the day it met, which involved such future luminaries as the famous writer Sukumar Ray (the father of film director Satyajit Ray), the statistician Prasantachandra Mahalanobis, the linguist Sunitikumar Chattopadhyay, and others. In Hirankumar Sanyal's description, "this was a regular club" with formal membership and a four-anna rate of subscription every month."[48] The activities included discussing "everything beginning from Plato-Nietzsche to Bankim-Vivekananda-Vaishnava poetry, Rabindra[nath's] poetry" as well as music, feasts, and picnicking.[49]

Rabindranath Tagore won the Nobel prize for literature in 1913. One can only imagine how this would have helped to embed literature in "ordinary" Bengali lives. Whereas the nineteenth-century cultivation of the literary self was mainly the province of the relatively well-to-do, the young nationalist, radical, or socialist writers of the 1920s and 1930s were not any longer the rich. They were, sociologically speaking, small people who often lived in financial difficulty, yet whose love for their own literature and that in other parts of the world had an unmistakable idealism about it. Tagore was a great believer in the Goetheian idea of "world literature," and his winning of the Nobel prize seems to have democratized the ideal of literature as a vocation. To be a literary person now—even if one were unemployed—was to be someone respectable, as literary activity was now by definition of cosmopolitan and global relevance. Or so, at least, the argument went for some.

Adda could thus become a space for the practice of literary cosmopolitanism by members of the middle and lower-middle classes. In 1921, two young men, Dineshranjan Das and Gokulchandra Nag, started a new organization called the Four Arts Club with the express intention of involving women. The "four arts" referred to literature, music, crafts, and painting. Neither Das nor Nag came from an aristocratic background. Das worked initially for a sports goods shop in the Chowringhee part of the city and later for a pharmacist's shop; Nag worked in a florist's shop in the New Market. The democratization, as well as a certain social radicalism, of this particular form of *adda* may be in seen in the fact that there was nobody's parlor available to them. As Jibendra Singha Ray, who has studied the history of this club, writes: "The chief problem after the establishment of the club was the venue. Many were reluctant to rent a room for the purpose of meetings that would involve both men and women. Faced with this situation, Dineshranjan's sister and her husband Sukumar Dasgupta . . . let out their lounge room for a small rent."[50]

Also remarkable was the idealism of the founders of this club, colored as it was with a heavy dose of a post-Tagore Bengali faith in the redemptive role of arts and literature in middle-class lives. Dineshranjan was later to describe the origin of the club in terms that bespoke an idealism seeking to take within its embrace nothing short of the whole world. He may have been an unknown Bengali writer but what he did, he assumed, was for the benefit of humanity at large. He saw himself as a citizen of the global literary cosmopolis. Das's description is a testimony to the way literature, male friendships, and a certain humanism came together to make literary *addas* of Calcutta of the 1920s spaces where a democratic and cosmopolitan vision of the world could be nurtured and sustained:

> The ideal and an imaginary [shape] of this club had been unfolding in my mind for many years. Witnessing the sign of a silent pain on the faces of many men and women of [this] idealistic country [would make my] heart wish that I could bring to light [my own] imagination from the dark caverns of my mind. . . . My pathos must have cast a shadow over my face. Gokul asked me one day, "What's going on in your mind? I feel as though I am also thinking the same thought as you are but cannot quite tell what the thought is." I said, "I imagine a [kind of] resting-house [an inn]—where people tired by the burden of their lives can come and rest, where *nationality, sex, and position will not be any barriers*, [where] men will make their own work joyful and by freely mixing with others and will find themselves fulfilled in the easy working out of their own desires. Gokul put his hand over mine, clapped, and cried out in joy, "That is the dream of my life, too, but I could not figure out its exact shape until now!"[51]

The growing book trade in the city—the market in global literature, that is—was itself organized around the culture and institution of *adda*. Conversation and orality remained important factors in the creation and dissemination of literary taste in a city where the production and consumption of books were based on relations that remained fundamentally personal. Every bookshop, every little office of a literary magazine hosted an *adda* at which writers, critics, editors, and readers gathered.[52] Nripendrakrishna Chattopadhyay gives us a lively sketch of this small but significant subculture:

> Right behind College Square was a big bookshop called The Book Company. A few new bookshops like this were established toward the beginning of this century around College Square. These shops played a very helpful role in spreading the culture [English word in the original] of the period. They began to import freshly produced books from Europe and America on various literary, poetic, and scientific subjects; it was through their efforts that the young and the writers of those times got an opportunity to get to know the trends in world literature and thinking.

Chattopadhyay reconstructs what might typically happen at this bookshop. His story, whether apocryphal or not, underlines the close connection that existed between *adda* and literary cosmopolitanism in Calcutta of the mid-twentieth century. In Chattopadhyay's somewhat dramatic narrative, the owner of this new shop, Girinbabu, suddenly calls out to a familiar customer he spots on the pavement outside. The customer happens to be none other than the reputed Bengali sociologist, professor at the University of Lucknow, and well-known correspondent of Tagore, Dhurjatiprasad Mukherjee. Girinbabu invites Mukherjee to go into the warehouse at the back of the shop, where an *adda* of a select group of book-crazy readers of Calcutta gathers regularly: "Go inside, Nadu was looking for you." Nadu, an employee of the shop, is in charge of opening the newly arrived shipping crates that contain the fresh imports of literature from overseas. He knows the readers by their personal reading tastes. Here is the scene, in Chattopadhyay's reconstruction, that Mukherjee witnesses on stepping inside the warehouse:

> Nadubabu is engaged in opening a crate that has just arrived. Around him are two *addadharis* [the central characters of an *adda*: see below] staring at the wooden box, their eyes thirsty like those of an alcohol lover eyeing a bottle of champagne. The younger of the two is very young. . . . The older person is middle-aged. An aristocrat from top to bottom, the latter is dressed in perfect Bengali attire, white as the feathers of a crane, holding—through sheer habit it seems—an empty, golden cigarette holder between two of his fingers. A closer look would reveal his fingers to be trembling a little—[this is] Pramatha Chaudhuri [a famous writer and critic of the 1920s and the editor of the avant-garde magazine, *Sabujpatra*]. Addressing the young man, he says, "You see, this new poetry now being written in England and France contains a very big tragedy behind all that seeming disorder of meter and rhyme. The Great War [1914] came and destroyed all the old-world beliefs in the minds of their young, their restless minds are seeking a new refuge. I will show you [an example] if the book has arrived by this mail . . . oh, here you are, Dhurjati, welcome!"[53]

Thus the market and taste in the consumption of literature are all mediated, as in this anecdote, by the conversation of the *adda*.

The practice of *adda* seems to have been critical in the creation and dissemination of taste in the areas of films and arts, as well. In remembering an *adda* that used to gather at "3-B, Kalighat South Park" in the 1950s and that revolved around the personality of Bimal Ghosh, "Kanuda" to his younger friends, the historian Arun Das Gupta says: "For as long as he lived among us, Kanuda was our expert, advisor, and guide in matters relating to films."[54] The Communist artist Debrabata Mukhopadhyay reminds us in his memoirs of the College Street Coffee House that it was from an *adda* at the Central Avenue Coffee House (of which Satyajit Ray and the future film critic Chidananda Das Gupta were regular members) that "the renewal of Bengali filmmaking began." And speaking of the education of his own taste, Mukhopadhyay is even more forthright in his insistence on the modernity of *adda*: "I have no academic training," he says. "My education, whether in art or culture generally, is largely a contribution of *adda*."[55]

These changes would have acted in tandem with other transformations in the nature of public space in the city. Two in particular deserve our attention. First, we need a history of parks in the city. The nineteenth-century material mostly does not mention "parks," at least not under that designation. *Hutom*, which is very good and detailed on streets, verandas, *baithakkhanas*, and opium-*addas*, has nothing on parks. Yet the park that Calcuttans usually call Hedo or Hedua (on Cornwallis Street) figures prominently in quite a few literary reminiscences of the twentieth century. Bipinbehari Gupta's *Puratan prasanga*, for example—an indispensable sourcebook on nineteenth-century history—is really a series of conversations between him and Krishnakamal Bhattacharya (a contemporary and an acquaintance of Bankim and the Tagores) that takes place at this park (Beadon Gardens/Hedua) around 1910/11.[56] When he was an undergraduate student, that is, in the 1910s, the physicist Satyendranath Bose was part of a literary *adda* that used to meet on the rooftop—yet another unresearched urban site in Calcutta—of the house of Girijapati Bhattacharya. Both Bose and Bhattacharya later became prominent members of another famous literary *adda* that formed around the magazine *Parichoy.* Sometimes, we are told, this *adda* would shift to the park at Hedua. Discussing Tagore's stories, reciting his poems, and singing songs written by him were the staple of this *adda*.[57] The journal *Prabashi*, in its later incarnation under the editorship of Ashok Chattopadhyay, was conceived at an *adda* at this same park in 1924. We need to find out more about rooftops and parks and the roles they played in the cultural life of the city in the twentieth century.[58]

The other important question is: When do tea shops, coffeehouses, and restaurants proliferate in Calcutta, and when do they begin to act as major sites for literary *addas*?[59] There have been, of course, places like "Puntiram's shop" near College Street in north Calcutta, which has now run for more than a hundred years, though its specific history needs research. The Communist author and leader Muzaffar Ahmad mentions in his reminiscences of the poet Kazi Nazrul Islam tea shops where he and others could drop in to sit down for a chat in the early 1920s.[60] But the reader will recall that Nirad Chaudhuri's comments suggested that *addas* in tea shops were relatively rare in the 1920s, compared to those in someone's parlor. In his introduction to Hirankumar Sanyal's reminiscences of the literary magazine *Parichoy* (started around 1932), the historian Sushobhan Sarkar writes: "In our college life, the streets and lanes of central Calcutta provided the chief meeting places. Eating out at restaurants was not yet a popular practice."[61]

These statements receive support from a remark of Radhaprasad Gupta. Gupta remembers how, in the late 1930s, many tea shops "from Shyambazar to Kalighat" (that is, from the north to the south of the city) used to advertise on red banners their desperately cheap rates: "Only two annas for a cup of tea, two pieces of toast, and an omelette made of two eggs."[62] Although it seems that there were indeed shops—Gupta mentions "Gyanbabu's tea shop," Favourite Cabin on Mirzapur Street, Basanta Cabin opposite the Calcutta University premises, and the College Street YMCA restaurant—that fostered a culture of *adda* among university students in the mid- to late 1930s, the chain of coffeehouses and Sangu Valley Restaurants that were to dominate the city's *adda* scene soon after independence did not appear until the late 1930s or during the war.[63] The big coffeehouses were started by the Indian Coffee Expansion Board as a way of marketing coffee to a city that belonged—and still does—predominantly to tea drinkers. However, the practice of drinking coffee, says Gupta, was introduced into the Bengali culture of Calcutta in the 1930s by the immigrant southerners (the Bengali word *dakshini* refers to people from the south—Tamilnad, Kerala, Andhra, and so on) in the city who set up small eating places around Ballygunge about this time. The drama of his first introduction to a "coffeehouse" is best captured in Gupta's own words:

> One evening in 1941–1942, I went to . . . Waterloo Street to see my childhood friend the dentist Gopal Banerjee. The young man Gopal,

though bred in . . . Konnagar, would in those days turn himself out sometimes as a full-fledged *sahib* and sometimes as a pure Calcutta-bred Bengali dandy. That day, when I showed up, he was ready [in English in the original] to go out, . . . dressed in a fine *dhoti* and *kurta*. On seeing me, he said, "Come, let me take you to a new place." When I asked him about this new place, he said, "Oh no, on that matter I should remain *speakti not* [a jocular Bengali expression which makes use of English to say 'I am not speaking']. It's close, why don't you just come along? You will soon see for yourself." So saying, he took me past . . . Bentinck Street to the just-opened India Coffee House at the crossing of Meredith Street and Central Avenue. Young people these days, even the children, do seem to be taken by surprise by anything. But my jaw dropped even in my "older" years at the sight of this coffee house, with its huge size, liveried bearers ["boys"] wearing badges, its clean appearance, polished tables and chairs, and nicely dressed customers at every table. . . . The College Street Coffee House started soon after this.[64]

Indeed, evidence from fiction would suggest that although *adda* may have been a general and plebeian practice among the residents of Calcutta, its more respectable form—self-consciously imitating a European coffeehouse form—made only tentative beginnings in the 1930s. Parashuram's celebrated story "Ratarati" (Overnight), written around 1931, creates a funny situation at a fictitious restaurant called The Anglo-Mughlai Cafe located somewhere in Dharmatola, the central business district of the city—its location itself signifying a degree of cultural distance from the everyday lives of the middle classes. The joke of the situation turns on many things. On the one hand, The Anglo-Mughlai Cafe is about the aspiration to Europeanize the *adda* form, to turn it into something like the conversation at a European cafe. At the same time, the Bengali lack of familiarity with European forms is suggested through the manager's ignorance as it reveals itself during an altercation with a customer, Bantlo, who prides himself on his superior knowledge of these things:

The Manager: Do you realize that this is Anglo-Moglai *kef*?

Bantlo cannot tolerate wrong pronunciation. He said, "It's not *kef*—*kaafe*."

The Manager: It is all the same. Do you realize that this is not an ordinary place, that this is a respectable res-tau-rant [says it phonetically]?

Bantlo: Restora [tries the French version].

Manager: It is all the same. Do you realize that this is a ren-des-vos for the educated people?

Bantlo: [using French] Rendezvous.[65]

ORALITY AND COMMUNITY IN *ADDA*

That there should be tension between the ideals of the *adda* and those of the modern civil society is understandable. They are mutually antithetical organizations of time and place. Civil society, in its ideal construction, builds into the very idea of human activity the telos of a result, a product and a purpose, and structures its use of time and place on that developmentalist and utilitarian logic (even when that logic is not simply linear). Conversations in an *adda*, on the other hand, are by definition opposed to the idea of achieving any definite outcome. Enjoying an *adda* is to enjoy a sense of time and space that is not subject to the gravitational pull of any explicit purpose. The introduction of a purpose that could make the conversation "instrumental" to the achievement of some object other than the social life of an *adda* itself, kills, it is claimed, the very spirit and the principle of *adda*. Buddhadev Bose says as much in his essay on *adda*: "Suppose we decide that we will convene a literary meeting once a week or twice a month, so that knowledgeable and talented people can come and discuss good things. . . . Good idea no doubt, and it is possible that the first few sessions will be so successful that we will ourselves be surprised. But we will observe after a while that the whole thing has fallen from the heaven of *adda* and has turned into the barren land of 'duty.' "[66]

The center of gravity of the *adda* lay in a direction away from the telos of productivity or development (in this case that of purposeful discussion). Hirankumar Sanyal recalls how food (and, I might add, a gendered division of labor) were once used in a meeting of the Monday Club to defeat Prasantachandra Mahalanobis's plans to inject into the proceedings a sense of purpose. Sanyal writes:

> Every . . . [meeting] included a feast. But one day, Prasantachandra turned obstinate [and said], "Eating makes discussion impossible. Why do you waste so much time just eating? I will serve you only tea and cheap biscuits." The meeting was at his place that day. There were some tiny little biscuits available those days called "gem" biscuits—usually offered to pet cats and dogs. Everybody raised a hue and cry. Tatada [Sukumar Ray] realized protesting would not achieve anything, for Pra-

> santa would not listen. He whispered to me, "Go inside [the house] and tell Prasanta's sister that Prasanta has invited a group of people for tea but has not arranged for any food. Just say this and come back." After about fifteen or twenty minutes a variety of food appeared. . . . Prasanta said, "What is this? Who got all this?" Tatada replied, "How does that concern you? The food is here, and we will eat it."[67]

Even without the aid of food, conversation in an *adda* could itself ensure that arguments never reached a terminal point. Take this entry for 24 January 1936 from Shyamal Ghosh's published diary in which he used to keep records of the conversations at the highbrow *adda* of people associated with the magazine *Parichoy.* The discussion here broaches large questions, but not with a view to solving them:

> Ayyub asked: Putting aside the matter of physical reactions, are there any qualitative differences between emotions such as anger, fear, love, and so on?
>
> Mallikda asked a counter-question: Can you isolate emotions if you leave the body out [of consideration]?
>
> It was not possible to reach a conclusion even after about an hour's argumentation.
>
> I heard Ayyub say once, "Let us assume that no feeling is possible without the mediation of the body, still I want to know why, if all emotions are of the same type, someone will be beside themselves when called a 'pig' at one time, and just brush it off at another . . . why does this happen?

Ghosh closes his entry with a matter-of-fact remark that suggests how used he was to such discussions: "There cannot be conclusions to such debates."[68]

Focused on the oral, Bengali *addas* represented a certain capacity on the part of their members to take pleasure in the pure art of conversation.[69] By its very nature, the pleasure was communal. The writer Hemendrakumar Ray's memoirs distinguish between the speaking style of a meeting and that of a *baithakkhana.* Pramatha Chaudhuri, the editor of *Sabujpatra,* was famous for his *bathaki* style of speech: "it was in small rooms that his *baithaki* style of conversation would become so captivating."[70] The life of the *adda* was always a person with some specialty to their speech, someone who could tell a good story, coin a new word, turn a phrase interestingly, or produce smart quips that made an impression on others. They were the people who could, as the Bengali expression goes, make an *adda* "congeal" or "thicken" (in the same way that a plot does). Hirankumar Sanyal says of Sukumar Ray in the context of the Monday Club: "[He] . . . had a remarkable capacity to help the *ashar* [*majlish*, convivial gathering] come into its own. On days on which the Monday Club had no specific subject to discuss, he kept us enthralled by telling us all kinds of stories."[71] The *adda*, in this way, must have drawn on older styles of speech such as those of *kathakata* (traditional practices of telling devotional stories).[72] The pleasure of conversation is also suggested by another story about Sukumar Ray told by Sanyal. The austere Brahmo teacher Herambachandra Maitra once asked Sukumar Ray, "Sukumar, can you tell me what life's ideal is [should be]?" Sukumar is said to have replied [in English]: "serious interest in life." Maitra was so pleased at this answer that he immediately ordered *sandesh* [a popular variety of Bengali sweet made out of ricotta cheese] for everybody present.[73] The communal nature of the pleasure exchanged by this verbal transaction is signified by the fact that everybody present celebrated the answer by making it an occasion for eating sweets—yet another exercise in public practices of orality.

The connection between orality and a certain kind of aesthetic/communal pleasure was thus already given in the form of the *adda*. The coming of English literature (or literature available in English) into the lives of the lower middle classes made possible certain distinct variations to this orality in the *adda* of the educated. *Adda* became an arena where one could develop techniques of presenting oneself as a character—from Wilde or Shaw or Joyce or Faulkner—through the development of certain mannerisms (meant for the enjoyment of others), habits of speech, and gestures. In the reminiscences of *addas*, people are typically remembered not in a way that "history" or "biography" as genres would represent them (in the round, as it were), but rather as relatively one-dimensional characters who are remembered for how they presented themselves to the *adda*. A case in point would be Radhaprasad Gupta's memories of a member of their *adda* called Amitabha Sen:

> His command over mathematics, science, literature, and arts used to leave us dazzled. All the developments in the [different] fields of knowledge-science [I have translated the Bengali expression literally] were at his fingertips, thanks to good books and foreign journals. It was through him that we first saw the ubiquitous ball[-point] pen of today. That perhaps was the first ball[-point] pen in the world, called Reynolds. We were rendered speechless by it. Everyone took his turn at writing with it. You

could write any way you wanted. Amitabhababu's face wore his familiar gentle smile. Watching us, he only made one remark [in English]: "Mankind at last has been freed from the tyranny of the pen-angle."[74]

WOMEN, *ADDA*, AND PUBLIC CULTURE

Was the space of the modern *adda*, the one that was opened up by the coming of universities, student dormitories, modern literary production, restaurants, tea shops, coffeehouses, and parks—was this a male space?

The Bengali cultural and literary critic Manashi Das Gupta has made the point to me that the very public acts of orality—speaking and eating—through which an *adda* created its sense of community tended to form "traditional" barriers to women's participation in a male *adda*. Women, if they were to adhere to nineteenth-century middle-class ideas about respectability in public (that is, avoid exposure to the gaze of men from beyond the confines of kinship), were barred from these practices of orality. Yet this does not mean that women did not enjoy or practice *adda*. First, one has to remember that the separation of spheres for men and women both before and after British rule in India meant that women could have their own *addas*, and that is in part is still the practice. The sites of such *addas* would have been different, being spaces where women could meet. The topics discussed may have also reflected the separation of social domains. The 1990 collection *Kolkatar adda* has female contributors on the subject as well as an essay on "women's *adda*." Women working in Calcutta and commuting to the city by train every day in their specially designated "women's compartments" develop their own sense of *adda*.[75]

But male *addas* of the mid-twentieth century were predicated, practically, on a separation of male and female spaces. As Nripendrakrishna Chattopadhyay bluntly asserted: "the biggest natural enemy of *adda* are women!" The statement is not as misogynist as it may seem. He actually also refers to the gender problem as a "defect" and takes a sympathetic view of the position to which women are relegated by the structure of *adda*: "A big natural defect of *adda* is that it is an intimate world for men. And yet this weakness is the amulet that also protects it. An *adda* breaks up if a woman comes within ten cubits of it. . . . Every married woman looks on *adda* with poisoned eyes. It is, after all, for the *addadhari* husband of hers that she has to sit up and wait into the silence of the night. Every husband who returns home from an *adda* comes back prepared to be asked this single [sarcastic] question: 'so the *adda* finally ended, did it?' "[76]

This (imagined) wifely hostility to *adda* drew on a culturally conceived opposition between the world and the word, between "worldly responsibilities"—the world of chores, dominated by needs—and the noninstrumental pleasure of company and conversation that an *adda* was. In speaking of role of the *addadhari*—literally, one who holds an *adda* together—Nripendrakrishna pictured him as a man who artfully and devotedly evaded everything to do with domestic and social duties. In words that in Bengali brim over with both humor and irony, Nripendrakrishna thus described the ideal *addadhari*:

> Every *adda* has a central personality, someone who could be called an *addadhari*. . . . [H]e is the sun of the solar system of an *adda*, it is around him that the *adda* revolves. The *addadhari* is like a stable center in a world that is otherwise restless. He has no office to go to, no wedding invitations to attend, no speeches to deliver at any meeting, no obsessions about going to the movies, no obligations to do with the marriage of his sister-in-law, no first-rice ceremonies of a son of his wife's brother, he has no Darjeeling, no Puri, his only job is to sit there like the immobile image of a deity lighting up the *adda*. The streets of Calcutta may be under water, the asphalt on them may have been melted by the sun, the Japanese may have dropped a few bombs, but every *addabaj* [*adda*-addicted person] has the assurance of knowing that there will be at least one person present at the *adda*. And that person is the *addadhari*.[77]

This could not, however, be the whole story. Women's education and their entry into public life—a historical process that started in the 1850s—made a difference. The tension between the old separation of male and female domains of life and the new ideals of companionate marriage is the subject of the Parashuram (Rajshekhar Bosu)'s humorous story "Dvandik kobita" (Dialectical poetry) written in 1957. "Dialectical poetry"—the name itself mocking some of the chantlike aspects of Bengali Marxism—is a tale told in an *adda*, and concerns a character called Dhurjati and his wife Shankari. Dhurjati lectures in mathematics but has devoted his life to writing love poems addressed, in the fashion of Bengali romanticism started by Tagore, to unknown, unseen, and completely imaginary women from imaginary foreign lands. Needless to say, this practice of addressing male romantic sentiments to fictional women consciously described as "unknown" (*ajana, achena*) itself reflected the distance between these sentiments and everyday, routine rounds of domesticity. After his marriage, the protagonist of Bose's story, Dhurjati, tried to make a dent in this tradition. For a while he deliberately made his wife the addressee of his expression of romantic and poetic love, but gave up the effort in frustration when he found that Shankari was more interested in the baby they had had soon after their marriage than in his poetic exuberance: "Dhurjati gradually realized that the 'ladylove' of his marriage had nothing in common with the beloved of his [poetic] fancy. Shankari does not understand the pleasure of poetry, there is no romance in her heart. She had received a lot of cheap presents . . . at the time of the wedding, she treated the poems that Dhurjati had written addressing her as though they were the same as these ordinary presents. She is just absorbed in domestic chores and in [their] newborn son." Dhurjati goes back to addressing his poems to his imaginary sweetheart, while Shankari devotes herself to domesticity.

If Bose's story had ended here, it would have depicted a nineteenth-century resolution of the tension between domesticity and the modern, expressivist male self: a man reserves his literary cosmopolitanism for his male friends and sustains a practical, mundane companionship with his wife. But Bose wrote in a period when literature was part of women's lives, as well. So, Bisakha, a friend of Shankari from her university days, steps in and plants doubt into Shankari's mind. She says one day:

> "Your husband is, after all, a famous poet. . . . Can you tell me for whom his poems of love are written? Surely not for you, for he wouldn't have written things like 'my unknown sweetheart [whom] I have met in dreams' in that case."
>
> Shankari said, "He writes for nobody. Poets are fanciful people, they erect somebody in their imagination and address her."
>
> — . . . Don't you feel angry?
>
> — I don't much care for it.
>
> — . . . You will have to regret later . . . take some *steps* now.
>
> — What do you suggest?
>
> — [That] you also start writing poems addressed to some imaginary man.

Shankari has never written poetry, so Bisakha offers to write for her. Soon poems appear in literary magazines in Shankari's name. They are addressed to such characters as the "belligerent young man of Red China" ("I want to take shelter in your hairless chest") or to "the young man of Pakhtunistan":

> Take me into your jungle-haired chest
> Hold me tight with those crank-shaft-like arms of yours
> Let the bones of my rib cage break and crumble
> Crush me, crush me.

And a male friend of Dhurjati says to him one day: "I say Dhurjati, isn't this Shankari Devi your wife? What extraordinary poetry she is writing, regular *hot stuff*. . . . Professor Bhar, the psychologist, said [the other day], this is *libido* gone wild." The subsequent conversation between Dhurjati and Shankari could not have taken place in the nineteenth century. Dhurjati said:

> "What is this rubbish you are writing? People are talking."
>
> Shankari said, "Let them talk. It is selling very well, I have given another book to the press."
>
> Dhurjati shook his head and said, "I am telling you this cannot go on."
>
> "That's funny. There's no harm if you write [this] but it's bad if I do!— . . . why do you write such rubbish?"
>
> "You compare yourself to me? It's all right if a man writes about imaginary women [lovers], but it's very bad for women to do so."
>
> "All right, you stop writing poetry and burn all your books, and I will do the same."

Unable to resolve the conflict on his own terms, Dhurjati gives up writing poetry and takes to writing books on algebra, while Shankari decides to write only recipes for magazine sections of Sunday newspapers.[78]

Bose's resolution to this problem is not one that completely destroys the division between male and female spaces even in modern public life. It is, however, one that would have made an *adda* laugh, and that laughter would have been a resource with which Bengalis could deal with the changes and tensions created by women's entry into public life. But although the laughter would have been such a resource, it was no answer to the question of why an implicit principle of gender segregation would continue to exist in public life.

The issue of friendship in public life between men and women is part of a complicated history of modern heterosexual practices in Bengal. In his magisterial survey of the history of the Bengali novel, the literary critic Srikumar Bandyopadhyay made the perceptive suggestion that it was within male—rather than male-female—friendship that European romantic and cosmopolitan sentiments made their initial home in our history and thus expanded and intensified the space of that friendship. Surveying the novels written at the turn of the century, Bandyopadhyay remarked:

> Given the closed-door nature of our social arrangements, friendship [between men, as opposed to romantic, heterosexual love] is the only opening through which external revolutions can enter the Bengali family. Only the claim of friendship or being a classmate of somebody allows us to overcome the barriers of . . . [women's space] of a different family and become intimate with them. The narrower the opportunities for free mixing between men and women, the greater the expanse of and the possibilities for male friendship. That is why Bengali novels see an excess of friendship [between men]—in the majority of cases complexity arises from the force and counterforce of the affection, sense of comfort, and yet at the same time the intense spirit of competition that such friendship generates.[79]

This is true not only of the nineteenth century. As recently as the 1960s, the sight of a woman engaged in *adda* with her male peers at the College Street Coffee House was rare enough to elicit this comment and sketch from the Communist artist Debabrata Mukhopadhyay: "Girls had just begun to come to the midday *adda* [at the Coffee House]. But they were extremely few in numbers. It was about this time a certain group of boys set up a regular *adda* around a particular girl. We, who had always been *addadharis* without the company of women, felt a little jealous. We named the girl 'the queen-bee.' One day, I captured her in a sketch" (see Figure 3).[80]

Bengali modernity, for complicated reasons, never quite transcended the structure of opposition between domestic space and that of *adda*. If I could take out of context an expression of Henry Lefebvre and give it a stronger sense of irony than Lefebvre intended, I might say that literary modernity and its attendant spaces of the school, university, coffeehouse, bookshops, magazines, and so on did indeed help to expand, deepen, and modernize the homosocial space of *adda*, and even allowed for women's participation in it. But its male character was never erased, and it often left the heterosexual men involved in literary endeavor with a sense of—that this is where I register my debt to Lefebvre's coinage—a "phallic solitude."[81] The "human" on whose behalf Gokul Nag and Dinesh Das dreamed their cosmopolitan dreams barely included Bengali women.

মক্ষিরাণী

Figure 3.

ADDA AND DWELLING IN CAPITALIST MODERNITY

The modern and hybrid space of Bengali *adda* thus does not in any way resolve the tensions brought about by the discourses of modernity and capitalism. The *adda*, thematically, is a site where several of the classic and endless debates of modernity are played out—discipline versus laziness, women's confinement in the domestic sphere versus their participation in the public sphere, separation of male and female domains versus a shared public life for both groups, leisure classes versus the laboring classes, an openness to the world versus the responsibilities of domestic life, and other related issues. Yet, as I said in the beginning of the chapter, the idea of *adda* now evokes in Bengali writings sentiments of mourning and nostalgia at the passing away of a familiar world.

It is possible that the world mourned today was never real. The cultural location of *adda* perhaps has more to do with a history in which the institution came to symbolize—in problematic and contested ways—a particular way of dwelling in modernity, almost a zone of comfort in capitalism. For all the claims made by the celebrants of *adda*, we know that it did not work equally well for everybody, that there were aspects of exclusion and domination in the very structure of *adda*. In spite of these problems, however, the institution played enough of a role in Bengali modernity for it to be tagged "Bengali." And Bengalis seemingly continue to invest *adda* with certain metaphysical talk: about life, vitality, essence, and youth. It could not be insignificant, after all, that the epigram to this chapter was penned by a woman, Manashi Das Gupta. Herself a trained academic and an active participant in many literary and political *addas* from the late 1940s to the present, Dr. Das Gupta is no stranger to the ways male *addas* tended to dominate if not exclude women. One would not expect her to "romanticize" *adda*. Yet the lines I quote from her:

> And it is a good sign that I still enjoy *adda*,
> for *adda* and youth are inseparable

were part of a poem she wrote home in 1957, describing her life at Cornell University, where she earned her Ph.D.[82] Why is it that even a cultural and feminist critic who is otherwise acutely aware of the male nature of the space of *adda* still associates that space with something as vitalist and metaphysical as youth, the sign of life? Why does the mention of *adda* generate such affection in most Bengali writing about the distinctiveness of their modernity?

The history sketched above attempts to answer this question. What remains buried in the current Bengali nostalgia for *adda*, I suggest, is an unresolved question of their present: how to be at home in a globalized capitalism now. An idealized image of *adda* points to the insistent pressures of that anxious question.

CHAPTER 8

Family, Fraternity, and Salaried Labor

RABINDRANATH TAGORE was not alone in finding the auspicious figure of the housewife, the *grihalakshmi*, much more deserving of poetry than the space of the office in which most employed middle-class Bengali men spent a large part of their waking hours. Bengali modernity has celebrated the home, the practice of *adda*, the production of plays, literature, films, and political mobilization; but modern office work and the requirements of capitalist work-discipline have seldom evoked affectionate or admiring sentiments in Bengali texts. Writing in 1874, when Tagore was still in his early teens, the Bengali intellectual Rajnarayan Bose complained: "We can never work as hard as the English. . . . The English style of exertion is not right for this land. The custom that the present rulers have introduced of working continuously from ten to four is not at all suited to this country. The body is quickly exhausted if one exerts oneself when the sun is still strong."[1]

This denigration of office discipline for men, however, was coupled in the late nineteenth century with an effusion of sentiments in praise of domestic work (*grihakarma* or *grihakarya*) by women. The *grihalakshmi*, the housewife imagined in the divine model of Lakshmi, the goddess of domestic well-being, became yet another site of nationalist aestheticization. An 1877 booklet on women's education, for instance, said that although "an uneducated woman cannot be skilled in *grihakarya* . . . a woman who neglects *grihakarya* for the sake of education will find her learning to be useless."[2] In fact, the same Rajnarayan Bose who complained that office work for men was too severe under British rule, also complained about "modern" Bengali housewives who did not work hard enough: "These days, women in well-to-do families are entirely dependent on [the labor of] their servants and are averse to *grihakarya*. The women of older times were not like that. . . . The educated women of our country now are reluctant to do physical labor or *grihakarya*."[3]

Historians have, with good reason, explained this aversion to *chakri* (salaried work) and the simultaneous glorification of housework for women in terms of either capitalism or patriarchy or both. Commenting on the disciplinary aspects of *chakri*, Sumit Sarkar has suggested that the

Bengali middle class's resistance to capitalist discipline was caused by the nature of colonial capitalism itself. Colonial rule, he contends, did not allow for a leisured pace of transition to capitalist production. And this, according to him, made it difficult to reproduce in Bengal the (supposedly) European experience of workers or employees who internalized over time the work ethic necessary for the successful functioning of capitalism. Sarkar writes: "What made *chakri* intolerable was—its connotation of impersonal cash nexus and authority, embodied above all in the new rigorous discipline of work regulated by clock-time. Disciplinary time was a particularly abrupt and imposed innovation in colonial India. Europe has gone through a much slower, and phased, transition spanning some five hundred years. . . . Colonial rule telescoped the entire process for India into one or two generations. . . . Chakri thus became a 'chronotype' [sic] of alienated time and space."[4]

A similar indictment of colonialism underlies Tanika Sarkar's (and some other scholars') explanation of why Bengali writers focused on domesticity and sentimental elaborations of housewifely virtues in the nineteenth century.[5] European domination of public life and civil society in Bengal, argues Tanika Sarkar, left the "home" as the only (conceptual) space in which nationalist Bengali men could act with some sense of autonomy and sovereignty over women and other social groups subordinate to them: "The Hindu home would be the one sphere where improvement could be made through our own initiative, changes could be wrought, where education would bring forth concrete, manipulable, desired results. The home, then, had to substitute for the world outside and for all the work and relations that lay there beyond one's comprehension and control."[6]

The Sarkars are right to emphasize the colonial context of Bengali modernity. It is no doubt true that, as in many other colonial situations, Bengali men experienced numerous instances of racial prejudice and humiliation at the hands of the Europeans as colonial rule became firmly entrenched. It understandable, therefore, as Partha Chatterjee and Tanika Sarkar have both suggested with insight, that the idea of the home should take on a special, compensatory significance in the modernity that Bengali nationalists experienced in the context of European colonial domination.[7]

It would perhaps not be controversial to say, then, that the Bengali modern was not classically bourgeois. Bengali modernity never developed anything like a Protestant ethic as a widely practiced value. It is also true that, for a long time, a romantic idealization of the extended family left little room for the development of a language of European-style individualism, whatever the actual practices of everyday life. Colonial rule brought about many of the desires and institutions of European bourgeois modernity but without, it would seem, the family romance of bourgeois Europe (see chapter 4 above). There is room for disagreement, however, as to why Bengali modernity implied a capitalist order without any hegemony of bourgeois thought.

Sumit Sarkar's explanation of why Bengalis have been historically averse to salaried work clearly takes certain received narratives of the history of industrialization in Europe as normative. There is, besides, an element of difficulty with the argument that Bengali problems with office space and "disciplinary time" followed from the nature of colonial capitalism. Contrary to what Sarkar's argument would lead one to expect, the most articulate Bengali critics of "discipline" and office work were themselves given to hard work and discipline in their personal lives. Rabindranath Tagore and Rajnarayan Bose, who found spoke derisively of the institution of the office, or Budhhadev Bose, who wrote in praise of *adda*, did not personally display any of the resistance to discipline that was supposedly symptomatic of a colonial political economy. The pace of transition to capitalism in the colony does not appear to have produced in them any aversion toward "labor." Yet they all found office work soul-killing and unattractive.

Arguments explaining the patriarchal character of Hindu Bengali nationalism generally highlight the "reactive" side of that discourse. Bengali nationalists, it is said, had to construct "home" as a space of autonomy because the Europeans left them no such space in public life. Eulogizing *griha* (home) and the *grihalakshmi* appears to have had a compensatory function for the nationalists. "Colonial masculinity," to use Mrinalini Sinha's apt phrase, may indeed appear to have driven Bengali men to wax lyrical on the virtues of the *grihalakshmi*.[8]

This is a powerful explanation, but to me it suffers from one major shortcoming. By seeking to explain the rhetoric and aesthetic of Bengali nationalist family romance in terms of their "feel-good" functions for colonized men and as some kind of a false consciousness when expressed by colonized women, it effectively reduces the aesthetic to its ideological functions alone. Nationalist discussions of *griha* and *grihalakshmi* then look like mere ideological ploys, tools in the politics of gender relations in colonial Bengal. It is, of course, impossible to deny the patriarchal nature of Bengali thought about home and the housewife in this period, and I will have more to say on this later. But to reduce popular categories of nationalist aesthetic to their ideological functions alone would be to miss out on the histories of contesting desires contained in them, even if we judged some of those desires to be reactionary by our standards today. Imagination and desire are always more than rationalizations of interests and power.

So if the housewife was declared beautiful and office space unattractive in the Bengali nationalist aesthetic of the nineteenth and early twentieth centuries, it might be profitable to look at this aesthetic for clues to the overall life form (including visions of the political) that this imagination sought to sustain. I want to suggest a supplementary explanation—beyond the prevailing functional ones—of why the twin figures of the *grihalakshmi* and the *griha* (home) were valorized over civil society in the particular strand of Bengali modernity under consideration here. I do not deny that these terms belonged to the evolving lexicon of the new patriarchy and gender relations that developed in Bengal under British rule. My aim is to make room for the proposition that Bengali modernity may have imagined life-worlds in ways that never aimed to replicate either the political or the domestic ideals of modern European thought. This problem goes to the heart of the project of this book. If the Bengali modern subject was not classically bourgeois, we must not look on this fact as a lack, however much and however justly we may need to criticize this modernity. A possible critique must proceed from other premises. To understand the Bengali valorization of the home and the *grihalakshmi* as part of a particular history of modernity and patriarchy involves an investigation of the possible imaginations of life that animated the creativity of this historical phenomenon, which now seems to have run its course.

Hindu Bengali nationalist writers of the late nineteenth century, much like nationalists anywhere in that period, did imagine the political community of the nation as a fraternity, a brotherhood of men, and in that sense as a structure of modern patriarchy. But the important point is that this was a conception of fraternity significantly different from the fraternity that, say, John Locke wrote about in his *Two Treatises of Government* (1690)—a text of that has long been identified as critical to the history of the modern bourgeois, "possessive," and patriarchal individual in the West.[9]

Fraternity in the Lockean schema was predicated on the emergence of private property and the political death of parental/paternal authority. The conceptual history of modern patriarchy in Bengali nationalism differs on these critical points. Although private property was a condition that enabled the new fraternity imagined in Bengali nationalism, it was never stipulated as a requirement in Bengali nationalist thought that the political authority of the father be destroyed before the brothers' compact could come into being. Fraternity in Locke's treatise was founded in the same principle/myth that underlies civil society, the myth of contract. Fraternity in Bengali nationalism was thought of as representing a natural rather than contractual solidarity of brotherhood. European bourgeois assumptions regarding autonomous personhood based in self-interest, contract, and private property were subordinated in Bengal to this idea of "natural" brotherhood. The Bengali (male) desire for a modern patriarchy was thus predicated on a rejection of the model of the "possessive individual" of Lockean thought.[10] The history of this nationalism thus allows us to analyze a colonial modernity that was intimately tied to European modernity but that did not reproduce the autonomous "individual" of European political thought as a figure of its own desire. This raises some critical questions about how one might think of the place of liberalism in this modernity. I shall return to this question at the end of this chapter and in the Conclusion to this book. But to think of this modernity as either incompletely bourgeois or merely as a compensatory move in the face of colonial rule, or to reject it as simply an ideological ruse for hiding the grosser facts of exploitation, oppression, and cruelties in Bengali society foreshortens the space for historical analysis.

I should make it clear, however, that I do not defend what I try to understand in these pages. Much of the nationalist construct discussed here has now outlived its utility. Much of it, as I shall endeavor to demonstrate, proved unworkable almost as soon as it was adumbrated. But it did succeed in elaborating a series of life practices around its central concepts and continued to do so well into the twentieth century. If contemporary criticism justly drives the last nail into the coffin of the imaginaire that underlay Bengali literary modernity, it does not thereby have to deny the life practices that this modernity once made historically possible.

ANCESTORS, GODS, AND THE SPHERE OF CIVIL SOCIETY

To write a history of Bengali refusal to valorize the civil society that European colonial rule brought in its train, I need to begin by recounting some of the strategies Bengali men deployed in negotiating British rule, long before the coming of modern nationalism. Prenationalist upper-caste Hindus who worked with and for the British in the early part of the nineteenth century possessed a distinctly developed pragmatism that helped them to accommodate some of important changes to lifestyle that British rule brought about. What shaped this pragmatism were the questions of quotidian life, in particular those relating to the ritual exchanges upper-caste men were expected to transact every day with both gods and the male ancestors of the particular lineages to which they belonged. This pragmatism is writ large, for instance, in Bhabanicharan Bandyopadhyay's book *Kalikata kamalalaya* (lit., Calcutta, the Abode of Kamala [Lakshmi]) published in 1823. Bhabanicharan, a Brahmin who edited the important Bengali news magazine *Samachar chandrika*, was a luminary of the "public sphere" that was emerging in Calcutta in this period.

Kalikata kamalalaya (hereafter *KK*) is written in the form of a dialogue between a "city dweller," a Brahmin who lives and works in Calcutta, and a "stranger," a newcomer from the country, who handles the city with a certain degree of anxiety and trepidation. "I hear that in Calcutta a large number of people have given up the right codes of conduct," says the stranger in *KK*. Is it true, he asks, that they eat too early, "spend the entire day working," return home late, and retire immediately after the evening meal?[11] The list of complaints was long. He said that he had heard that the upper-caste men of Calcutta had given up all rules appropriate to their castes:

> [They] do not any longer observe the life-cycle ceremonies . . . have abandoned the daily rite of *sandhyabandana* [evening prayers] and other similar actions. . . . They give no thought to what they wear or eat and just please themselves. . . . They have stopped reading the scriptures and learn only Persian and English. They cannot read or write Bengali and do not consider sacred texts written in Bengali worthy of their attention. . . . On the death of their parents, they participate in the funeral ceremonies only by proxy as they find these ceremonies repulsive. . . . Uncut hair is the only sign of mourning they wear, some even going to the length of shaving their beards on the pretext that they have to attend office. . . . They have given up the *dhoti* and have taken to wearing tunic, pants, and black leather boots . . . with shoe laces. They would employ any stranger that came along and claimed to be a Brahmin cook. . . . Their speech is a mixture of their own language and those of foreign races. . . . Perhaps they have not read any *shastras* [scriptures] in Sanskrit, why else would they want to use *yavanik* [Muslim/foreign] speech when one's own language would serve just as well?[12]

These charges brought against the fledgling middle classes of Calcutta are self-explanatory. But let me highlight the ones important for our analysis: salaried work that demands long and fixed hours; impurity of language, food, and clothes; and the neglect of daily ritual observances to do with ancestral spirits and the Hindu divinities. The city dweller in *KK* responds first by conceding the validity of these charges. "What you have heard is true," he says, and adds, "but a Hindu who behaves like this is a Hindu only in appearance." He explained that in spite of the new structuring of the day required by colonial civil society, the true Hindu strove to maintain a critical symbolic boundary between the three spheres of involvement and action (*karma*) that defined life. These spheres were: *daivakarma* (action to do with the realm of gods), *pitrikarma* (action to pertaining to one's male ancestors), and *vishaykarma* (actions undertaken in pursuit of worldly interests such as wealth, livelihood, fame, and secular power). The commendable members of the *vishayi bhadrolok* (that is, respectable people with worldly interests), said the city dweller, were able to separate their involvement in *vishaykarma* from the other two spheres of daily transactions:

> People with important occupations such as *dewani* [financial stewardship] or mutasuddiship [commercial agency] wake up early and meet with . . . different kinds of people after completing their morning ablutions. . . . Later on they rub their bodies with oil. . . . Before eating, they engage in different *puja* [worship] rituals including *homa* sacrifice, *vali-vaishya*, etc. . . . They do not stay at work any longer than necessary. . . . On returning home, they change into a fresh set of clothes, wash themselves, and touch Ganga water to purify themselves. . . . Middle-class people who are not wealthy . . . follow the same pattern, with the difference that they work harder, have less to give away in charity, and can afford to entertain a smaller number of [importunate] visitors. The more indigent *bhadralok* also live by the same ideas. But they have to work even harder and have even less to eat or give away.[13]

Of particular interest to us is how the city dweller handled the question of the polluting effects of using foreign languages. True, he said, many foreign words had equivalents in Bengali or Sanskrit and the Calcutta middle classes were indeed at fault for not using them. But "what should we do," he asked, "when dealing with words that do not translate into Bengali or Sanskrit?" *KK* actually produces a list of such unavoidable words. Of them, the following are in English: "non-suit, summons, common law, company, court, attachment, double, decree, dismiss, due, premium, collector, captain, judge, subpoena, warrant, agent, treasury, bills, surgeon [sergeant?], discount."[14] These words suggest the growing presence in Bengali lives of British law, and a fledgling civil society within which the middle classes had to find their livelihood. The words quoted all belonged to the sphere in which one had to earn one's livelihood, the domain of *vishaykarma*. British rule itself, one might say, belonged to that domain, as did any other rule, and the city dweller's aim was to prevent these words from polluting the ritually purer domains in which one transacted with gods and ancestors (*daivakarma* and *pitrikarma*). Using Ganga water, clothes, and other objects to mark the boundaries between the domains seems to have been a common practice among the upper castes of Calcutta during the early part of the nineteenth century. A description of Calcutta in the days of Rammohun Roy (1784–1833) said:

> The *vishayi* Brahmins of Calcutta conducted their *vishaykarma* under the British but took special care to protect the dominance and prestige of the Brahmins in the eyes of their own people. They washed themselves every evening on returning home from work and thus cleansed themselves of the bad effects (*dosha*) born of contact with the *mlechha* [the untouchable, the British]. They would then complete their *sandhya* [evening prayers] and other [rituals of] *puja* [worship], and eat in the eighth part of the day. Those who found this routine too difficult made a habit of completing their evening prayer, *homa*, and other *pujas* in the morning before they left for work.[15]

Where would the state, the public sphere, and the civil society—or even that which later came to be regarded as the political work of nationalism—belong in this "art of living" that Bhabanicharan and his contemporaries devised to cope with the demands of a modern but colonial civil-political society? In the first place, one has to note that the worldly, *vishayi*, self of Bhabanicharan's construction cannot be a nationalist self, for it has at the outset abnegated the capacity to rule in the material world (without giving up the desire to be materially successful in it). In the face of British rule, the author of *KK* can only plead his lack of power and the force of circumstances. The king must uphold *dharma*, and it was the duty of the Brahmin to assist the king in this task, so the latter must learn the ways of the foreign king—so went the argument in *KK* regarding English education for Indians. "I see no *dosha* [bad effects] coming from learning the language of the rulers of the land, as otherwise the business of the state (*rajkarma*) would be impossible to pursue."[16] Very similar was his defense of the use of English words by Bengalis: "Rulers of every race (*jati*) put into circulation words or expressions belonging to their own tongue. What else can one do but adopt them, especially in matters to do with the administration of royal justice (*rajbichar*)?"[17] Or mark his pragmatism as well as the somewhat pathetic declaration of helplessness in handling English words that did not translate into Bengali or Sanskrit but which were nevertheless unavoidable in the pursuit of material well-being. *KK* argues: "*Dosha* accrues to a person if he uses those [English, Arabic, and Persian] words in the conduct of *daivakarma* and *pitrikarma*. But what harm is done is using them in conducting *vishaykarma* or indeed in the context of jokes and lighthearted conversations?"[18]

KK thus does not share the later nationalist urge to translate into Indian languages English words that have to do with modern statecraft, institutional government, and technology. An unmistakable expression of the nationalist and civic desire to appropriate the instruments of modern rule is absent from this text. *KK* instead marginalizes the state (and by implication the nation) by making them inferior to the ritually purer aspects of the (male) householder's duties toward gods and ancestors. The state and civil society are seen here as a contingency and an external constraint, one of the many one has to negotiate in the domain of *vishaykarma*. Another publication on the moral conduct of the male Hindu householder put it thus: "one may engage in improper *karma* if that is essential to the maintenance of one's family."[19]

There is, in addition, nothing in *KK* that suggests any attraction to the idea that the time of the household should keep pace with the time of the civil-political society. The themes of discipline, routine, punctuality—all those particular aspects of human personality that the themes of "progress" and "civilization" made both desirable and necessary, and that characterize what later nationalists wrote on domestic life—are absent from *KK*. If anything, there was an emphasis to the contrary. In the world *KK* depicted, the householder never spent more time at office than was minimally needed and concentrated on ministering to the needs of gods and ancestors. The self, in its highest form, was visualized as part of the male lineage, *kula*, and was thus more tied to a mytho-religious practice of time than to the temporality of secular history. The civil society here was a matter of compulsion, of unfreedom, a forced interruption of more important and higher performances.

Nationalism would have been an anomaly for the framework that Bhabanicharan elaborated in *KK*. The pure pragmatism within which the city dweller of *KK* located his involvement in civil and political society could not provide sufficient ground for nationalist involvement in these spheres. For nationalist politics meant participation in public life, an involvement with the instruments of worldly power, working through the institution of civil society. And yet it was as such neither *vishaykarma* nor *daiva* nor *pitrikarma*. Nationalism entailed an unmistakable and secular engagement with the world but it had to be above the pursuit of pure and narrow self-interest. In fact, the framework in *KK* would not even explain Bhabanicharan's own involvement in a contemporary voluntary association such as the Gauradeshiya Samaj, which was expressly set up to imitate European "societies," followed European rules of public meetings, and was dedicated to the European theme of "social improvement."[20]

NATIONALISM AND THE THEME OF DOMESTICITY

The intellectual framework of *KK* was never completely displaced from Bengali upper-caste male practices. Born into an upper-caste and middle-class Bengali family in independent India, I grew up around rituals, practices, and attitudes that in retrospect seem much like those of the city dweller in *KK*. The nineteenth-century writer Bhudev Mukhopadhyay's essays on Hindu rituals, *Achara prabandha*, contain a strand of argument reminiscent of *KK*. Bhudev's critique of what British rule meant for the daily and the life-cycle rituals of upper-caste Hindus also doubles as a powerful critique of civil-political society itself, of capitalism, and of bourgeois regimes of modern work and historical time. Bhudev groups all of them together as simply so many external and historical constraints imposed on a more permanent and deeper rhythm of life assumed in the Hindu cycles of *nityachar* (everyday rituals) and *naimittikachar* (rites of passage). This is how, for instance, Bhudev handled the problem of "salaried work" that took up the whole day:

> It is the first half of the third part of the day, that is, from 9 to 10:30 [A.M.] that is the time [assigned in the scriptures] for work related to the earning of one's livelihood. How different are our circumstances now from those of the ancients! One and a half hours' work was enough for earning money. Nowadays even twenty-four hours do not seem enough. . . . These days people on salaries (*chakuria*) are *forced* to have their [midday] meal between 9 and 10:30 so that they can be at work on time. Many of them, therefore, *have to* complete their afternoon and evening prayers in the morning itself.[21]

Written about sixty years after *KK*, these words acknowledge the powerful and inexorable presence of the new order of work and civil society and their capacity to disrupt violently the *dharma*-related arrangement of time for the male upper-caste householder. Bhudev accepts the civil society but does not place it within the higher realms of life. One had to bend to its compulsion but not let it enter one's soul. There is no better example of this theme in *bhadralok* history than the teachings of the nineteenth-century Hindu saint Ramakrishna, who consistently denigrated the regimen of salaried work as a conflicted and corrupting world.[22]

Yet nationalism made a difference to this framework of understanding. Nationalist writers, even when they criticized the requirements of the civil society, wrote within an overarching frame that embraced the European idea of "improvement," both of the nation and of its members.[23] This is also what made "nationalism" modern, for it could not do without deploying some variant of the "public/private" opposition that does not exist at all in *KK*. This becomes clear in the literature on "domesticity" and women's education that was produced in Bengal in the second half of the nineteenth century. The "home" emerged in this literature as a space for reforms, where an educated and reformed mother was expected to prepare the Bengali Indian child to be the proper subject of nationalism. In that sense, this new "domestic" space was by definition oriented to a "public" realm. For even if the Europeans dominated the arena of salaried employment, nationalist activity would constitute a form of "public arena" for the nationalist. The "home" itself was in this sense a public arena of action. As a writer on "women's duties" wrote in the nineteenth century: "There cannot be any improvement in the state of the nation without improvement first in the domestic and political spheres. Obedience is the fundamental aspect of life in both politics and the family; in the latter the father and the husband is the master. The degree to which a society will obey rules depends on [practices] at more fundamental levels."[24]

The Victorian fetishes of discipline, routine, and order became some of the most privileged and desired elements in Bengali imaginings on domestic and personal arrangements. This is another reason why, Sumit Sarkar to the contrary, a critique of the discipline of office work was not necessarily a critique of the idea of discipline as such. Even Bhudev's enthusiasm for Hindu rituals of domesticity, on the basis of which he criticized the requirements of civil society, was derived from a nationalist desire for disciplined subjects. By using the English words "drill" and "discipline," he sought to explain how the practice of the daily Hindu upper-caste rituals might actually enhance "one's vitality and capacity for work."[25] The internal order of "the European home" was praised in nationalist writings and seen as a key to European prosperity and political power.[26] Order itself was linked to notions of health, cleanliness, and hygiene. As Anukulchandra Datta, the author of an early text on "domestic science," wrote: "Well-trained children are the pride of the country. . . . "With bad training and corrupt morals, they only bring disgrace to the family and . . . the nation."[27] The housewife was now being called to administer a regimen regulating children's eating habits, games, work, and manners.[28]

Time was of the essence of this regimen. Its proper management was now extolled as critical to the civilization of the country. In Datta's book on home science, a mother tells her daughter: "How the English appreciate the value of time! They work at the right time, eat at the right time, attend office at the right time, and play at the right time. Everything they do is governed by rules. . . . It is because of this quality that the English get the time to accomplish so much. Nowhere among the educated, civilized nations are instances to be found of a people disregarding the value of time and misusing it as we do."[29] Without a sense of time, said another author, even nursing the sick was difficult. In administering doses of medicine, he said, "one should not deviate from the intervals prescribed by the doctor. . . . This is why it is absolutely essential that there be a clock in every house and that . . . the women are taught to read it."[30] Several authors deplored the fact that there were not many books written in Bengali on the subject of domestic science. "In our country," said Datta, "we do not have 'home-training.' Yet the prospects of our improvement depend 100 percent on this." "The country needs nothing so much to promote its regeneration as good mothers," declared an epigraph on the title page of his book.[31]

This Bengali nationalist adaptation of the bourgeois and modern distinction between the public and the private was modified, however, by another aspect of these discussions on domesticity and the new woman. A single, obsessive point of focus of the nineteenth-century literature on Bengali women's education was on the production of "pleasantness" as part of the modern woman's charm and beauty. That is why both the lack of education that supposedly made women quarrelsome as well as too much education, which could make them defiant of authority, were dangers these texts constantly harped on. Education was meant to correct the feelings of "malice and hostility," the "terrible disposition to quarrel," that were allegedly found "especially in the uneducated."[32] But Western education in "improper" doses could also make women *mukhara* (sharp-tongued), selfish, and neglectful of domestic duties. When formally educated women were perceived as behaving thus, they were compared to memsahibs or European women. Kundamala Devi, a woman writing in a magazine for women in 1870 said: "Oh dear ones! If you have acquired real knowledge, then give no place in your heart for memsahib-like behaviour. This is not becoming in a Bengali housewife."[33] Grace/modesty (*lajja*) and obedience were described in this literature as the two signs of auspiciousness in a woman. "True modesty," said a book on women's education, was to be distinguished from the "uncivilized" modesty of the women who were not educated. The properly educated could be told by their "downcast eyes" and their disposition to "speak softly and little."[34]

This association between womanly attraction and pleasantness is spelled out directly in several contemporary tracts on the "new" Bengali woman. A woman's demeanor, speech, name—all had to convey that she was not a "shrew." "*Mukhara* [sharp-tongued] is another name for women of unpleasant speech," said one book entitled *Bangamahila* (the Bengali Woman). "Even the presence of a single *mukhara* woman can drive peace away from a household forever."[35] A booklet on methods of examining prospective brides warned that women with names that evoked feelings of terror should not be married.[36] Some texts quoted the ancient lawgiver Manu to emphasize the connection between the pleasant and the auspicious in the desirable aspects of the feminine: "A girl should be given a name that is pleasant to pronounce and that has no oblique meanings. . . . The [name] should fill the heart with feelings of affection and joy. It should signify *mangal* [auspiciousness and well-being], end in a long vowel, and bring to [the bearer of the name] blessings from those who utter it." That is why, our author explained, all the Sanskrit terms for wife were meant to sound pleasant, and all significantly ended with a long vowel—*jaya*, *bharya*, *grihalakshmi*, *ankalakshmi*, *grihini*, *sahadharmini*, *ardhangarupini*, and so on.[37]

The word *ghihalakshmi* summed up the aesthetic figure of the ideal housewife by associating her with the beauty of the goddess Lakshmi, who has long been upheld in Hindu mythical texts as the model wife. The goddess Sri-Lakshmi, as David Kinsley points out, "is today one of the most popular and widely venerated deities of the Hindu pantheon. Her auspicious nature and her reputation for granting fertility, luck, wealth and well-being seem to attract devotees in every village."[38] Paul Greenough and Lina Fruzetti have dealt at length with the role that religious rituals having to do with Lakshmi play in contemporary Hindu-Bengali domestic life, and the continuing association of this goddess with notions of abundance, wealth, auspiciousness, and prosperity.[39]

The goddess Lakshmi has a reverse side, Alakshmi (Anti-Lakshmi), her dark and malevolent other. Those heterogenous and mythical Hindu texts, the Puranas, ascribe the origins of this malicious female antigoddess to diverse sources. Her genealogy is complex and is embedded, as Upendranath Dhal shows, in the claims and contestations of caste divisions and the question of the ritual supremacy of the Brahmins: "The Lingapurana . . . says that Visnu created the universe in two-fold ways. One part consisted of Sri-Padma, four Vedas, the rites prescribed by the Vedas and Brahmanas. And the other part consisted of Alakshmi, Adharma and rites deprecated by the Vedas."[40]

However she originated, Alakshmi came to embody a gendered and elitist conception of inauspiciousness, and the opposite of all that the Hindu lawgivers upheld as *dharma* (proper moral conduct) of the householder. It was said that when she entered a household, Alakshmi brought jealousy and malice in her trail. Brothers fell out with each other, families and their male lineages (*kula*) faced ruin and destruction. As Dhal puts it on the basis of *Padmapurana*: "The choice of Alakshmi rests with a residence where there is constant family feud, where the guests are not honoured, where thieves and scoundrels are in plenty, where people . . . [engage in] illicit love [—] in other words, whatever has been proscribed by lawmakers like Manu, Yajnavalkya has been portrayed as the most cherished thing for Alakshmi."[41] Lakshmi and Alakshmi were thus mutually exclusive figures. A house where the spirit of Alakshmi prevailed was said to be unbearable for Lakshmi, who always left such a household and bestowed her favors on others who, and in particular whose women, did not flout the rules and rituals that made them auspicious.

The stories of Lakshmi and Alakshmi, however, were—and still are in many households—part of religious rituals that marked the daily, weekly, and annual calendars of women's religious activities in Hindu Bengali families. Ever since printing technology became available, books carrying stories of Lakshmi and Alakshmi, meant for use by women in ritual contexts, have been in continuous supply from the small and cheap presses of Calcutta.[42] What is significant about Bengali discussion of women's education in the late nineteenth century was the secularization of the twin figures of Lakshmi and Alakshmi, whereby Lakshmi came to stand for all that was beauteous, harmonious, and feminine about the Bengali home and Alakshmi for its opposite. Nineteenth-century Bengali texts on modern domesticity emphasize this association: "Women are the Lakshmis of society. If they undertake to improve themselves in the spheres of *dharma* and knowledge . . . there will be an automatic improvement in social life."[43]

The very presence of words like Lakshmi and Alakshmi in the literature on women's education alerts us that this is a discussion, ultimately, about the ideals of modern Bengali patriarchy. The modern woman had to be pleasant because quarrelsome and jealous wives, it was thought, pitted brother against brother in a spirit of competition, and thus broke up the solidarity of the clan or *kula*. In his study of Bengali kinship and ranking systems, Ronald Inden defined *kula* as a collectivity of "persons who share the body of the same ancestral male."[44] The task of the *grihalakshmi* was fundamentally to maintain the unity of the *kula*. *Grihalakshmi* thus became synonymous with *kulalakshmi*, a word that once connoted "the goddess of family and clan well-being" but now could be used to refer to mortal women in their married state.[45] In his well-known essays on the family, *Paribarik prabandha* (1882), Bhudev Mukhopadhyay advised parents to select as daughters-in-law women who showed early signs of their capacity to become *kulalakshmi*(s) one day. This, said Bhudev, would be one way of preventing the divisions that often arose among brothers on the death of their parents.[46] Indeed, in the discussions of this period, the difference between a *kulastree* (a woman who has married into a *kula*) and a *kulata* (a woman who has lost, or has been lost to, her *kula*; a prostitute) was an axis around which arguments turned in debates on women's education. This is how one text laid the out the differences between the two categories:

> *Kulastree*: calm and composed movements; measured speech; eyes downcast; avoids men; covers up her body; without lust; dresses simply.
> *Kulata*: restless, garrulous; looks everywhere; seeks male company; parts of body exposed; lustful, dresses up.[47]

Bengali nationalist thought on new domesticity and women's education in the nineteenth century thus combined the bourgeois distinction of public and private, of domestic and national, with the idea of the male lineage, *kula*. Herein lay a crucial difference between the ideology of Bengali modernity and some of the critical assumptions of patriarchal liberalism in Europe. The following section addresses this problem.

FRATERNITY, PATRIARCHY, AND POLITICAL THOUGHT

The aestheticization—and consequent secularization—of goddesses helped produce some historically enduring markers of modern Bengali nationalist identity. We have seen how Bengal itself could be portrayed in nationalist poetry as Bangalakshmi, Bengal as the goddess Lakshmi herself. Even the formally atheist, Communist, Bengali poet Shubhash Mukhopadhyay could express his sense of being Bengali by representing a religious ritual of domestic well-being—the practice of painting Lakshmi's footprints, thus indicating Lakshmi's advent into the space of domesticity—as a secular insignia of identity. To recall the lines I quoted before:

> However far I go
> attached to my eyelids
> remain
> rows of footprints of Lakshmi
> painted on a courtyard
> mopped clean with cowdung and water.[48]

An assumed fraternal compact underlay the tendency—pervasive in Bengali and Indian nationalism—to think of the country as Mother. From Bankimchandra on, Hindu nationalists portrayed themselves as children, *santan*, of the mother. Popular nationalist songs written by Tagore or Dwijendralal Roy at the turn of the century capture the affective side of the brotherly unity on which this patriarchal nationalism was based:

> What brings us together is the Mother's call.
> For how long can brothers from the same home
> stay apart as if they were unrelated?[49]

Or:

> For once, cry out "Mother,"
> cry out "Mother" in a full-throated way.
> . . .
> Let us see how long the Mother can ignore
> the cry of her sons.[50]

The myth of a fraternity based in the idea of a natural unity of brothers is one critical difference between the patriarchal assumptions of nationalist politics in Bengal and the classical themes of European political thought. Bengali writers had otherwise embraced many important aspects of the European bourgeois self. The public/private distinction, as we have seen, was adapted into their discussions of domesticity. Even the idea of "individual property" or "natural rights" of women in paternal property were acceptable to a so-called conservative thinker such as Bhudev Mukhopadhayay, who wrote: "By the laws of nature women have some rights in paternal property. Our legal texts do not deny such a natural right."[51] He also recommended equal division of property and, if need be, even an amiable breakup of the joint family. But all these liberal-sounding moves were subordinated to the higher cause of preserving the unity between brothers, the fraternal compact on which nationalism was based:

> Separate kinship from all material connections of self-interest. . . . You and [your] younger brother are devotees of the same god and goddess in the shape of your father and mother. The two of you should sit down together in private and remember your parents—what sacred feelings you will have![52]
>
> Brothers separate when they get married and when the parents are gone. But this often does not happen to families that are well managed and in which the paternal property has been clearly divided. If the brothers are truly united in their hearts, their wives cannot be ill disposed toward each other.[53]

Brothers in John Locke's essay on "civil government" are autonomous individuals with rights of property in their own person who come together to form a "political or civil society" by contract for the sake of preservation of their life and property.[54] What induces brothers to form this contract and honor it is a very special gift of God to humanity: reason. As Locke put it: "God, who hath given the world to men in common, hath also given them reason to make use of it to the best advantage of life and convenience."[55] Indeed, it was this gift of reason that allowed God to withdraw and let humans be in charge of their own history, knowing that reason would align that history with divine intention. Thus began a secular history of human sovereignty on earth for "the earth and all that is therein [was] given to men for the support and comfort of their being."[56]

Not only does God withdraw from human affairs, leaving only in his gift of "reason" a trace of his continuing presence, but reason itself cannot work in Locke's schema until parental (that is, paternal) political authority—which is to say the authority to punish—ceases to be. Locke contends that humans endowed with reason are autonomous adults, and they enter political-civil society as such. Parental/parental authority is temporary. It is there to help children imbibe reason through education, and parents deserve gratitude and honor throughout their lives for what they do for the child. But their political authority, the right to punish, must cease for the fraternal contract to come into its own: "The first part, then, of paternal power, or rather duty, which is education, belongs so to the father that it terminates at a certain season. When the business of education is over it ceases of itself. . . . To conclude, then, . . . the father's power of commanding extends no farther than the minority of his children, and [is] to a degree only fit for the discipline and government of that age."[57]

In her incisive book, *The Sexual Contract*, Carol Pateman has pointed out that the Lockean story of the death of the father's authority was precisely the origin myth of modern patriarchy of the Christian West, which was born under the sign of the formal equality of all humans (that is, brothers).[58] Such a death of parental authority, however, is never imagined in the Bengali fraternal compact. The capacity to command—to give order (*adesh*, *ajna*)—belongs to parents and through them to the male ancestral line, with no age limit. Political authority in this modernity was modeled on parental authority, which never ceased to be. Consider, again, Bhudev Mukhopadhyay on the point:

> Without submission, there is no unity. . . . Bengalis are not a martial race. That is why the true spirit of submission is rarely to be found in Bengalis. The obedience and politeness that the weak shows to the strong cannot be called submission. . . . Submission is based on devotion—it has to be learned in childhood. And parents being the recipient of the [child's] devotion can plant and nurture that sentiment. The Bengali who has learned to feel both fear and devotion to his parents will also be capable of submitting to a leader.[59]

We should note how different this view of paternal authority is from the Lockean understanding of it. The basis of the child's submission to the father/parent in Bhudev's text is *bhakti*, the sentiment of devotion and adoration. This is why even an adult son, in this model, remains submissive to the father. *Bhakti* signifies a wilful submission born out of devotion and adoration. The father in Locke's schema, however, is a different kind of father. He wields absolute power. In his *Some Thoughts Concerning Education*, Locke says: "I imagine everyone will judge it reasonable that their children, when little, should look upon their parents as lords, their absolute governors, and as such stand in awe of them."[60] The basis of submission on the part of the child here is his awe of the father's power, exactly the feeling that Bhudev would not have regarded as a proper basis for the son's lifelong submission to paternal authority. Nationalist authors such as Bhudev made *bhakti* (loving and worshipful devotion) into a modern political sentiment.

Political unity in Bhudev's understanding, then, was founded in the cultivation of "natural" sentiments of the family: love between brothers and submission to parents. Unity was not to be found in the pursuit of contract, competition, or self-interest.[61] As Tapan Raychaudhuri puts it in his study of Bhudev, "an excessive preoccupation with money was, to Bhudev, one of the least acceptable features of Western society. . . . The apotheosis of money made the westerner hesitant to accept or give financial help even where close relatives were concerned."[62] Indians would come together because as children (sons) of the same Mother they had a natural bond. In one of his fictional pieces, Bhudev made a Maratha leader say this:

> This motherland of ours has always been burnt by the fire of internal strife; that fire will be put out today. . . . Even though India is truly the motherland of the Hindus alone, . . . still the Muslims are no longer alien to her for long has she held them to her heart and nourished them. Therefore the Muslims too are her foster children. If a child is born of the mother's womb and another child is breastfed . . . by her, are not the two siblings?. . . Hence Hindus and Muslims who live in India have become brothers. The relationship is destroyed if there are quarrels.[63]

CONCLUSION

Our contemporary disapproval should not blind us to the creative sides of this patriarchal, nonliberal, and yet modern humanism constructed by the subjects of the modernity under discussion. The theme of "natural brotherhood" that underlies the nationalist use of older patrilineal categories—*kula*, *vamsa*, *purbapurush*—actually continued to speak to many middle-class, *bhadralok* Bengalis in the twentieth century. Some of the most popular novels of the 1920s and 1930s (later made into films) elaborated on the themes of crisis of brotherly love and the extended family.[64]

It would also be wrong to think of this modernity that consolidated the question of women's education within the ideology of the *grihalakshmi* as an iron cage of unfreedom. A telling case in point is an obscure but by no means atypical text from the nineteenth century: a booklet entitled *Patibrata dharma* (with the English subtitle *A Treatise on Female Chastity*) written around 1870 by a woman called Dayamayi Dasi. A certain stamp of the bourgeois project of European modernity, of educating women to be both companions and loyal to their husbands, is unmistakably present in this book. The very title of the book and its rendition into English place it in the tradition of Bengali Victoriana. Encouraged by her husband to read and write, Dayamayi Dasi wrote this tract on *kulaka-*

minir kartabya (duties of the woman who belongs to a *kula*). *Kula* in this text is a term that articulated the domestic with the national. Dasi quoted from the *Brahmavaivartapurana* to express her sense of nationalism: "The land blessed with women [devoted to their husbands] . . . is comparable to heaven, and the people of that country should treat their women as goddesses."[65]

The very writing of such books meant participation not only in the patriarchal model of the "new woman" but in the public sphere itself. And even though women often seem to repeat the language of patriarchy, they could use it as a screen language, performing "modesty" for the gaze of the public but expressing through that performance sentiments of individuality that would never be authorized by the dominant ideology of men. For instance, Dayamayi wrote the following passage in praise of the general figure of the husband. At one level, the passage speaks the sanctioned language of the patriarchal modern subject. At another, it have may been a coded way of speaking intimately in public to her own husband, expressing her own personal desire and eroticism. One will never know. The passage reads:

> A woman has no better friend than her husband. It is because he helps cover [a woman's shame] that he is called *bharta*. He is *pati* because he nurtures. He is *swami* because it is to him that the body belongs. . . . [H]e fulfills [woman's] desires, that it why he is called *kanta*. He is a *bandhu* as he shares happiness, *parampriya* as he gives affection, and *raman* because he gives pleasure. It is he who, through his own semen, returns as the son. That is why the son is valued. But to a *kulastree*, the husband is dearer than even a hundred sons.[66]

In the preface to this book, which otherwise remains within the ideology of the fraternal compact of the Bengali modern subject, Dayamayi Dasi creates a surprising moment of individuality that is so radical it cannot be harnessed to any social-political project at all. She records the exhilarating feeling of pure liberation that the acquisition of literacy brought her. But that is not all. She also records in a cryptic sentence how the joy of this freedom made her forget the world, including her duties toward her husband. The thought is not completed, and we will never have a fuller history of that moment. But her words remain a testimony to the possibilities of alternative subject positions breaking out of, or at least interrupting, the voice of the modern Bengali. Dayamayi Dasi wrote: "I had never entertained the thought that I could ever learn to recognize the alphabet or be able to read books. . . . But, in the end, I developed such a thirst for prose and poetry that I began to neglect my duties toward the *samsar* [the world, the household, the family] and my husband."[67]

The Swadeshi movement (1905–1908)—the agitation against the first partition of Bengal effected in 1905—dramatically brought to light both the creative aspects and the limitations of the political possibilities of this Bengali modernity. This movement was rich in the symbolism of the country imagined as a Mother and national unity as fraternal bond. Women's rites and activities having to do with the well-being of the *kula*—such as religious vows and overseeing the family hearth—were used to express a national sense of mourning at the partition of the province.[68] When the movement started, Rabindranath Tagore suggested that a traditional Hindu ritual of brotherhood—sisters tying strings around brothers' wrists as a mark of protection—be made "into a symbol of the brotherhood and unity of the people of Bengal." Sumit Sarkar, who has extensively researched this movement, comments: "Bengal, and particularly Calcutta, witnessed truly memorable scenes of fraternisation on that day [16 October 1905], from which Muslim mullas, policemen and even whites were not excluded. From early morning huge crowds walked barefoot (the traditional sign of mourning) to the Ganga to bathe in its holy waters which too knew no caste. Year after year these rites were kept up, though may be on a diminishing scale—till the partition was abrogated."[69]

Sarkar himself is moved by this articulation of the political with the aesthetic. Commenting on the political use of "traditional" rites of brotherhood, he says: "The imagination of India's greatest poet had bestowed on a political movement a beauty which is rare indeed."[70] Yet, as he shows in his own book, the theoretical apparatus of this modernity was not powerful enough to cope with the problems of political representation and Hindu-Muslim unity that elections and other mechanisms of an emerging democracy soon posed to Indian nationalism. Muslims did not buy this largely Hindu, upper-caste rhetoric of natural brotherhood. Nor did the lower castes, as the twentieth century progressed. Bengal was divided once again at independence in 1947, broadly between Hindus and Muslims, with the lower castes working out a complex strategy of participating in this divisive history.[71]

The theoretical failure of the upper-caste (male) Bengali modernity is not far to seek. A theory of natural fraternity had no way of accommodating historical differences of class, gender, or religion without absorbing/retaining them in a natural image of unity. A Bhudev could preach to the Muslim that he, the Muslim, was also a son of the motherland. But that still left him a Muslim. The Lockean liberal contractual fraternity, on the other hand, had at least theoretically the advantage of positing brotherhood as a collection of unmarked, universal individuals—male, no doubt, but still (potentially) universal—and one could use the universal (the human, the individual) to try to transcend historical difference. Locke grounded this universal in reason, a defining property of the adult, autonomous, contractual human. Reason, in turn, was grounded in a Christian conception of God. It was a gift of this particular god to humans. The history of the secularization of reason is the history of secularized Christianity.

There are also different kinds of authority that the past has in the two narratives of brotherhood considered here. In the Lockean case, brotherhood is founded on a contract made possible by the death of paternal authority. In the death of paternal authority, history, it may be said, dies and creates room for the heroic act of "making history." Every generation of brothers makes history afresh. In the modern Bengali story of brotherly solidarity, however, brotherhood stands not for the death but for the transmission over time of the authority of the male ancestors, a long and mythical line of fathers—*purbapurush*, the line of men to which the mother also belongs. Men, past and present, together constitute the line of the *kula*. That situates the whole question of tradition rather differently in the Bengali case. In their political thought having to do with civil society and its relationship to domestic life, Bengali nationalists did not repeat the Lockean theme of the separation of parental from political authority. Rather than sentiments of individual autonomy, the feeling of *bhakti* was what they made into a modern political sentiment.

Conventional historical explanations of these differences between the European bourgeois and the Bengali modern fall back onto some mode of historicism. It is tempting to see Bhudev and his likes as "reactionaries" who offered resistance, futile in the long run, to the onward march of progress. There is, however, a major problem with this view. The coming of "mass democracy" in India, which necessarily undermined in the twentieth century the pedagogical, top-down project of modernity that the upper-caste Hindus had initiated in the nineteenth, did not mean anything like a final triumph of reason and emancipatory political thought from Europe. As Sudipta Kaviraj has written: "the more modernity unfolds [the more] it seems to appear inescapably plural. . . . Transition narratives create the increasingly untenable illusion that given all the right conditions, Calcutta would turn into London, and the Bengali rich and poor would 'understand' the principles of being private and public in the right ways. In fact, what these strong transition narratives do is to blind us to the responsibility of looking at the shapes and forms our modernity is taking."[72]

I could not agree more with Kaviraj. The problem, however, is that our systems of knowledge tend toward an a priori valorization of "reason." Most professional social scientists write on behalf of some kind of liberal-secular form of reasoning, not because they personally embody liberal goodness any more than any other mortal, but because that is the position built into their knowledge protocols and institutional procedures. The question is: In what do we ground the "reason" that unavoidably marks the social sciences, if not in a historicist understanding of history? How do we find a home for reason even as we acknowledge the plural of ways of being human that we ourselves inhabit?

The connection between reason and the autonomous, sovereign, and propertied individual that Locke posited was rooted in Christian theological understandings of the relationship between humans and their creator. Over time, as many commentators have noted, the theological propositions of Locke became secularized into some of the fundamental axioms of modern European liberal and Marxist political thought.[73] But the history of secularization of thought in Bengal was not the same as in Europe. Nor were the gods and goddesses secularized in Bengali modernity in any way like the reason-endowed God of Christianity. One could argue that these theological differences did not matter. Reason was transcendental and could be shared by all humans because of their shared ability to communicate. But even if one granted that proposition for argument's sake, would it follow that the story of the relationship between reason and theological thought and imagination would be the same the world over? Can we give to reason the same historical mission all over the world? Does the coming of reason necessarily give us the same universal way of being human—liberal and rational? Historicist thought makes out this development to be the story of modernity. Many times the history of the nineteenth-century "Bengal renaissance," for instance, has been written up as the story of a repetition of a theme popular in European history: "the liberation of the mind from a blinding bondage to the superstitions and customs of the middle ages."[74] To struggle against historicism, then, is to try and tell a different history of reason.

EPILOGUE

Reason and the Critique of Historicism

SCHOLARS contemplating the subject called "Indian history" have often relived, as it were, the old passions of the "the struggle of the Enlightenment with superstition" that Hegel writes about in his *Phenomenology*.[1] They have assumed that for India to function as a nation based on the institutions of science, democracy, citizenship, and social justice, "reason" had to prevail over all that was "irrational" and "superstitious" among its citizens. Historicism has been a very close ally of such thought. For instance, peasants' lives, including their politics, are replete with practices that could seem "superstitious" to the rational and secular observer. How would history, the rational-secular discipline, understand and represent such practices? Where would the polytheism that marks everyday life in the subcontinent find its place in such a frame of thought? Depending on the political dispositions of their authors, historicist narratives by secular and rational scholars have produced either harshly judgmental or sympathetic accounts of subaltern social groups' tendency to treat gods, spirits, and other supernatural entities as agential beings in the worlds of humans. But, sympathetic or not, these accounts all foreground a separation—a subject-object distinction—between the academic observer-subject and the "superstitious" persons serving as the objects of study.

There is an honored tradition, both in Europe and elsewhere, of regarding "rational outlook," the "spirit of science" and of "free enquiry" as constituting the "progressive" aspects of modernity. Secular and Marxist Indian intellectuals have long held this view.[2] Soon after the war, some leading Bengali academic intellectuals of left-liberal persuasion organized a series of lectures in Calcutta to discuss the nature of modernity in India. Their deliberations were published in 1950 as a collection of essays, *Modern Age and India*.[3] One of the authors, Tripurari Chakravarti, typically connected modernity with European developments: "the Modern Age all over the world undeniably stem[med] from modern European history."[4] The physicist Satyendranath Bose characterized science as knowledge that "was obliged to oppose religion whenever religion [presumed to] speak about things on this earth."[5] The recent memory of the atom bomb at Hiroshima and Nagasaki muted to some degree what could have been otherwise an unqualified enthusiasm for science on the part of the contributors to this book (see the essays by Satyendranath Bose and Nareshchandra Sen Gupta, in particular). But a faith in the capacity of scientific spirit to deliver humankind from all terrestrial problems and superstitious attitudes ran intact through the entire volume.

This tendency to identify reason and rational argumentation as a modernist weapon against "premodern" superstition ends up overdrawing the boundary between the modern and the premodern. For the question of pitting "reason" against that which seems irrational was not just an issue in the battle between the educated and the peasant classes in Bengali modernity. Reason has found other objects of domination besides the peasant. Gender relations in the middle classes, for instance, have as often borne the brunt of this history as has the supposedly superstitious peasant. In his personal reminiscences, the Bengali intellectual Dilipkumar Ray recounts the story of his conversion to rationalism in his youth early in this century. The story is common enough—many of my own generation went through similar stages in their conversion to a rationalist and atheist Marxism—but it is also a sad and comic story. As in the lives of many Bengali men before and after him, Ray's conversion to rationalism and atheism in his teens was accompanied by his immediate discovery that the women of the household—his aunt and his grandmother in particular—were the "irrational" people whose company he needed to avoid.[6] Ray's misogyny is typical of the history of the "scientific temper" in modern Bengal.

I do not mean to suggest that reason as such is elitist. Reason becomes elitist whenever we allow unreason and superstition to stand in for backwardness, that is to say, when reason colludes with the logic of historicist thought. For then we see our "superstitious" contemporaries as examples of an "earlier type," as human embodiments of the principle of anachronism. In the awakening of this sense of anachronism lies the beginning of modern historical consciousness. Indeed, anachronism is regarded as the hallmark of such a consciousness.[7] Historical evidence (the archive) is produced by our capacity to see something that is contemporaneous with us—ranging from practices, humans, institutions, and stone-inscriptions to documents—as a relic of another time or place. The person gifted with historical consciousness sees these objects as things that once belonged to their historical context and now exist in the observer's time as a "bit" of that past. A particular past thus becomes objectified in the observer's time. If such an object continues to have effects on the present, then the historically minded person sees that as the effect of the past. It is through such objectification—predicated on the principle of anachronism—that the eye of the participant is converted into the eye of the witness. This is how a participant in an historical "event" becomes an "eyewitness" for the historian, affirming the "rule of evidence" of historiography. Ethnographic observation, similarly, is based on the ethnographer himself or herself shuttling between the two distinct roles of the participant and the observer, but here also analysis entails the conversion of the participant's involved and engaged eye into the distant and disinterested eye of the observer.

If historical or anthropological consciousness is seen as the work of a rational outlook, it can only "objectify"—and thus deny—the *lived* relations the observing subject already has with that which he or she identifies as belonging to a historical or ethnographic time and space separate from the ones he or she occupies as the analyst. In other words, the method does not allow the investigating subject to recognize himself or herself as also the figure he or she is investigating. It stops the subject from seeing his or her own present as discontinuous with itself.[8] We shall see that what blocks the path of this thought is the idea that the analytical gives us some kind of x-ray vision into the social, that it gives us access to a level of reality somehow deeper than the everyday. This epistemological primacy routinely assigned in social science thought to one's analytical relationships to the world (Heidegger's "present-at-hand") over lived, preanalytical ones (the "ready-to-hand" in Heideggerian terms) produces, in Marxist and liberal histories, versions of the "uneven development" thesis.[9] Some relations of everyday transactions can now take on the character of "unvanquished remnants" of the past (to recall Marx's phrase). But that only reproduces ultimately, as we have already discussed in the first part of this book, the useful but empty and homogeneous chronology of historicism.[10]

In drawing this book to a close, I want to raise the question of how we might find a form of social thought that embraces analytical reason in pursuit of social justice but does not allow it to erase the question of heterotemporality from the history of the modern subject. To do this, however, I want to begin by identifying certain common analytical strategies in the social sciences that seek to hide from view the fragmentary nature of the "now" the investigating subject inhabits. For this purpose, I shall draw on the writings of three intellectuals important for postcolonial thinking: Jomo Kenyatta, Anthony Appiah, and D. D. Kosambi.

READING KENYATTA, APPIAH, AND KOSAMBI

Consider the question of superstition and magic as it comes up in the Kenyan nationalist leader Jomo Kenyatta's classic book *Facing Mount Kenya*. Long before he trained in anthropology in London, Kenyatta had developed an intimate relationship to practices that early European anthropological thought classified as "magical" and "superstitious." His was truly a participant's eye that was called upon to "witness," as well. Mixing the two modes of relating to the "object"—as an "apprentice" and as a "witness"—Kenyatta writes: "As for magic, I have *witnessed* the performance of magic rites in my own home and elsewhere. My grandfather was a seer and a magician, and in travelling about with him and in carrying his bag of equipment I served a kind of *apprenticeship* in the principles of the art."[11]

Yet the mixing of the two modes in a context where Kenyatta's lived, preanalytical involvement in the world of "magic" constantly cut across the lines of the objectifying gaze of the anthropologist in the end produced a consciousness that was inherently double. The practices of his grandfather to whom he had served as kind of apprentice could never be a completely objectified past for him. Yet he was distant enough to seek a justification for them in terms his grandfather would not have needed. The doubling of his voice is clear in these lines he wrote on the subject of magic:

> From personal experience . . . in various branches of magical treatment, it can be safely said that this is one way of transmitting thoughts telepathically from one mind to another. . . . [T]he magician's suggestions are easily transmitted by means of vibrations to the brain, and thence to the mind. If the functions and the methods of magic are studied carefully and scientifically, it will most probably be proved that there is something in it which can be classified as occultism, and, as such, cannot be dismissed as mere superstition.[12]

This passage actually caused great embarrassment to the anthropologist Malinowski, Kenyatta's professor in London, whom Kenyatta had invited to write an introduction to the book. Malinowski obliged, but the tension around the subject of "magic"—between Kenyatta, the "native-turned-anthropologist" and Malinowski, the intellectual with no (acknowledged) lived relationship to the object of study—is palpable from the way Malinowski's introduction and Kenyatta's own preface to the book diverge from one another. The doubling of the voice in Kenyatta contrasts strongly with the single voice of disapproval with which Malinowski expressed his sense of discomfiture. "Some anthropologists," he wrote, maintaining a critical but polite distance from the text he had been accorded the honor of introducing, "may question here the reinterpretation of the real processes which underlie magic. . . . Mr. Kenyatta would still have to supply some evidence as to how these 'vibrations' are produced, how they act on the brain, and thence on the mind." It was in Kenyatta's reference to "occultism," a European practice, that Malinowski finally found a way out of his discomfiture of having to criticize an African anthropologist and a former student whom he had generously agreed to introduce to the reader. "For indeed," he said, "how can *we* [Europeans] criticise Mr. Kenyatta for believing in . . . occultism" when "Europe is as deeply immersed" in it? Malinowski could now make his criticism seem fair by saying that "superstition, blind faith and complete disorientation are as dangerous a canker in the heart of our Western civilisation as in Africa."[13] The closer one gets to Malinowski's end of things, the more the language of social science obliterates the plural ways of being human that are contained in the very different orientations to the world—the "worlding" of the earth, in Heidegger's language—that "participation" and "observation" connote.

The doubling of the "voice" is almost inaudible but not quite silenced, for instance, in Kwame Anthony Appiah's discussion of some Asante practices that resembled what Kenyatta called "communion with ancestors."[14] "When a man opens a bottle of gin," writes Appiah, "he will pour a little on the earth, asking his ancestors to drink a little and to protect the family and its doings." Appiah, again, had some kind of lived relationship to this practice. For it was a practice of his father, he says, to casually pour "a few drops from top of a newly opened bottle of Scotch onto the carpet" as offering to ancestors. Appiah had grown up around this practice as a child. This was how a certain way of being-in-the-world, an Asante way, came into the formation of the modern, cosmopolitan, formally educated Appiah. However, a child's sense of being around a repeated set of practices is converted into a statement of the anthropologist in Appiah's text that converts the participant's eye into that of the eyewitness: "All my life, I have seen and heard ceremonies [that involve] . . . ritual appeal to unseen spirits." Unlike Kenyatta's text, the phenomenology of Appiah's having been in a preanalytic relation to the practice under observation, long before he had learned to be an observer of it, is thoroughly written over by the voice of the anthropologist, a voice amplified in this case by a reference to Tylor. "If I am right," writes Appiah, in a move to "explain" his father's habit of offering scotch to ancestors, "it is (as Tylor claimed) a commitment to disembodied agency that crucially defines the religious beliefs that underlie rituals like the one I have described," and so on.[15] Needless to say, the giveaway word "belief" is what takes the Asante Appiah and his father out of lived, preanalytical relationships and inserts them here into an objectifying relationship of social science within which the son and father face each other as the subject and the object.

A similar privileging of the analytical over the lived tames the radical potential of the Indian historian D. D. Kosambi's magnificently imaginative attempts to write Indian history out of the material practices of everyday life. Kosambi, for instance, pondered the historical significance of something so ubiquitous and familiar in the context of the kitchen in South Asian homes as the saddle-quern, the stone implement commonly used to grind spices. It intrigued Kosambi that such an ancient-looking object should exist in the same space that was also occupied by the electric stove, a veritable symbol of modernization in India of the 1950s. Not only was the saddle-quern in everyday use in the kitchen, Kosambi reports that around it had developed "rituals" in which the women and babies of Brahmin families such as Kosambi's participated. He writes: "With the implement [saddle-quern] . . . is performed a ceremony in force even among brahmins, yet without sanction in any of the brahminical scriptures which prescribe rites from birth to death. Before or on the name-day of a child, . . . the top roller stone is dressed up, passed around the cradle containing the child and finally deposited at the foot of the infant in the cradle. The theory given is that of sympathetic magic, namely that the child would grow up as strong and unblemished as the stone, to be as long-lived and free from infirmity."[16]

Kosambi thus extracted an interesting social fact from this stone object, a fact that actually surprised him. His sense of surprise is contained in the expression "even among brahmins"—for the saddle-quern had found use in rituals not authorized by any sacred texts. Kosambi's historicizing instincts told him that there must have been some interesting social history going on here. But what did it mean for Kosambi's own sense of the present when he wrote his book in the 1950s? He is not describing some dead practice from the past; he is writing about his own class, about "magical" practices in the lives of women from the educated middle classes, the users of modern technology. For all one knows, Kosambi himself may have helped in the organization of these rites. The saddle-quern of Kosambi's description belongs, therefore, in our terms, to the problem of entangled times, to what I have called the "timeknot."[17] It is made of stone, it resembles stone-age implements and therefore may have had a relationship to another period, and yet it shares in the time of the electric or kerosene stove as well. Moreover, it mediates in the relationship between upper and lower castes and locates them in some shared practices: "The implication is that a stone-age ceremony has come down with the implement, and has been borrowed by the brahmin families from the surrounding population."[18] His historicism makes Kosambi blind to the problem of temporality posed by the saddle-quern. He could see the implement only as something that "developed with the first agriculture before the end of the stone age." The relationship between the cooking stove and the saddle-quern, for him, could then be only that of a one-way flow of time.

With hindsight, one can see that Kenyatta's relationship to his grandfather's magic, Appiah's relationship to his father's habit of offering scotch to ancestors, and Kosambi's relationship to the saddle-quern all point to the same problem. They refer us to the plurality that inheres in the "now," the lack of totality, the constant fragmentariness, that constitutes one's present. Over against this stands our capacity to deploy the historicist or ethnographic mode of viewing that involves the use of a sense of anachronism in order to convert objects, institutions, and practices with which we have lived relationships into relics of other times. As we have already said, this capacity to construct a single historical context for everything is the enabling condition of modern historical consciousness, the capacity to see the past as gone and reified into an object of investigation. It is this ability to see the past as genuinely dead, as separate from the time of the observer, that has given rise to the utopian and hermeneutic (but nevertheless ethical) struggles of the modern historical imagination—to try to get inside the skin of the past, to try to see it "as it really was," to try and reenact it in the historian's mind, and so on. I do not mean to devalue this struggle or the intense sense of craftsmanship to which it gives rise.[19] But it is also true—as I hope my examples have demonstrated—that the modern sense of "anachronism" stops us from confronting the problem of the temporal heterogeneity of the "now" in thinking about history. We need to consider why we find anachronism productive.

WHAT IS INVESTED IN ANACHRONISM?

Because I do not wish to suggest that "anachronism" is a simple error of the mind, the question arises: What is invested in the practice of anachronism that allows us to reify the past into an object of study? Let me offer a very general answer. If the rise of the modern historical consciousness speaks of the coming of a certain modern and political way of inhabiting the world, I suggest that it also speaks of a very particular relation to the past. This is the desire on the part of the subject of political modernity both to create the past as amenable to objectification and to be at the same time free of this object called "history." In fact, one can argue that the attempt to objectify the past is an expression of the desire to be free of the past, the desire to create what Paul de Man once called "the true present." What is the "true present?" The " 'full power of the idea of modernity,' " writes Marshall Berman quoting de Man, "lay in a 'desire to wipe out whatever came earlier,' so as to achieve a 'a radically new departure, a point that could be a true present.' "[20] The true present is what is produced when we act as if we could reduce the past to a nullity. It is a kind of a zero point in history—the pastless time, for example, of a *tabula rasa*, the *terra nullius*, or the blueprint. It reflects the desire of the modern political subject to practice, in pursuit of the goal of social justice, a certain degree of freedom with respect to the past.

Since the beginning of the nineteenth century, embracing political modernity has posed a number of anxious questions about the past to socially radical Indian intellectuals. Are "modernity" and the realization of "reason" possibilities inherent in our history? Or are they grounded in something outside of histories that are specific to any time or place, for example, in the "moral disposition" or the "communicative competence" of the human? How does one comport oneself toward those "unjust" social practices that are often justified in the name of tradition, custom, or indeed the past itself? Caste, *sati*, untouchability, religious conflicts—examples abound. Indeed, from what position does the modern intellectual contemplate the past?

There is no single answer to this question. In the Lockean fable of the fraternal contract underlying civil-political society, political freedom itself was freedom from the rule of the past. The father, insofar as he represents a part of the history of the sons' childhood, is to be honored but has no "power of command" over his sons who, when they attain adulthood and reason, enjoy the "liberty of acting according to [their] own will." Their freedom is grounded in their reason.[21] Reason here is external to history, and its attainment signals a freedom from any political authority of the past (embodied in the father). On the cessation of childhood, a Lockean individual begins life from this zero point in history. He constantly seeks to bring into being the "true present." Historical possibilities now are created by reason alone. Likewise, the modern individual is not bound by the past. Custom has no "power to command" or punish him. John Locke's fable about the fraternal contract that underlies the modern civil-political society has been justly described as nonhistorical or antihistorical.[22]

In Marxist and social-science historiography, on the other hand, the possibilities one fights for are seen as emerging out of the conflicts of history. They are not completely external to it, but they are not completely determined by it, either. In this framework, the undecidable question of how much power the past possesses could produce an extreme degree of ambivalence in the modern individual. For in this mode of thinking, the past could appear to be both an enabling resource and a disabling constraint. Marx himself exemplified this ambivalence when he wrote: "The tradition of all the dead generations weigh like a nightmare on the brain of the living." Why "nightmare"? Why such an anxiety-ridden description of the dead generations? The anxiety arises because the modern individual in Marx's position is never as completely free of the past as are the brothers in Locke's theory of civil-political rule. Marxian modernity is caught in a contradiction with respect to the past. On the one hand, the revolutionary in every modern person desires to exceed and excise the past, to create "something that has never existed." Yet the new can be imagined and expressed only through a language made out of the languages already available. Political action is thus loaded with the risk that what was meant to be a break with the past—"something that has never existed"—could end up looking like a return of the dead. The uncertainty of this break is what makes the voice of the modern in Marx's text sound anxious. As Marx wrote, "And just when they seem engaged in revolutionising themselves and things, in creating something that has never existed, precisely in such periods of revolutionary crisis they anxiously conjure up the spirits of the past to their service and borrow from them names, battle cries and costumes in order to present the new scene of world history in this time-honoured disguise and this borrowed language."[23]

In their debate in the 1930s on the "caste system" in India, Mahatma Gandhi and B. R. Ambedkar, the leader of the so-called "untouchables," both reproduced—for all their well-publicized disagreements—elements of the two positions outlined above. They both saw their pursuit of social justice as creating possibilities that were independent of the past. Gandhi, for instance, made it clear that his criticisms of caste had very little to do with the history of the practice. "Caste," he said, "has nothing to do with religion. It is a custom whose origin I do not know and *do not need to know* for the satisfaction of my spiritual hunger. But I do know that it is harmful both to spiritual and national growth."[24] And Ambedkar recommended a complete overhaul of Hinduism to bring it in into line "with Democracy." He called for a "complete change in the fundamental notions of life," in "outlook and attitude towards men and things," for the "annihilation of caste," and for Indian society to be entirely rebuilt on the basis of the three principles of "*Liberty*, *Equality* and *Fraternity*."[25]

This very sense of freedom with regard to the past that both Ambedkar and Gandhi articulated suggested, however, another possible relationship to it. Freedom from the past could also mean that the past could be treated as though it were a pool of resources, a standing reserve, on which the subject of political modernity could draw as needed in the struggle for social justice. Gandhi's attitude to the scriptures contained this sense of freedom. "The scriptures, properly so called," wrote Gandhi, "can only be concerned with internal verities and must appeal to any conscience. . . . Nothing can be accepted as the word of God which cannot be tested by reason or be capable of being spiritually experienced." He argued that one had a choice in the matter of religion: "A religion has to be judged not by its worst specimen but by the best it might have produced. For that and that alone can be used as the standard to aspire to, if not to improve upon."[26]

Ambedkar in his turn quoted John Dewey—"my teacher and to whom I owe so much"—to say: "Every society gets encumbered with what is trivial, with dead wood from the past, and with what is positively perverse." The task of an "enlightened" society was "*not* to conserve and transmit the whole of its existing achievements, but only such as make for a better future society." The Hindus, therefore,

> must consider whether they must not cease to worship the past as supplying [their] ideals. . . . Prof. Dewey . . . says: "An individual can live only in the present. The present is not just something which comes after the past; much less something produced by it." . . . The Hindus must consider whether the time has not come for them to recognize that there is nothing fixed, nothing eternal, nothing *sanatan*; that everything is

> changing . . . there must be a constant revolution of values and the Hindus must realize that if there must be standards to measure the acts of men there must also be a readiness to revise those standards.[27]

There are, then, two kinds of relationship to the past being professed in these passages. One is historicism, the idea that to get a grip on things we need to know their histories, the process of development they have undergone in order to become what they are. Historicism itself promises to the human subject a certain degree of autonomy with respect to history. The idea is that once one knows the causal structures that operate in history, one may also gain a certain mastery of them. The other relationship to the past professed here is what I would call a "decisionist" relationship. By "decisionism," I mean a disposition that allows the critic to talk about the future and the past as though there were concrete, value-laden choices or decisions to be made with regard to both. There is no talk of historical laws here. The critic is guided by his or her values to choose the most desirable, sane, and wise future for humanity, and looks to the past as a warehouse of resources on which to draw as needed. This relationship to the past incorporates the revolutionary-modernist position in which the reformer seeks to bring (a particular) history to nullity in order to build up society from scratch. Decisionism, however, does not have to connote an iconoclastic attitude to the past. It allows one to entertain a variety of attitudes toward the past—from respect to disgust—and yet not be bound by it. It uses "tradition," but the use is guided by a critique of the present. It thus represents a freedom from history as well as a freedom to respect the aspects of "tradition" considered useful to building the desired future.

Decisionism and historicism may initially seem opposed to each other. The noted Indian critic Ashis Nandy, for example, has sometimes powerfully opposed historicism positions that in my terms are "decisionist." In a recent essay entitled "History's Forgotten Doubles," Nandy criticizes history's methods. Unlike the subjects of anthropology, "the subjects of history almost never rebel, for they are mostly dead."[28] What fundamentally troubles Nandy is the nondialogical nature of the "conversation" between the past and the present that goes on in the texts of the historian. He advocates instead the idea of "principled forgetfulness and silences." In explaining what he means by this, Nandy comes close to what I have described as the decisionist position. Desirable constructions of the past, he says, "are primarily *responsible to the present* and to the future; they are meant neither for the archivist nor for the archaeologist. They try *to expand human options* by reconfiguring the past and transcending it through *creative improvisations*. . . . [T]he past shapes the present and future but the present and the future also shape the past. Some scholars . . . are . . . willing to redefine, perhaps even transfigure, the past to open up the future. The *choice* is not cognitive, but moral and political, in the best sense of the terms."[29]

Presenting the past as a matter of "moral and political" choice to the modern subject is what makes Nandy's position decisionist. He clearly deploys it in opposition to what may be called social-science history, which sees historical processes as setting limits to human freedom. He writes: "One wonders if some vague awareness of this asymmetry between the subjects and the objects [in the discipline of history], and between the knowers and the known, prompted Gandhi to reject history as a guide to moral action and derive such guidance from his reading of texts and myths. . . . Gandhi, like Blake and Thoreau before him, defied this new fatalism [that is, the idea of historical laws] of our times."[30]

Although in some kind of tension with each other, in particular over the question of historical evidence, decisionism and historicism are not mutually exclusive options for the subject of political modernity. As the quotes from Ambedkar show, he coupled his decisionist attitude to the past with the modern view that history as a discipline was primarily about explaining the processes and origins of social change. He stood for scrapping the caste-ridden past of India; in that, he was a decisionist. But the modern person in Ambedkar was not against the discipline of history. Everything changes, he said. Nothing is "fixed" or "eternal." The main task of the historical sciences is to answer "why." This understanding of history was historicist. In an early essay on "Castes in India," read before the "Anthropology seminar of Dr. A. A. Goldenweizer of Columbia University" in 1916, he deplored the absence of proper histories of the practices of *sati*, "enforced widowhood," and "girl marriage" in India. "We have plenty of philosophy to tell us why these customs were honoured, but nothing to tell us the *causes of their origin* and existence."[31]

Decisionism thus cannot constitute a fundamental critique of historicism. They are both invested in the modernist dream of the "true present" that always looks to, and is in turn determined by, the blueprint of a desirable future. Anachronism is an integral part of the historicist sensibility that accompanies such a political program. It accompanies our search for social justice. But historicism and the accompanying idea of anachronism also produce a problem for what we have called the project of provincializing Europe. Historicism can circulate only in a mood of frustration, despair, and ressentiment.[32] For so long as we have historicism in place, the task of conceptualizing the nature of political modernity in colonial and postcolonial India baffles us. The peasant as citizen keeps looking like a relic of another time, although we know that he belongs squarely to the same present as that of the modern citizen. The challenge is to reconceptualize the present. To redefine our project as seeking to go beyond ressentiment toward European thought, we need to think beyond historicism. To do this is not to reject reason but to see it as one among many ways of being in the world. The following section elaborates on this point.

BEYOND HISTORICISM

To critique historicism in all its varieties is to unlearn to think of history as a developmental process in which that which is possible becomes actual by tending to a future that is singular. Or, to put it differently, it is to learn to think the present—the "now" that we inhabit as we speak—as irreducibly not-one. To take that step is to rethink the problem of historical time and to review the relationship between the possible and the actual. The following thoughts derive from the discussion presented in the second division of Martin Heidegger's *Being and Time*. At the core of this exercise is a concern about how one might think about the past and the future in a nontotalizing manner.

Usually—Heidegger reminds us—we think of the possible as an unrealized actual. However, to see the present as radically not-one and thus plural is to see its "now" as a state of partial disclosedness, without the suggestion or promise of any principles—such as *dharma*, capital, or citizenship—that can or will override this heterogeneity and incompleteness and eventually constitute a totality. Such plural possibilities therefore cannot be considered to be merely waiting to become actual—like the possibility of ripening inherent in a fruit. Nor can the plurality of possibilities be captured by the thought of "lack" or "incompleteness" that assumes an additive view of totality. We can see something as "merely incomplete" if we subscribe to the principle of a totality that can be brought into view by the addition of certain elements in the chronological time that follows the "now." We have encountered such thought before in certain Marxist versions of Indian history that speak of "incomplete transitions" to capitalism and modernity.[33] To think of the "not yet," of the "now," as a form of "unrealized actual" would be to remain trapped entirely within historicism. For a possibility to be neither that which is waiting to become actual nor that which is merely incomplete, the possible has to be thought of as that which already actually *is* but is present only as the "not yet" of the actual. In other words, it is what makes not-being-a-totality a constitutional characteristic of the "now." It is in this radical sense of never being a totality that the "now" is "constantly fragmentary" and not-one.[34]

Heidegger also helps us to see how the problem of the past cannot be thought about until we think about the question of the future as well. A human being simply cannot avoid being oriented toward the future. Yet the fact of having been there already—what Heidegger calls "I am as having been"—is also beyond the control of the human. All our pasts are therefore futural in orientation. They help us make the unavoidable journey into the future. There is, in this sense, no "desire for going back," no "pathological" nostalgia that is also not futural as well. Being futural is something that is with us, at every moment, in every action that the human being undertakes.[35]

But one has to make a distinction between the conscious thought of "a future" that we address in our pursuit of social justice and the futurity that laces every moment of human existence. The first kind of "future" is what both the historicist and the decisionist address. Recall Nandy's words: "such constructions [of the past] are primarily responsible to the present and the future."[36] This is a future of which we know at least the constitutive principles, even if we do not have a blueprint for it. Let us call this future, the future that "will be." This is different from the futurity that already *is* in our actions at every moment. This other futurity we could refer to as the futures that already "are."[37]

The future that "will be" aligns itself with what I called History 1 in my chapter on "The Two Histories of Capital." This is the universal and necessary history posited by the logic of capital. In this history inhere the Enlightenment universals. As moderns desirous of social justice and its attendant institutions, we, whether decisionist or historicist, cannot but have a shared commitment to it (in spite of all the disagreements between liberalism and Marxism). It is through this commitment that is already built into our lives that our jousting with European thought begins. The project of "provincializing Europe" arises from this commitment. But this beginning does not define the project. The project has to be defined with reference to other pasts, that is to say, with reference to History 2s—pasts "encountered by capital as antecedents but not as belonging to its own life-process."

Futures that already *are* there, the futurity that humans cannot avoid aligning themselves with, are what I have called History 2. These futures are plural and do not illustrate any idea of the whole or one. They are what makes it impossible to sum up a present through any totalizing principle. They make the "now" constantly fragmentary, but the fragments are not additive; they do not suggest a totality or a whole. The constant and open-ended modification of the future that "will be" by the futures that "are" parallels the ongoing modification of History 1 by History 2s, as argued in Chapter 2.

These futures that already "are" do not necessarily look to the future that "will be," which forms itself in the calculations and the desires of the subject of political modernity. The futures that "are" are plural, do not lend themselves to being represented by a totalizing principle, and are not even always amenable to the objectifying procedures of history writing. For my "I am as having been" includes pasts that exist in ways that I cannot see or figure out—or can do so sometimes only retrospectively. Pasts *are* there in taste, in practices of embodiment, in the cultural training the senses have received over generations. They are there in practices I sometimes do not even know I engage in. This is how the archaic comes into the modern, not as a remnant of another time but as something constitutive of the present. Whatever the nature of these pasts that already "are," they are always oriented to futures that also already "are." They exist without my being decisionist about them. The modern Bengali poet Arunkumar Sarkar writes, for instance, of his childhood: "Ever since I was a child, I was attracted to [the] sound [of language], and it was this attraction that gave rise to the desire to write poetry. My mother used to recite different kinds of poems, my father Sanskrit verses of praise [to deities], and my grandmother the hundred and eight names of [the god] Krishna. I did not understand their meanings but I felt absorbed in the sounds."[38]

Arun Sarkar's statement nicely captures the nondecisionist aspect of his relationship to both the past and future within which the "now" of his "writing poetry" moves. The "having been" of his mother's recitation of poetry, his father's of Sanskrit verses, and his grandmother's of the names of the Hindu god Krishna is (re)collected here in a movement of existence whose direction is futural. The futural direction of the movement is indicated by the phrase "the desire to write poetry." It is within this futurity that Arun Sarkar's poetry writing happens.

As against this plurality of the futures that already "are," there is the future of the politically modern position. This is the future that "will be."

This future posits a "now" where we are required to see the present as capable of yielding a principle of totalization. This in turn calls on us to be decisionist and/or objectifying about the past. This is the unavoidable gesture of the modern political subject. There is no reason to reject it as such. But we have to recognize the limitations of such methods in matters of thinking about the past. The past, for reasons adduced above, is never completely amenable to the objectifying protocols of historiography. To say this, incidentally, is not to deny the heuristic value of class, patriarchy, or technology in social-critical analysis of the past. But the clarity of the model is not the same as the clarity in the object for which the model stands.

We always have, in Heideggerian terms, a fore-conception of the fact that we live amid "futures" that already are and that cut across the future, which is cast in the mold of a "will be." Ultimately, this is the question of the diverse ways the human finds of being-in-the-world. Of these many modes of being, the "objectifying" one is simply one, albeit a globally dominant one at present. A problem arises when the demand is made that the objectifying relationship to the past be our only relationship, for then any return of other relationships seem like a "nightmare of the dead," as Marx put it. For those who give themselves over completely to objectifying modes of thought, the past retains a power to haunt and deliver the shock of the uncanny.[39] Listen, for instance, to the French Marxist-theorist Henri Lefebvre's thoughts and experience—ironic in the case of this trenchant critic of capitalist objectification—when he visited a little church near Navarrenx (his "native country-town"), a church that belonged to his childhood: "I know what I shall find: an empty, echoing space, with hidden recesses crammed with hundreds of objects, each uttering the silent cry that makes it a sign. What a strange power! I know I cannot fail to understand their 'meanings' because they were explained to me years ago. It is impossible to close your eyes and ears to these symbols. . . . It is impossible to free myself from it." The "having been's" that create this "now" for Lefebvre in the church orient that "now" toward the future that his childhood once was. His Marxism, however, enjoins him to close off this moment and the plurality of it. Instead he wants to be consumed by a future that "will be," the future called "socialism." So a struggle ensues in Lefebvre's text at this point: "But precisely because I feel this obscure emotion I can begin to understand its obscure causes. So I must not despair, the fight goes on . . . religion . . . is a reactionary destructive critique. Marxism offers an effective, constructive critique of life. And Marxism alone!"[40]

The "constantly fragmentary" and irreducibly plural nature of the "now" is a problem to a social science that formulates human future as a project in which reason is realized in some form or other (more democracy, liberalism, rights, socialism, and so on). This in turn makes the life practices we do not approve of—practices that seem superstitious or that ascribe agency to gods and spirits—seem anachronistic if not reactionary. This happens, as we have seen, even when the investigating subject has lived an everyday relationship to these practices. Reason here assumes the form of a totalizing principle with the help of which the social-science investigator can only create an anthropologizing relationship, even to that with which he or she may have a connection prior to, during, and after the process of the investigation.

Interestingly, practicing Indian scientists—and I suppose scientists elsewhere as well—often have not felt any intellectual or social obligation to find one single overarching framework within which to contain the diversity of their own life practices (as distinct from their practices as scientists). In other words, the practice of "science" does not necessarily call on the researcher to develop a "scientific temper" beyond the practice of science itself. A. K. Ramanujan, the folklorist, once wrote about his astronomer father who had no difficulty being an astrologer as well:

> He was a mathematician, an astronomer. But he was also a Sanskrit scholar, an expert astrologer. He had two kinds of exotic visitors: American and English mathematicians who called on him when they were on a visit to India, and local astrologers, orthodox pundits who wore splendid gold-embroidered shawls dowered by the Maharajah. I had just been converted by Russell to the "scientific attitude." I . . . was troubled by his holding together in one brain both astronomy and astrology; I looked for consistency in him, a consistency he did not seem to care about, or even think about. When I asked him what the discovery of Neptune and Pluto did to his archaic nine-planet astrology, he said, "You make the necessary corrections, that's all." Or, in answer to how he could read the Gita religiously having bathed and . . . later talk appreciatively about Bertrand Russell and even Ingersoll, he said, ". . . don't you know, the brain has two lobes?"[41]

Ramanujan's father's strategy for living precisely in a "now" that lacked totality—his metaphor of the two contradictory lobes effectively reduced the unity of the brain to merely an empty, contingent shell—was apparently also practiced by the Indian Nobel laureate physicist C. V.

Raman. Raman, it is said, would rush home from his laboratory in Calcutta in the 1930s to "take a ritual bath ahead of a solar eclipse." When questioned about this, the physicist is reported to have simply quipped, "The Nobel Prize? That was science, a solar eclipse is personal."[42]

We do not have to accept these two anecdotes about two Indian scientists as perfectly true. But these possibly apocryphal stories about Ramanujan's father and Sir C. V. Raman help me to imagine an alternative location for "reason" as we think about the subject of "Indian history." These stories suggest, in Heideggerian sense, a fore-conception of how we might provincialize the Europe of our desire to be modern by giving reason a place different from the one assigned to it in historicist and modernist thought. The senior Ramanujan and Raman were both serious scientists. Yet they did not need to totalize through the outlook of science all the different life-practices within which they found themselves and to which they felt called. These stories—even if they are not true of the individuals named—speak of possible thought practices in which the future that "will be" never completely swamps the futures that already "are."

To provincialize Europe in historical thought is to struggle to hold in a state of permanent tension a dialogue between two contradictory points of view. On one side is the indispensable and universal narrative of capital—History 1, as I have called it. This narrative both gives us a critique of capitalist imperialism and affords elusive but necessarily energizing glimpses of the Enlightenment promise of an abstract, universal but never-to-be-realized humanity. Without such elusive glimpses, as I have said before, there is no political modernity. On the other side is thought about diverse ways of being human, the infinite incommensurabilities through which we struggle—perennially, precariously, but unavoidably—to "world the earth" in order to live within our different senses of ontic belonging. These are the struggles that become—when in contact with capital—the History 2s that in practice always modify and interrupt the totalizing thrusts of History 1.

Although this book is not committed to either Marx or Heidegger in any doctrinaire or dogmatic sense, the spirit of their thinking and their guiding concepts preside over the two poles of thought that direct the movements of this book. As I said at the beginning, Marx and Heidegger represent for me two contradictory but profoundly connected tendencies that coexist within modern European social thought. One is the analytical heritage, the practice of abstraction that helps us to universalize. We need universals to produce critical readings of social injustices. Yet the universal and the analytical produce forms of thought that ultimately evacuate the place of the local. It does not matter if this is done in an empirical idiom, for the empirical can often be a result of the universal, just as the particular follows from the general. Such thought fundamentally tends to sever the relationship between thought and modes of human belonging. The other European heritage is the hermeneutic tradition that tends to reinstitute within thought itself this relationship between thought and dwelling. My attempt in this book has been to write some very particular ways of being-in-the-world—I call them Bengali only in a provisional manner—into some of the universal, abstract, and European categories of capitalist/political modernity. For me, provincializing Europe has been a question of how we create conjoined and disjunctive genealogies for European categories of political modernity as we contemplate the necessarily fragmentary histories of human belonging that never constitute a one or a whole.

As I hope is obvious from what has been said, provincializing Europe cannot ever be a project of shunning European thought. For at the end of European imperialism, European thought is a gift to us all. We can talk of provincializing it only in an anticolonial spirit of gratitude.[43]

Notes

Introduction
The Idea of Provincializing Europe

1. See, for instance, Oscar Halecki, *The Limits and Divisions of European History* (Notre Dame, Indiana: University of Notre Dame Press, 1962), chapter 2 and *passim.*

2. Janet Abu-Lughod, *Before European Hegemony: The World System A.D. 1250–1350* (New York and Oxford: Oxford University Press, 1989); Eric Wolf, *Europe and the People without History* (Berkeley and Los Angeles: University of California Press, 1982); K. N. Chaudhuri, *Asia before Europe: Economy and Civilisation of the Indian Ocean from the Rise of Islam to 1750* (Cambridge: Cambridge University Press, 1990). Among more recent titles, see J. M. Blaut, *The Colonizer's Model of the World: Geographical Diffusionism and Eurocentric History* (New York, London: Guilford Press, 1993); Martin W. Lewis and Karen E. Wigen, *The Myth of Continents: A Critique of Metageography* (Berkeley and Los Angeles: University of California Press, 1997). See also Sanjay Subrahmanyam, "Connected Histories: Notes towards a Reconfiguration of Early Modern Eurasia," *Modern Asian Studies* 31, no. 3 (1997), pp. 735–762.

3. Michael Roth, "The Nostalgic Nest at the End of History," in his *The Ironist's Cage: Memory, Trauma and the Construction of History* (New York: Columbia University Press, 1995), pp. 163–174.

4. Immanuel Kant, "An Old Question Raised Again: Is the Human Race Constantly Progressing?" in his *The Conflict of Faculties*, translated by Mary J. Gregor (Lincoln and London: University of Nebraska Press, 1992), p. 153. Jean Hyppolite, *Genesis and Structure of Hegel's "Phenomenology of Spirit,"* translated by Samuel Cherniak and John Heckman (Evanston: Northwestern University Press, 1974), p. 426. See also Charles Taylor, *Hegel* (Cambridge: Cambridge University Press, 1978), pp. 416–421.

5. It is important to keep in mind that it is not my purpose here to discuss the long history and genealogy of the fundamental categories of European social and political thought. Two such possible genealogies, for example, of the "public sphere" and the "civil society" are Jurgen Habermas, *The Structural Transformation of the Public Sphere: An Inquiry into a Category of Bourgeois Society*, translated by Thomas Burger and Frederick Lawrence (Cambridge: MIT Press, 1989), and Dominique Colas, *Civil Society and Fanaticism: Conjoined Histories*, translated by Amy Jacobs (Stanford: Stanford University Press, 1997). But these genealogies are completely "internalist" accounts of European intellectual history. For a postcolonial history of European (French) thought, see Alice Bullard, *Constella-*

tions of Civilization and Savagery: New Caledonia and France 1770–1900 (forthcoming).

6. I distinguish here between thought and practice. To be a member of the parliamentary body in India does not require one to know the history of anything called "the parliament" in any depth. Yet a textbook explaining to the children of India what the role of "the parliament" is would find it impossible to address this task without some engagement with European history.

7. Tapan Raychaudhuri, *Europe Reconsidered: Perceptions of the West in Nineteenth Century Bengal* (Delhi: Oxford University Press, 1988), p. ix.

8. On Rammohun Roy, see V. C. Joshi, ed., *Raja Rammohun Roy and the Process of Modernization in India* (Delhi: Nehru Memorial Museum and Library, 1973); on M. N. Roy, see Sanjay Seth, *Marxist Theory and Nationalist Politics: The Case of Colonial India* (Delhi: Sage Publications, 1995).

9. See the last chapter of this book.

10. Hichem Djait, *Europe and Islam: Cultures and Modernity*, translated by Peter Heinegg (Berkeley and Los Angeles: University of California Press, 1985), p. 101.

11. See the conclusion to Frantz Fanon, *The Wretched of the Earth*, translated by Constance Farrington (New York: Grove Press, 1963).

12. See Martin Bernal, *The Black Athena: The Afroasiatic Roots of Classical Civilization*, vol. 1 (London: Vintage, 1991); Samir Amin, *Eurocentrism*, translated by Russell Moore (New York: Zed, 1989), pp. 91–92, on "the myths of Greek ancestry." I understand that several of Bernal's claims are being disputed in the scholarship today. But his point about the contributions made by non-Greek persons to so-called "Greek" thought remains.

13. This is not to deny the fact that Sanskrit learning enjoyed a brief renaissance under British rule in the early part of the nineteenth century. But this revival of Sanskrit should not be confused with the question of survival of an intellectual tradition. Modern research and studies in Sanskrit have on the whole been undertaken within the intellectual frameworks of the European human sciences. Ṣheldon Pollock's forthcoming book, "The Language of the Gods in the World of Men: Sanskrit and Power to 1500," directly engages with the problematic intellectual legacies of this practice. See also Pollock's forthcoming essays "The Death of Sanskrit," in *Comparative Studies in Society and History*, and "The New Intellectuals of Seventeenth-Century India," in *Indian Economic and Social History Review*. See also John D. Kelly, "What Was Sanskrit for? Metadiscursive Strategies in Ancient India"; Sheldon Pollock, "The Sanskrit Cosmopolis, 300–1300 C.E.: Transculturation, Vernacularization, and the Question of Ideology"; and Saroja Bhate, "Position of Sanskrit in Public Education and Scientific Research in Modern India," all in Jan E. M. Houben, ed., *Ideology and Status of Sanskrit* (Leiden, New York, Cologne: E. J. Brill, 1996), pp. 87–107, 197–247, and 383–400, respectively. The very use of the word "ideology" in the title of this book would appear to support my thesis. Similar points could be made with respect to scholar-

ship and intellectual traditions available, say, in the eighteenth century in Persian and Arabic. I am, unfortunately, less aware of contemporary research of this problem with respect to these two languages. I also acknowledge the highly respectable line of modern scholars of Indian philosophy who over generations have attempted conversations between European and Indian traditions of thought. Two contemporary exemplars of this tradition would be J. N. Mohanty and the late B. K. Matilal. But, sadly, their thinking has yet to have any major impact on social-science studies of South Asia.

14. I document some instances of this in Chapter 5 below.

15. Robert Young, *White Mythologies: History Writing and the West* (London and New York: Routledge, 1990).

16. Frederic Jameson, *Postmodernism or, the Cultural Logic of Late Capitalism* (Durham: Duke University Press, 1991), chapter 1.

17. Lawrence Grossberg cited in Meaghan Morris, "Metamorphoses at the Sydney Tower," *New Formations* 11 (Summer 1990), pp. 5–18. See the larger discussion in my "The Death of History? Historical Consciousness and the Culture of Late Capitalism," *Public Culture* 4, no. 2 (Spring 1992), pp. 47–65. See also Lawrence Grossberg, "History, Imagination and the Politics of Belonging: Between the Death and Fear of History," in Paul Gilroy, Lawrence Grossberg, and Angela McRobbie, eds., *Essays in Honor of Stuart Hall* (London and New York: Verso, forthcoming); Meaghan Morris, *Too Soon Too Late: History in Popular Culture* (Bloomington: Indiana University Press, 1998).

18. David Harvey, *The Condition of Postmodernity: An Enquiry into the Origins of Cultural Change* (Oxford: Basil Blackwell, 1990), chapters 8 and 9.

19. "Introduction" to Lisa Lowe and David Lloyd, eds., *The Politics of Culture in the Shadow of Capital* (Durham: Duke University Press, 1997). Gyan Prakash, "Introduction" to Prakash, ed., *After Colonialism: Imperial Histories and Postcolonial Displacements* (Princeton: Princeton University Press, 1995), pp. 3–17.

20. "Preface to the First Edition" in Karl Marx, *Capital: A Critique of Political Economy*, vol. 1, translated by Ben Fowkes (Harmondsworth, 1990), p. 91. Bob Jessop and Russell Wheatley, eds., *Karl Marx's Social and Political Thought: Critical Assessments—Second Series*, vol. 6 (London and New York: Routledge, 1999) is an excellent collection of reprints of recent essays on the issue of Eurocentrism in Marx.

21. Phyllis Deane, *The First Industrial Revolution* (Cambridge: Cambridge University Press, 1979).

22. Both Naoki Sakai, in his *Translation and Subjectivity: On "Japan" and Cultural Nationalism* (Minneapolis: University of Minnesota Press, 1997), and Samir Amin in *Eurocentrism* make this point.

23. Uday Singh Mehta, *Liberalism and Empire: A Study in Nineteenth-Century British Liberal Thought* (Chicago: University of Chicago Press, 1999), pp. 99–100, offers a relevant reading of John Stuart Mill's essay on "civilization." For an analysis of the role of the idea of "civilization" in the American academic

organization of "area studies," see Andrew Sartori, "Robert Redfield's Comparative Civilizations Project and the Political Imagination of Postwar America" in *Positions: East Asia Cultures Critique* 6, no. 1 (Spring 1998), pp. 33–65.

24. See Fernando Coronil, *The Magical State: Nature, Money and Modernity in Venezuela* (Chicago: University of Chicago Press, 1997), pp. 387–388. Enrique Dussel, *The Invention of the Americas: Eclipse of "the Other" and the Myth of Modernity*, translated by Michael D. Barber (New York: Continuum, 1995) is a powerful attempt to question Eurocentricism.

25. Johannes Fabian, *Time and the Other: How Anthropology Makes Its Object* (New York: Columbia University Press, 1983), chapters 1 and 2. For a related and powerful reading of nineteenth-century anthropology that furthers this line of argumentation, see Patrick Wolfe, *Settler Colonialism and the Transformation of Anthropology: The Politics and Poetics of an Ethnographic Event* (London and New York: Cassell, 1999).

26. On the European origins of the academic discipline of "history," see Peter Burke, *The Renaissance Sense of the Past* (London: Edward Arnold, 1969); J.G.A. Pocock, *The Ancient Constitution and the Feudal Law: A Study of English Historical Thought in the Seventeenth Century* (Cambridge: Cambridge University Press, 1990); and Reinhart Kosselleck, *Futures Past: On the Semantics of Historical Time*, translated by Keith Tribe (Cambridge: MIT Press, 1985). Kosselleck writes (p. 200) : "Our contemporary concept of history, together with its numerous zones of meaning . . . was first constituted towards the end of the eighteenth century. It is an outcome of the lengthy theoretical reflections of the Enlightenment. Formerly there had existed, for instance, the history that God had set in motion with humanity. But there was no history for which humanity might have been the subject or which could be thought of as its own subject." Before 1780, Kosselleck adds , "history" would have always meant the history of something particular. The idea of being, say, a "student of history"—that is, the idea of a history-in-general—is clearly a modern, post-Enlightenment exercise.

27. "On Liberty," chapter 1 (especially p. 15) and "Considerations on Representative Government," chapter 18, pp. 409–423 in particular, in John Stuart Mill, *Three Essays* (Oxford and New York: Oxford University Press, 1975). See also the stimulating discussion on Mill in Mehta's *Liberalism and Empire*, chapter 3.

28. Mill, "Representative Government," p. 278. Mill produces a list of topics knowledge of which "could be required from all electors."

29. *Report of the Indian Franchise Committee* (Calcutta: Government of India, 1932), vol. 1, pp. 11–13.

30. Radhakrishnan's speech to the Constituent Assembly on 20 January 1947, reprinted in B. Shiva Rao, et al., eds., *The Framing of India's Constitution: Select Documents* (Delhi: Indian Institute of Public Administration, 1967), vol. 2, p. 15.

31. See Akhil Gupta, *Postcolonial Development: Agriculture in the Making of Modern India* (Durham: Duke University Press, 1998), James Ferguson, *The Anti-*

Political Machine: "Development," Depoliticization, and Bureaucratic Power in Lesotho (Minneapolis: University of Minnesota Press, 1994), and Arturo Escobar, *Encountering Development: The Making and Unmaking of the Third World* (Princeton: Princeton University Press, 1995) document the historicism that underlies the language of development administration.

32. Homi K. Bhabha, "DissemiNation: Time, Narrative and the Margins of the Modern Nation," in Homi K. Bhabha, *The Location of Culture* (London: Routledge, 1994), pp. 139–170.

33. Ranajit Guha, ed., *Subaltern Studies: Studies in Indian Society and History* (Delhi: Oxford University Press, 1983–1993), vols. 1–6. Later volumes, 7–10, have been edited, respectively, by editorial teams consisting of Gyan Pandey and Partha Chatterjee; David Arnold and David Hardiman; Shahid Amin and Dipesh Chakrabarty; and by Susie Tharu, Gautam Bhadra, and Gyan Prakash.

34. Ranajit Guha, *Elementary Aspects of Peasant Insurgency in Colonial India* (Delhi: Oxford University Press, 1983), p. 6.

35. I ignore here the literature in rational choice theory, as few historians use rational choice frameworks in writing histories of human consciousness or cultural practices. Rational choice has been a more dominant framework in economics and political science departments.

36. E. J. Hobsbawm, *Primitive Rebels: Studies in Archaic Forms of Social Movement in the 19th and 20th Centuries* (Manchester: Manchester University Press, 1978; first pub. 1959), pp. 2–3.

37. Neil Smith, *Uneven Development: Nature, Capital and the Production of Space* (Oxford: Basil Blackwell, 1990). Smith's own understanding of uneven development remains historicist. Marx's distinction between "formal" and "real" subsumption of labor, for example, is treated by Smith mainly as a question of historical transition (p. 140). James Chandler, *England in 1819* (Chicago: University of Chicago Press, 1998), p. 131, dates the idea of uneven development back to the Scottish Enlightenment.

38. Ernst Bloch's imaginative discussion of Nazism in terms of the "synchronicity of the non-synchronous" assumes a "totality" within which the "now" belongs to the capitalist mode and the peasant remains an "earlier type," an example of the "genuinely non-synchronous remainder." Ernst Bloch, "Non-synchronism and the Obligation to Its Dialectics," *New German Critique* 11, translated by Mark Ritter (Spring 1977), pp. 22–38. Bloch, as Martin Jay points out, later developed his own critique of empty, secular historical time by seriously thinking through the so-called religious. See Martin Jay, *Marxism and Totality: The Adventures of a Concept from Lukacs to Habermas* (Berkeley and Los Angeles: University of California Press, 1984), pp. 189–190.

39. James Chandler, *England in 1819*, p. 131.

40. On this point, see my essay, "A Small History of Subaltern Studies" (forthcoming).

41. See below, Chapter 4.

42. Guha, *Elementary Aspects*, p. 6.

43. Ibid., p. 75.

44. Ibid., chapters 1 and 2. Conservative historians ignored this phase of peasant rebellion as the "traditional reaching out for sticks and stones," and therefore devoid of politics. Anil Seal, *The Emergence of Indian Nationalism: Competition and Collaboration in the Later 19*th Century (Cambridge: Cambridge University Press, 1968), chapter 1. Marxist historians of India, on the other hand, typically emptied religion of all its specific content by assigning to its core a secular rationality. See Guha's essay "The Prose of Counter-Insurgency" in Ranajit Guha and Gayatri Chakravorty Spivak, eds., *Selected Subaltern Studies* (New York: Oxford University Press, 1988), pp. 45–86.

45. Talal Asad's *Genealogies of Religion: Discipline and Reason of Power in Christianity and Islam* (Baltimore and London: Johns Hopkins University Press, 1993) contains many perceptive remarks on the secularized life of Christianity in Western democracies.

46. With its many limitations, this was one of the arguments attempted in my book *Rethinking Working-Class History: Bengal 1890–1940* (Princeton: Princeton University Press, 1989).

47. Ranajit Guha, "On Some Aspects of Indian Historiography," in Guha and Spivak, eds., *Selected Subaltern Studies*, p. 4.

48. Ibid., pp. 5–6.

49. This is how Indian nationalist leaders such as Jawaharlal Nehru argued in the 1930s. See Jawaharlal Nehru, *India's Freedom* (London: Allen and Unwin, 1962), p. 66. Bipan Chandra reproduces a similar argument in his *Nationalism and Colonialism in Modern India* (Delhi: Orient Longman, 1979), p. 135.

50. Ranajit Guha, "Colonialism in South Asia: A Dominance without Hegemony and Its Historiography," in his *Dominance without Hegemony: History and Power in Colonial India* (Cambridge: Harvard University Press, 1997), pp. 97–98.

51. I say the "the *question* of being human" because this question, as we know from Heidegger, could only ever be asked as a question and not posed as an answer. Any attempted answer based on the positive sciences would end up dissolving the category "human." See the section entitled "How the Analytic of Dasein Is to Be Distinguished from Anthropology, Psychology and Biology," in Martin Heidegger, *Being and Time*, translated by John Macquarrie and Edward Robinson (Oxford: Basil Blackwell, 1985), pp. 71–75.

52. Ramachandra Gandhi, *The Availability of Religious Ideas* (London: Macmillan, 1976), p. 9.

53. Leela Gandhi, *Postcolonial Theory: An Introduction* (Sydney: Allen and Unwin, 1998), p. x.

54. For Spanish mediation of European thought in Latin America, see Walter Mignolo, *The Darker Side of the Renaissance: Literacy, Territoriality, and Colonization* (Ann Arbor: University of Michigan Press, 1995), and Fernando Coronil's

"Introduction" to Fernando Ortiz's *Cuban Counterpoint: Tobacco and Sugar* (Durham: Duke University Press, 1995), p. xix. For Latin American perspectives on postcolonial social sciences, see Fernando Coronil, *The Magical State: Nature, Money, and Modernity in Venezuela* (Chicago: University of Chicago Press, 1997); Sara Castro-Klaren, "Historiography on the Ground: The Toledo Circle and Guaman Poma" (unpublished); Peter Hulme, *Colonial Encounters: Europe and the Native Caribbean 1492–1797* (London and New York: Routledge, 1986) ; Enrique Dussel, "Eurocentrism and Modernity," *Boundary* 2 20, no. 3 (1993), pp. 65–76.

55. Xudong Zhang's *Chinese Modernism in the Era of Reforms* (Durham: Duke University Press, 1997), chapter 2, contains a lively discussion of the disputed status of postcolonial studies among China scholars. See also his "Nationalism, Mass Culture, and Intellectual Strategies in Post-Tiananmen China," *Social Text*, 6, no. 2 (Summer 1998), pp. 109–140. Rey Chow's writings, significantly, mark a somewhat different trajectory. See her *Women and Chinese Modernity: The Politics of Reading between East and West* (Minneapolis: University of Minnesota Press, 1991).

56. See, for example, Stefan Tanaka, *Japan's Orient: Rendering Pasts into History* (Berkeley and Los Angeles: University of California Press, 1993), chapter 1; Vincente L. Rafael, *Contracting Colonialism: Translation and Christian Conversion in Tagalog Society under Early Colonial Rule* (Durham: Duke University Press, 1993); Tessa Morris-Suzuki, *Re-inventing Japan: Time, Space, Nation* (New York and London: M. E. Sharpe, 1998), chapter 7; Ann Stoler, *Capitalism and Confrontation in Sumatra's Plantation Belt, 1870–1979* (Ann Arbor: University of Michigan Press, 1995), see in particular Stoler's new "Preface"; idem., *Race and the Education of Desire: Foucault's "History of Sexuality" and the Colonial Order of Things* (Durham: Duke University Press, 1995); V. Y. Mudimbe, *The Idea of Africa* (Bloomington and London: Indiana University Press and James Currey, 1994). Naoki Sakai's work would clearly belong to this list, and I myself have attempted to raise the question of non-Eurocentric history in Japan's case in my brief "Afterword" to Stephen Vlastos, ed., *Mirror of Modernity: Invented Traditions of Modern Japan* (Berkeley and Los Angeles: University of California Press, 1998), pp. 285–296.

57. As Meaghan Morris has said with great clarity in her "Foreword" to Naoki Sakai, *Translation and Subjectivity: On "Japan" and Cultural Nationalism* (Minneapolis: University of Minnesota Press, 1997), p. xiii: "Sakai clearly shares with other theorists a conception of translation as a practice producing difference out of incommensurability (rather than equivalence out of difference)." See also Gayatri Chakravorty Spivak, "The Politics of Translation" in her *Outside in the Teaching Machine* (London and New York: Routledge, 1993), pp. 179–200; Vincente L. Rafael, *Contracting Colonialism*, chapter 1, "The Politics of Translation"; Talal Asad, "The Concept of Cultural Translation in British Anthropology," in his *Genealogies of Religion*, pp. 171–199; Homi K. Bhabha, "How New-

ness Enters the World: Postmodern Space, Postcolonial Times and the Trials of Cultural Translation," in his *The Location of Culture*, pp. 212–235.

58. I am grateful to Homi Bhabha for this expression. The relationship between the analytic and the hermeneutic traditions receives clear discussion in Richard E. Palmer, *Hermeneutics: Interpretation Theory in Schleirmacher, Dilthey, Heidegger and Gadamer* (Evanston: Northwestern University Press, 1969). One cannot, however, be dogmatic about this division.

59. "Postcoloniality and the Artifice of History: Who Speaks for "Indian" Pasts?" *Representations* 37 (Winter 1992), pp. 1–26.

60. Friedrich Nietzsche, "On the Uses and Disadvantages of History for Life" (1874) in his *Untimely Meditations*, translated by R. J. Hollingdale (Cambridge: Cambridge University Press, 1989), pp. 57–123.

61. See the discussion in my essay, "Reconstructing Liberalism? Notes toward a Conversation between Area Studies and Diasporic Studies," *Public Culture* 10, no. 3 (Spring 1998), pp. 457–481.

62. J. H. Broomfield, "The Forgotten Majority: The Bengal Muslims and September 1918," in D. A. Low ed., *Soundings in Modern South Asian History* (London: Weidenfeld and Nicolson, 1968), pp. 196–224.

63. See H. Aram Veeser, ed., *The New Historicism Reader* (New York and London: Routledge, 1994).

64. See Georg G. Iggers, *The German Conception of History: The National Tradition of Historical Thought from Herder to the Present* (Hanover, N. H.: University Press of New England, 1983).

65. Ian Hacking, "Two Kinds of 'New Historicism' for Philosophers," in Ralph Cohen and Michael S. Roth eds., *History and . . . Historians within the Human Sciences* (Charlottesville and London: University of Virginia Press, 1995), p. 298.

66. Maurice Mandelbaum, *History, Man and Reason* (Baltimore, 1971), p. 42 quoted in F. R. Ankersmit, "Historicism: An Attempt at Synthesis," *History and Theory* 36 (October 1995), pp. 143–161.

67. I depend here on Ankersmit, "Historicism"; Friederich Meinecke, *Historism: The Rise of a New Historical Outlook*, translated by J. E. Anderson (London: Routledge and Kegan Paul, 1972); Hayden White, *Metahistory: The Historical Imagination in Nineteenth-Century Europe* (Baltimore: Johns Hopkins University Press, 1985), and "Droysen's *Historik*: Historical Writing as a Bourgeois Science" in his *The Content of the Form: Narrative Discourse and Historical Representation* (Baltimore: Johns Hopkins University Press, 1990), pp. 83–103; Leopold von Ranke, "Preface: *Histories of Romance and Germanic Peoples*," and "A Fragment from the 1830s" in Fritz Stern, ed., *The Varieties of History: From Voltaire to the Present* (New York: Meridian Books, 1957), pp. 55–60; Hans Meyerhoff, ed., *The Philosophy of History in Our Own Time: An Anthology* (New York: Doubleday Anchor Books, 1959), see "Introduction," pp. 1–24 and the section entitled "The Heritage of Historicism"; and Paul Hamilton, *Historicism* (London

and New York: Routledge, 1996). James Chandler's discussion of historicism in *England in 1819* is enormously helpful. I choose not to discuss Karl Popper's formulations on "historicism," as his use of the term has been acknowledged to be idiosyncratic.

68. "History is the subject of a structure whose site is not homogeneous, empty time, but time filled by the presence of the now." Walter Benjamin, "Theses on the Philosophy of History" in his *Illuminations*, translated by Harry Zohn (New York: Fontana/Collins, 1982), p. 263. For a critique of Benjamin in terms of his failure to acknowledge why chronologies retain their significance for historians, see Siegfried Kracauer, *History: The Last Things before the Last* (Princeton: Markus Wiener, 1995), chapter 6 in particular.

Chapter 1
Postcoloniality and the Artifice of History

1. Ronald Inden, "Orientalist Constructions of India," *Modern Asian Studies* 20, no. 3 (1986), p. 445.

2. I am indebted to Jean Baudrillard fot the term "hyperreal" but my use differs from his. See his *Simulations*, translated by Paul Foss, Paul Patton, and Philip Batchman (New York: Semiotext[e], 1983).

3. Linda Hutcheon, *The Politics of Postmodernism* (London: Routledge, 1989), p. 65.

4. Edmund Husserl, *The Crisis of European Sciences and Transcendental Philosophy*, translated by David Carr (Evanston: Northwestern University Press, 1970), pp. 281–285. See also Wilhelm Halbfass, *India and Europe: An Essay in Understanding* (New York: State University of New York Press, 1988), pp. 167–168.

5. See the discussion in Karl Marx, *Grundrisse: Foundations of the Critique of Political Economy*, translated by Martin Nicholas (Harmondsworth: Penguin, 1973), pp. 469–512, and in Karl Marx, *Capital: A Critique of Political Economy*, vol. 3 (Moscow: Foreign Languages Publishing House, 1971), pp. 593–613.

6. See my *Rethinking Working-Class History: Bengal 1890–1940* (Princeton; Princeton University Press, 1989), chapter 7.

7. Marx, *Capital*, vol. 1 (Moscow: Foreign Languages Publishing House, n.d.), p. 60.

8. *Grundrisse*, p. 105.

9. See *Rethinking Working-Class History*, chapter 7 in particular.

10. Sumit Sarkar, *Modern India 1885–1947* (Delhi: Macmillan, 1985), p. 1.

11. Ibid., p. 4.

12. Ranajit Guha and Gayatri Chakravorty Spivak, eds., *Selected Subaltern Studies* (New York: Oxford University Press 1988), p. 43, emphasis added. The words quoted here are Guha's. But I think they represent a sense of historio-

graphical responsibility that is shared by all the members of the Subaltern Studies collective.

13. See L. T. Hobhouse, *Liberalism* (New York: Oxford University Press, 1964), pp. 26–27.

14. Nirad C. Chaudhuri, *The Autobiography of an Unknown Indian* (Berkeley and Los Angeles: University of California Press, 1968 [1951]), dedication page.

15. Partha Chatterjee, *Nationalist Thought and the Colonial World: A Derivative Discourse?* (London: Zed, 1986).

16. *Madhusudan rachanabali* (in Bengali), (Calcutta: Sahitya Samsad, 1965), p. 449. See also Jogindranath Basu, *Michael Madhusudan Datter Jibancharit* (in Bengali) (Calcutta: Ashok Pustakalay, 1978), p. 86.

17. My understanding of this poem has been enriched by discussions with Marjorie Levinson and David Bennett.

18. I am not making the claim that all of these genres necessarily emerge with bourgeois individualism. See Natalie Zemon Davis,"Fame and Secrecy: Leon Modena's *Life* as an Early Modern Autobiography," *History and Theory* 27 (1988), pp. 103–118, and "Boundaries and Sense of Self in Sixteenth-Century France," in Thomas C. Heller et al., eds., *Reconstructing Individualism: Autonomy, Individuality, and the Self in Western Thought* (Stanford: Stanford University Press, 1986), pp. 53–63. See also Philippe Lejeune, *On Autobiography*, translated by Katherine Leary (Minneapolis: University of Minnesota Press, 1989), pp. 163–184.

19. See Chatterjee, *Nationalist Thought*, chapter on Nehru.

20. M. K. Gandhi, *Hind Swaraj* (1909) in *Collected Works of Mahatma Gandhi*, vol. 10 (New Delhi: Publications Division, Ministry of Information and Broadcasting, Government of India, 1963), p. 15.

21. See the discussion in Gauri Viswanathan, *Masks of Conquest: Literary Studies and British Rule in India* (New York: Columbia University Press, 1989), pp. 128–141.

22. Ranajit Guha, *Elementary Aspects of Peasant Insurgency in Colonial India* (Delhi: Oxford University Press, 1983), chapter 2.

23. William E. Connolly, *Political Theory and Modernity* (Oxford and New York: Basil Blackwell, 1989).

24. Jurgen Habermas, *The Structural Transformation of the Public Sphere: An Inquiry into a Category of Bourgeois Society*, translated by Thomas Burger and Frederick Lawrence (Cambridge: MIT Press, 1989), p. 49.

25. See Sumit Sarkar, "Social History: Predicament and Possibilities," in Iqbal Khan, ed., *Fresh Perspective on India and Pakistan: Essays on Economics, Politics and Culture* (Lahore: Book Traders, 1987), pp. 256–274.

26. For reasons of space, I shall leave this claim here unsubstantiated, though I hope to have an opportunity to discuss it in detail elsewhere. I should qualify the statement by mentioning that it refers in the main to autobiographies published

between 1850 and 1910. Once women join the public sphere in the twentieth century, their self-fashioning takes on different dimensions.

27. Nirad C. Chaudhuri, *Thy Hand, Great Anarch! India 1921–1952* (London: Chatto and Windus, 1987), pp. 350–351.

28. See Marx, *On the Jewish Question* in his *Early Writings* (Harmondsworth: Penguin, 1975), pp. 215–222.

29. Ramabai Ranade, *Ranade: His Wife's Reminiscences*, translated by Kusumavati Deshpande (Delhi: Publications Division, Ministry of Information and Broadcasting, Government of India, 1963), p. 77.

30. Ibid., pp. 84–85.

31. Meaghan Morris, "Metamorphoses at Sydney Tower," *New Formations*, 11 (Summer 1990), p. 10. Emphasis in original.

32. Amiya Chakravarty quoted in Bhikhu Parekh, *Gandhi's Political Discourse* (London: Macmillan, 1989), p. 163.

33. Gayatri Chakravorty Spivak, "Can the Subaltern Speak?" in Cathy Nelson and Lawrence Grossberg, eds., *Marxism and the Interpretation of Culture* (Urbana and Chicago: University of Illinois Press, 1988), p. 277.

34. See *Subaltern Studies*, vols. 1–7 (Delhi: Oxford University Press, 1982–1991), and Ashis Nandy, *The Intimate Enemy: Loss and Recovery of Self under Colonialism* (Delhi: Oxford University Press, 1983).

35. See various essays in *Subaltern Studies* and Ranajit Guha, *Elementary Aspects*.

36. Homi K. Bhabha, "Of Mimicry and Man: The Ambivalence of Colonial Discourse," in Annette Michelson, et al., eds., *October: The First Decade 1976–1986* (Cambridge: MIT Press, 1987), pp. 317–326; also Homi K. Bhabha, ed., *Nation and Narration* (London: Routledge, 1990).

37. Spivak, "Can the Subaltern Speak?" Also see Spivak's interview published in *Socialist Review* 20, no. 3 July-September 1990.

38. On the close connection between imperialist ideologies and the teaching of history in colonial India, see Ranajit Guha, *An Indian Historiography of India: A Nineteenth-Century Agenda and Its Implications* (Calcutta: K. P. Bagchi, 1988).

39. Without in any way implicating them in the entirety of this argument, I may mention that there are parallels here between my statement and what Gyan Prakash and Nicholas Dirks have argued elsewhere. See Gyan Prakash, "Writing Post-Orientalist Histories of the Third World: Perspectives from Indian Historiography," *Comparative Studies in Society and History* 32, no. 2 (April 1990), pp. 383–408; Nicholas B. Dirks, "History as a Sign of the Modern," *Public Culture* 2, no. 2 (Spring 1990) pp. 25–33.

40. See Amartya Kumar Sen, *Of Ethics and Economics* (Oxford and New York: Basil Blackwell, 1987). Tessa Morris-Suzuki's *A History of Japanese Economic Thought* (London: Routledge, 1989) makes interesting reading in this regard. I am grateful to Gavan McCormack for bringing this book to my attention.

41. Carole Pateman, *The Sexual Contract* (Stanford: Stanford University Press, 1988), p. 184.

42. Fredric Jameson, "Cognitive Mapping," in Nelson and Grossberg, eds., *Marxism and the Interpretation of Culture*, p. 354.

43. David Arnold, "The Colonial Prison: Power, Knowledge, and Penology in Nineteenth-Century India," in D. Arnold and D. Hardiman, eds., *Subaltern Studies* 8 (Delhi: Oxford University Press, 1995). I have discussed some of these issues in a Bengali article: "Sarir, samaj o rashtra—oupanibeshik bharate mahamari o janasangskriti," *Anustup*, annual no. (1988).

44. Lawrence Brilliant with Girija Brilliant, "Death for a Killer Disease," *Quest*, May/June 1978, p. 3. I owe this reference to Paul Greenough.

45. Richard Rorty, "Habermas and Lyotard on Postmodernity," in Richard J. Bernstein, ed., *Habermas and Modernity* (Cambridge: MIT Press, 1986), p. 169.

46. For an interesting and revisionist reading of Hegel in this regard see the exchange between Charles Taylor and Partha Chatterjee in *Public Culture* 3, no. 1 (1990). My book *Rethinking Working-Class History* attempts a small beginning in this direction

Chapter 2
The Two Histories of Capital

1. This chapter is concerned with the production—and not the circulation—side of capital. I concentrate mostly on *Capital*, vol. 1, the *Grundrisse*, and sections of *Theories of Surplus Value*. Considerations from the circulation side should not contradict my basic argument.

2. See my "Marxism and Modern India," in Alan Ryan, ed., *After the End of History* (London: Collins and Brown, 1992), pp. 79–84.

3. E. P. Thompson, "Time, Work-Discipline and Industrial Capitalism," in M. W. Flinn and T. C. Smout, eds., *Essays in Social History* (Oxford: Clarendon, 1974), pp. 66, 61.

4. *Wall Street Journal*, 11 October 1996. Thanks to Dipankar Chakravarti for drawing my attention to this article.

5. Ibid.

6. Sasthi Brata, *India: Labyrinths in the Lotus Land* (New York: William Morrow, 1985), p. 21, cited in S. N. Balagandhara, *"The Heathen in His Blindness": Asia, the West and Dynamic of Religion* (Leiden: E. J. Brill, 1994), p. 21. I have discussed this trope and its use by the Indian Marxist historian D. D. Kosambi in my essay in Bengali, "Bharatbarsher adhunikatar itihash o shomoy-kalpana," *Aitihashik* 6, no. 2 (September 1997), pp. 121–128.

7. For Marx's idea regarding real and formal subsumption of labor under capital, see his "Results of the Immediate Process of Production," Appendix to Karl Marx, *Capital: A Critique of Political Economy*, vol.1 [hereafter *Capital* I], translated by Ben Fowkes (Harmondsworth: Penguin, 1990), pp. 1,019–1,049.

8. My book *Rethinking Working-Class History: Bengal 1890–1940* (Princeton: Princeton University Press, 1989), discusses this proposition and takes it as its foundational gesture.

9. Aristotle, *Nichomachean Ethics*, translated by Martin Ostwald (Indianapolis: Liberal Arts Press, 1981), Book 5, pp. 125–127.

10. Ibid., p. 125.

11. Ibid., p. 126; see Cornelius Castoriadis, "Value, Equality, Justice, and Politics: From Marx to Aristotle and from Aristotle to Ourselves," in his *Crossroads in the Labyrinth*, translated by Kate Soper and Martin H. Ryle (Cambridge: MIT Press, 1984), pp. 260–339, and in particular pp. 282–311.

12. Aristotle, *Nichomachean Ethics*, p. 126n35.

13. Marx, *Capital* I, p. 151.

14. Ibid., p. 152

15. Karl Marx, *Grundrisse: Foundations of the Critique of Political Economy*, translated by Martin Nicholas (Harmondsworth: Penguin, 1973), p. 105.

16. *Capital* I, p. 134.

17. Ibid., p. 137.

18. I. I. Rubin, *Essays on Marx's Theory of Value*, translated by Milos Samardźija and Fredy Perlman (Montreal: Black Rose Books, 1975 [1928]), pp. 131–138; Moishe Postone, *Time, Labor, and Social Domination: A Reinterpretation of Marx's Social Theory* (Cambridge: Cambridge University Press, 1993), pp. 144–146; Castoriadis, "Value, Equality, Justice, and Politics," pp. 307–308; Jon Elster, *An Introduction to Karl Marx* (Cambridge: Cambridge University Press, 1995), chapter 4 rejects Marx's labor theory of value as unobjective and Hegelian (see p. 68 in particular).

19. *Capital* I, p. 128. Emphasis added.

20. Ibid., pp. 139, 165.

21. *Grundrisse*, p. 104

22. Ibid., pp. 104–105.

23. *Capital* I, p. 128. Emphasis added.

24. Ibid., pp. 166–167.

25. Cf. Ronald L. Meek, *Studies in the Labour Theory of Value* (London: Lawrence and Wishart, 1979), p. 168: "The 'averaging' process, Marx's argument implies, takes place in history before it takes place in the minds of economists."

26. Castoriadis, "Value, Equality, Justice, and Politics," pp. 328–329: "to propose another institution of society is a matter of a political project and political aim, which are certainly subject to discussion and argument, but cannot be 'founded' in any kind of Nature or Reason. . . . Men are born neither free nor unfree, neither equal nor unequal. *We will them to be* (we will ourselves to be) free and equal." Emphasis in original.

27. *Capital* I, p. 465.

28. Ibid., p. 550.

29. Ibid., p. 635.

30. Ibid., pp. 342–343.

31. This is reminiscent of Lukács's contention that "class consciousness" was not a category that referred to what actually went on inside the heads of individual, empirical workers. Georg Lukács, "Class Consciousness," and "Reification and the Consciousness of the Proletariat," in his *History and Class Consciousness*, translated by Rodney Livingstone (London: Merlin Press, 1971), pp. 51, 197. David Harvey, *The Limits of Capital* (Oxford: Basil Blackwell, 1984), p. 114, writes: "[T]he duality of worker as 'object for capital' and as 'living creative subject' has never been adequately resolved in Marxist theory." I have criticisms of Harvey's reading of Marx on this point—one could argue, for instance, that for Marx, the worker could never be a thing-like "object for capital" (see below)—but Harvey's statement has the merit of recognizing a real problem in Marxist histories of "consciousness."

32. Spivak, "Can the Subaltern Speak?" in Cathy Nelson and Lawrence Grossberg, eds., *Marxism and the Interpretation of Culture* (Urbana and Chicago: University of Illinois Press, 1988), p. 277. The opposition of class-in-itself and class-for-itself, Spivak clarifies, does not define a program of "an ideological transformation of consciousness on the ground level."

33. *Capital* I, p. 468

34. Ibid, p. 549. See also p. 535. Sometimes Marx's examples allow us tantalizing glimpses of how one might construct a possible history of the modern machine incorporating into itself the live, physical, and animate body. "[B]efore the invention of the present locomotive," writes Marx, "an attempt was made to construct a locomotive with two feet, which it raised from the ground alternately, like a horse. It is only after a considerable development of the science of mechanics, and an accumulation of practical experience, that the form of a machine becomes settled entirely in accordance with mechanical principles, and emancipated from the traditional form of the tool from which it has emerged." *Capital* I, p. 505n18.

35. *Grundrisse*, p. 704.

36. *Capital* I, p. 504.

37. Ibid., p. 497.

38. *Capital* I, pp. 517, 526, 546, 547, 518n39.

39. Ibid., p. 395.

40. Ibid., pp. 489–490.

41. *Grundrisse*, p. 410. Emphasis added.

42. *Capital* I, pp. 549–550.

43. Ibid., p. 450. Michel Foucault, *Discipline and Punish: The Birth of the Prison*, translated by Alan Sheridan (Harmondsworth: Penguin, 1979), p. 163, comments on these military analogies in Marx. But whereas disciplinary power, for Foucault, creates "the docile body," Marx posits the living body as a source of resistance to discipline.

44. *Grundrisse*, p. 548. Emphasis added.

45. Ibid., p. 296. This is why Harvey's contention that Marx's "theory shows that, from the standpoint of capital, workers are indeed objects, a mere 'factor' of production . . . for the creation of surplus value" seems mistaken to me; Harvey, *Limits*, p. 113. The worker is a reified category, but the reification includes an irreducible element of life and (human) consciousness.

46. *Grundrisse*, p. 298. Emphasis added.

47. Ibid., pp. 703–704.

48. Ibid., pp. 298, 323.

49. *Hegel's Logic*, translated by William Wallace (Oxford: Clarendon Press, 1975), p. 280 (Article 216, additions).

50. Charles Taylor, *Hegel* (Cambridge: Cambridge University Press, 1978), p. 332.

51. See *Hegel's Logic*, p. 281 (Article 219, addition). I prefer Taylor's translation of this passage to that of Wallace.

52. *Grundrisse*, pp. 500–501.

53. Ibid., p. 701.

54. The quotations in this paragraph are from ibid., pp. 700, 705, 706.

55. Ibid., pp. 460, 461; see also pp. 471–472, 488–489, 505.

56. Ibid., p. 459. Nothing in this sense is inherently "precapitalist." Precapitalist could only be a designation used from the perspective of capital.

57. Ibid., p. 459. Emphasis in original.

58. Karl Marx, *Theories of Surplus Value*, vol. 3 (Moscow: Progress Publishers, 1978), p. 491. Emphasis in original. See also *Grundrisse*, p. 105.

59. *Theories of Surplus Value*, 3, p. 491.

60. Ibid., p. 468.

61. Marx, *Capital* I, Preface to the First Edition: "for bourgeois society, the commodity-form of the product of labour, or the value-form of the commodity, is the economic cell-form" (p. 90).

62. *Theories of Surplus Value*, 3, p. 468.

63. *Grundrisse*, pp. 105–106.

64. *Grundrisse*, p. 459.

65. Ibid., p. 410.

66. Max Horkheimer, "The Concept of Man," in his *Critique of Instrumental Reason*, translated by Matthew J O'Connell et al. (New York: Continuum, 1994), p. 22.

67. Marxist arguments have often in the past looked on advertising as merely an instance of the "irrationality" and "waste" inherent in the capitalist mode of production. See Raymond Williams, "Advertising: The Magic System," in Simon During, ed., *The Cultural Studies Reader* (London and New York: Routledge, 1993), pp. 320–326.

68. The excellent discussion of "use value" in Roman Rosdolsky, *The Making of Marx's "Capital,"* translated by Pete Burgess (London: Pluto Press, 1977), pp. 73–95 helps us appreciate how, as a category, "use value" moves in and out of

Marx's political-economic analysis. Spivak puts it even more strongly by saying that as a category of political economy, use value can appear "only *after* the appearance of the exchange relation." Gayatri Chakravorty Spivak, "Limits and Openings of Marx in Derrida," in her *Outside in the Teaching Machine* (London and New York: Routledge, 1993), p. 106. Spivak categorically states, rightly I think, that "Marx left the slippery concept of 'use value' untheorized" (p. 97). My point is that Marx's thoughts on use value do not turn toward the question of human belonging or "worlding," for Marx retains a subject-object relationship between man and nature. Nature never escapes its "thingly" character in Marx's analysis.

69. As Marx defines it in the course of discussing Adam Smith's use of the category "productive labor," "only labour which produces capital is productive labour." Unproductive labor is that "which is not exchanged with capital but *directly* with revenue." He further explains: "An actor, for example, or even a clown, . . . is a productive labourer if he works in the service of a capitalist." Marx, *Theories of Surplus Value*, vol. 1 (Moscow: Progress Publishers, 1969), pp. 156–157.

70. *Grundrisse*, p. 305. Emphasis in original.

71. Martin Heidegger, *Being and Time*, translated by John Macquarrie and Edward Robinson (Oxford: Basil Blackwell, 1985), division I, chapter 3, "The Worldhood of the World," explains these terms. The more recent translation by Joan Stambaugh (*Being and Time* [Albany: State University of New York Press, 1996]) replaces "ready-to-hand" with "handiness" and "present-at-hand" with the expression "objectively present" (pp. 64, 69).

72. See the classic study on this theme, Syed Hussein Alatas, *The Myth of the Lazy Native: A Study of the Image of Malays, Filipinos, and Javanese from the Sixteenth to the Twentieth Centuries and Its Function in the Ideology of Colonial Capitalism* (London: Frank Cass, 1977). The theme of laziness, however, is a permanent theme within any capitalist structure, national or global. What would repay examination is the business (and business-school) literature on "motivation" in showing how much and how incessantly business wrestles with an unsolvable question: What motivates humans to "work"?

Chapter 3
Translating Life-Worlds into Labor and History

1. J.B.S. Haldane, *Everything Has a History* (London: Allen and Unwin, 1951).

2. See Peter Burke, *The Renaissance Sense of the Past* (London: Edward Arnold, 1970); E. H. Carr's classic *What Is History?* (Harmondsworth: Penguin, 1970) is a discussion of how the genre had changed in Carr's own lifetime; R. G. Collingwood's *The Idea of History* (Oxford: Oxford University Press, 1976; first pub. 1936) distinguishes "the modern European idea of history" from other his-

torical sensibilities or the lack thereof; Marc Bloch in his *The Historian's Craft* (Manchester: University of Manchester Press, 1984; first pub. 1954) relates the historian's method to the modern "method of doubt." Fernand Braudel, *On History*, translated by Sarah Matthews (Chicago: University of Chicago Press, 1980) describes "history" as making up "one single intellectual adventure" in partnership with sociology (p. 69); J.G.A. Pocock's *The Ancient Constitution and the Feudal Law* (Cambridge: Cambridge University Press, 1990; first pub. 1957) gives the modern historical method a specific origin in seventeenth-century juridical thought.

3. An exception is Giorgio Agamben's essay, "Time and History: Critique of the Instant and the Continuum," in his *Infancy and History: Essays on the Destruction of Experience*, translated by Liz Heron (London and New York: Verso, 1993), pp. 89–108.

4. Paul Davis and John Gribbin, *The Matter Myth: Beyond Chaos and Complexity* (Harmondsworth: Penguin, 1992), pp. 103–104.

5. Joyce Appleby, Lynn Hunt, and Margaret Jacobs, *Telling the Truth about History* (New York: Norton, 1994).

6. D. H. Buchanan, *The Development of Capitalist Enterprise in India* (New York, 1934), p. 409, quoted in Chakrabarty, *Rethinking Working-Class History: Bengal 1890–1940* (Princeton: Princeton University Press, 1989), pp. 89–90.

7. For an analysis and description of this festival in its present-day form, see Leela Fernandes, *Producing Workers: The Politics of Gender, Class and Culture in the Calcutta Jute Mills* (Philadephia: University of Pennsylvania Press, 1997).

8. Slavoj Žižek, *The Sublime Object of Ideology* (London and New York: Verso, 1989), pp. 30–34.

9. Gyanendra Pandey, *The Construction of Communalism in North India* (Delhi: Oxford University Press, 1992).

10. Ibid., pp. 71, 74; E. P. Thompson, *The Making of the English Working Class* (Harmondsworth: Penguin, 1968), p. 297.

11. Ibid., pp. 99, 102.

12. See Thompson, *Making*, pp. 302, 303, 305.

13. Ibid., pp. 305, 323.

14. Pandey, *Communalism*, pp. 88, 97–98. Also Deepak Mehta, "The Semiotics of Weaving: A Case Study," *Contributions to Indian Sociology* 26, no. 1 (January-June 1992), pp. 77–113.

15. Pandey, *Communalism*, pp. 98–99.

16. Ibid., p. 97.

17. Richard Maxwell Eaton, *Sufis of Bijapur 1300–1700: Social Role of Sufis in Medieval India* (Princeton: Princeton University Press, 1978).

18. Ibid., p. 161.

19. Ibid., pp. 163–164.

20. Gyan Prakash, *Bonded Histories: Genealogies of Labor Servitude in Colonial India* (Cambridge: Cambridge University Press, 1990), p. 216.

21. Paul Veyne, *Writing History: Essay on Epistemology*, translated by Mina Moore-Rinvolucri (Middletown, Conn.: Wesleyan University Press, 1984), p. 56.

22. This translation is by Dinesh Chandra Sen. See his *History of Bengali Language and Literature* (Calcutta: Calcutta University Press, 1911), pp. 36–37. The passage is also discussed in Sukumar Sen, *Bangala sahityer itihas* (in Bengali), vol. 1 (Calcutta: Ananda Publishers, 1991), pp. 114–116, and in Gautam Bhadra, "The Mentality of Subalternity: *Kantanama* or *Rajadharma*," in Ranajit Guha, ed., *Subaltern Studies: Writings on South Asian History and Society* (Delhi: Oxford University Press, 1994), pp. 54–91.

23. Richard M. Eaton, *The Rise of Islam and the Bengal Frontier, 1204–1760* (Berkeley and Los Angeles: University of California Press, 1993), p. 275.

24. Ibid., p. 276.

25. Carl W. Ernst, *Eternal Garden: Mysticism, History and Politics at a South Asian Sufi Center* (New York: State University of New York Press, 1992), p. 52.

26. Bhadra, "Mentality," p. 65.

27. Ernst, *Eternal Garden*, pp. 32–33.

28. See the discussion in the preceding chapter.

29. Eaton, *Rise of Islam*, p. 305.

30. Simon During, "Is Literature Dead or Has It Gone to the Movies?" *Age* (Melbourne), 19 June 1993.

31. See Ranajit Guha, "The Migrant's Time," *Postcolonial Studies* 1, no. 2 (July 1998).

32. Jean-François Lyotard, *The Postmodern Condition*, translated by Geoff Bennington and Brian Massumi (Manchester: Manchester University Press, 1984), pp. 31–37.

33. See Gayatri Chakravorty Spivak, "Politics of Translation," in her *Outside in the Teaching Machine* (New York and London: Routledge, 1993), p. 182, and the chapter entitled "Untranslatability and the Terms of Reciprocity" in Vincente L. Rafael, *Contracting Colonialism: Translation and Christian Conversion in Tagalog Society under Early Spanish Rule* (Durham: Duke University Press, 1993), pp. 110–135.

34. Spivak, "Politics of Translation," p. 182.

35. Michael Gelven, *A Commentary on Heidegger's "Being and Time"* (De Kalb: Northern Illinois University Press, 1989), p. 41.

36. The phrase is Benjamin's. See "Theses on the Philosophy of History," in Walter Benjamin, *Illuminations*, translated by Harry Zohn (New York: Fontana, 1982), p. 265.

37. Drucilla Cornell, *The Philosophy of the Limit* (New York and London: Routledge, 1992), pp. 72–77, discusses the idea of the "trace."

38. Michel Henry, *Marx: A Philosophy of Human Reality* (Bloomington: Indiana University Press, 1983), and I. I. Rubin, *Essays on Marx's Theory of Value* (Montreal: Black Rose Books, 1975).

39. Chakrabarty, *Rethinking Working-Class History*, pp. 225–226.

40. Michael T. Taussig, *The Devil and Commodity Fetishism in South America* (Chapel Hill: University of North Carolina Press, 1984).

41. See Michel Foucault, "Governmentality," in Graham Burchell, Colin Gordon, and Peter Miller, eds., *The Foucault Effect: Studies in Governmentality* (London: Wheatsheaf, 1991), pp. 87–104.

Chapter 4
Minority Histories, Subaltern Pasts

1. Eric Hobsbawm, "Identity History Is Not Enough" in his *On History* (London: Weikenfeld and Nicholson, 1997), p. 277. Hobsbawm unfortunately overlooks the point that modern European imperialism in India and elsewhere used "good history" to justify the subjugation of peoples who, according to European thinkers, had "myths" but no sense of history.

2. Joyce Appleby, Lynn Hunt, and Margaret Jacob, *Telling the Truth about History* (New York: W. W. Norton, 1994).

3. Cf. Georg G. Iggers, *Historiography in the Twentieth Century: From Scientific Objectivity to the Postmodern Challenge* (Hanover, N. H., and London: Wesleyan University Press, 1997), p. 145. Emphasis added.

4. Hobsbawm, "Identity History," p. 271.

5. Immanuel Kant, "An Answer to the Question: What Is Enlightenment?" (1784) in Immanuel Kant, *Perpetual Peace and Other Essays*, translated by Ted Humphrey (Indianapolis: Hackett, 1983), pp. 41–48.

6. See David Lloyd, *Nationalism and Minor Literature: James Clarence Mangan and the Emergence of Irish Cultural Nationalism* (Berkeley and Los Angeles: University of California Press, 1987), pp. 19–20. Also Gilles Delueze and Felix Guattari, *Kafka: Toward a Minor Literature*, translated by Dana Polan (Minneapolis: University of Minnesota Press, 1986), chapter 3.

7. See also Gyan Prakash, "Subaltern Studies as Postcolonial Criticism," *American Historical Review* 99 no. 5 (December 1994), pp. 1,475–1,491.

8. Ranajit Guha, "The Prose of Counter-Insurgency," in Ranajit Guha and Gayatri Chakravorty Spivak eds., *Selected Subaltern Studies* (New York: Oxford University Press, 1988), pp. 46–47.

9. Ibid., p. 80.

10. Ibid., p. 78.

11. Rudolf Bultmann, "Is Exegesis without Presuppositions Possible?" in Kurt Mueller-Vollmer, ed., *The Hermeneutics Reader: Texts of the German Tradition from the Enlightenment to the Present* (New York: Continuum, 1985), p. 244.

12. Guha and Spivak, eds., *Selected Subaltern Studies*, p. 78.

13. Shahid Amin, *Events, Memory, Metaphor* (Berkeley and Los Angeles: University of California Press, 1995).

14. Greg Dening, "A Poetic for Histories," in his *Performances* (Melbourne: Melbourne University Press, 1996), pp. 35–63; David Cohen, *The Combing of*

History (Chicago: University of Chicago Press, 1994); Ashis Nandy, "History's Forgotten Doubles," *History and Theory* 34 (1995), pp. 44–66; Klaus Neumann, *Not the Way It Really Was: Constructing Tolai Past* (Honolulu: University of Hawaii Press, 1992); Chris Healy, *From the Ruins of Colonialism: History as Social Memory* (Melbourne: Cambridge University Press, 1997); Stephen Muecke, "The Sacred in History," *Humanities Research* 1 (1999), pp. 27–37; Ann Curthoys and John Docker, "Time, Eternity, Truth, and Death: History as Allegory," *Humanities Research* 1 (1999), pp. 5–26.

15. The question of alternative pasts is highlighted in the following recent works in Indian history: Amin, *Events, Memory, Metaphor*; Ajay Skaria, *Hybrid Histories: Forests, Frontiers, and Wildness in Western India* (Delhi: Oxford University Press, 1999); and Saurabh Dube, *Untouchable Pasts: Religion, Identity, and Power among a Central Indian Community, 1780–1950* (Albany: State University of New York Press, 1998), chapters 5, 7, 8.

16. Hobsbawm, "Identity History," p. 272.

17. See Ashis Nandy's essay "From Outside the Imperium" in his *Traditions, Tyranny and Utopia: Essays in the Politics of Awareness* (Delhi: Oxford University Press, 1987), pp. 147–148, and my discussion in "The Modern Indian Intellectual and the Problem of the Past: An Engagement with the Thoughts of Ashis Nandy," in *Emergences* 7/8 (1995–96), special issue on Nandy, guest edited by Vinay Lal, pp. 168–177.

18. Soren Kierkegaard, *Fear and Trembling: Dialectical Lyric by Johannes de Silentio*, translated by Alastair Hannay (Harmondsworth: Penguin, 1985), p. 60.

19. Wilhelm von Humboldt, "On the Task of the Historian," in Mueller-Vollmer, ed., *The Hermeneutics Reader*, p. 112.

20. Peter Burke, "Editorial Preface" to Aron Gurevich, *Medieval Popular Culture: Problems of Belief and Perception*, translated by Janos M. Back and Paul A. Hollingsworth (Cambridge: Cambridge University Press, 1990), p. vii.

21. Jacques Le Goff, ed. *The Medieval World*, translated by Lydia G. Cochrane (London: Collins and Brown, 1990), pp. 28–29.

22. "Preface" to Fredric Jameson, *The Political Unconscious: Narrative as a Socially Symbolic Act* (Ithaca: Cornell University Press, 1981), p. 9.

23. See Jacques Derrida, *Specters of Marx: The State of the Debt, the Work of Mourning, and the New International*, translated by Peggy Kamuf (New York and London: Routledge, 1994).

24. In using the idea of "disenchantment" I do not deny what has been said about the "magic" of commodities or about the magical aspects of modernity itself. That the so-called moderns can be nonmodern as well is, of course, what I myself am arguing. For a critical discussion of "disenchantment," see Jacques Rancière, "The Archeomodern Turn," in Michael P. Steinberg, ed., *Walter Benjamin and the Demands of History* (Ithaca: Cornell University Press, 1996), pp. 24–40.

25. Personal communication from David Lloyd.

26. Robin Horton's illuminating studies of "African thought" define "religion" on the basis of this very European, perhaps Protestant, category, "belief." Robin Horton, *Patterns of Thought in Africa and the West* (Cambridge: Cambridge University Press, 1995).

27. Ranajit Guha reminded me of the Bengali word *shomoy-granthi*, literally, "time-knot."

28. Hans-Georg Gadamer, "Kant and the Hermeneutical Turn," in his *Heidegger's Ways*, translated by John W. Stanley (New York: State University of New York Press, 1994), p. 58. Emphasis in original.

Chapter 5
Domestic Cruelty and the Birth of the Subject

1. Kalyani Datta, "Baidhabya kahini" (Tales of Widowhood), *Ekshan* 20 (Autumn 1991); reprinted in Kalyani Datta, *Pinjare boshiya* (Calcutta: Stree, 1997).

2. Muhammad Abdul Jalil, *Madhyajuger bangla shahitye bangla o bangali shamaj* (Dhaka: Bangla Akademi, 1986), chapter 6, pp. 149–167.

3. The following recent writings study the problem of widowhood in colonial India: Lata Mani, *Contentious Traditions: The Debate on Sati in Colonial India, 1780–1833* (Berkeley and Los Angeles: University of California Press, 1998); Lucy Caroll, "Law, Custom and Statutory Social Reform: The Hindu Widows' Remarriage Act of 1856," *Indian Economic and Social History Review* 20, no. 4 (1983); Sudhir Chandra, "Conflicted Beliefs and Men's Consciousness about Women: Widow Remarriage in Later Nineteenth Century Indian Literature," *Economic and Political Weekly*, 31 October 1987, pp. 55–62; Rosalind O'Hanlon, "Issues of Widowhood: Gender and Resistance in Colonial Western India," in Douglas Haynes and Gyan Prakash, eds., *Contesting Power: Resistance and Everyday Social Relations in South Asia* (Delhi: Oxford University Press, 1981), pp. 62–108.

4. Rammohun Roy, "Brief Remarks Regarding Modern Encroachments on the Ancient Rights of Females," in Ajitkumar Ghosh, ed., *Rammohan rachanabali* (Calcutta: Haraf Prakashani, 1973), pp. 496–497.

5. Ibid., pp. 496–497, 500–501.

6. "Prabartak o nibartaker dvitiyo shombad," in *Rammohun rachanabali*, p. 203.

7. *Rammohan rachanabali*, p. 575. This is Rammohun's own translation of his 1818 text "sahamaran bishaye prabartak o nibartaker shombad," ibid., p. 175.

8. Ibid. Distinguishing between "custom" and "reason," Hume equated the former with "habit." David Hume, *Enquiries Concerning Human Understanding and Concerning the Principles of Morals* (1777), introduction by L. A. Sigby-Bigge (Oxford: Clarendon Press, 1990), p. 43. In his *Treatise*, he argues that it is "custom or repetition" that can convert "pain into pleasure." See idem, *A Treatise*

of Human Nature (1739–1740), edited by L. A. Selby-Bigge, revised by P. H. Nidditch (Oxford: Clarendon, 1978), p. 422.

9. Vidyasagar's intellectual positions are discussed with insight and critical sympathy in Asok Sen, *Iswarchandra Vidyasagar and His Elusive Milestones* (Calcutta: Ridhhi, 1975).

10. I have followed and modified the translation provided in Isvarchandra Vidyasagar, *Marriage of Hindu Widows*, edited by Arabindo Poddar (Calcutta, 1976), pp. 107–108.

11. Adam Smith, *The Theory of Moral Sentiments*, edited by D. D. Raphael and A. L. Macfie (Indianapolis: Liberty Fund, 1984), p. 9. See also p. 22. Raphael and Macfie explain (p. 14n) that Smith's theories were in part a refutation of Hobbes's and Mandeville's contention that all sentiments arose from self-love.

12. Hume, *Treatise*, pp. 316, 369.

13. Nagendranath Chattopadhyay, *Mahatma Raja Rammohon rayer jibancharit* (Calcutta: Deys, 1991), p. 273.

14. Subal Chandra Mitra, *Isvar Chandra Vidyasagar: A Story of His Life and Work* (New Delhi: Ashish Publishing House, 1975; first pub. 1902), p. 116.

15. Chandicharan Bandyopadhyay, *Vidyasagar* (Calcutta: Anandadhara Prakashan, 1970), pp. 48–49.

16. Mitra, *Isvar Chandra*, pp. 78–79.

17. Bandyopadhyay, *Vidyasagar*, p. 49. See also p. 187.

18. Mitra, *Isvar Chandra*, pp. 272–273.

19. See Binoy Ghosh, *Bidyasagar o bangali samaj* (Calcutta: Orient Longman, 1973), p. 363. Vidyasagar was sometimes called *dayar sagar* (ocean of kindness) as well.

20. Sivanath Sastri, "Rammohun Roy: The Story of His Life" in Satis Chandra Chakravarti, ed., *The Father of Modern India: Commemoration Volume of the Rammohun Roy Centenary Celebrations, 1933* (Calcutta: Rammohun Roy Centenary Committee, 1935), part 2, p. 20.

21. Mitra, *Isvar Chandra*, p. 261.

22. Smith, *Moral Sentiments*, p. 12.

23. Ibid., p. 22. Hume also saw sympathy as universal to human nature.

24. For a general discussion of Sanskrit aesthetics, see Ranerio Gnoli's *The Aesthetic Experience According to Abhinavagupta* (Varanasi: Chowkhamba Sanskrit Series Office, 1968).

25. Smith, *Moral Sentiments*, pp. 45, 50. For a Bengali criticism of the practice of crying in public, see Bankimchandra Chattopadhyay, "Uttarcharit" in *Bankimrachanabali* (Calcutta: Sahitya Samsad, 1973), vol. 2, pp. 159–185.

26. See Hans-Georg Gadamer, *Truth and Method* (London: Sheed and Ward, 1979), pp. 239–253.

27. Bandyopadhyay, *Vidyasagar*, p. 478.

28. Ibid., p. 278.

29. Ibid., preface, p. 6.

30. C. B. Macpherson, *The Political Theory of Possessive Individualism: Hobbes to Locke* (Oxford: Oxford University Press, 1974), pp. 137–142.

31. See *On the Jewish Question* in Karl Marx, *Early Writings*, introduction by Lucio Colletti, translated by Rodney Livingstone and Gregor Benton (Harmondsworth: Penguin, 1975), pp. 211–241.

32. William E. Connolly, *Political Theory and Modernity* (Oxford: Basil Blackwell, 1989), p. 71.

33. Ibid., pp. 57–58.

34. Timothy Mitchell, *Colonising Egypt* (Berkeley and Los Angeles: University of California Press, 1991), p. 121.

35. Emphasis added.

36. Nineteenth-century plays on widow remarriage understood the widow's own problems through such Bengali expressions as *joubanjontrona* (lit., the agony of the body in youth) and *joubonjvala* (lit., the burning sensation produced by the onset of youth): Anonymous, *Bidhaba bisham bipad* (Calcutta, 1856); Radhamadhab Mitra, *Bidhabamonoranjan natak*, Part 1 (Calcutta, 1857); Anonymous, *Bidhaba shukher dasha* (Mirzapur, 1861); Umacharan Chattopadhyay, *Bidhabodbaho natak* (Calcutta, 1857); and Jadunath Chattopadhyay, *Bidhababilash* (Serampore, 1864). I have consulted copies of these tracts available at the India Office Library, London.

37. Cf. Thomas W. Laqueur, "Bodies, Details and the Humanitarian Narrative," in Lynn Hunt, ed., *The New Cultural History* (Berkeley and Los Angeles: University of California Press, 1989), pp. 177–204.

38. Rabindranath Tagore, *Chokher bali* in *Rabindrarachanabali* (Calcutta: Government of West Bengal, 1962), vol. 8, Preface.

39. Dayananda, Vivekananda, and Gandhi were the nationalist leaders who played a key role in disseminating these ideas.

40. "It was the Bengali weekly Amritabazar Patrika (28 March 1870) that first drew the attention of the education-proud Bengalis to Vaishnav poetry. But the first collection of these poems in a book-form was edited by Jagabandhu Bhadra (1870)." Prabhatkumar Mukhopadhyay, *Rabindrajibani o rabindrasahitya prabeshak* (Calcutta: Visva Bharati, 1960), vol. 1, p. 68. See also Ramakanta Chakrabarti, *Vaisavism in Bengal 1486–1900* (Calcutta: Sanskrit Pustak Bhandar, 1985), chapters 21 and 22.

41. "Bidyapati o Jaydeb" in *Bankimrachanabali* (Calcutta: Sahitya Samsad, 1973), vol. 2, p. 191.

42. Sukumar Sen, *Bangla sahityer itihas* (Calcutta: Ananda Publishers, 1991), vol. 1, p. 126, says that the story of Chandidasa and Rami became popular from the seventeenth century on.

43. "Chandidas o bidyapati" in *Rabindrarachanabali* (Calcutta: Government of West Bengal, 1962), vol. 13, p. 635.

44. See Dinesh Chandra Sen, *History of Bengali Language and Literature* (Calcutta: Calcutta University Press, 1911), p. 149, and Asitkumar Bandyopadhyay,

Bangla shahityer shompurno itibritto (Calcutta: Modern Book Agency, 1992), pp. 100–101.

45. "Kamalakanter daptar" in *Bankimrachanabali*, vol. 2, p. 58. See also the discussion in Sudipta Kaviraj, *The Unhappy Consciousness: Bankimchandra Chattopadhyay and the Formation of Nationalist Discourse in India* (Delhi: Oxford University Press, 1995).

46. Bankimchandra Chattopadhyay, *Bishabriksha* in *Bankimrachanabali*, vol. 1, p. 261. See Marian Maddern's translation of *Bishabriksha* (The Poison Tree) in Bankim Chandra Chatterjee, *The Poison Tree: Three Novellas* translated by Marian Maddern and S. N. Mukerjee (New Delhi: Penguin, 1996), p. 113.

47. Ibid., p. 114

48. See Mohitlal Majumdar's discussion in *Bankimchandrer upanyash* (Calcutta: Bidyoday Library, 1979), pp. 21–51.

49. Tagore, "Chokher bali," p. 316

50. Ibid., pp. 302–3

51. Gopalchandra Ray, *Saratchandra*, vol. 2 (Calcutta: Sahitya sadan, 1966), pp. 201–2.

52. Cited in Khondkar Rezaul Karim, *Bangla upanyashe bidhaba* (Dhaka, 1979), p. 71.

53. Many today are sceptical of this fiction of the autonomous subject, but for the period we are considering this *was* the guiding fiction.

54. Tagore, "Chokher bali," p. 232.

55. Quoted in Gopalchandra Ray, *Saratchandra*, vol. 2, pp. 18–19.

56. Manashi Dasgupta, *Kom boyosher ami* (Calcutta: Ramayani prakash bhaban, 1974), p. 49.

57. Kalyani Datta, "Baidhaibya kahini," p. 41.

58. Prasannamayi Devi, *Purba katha*, edited by Nirmalya Acharya (Calcutta: Subarnarekha, 1982; first pub. 1917), pp. 80–81.

59. Drawing on the work of Maurice Halbwachs, Paul Conerton discusses this problem of articulation of social and familial memories in his *How Societies Remember* (Cambridge: Cambridge University Press, 1989), pp. 38–39.

60. Michel Foucault, *History of Sexuality* Vol.1. *An Introduction*, translated by Robert Hurley (New York: Vintage, 1980), Part 2, chapter 1.

61. Kalyani Datta, "Baidhabya kahini," p. 43. Emphasis added.

62. Ibid., pp. 50–51.

63. These familiar words paraphrase Marx.

64. See Ramachandra Gandhi, *The Availability of Religious Ideas* (London: Macmillan, 1976), p. 9.

65. "Baidhabya kahini," p. 53.

66. For similar accounts see also ibid., pp. 49–50; Nistarini Devi, *Shekele katha* (1913), in Nareshchandra Jana et al., eds., *Atmakatha* (Calcutta: Ananya Prakashan, 1982), vol. 2, pp. 33, 35.

67. Datta, "Baidhabya kahini," p. 48.

68. See the discussion in Ronald B. Inden and Ralph W. Nicholas, *Kinship in Bengali Culture* (Chicago: University of Chicago Press, 1977), pp. 3–34.

69. A similar point is made in the autobiography of the mother of the Bengali reformer Keshub Sen, Sarasundari Devi (1819–1907). Even when she suffered at the hands of her in-laws following the death of her husband, Saradasundari was concerned to put her loyalty to her dead husband's ancestral line over her concern for property. See Saradasundari Devi, *Atmakatha* (1913), reprinted in Nareshchandra Jana, et al., eds., *Atmakatha* (Calcutta: Ananya Prakashan, 1981), vol. 1, pp. 14, 26.

70. Michel Foucault, "Nietzsche, Genealogy, History" in Foucault, *Language, Counter-memory, Practice: Selected Essays and Interviews*, translated by Donald Bouchard and Sherry Simon, edited by Donald Bouchard (Ithaca: Cornell University Press, 1980), pp. 139–184.

71. Nietzsche cited ibid., p. 143.

Chapter 6
Nation and Imagination

1. Benedict Anderson, *Imagined Communities: Reflections on the Origin and Spread of Nationalism* (London: Verso, 1983).

2. Ibid., p. 15.

3. Rabindranath Tagore, "Bhagini nibedita" in *Rabindrarachanabali* (hereafter *RR*) (Calcutta: Government of West Bengal, 1962), vol. 13, p. 198. Unless otherwise stated, all references to *RR* will be to the centenary edition bearing the publication date of 1962.

4. Ibid.

5. Ibid.

6. I owe this point to Jon Mee.

7. Robin Pal, *Kolloler kolahol o onnanno probondho* (Calcutta, 1980), pp. 9, 13. See also Ujjval Majumdar's essay "Gapaguchher nari: abarodh theke mukti" in his *Rabindrashanga* (Calcutta: Sahitya Samidha, 1977), pp. 10–14.

8. Rabindranath Tagore, *Galpaguchha* (Calcutta: Visva Bharati, 1973), p. 1,004.

9. "Sahityabichar" in *RR*, vol. 14, pp. 531–532.

10. "Grambashider proti" (c.1930) in his *Palliprakriti* in *RR*, vol. 13, p. 524.

11. "Abhibhasan," ibid., p. 532. For instances of both historicism and nostalgia in Tagore's writings on villages, see "Protibhashan" (1926) and "Pallisheba" (1940), ibid., pp. 540, 560.

12. Bibhutibhushan Bandyopadhyay's novel *Pather panchali*, published in 1927, clearly occupied a middle ground between these two extremes in being able to sustain the image of the village as the home for tender sentiments without denying either the grinding poverty or the petty conflicts of village lives. See my "Remembered Villages: Representations of Hindu-Bengali Memories in the After-

math of the Partition" in *South Asia* 18 (1995), special issue on "North India: Partition and Independence" (guest edited by D. A. Low), pp. 109–129.

13. See Tagore's essays on "Loka-sahitya" in *RR*, vol. 13, pp. 663–734.

14. Translation by Clinton Seely in his *A Poet Apart: A Literary Biography of the Bengali Poet Jibanananda Das (1899–1954)* (Newark: University of Delaware, 1990), p. 15.

15. Prasanta Pal, *Rabijibani* (Calcutta: Ananda Publishers, 1989), vol. 4, p. 67. For a historical background to the poem, see Sachindranath Adhikari, *Shilaidaha o Rabindranath* (Calcutta: Jijnasha, 1974), pp. 317–321.

16. Srikumar Bandyopadhyay, *Bangasahitye upanashyer dhara* (Calcutta: Modern Book Agency, 1988; first pub. 1939).

17. Ibid., p. 1.

18. Ibid., p. 3.

19. Ibid., p. 13.

20. Humayun Kabir, *The Novel in India* (Calcutta: Firma K. L. Mukhopadhyay, 1968), p. 2.

21. Ibid., pp. 3, 4, 5.

22. Hari Ram Mishra, *The Theory of Rasa* (Chhattarpur, M.P.: Vindhyachal Prakashan, 1964), p. 10.

23. Sukanta Bhattacharya, "He mahajibon" in his *Chharpatra* (Calcutta: Saraswat Library, 1967; first pub. 1948). The poems of this book were written between 1943 and 1947.

24. See Budhhadev Bose's discussion on Sukanta Bhattacharya in the contemporary journal *Kabita* in Minakshi Datta, ed., *Budhhadev bosu shampadita kabita* (Calcutta: Papyrus, 1989), vol. 2, p. 104.

25. Marshall Berman, *All That Is Solid Melts into Air* (New York: Penguin, 1988), chapter 1.

26. Charles Baudelaire, *Paris Spleen*, translated by Louise Varese (New York: New Directions, 1970). See also the discussion in Walter Benjamin, *Charles Baudelaire: A Lyric Poet in the Era of High Capitalism*, translated by Harry Zohn (London: Verso, 1985) and in Berman, *All That Is Solid*, chapter 3.

27. Quoted in Aditya Ohadedar, *Rabindra-bidushan itibritta* (Calcutta: Basanti Library, 1986), p. 10.

28. Ibid., p. 28.

29. Ibid., p. 27.

30. Ibid., p. 52. See also pp. 54, 59. These texts are also discussed in Dipan Chattopadhyay, *Rabindrabirodhi shomalochona* (Calcutta: Annapurna Prakashani, 1994).

31. Ohadedar, *Rabindra-bidushan*, pp. 108–09, 112.

32. Achintyakumar Sengupta, *Kallolyug* (Calcutta: M. C. Sarkar and Sons, 1988), p. 47.

33. Cited and discussed in Ujjvalkumar Majumdar, "Rabindranath, shamashamay o jibanananda," in his *Rabindrashanga*, pp. 25–26 . See also Sutapa Bhatta-

charya, *Kabir chokhe kabi: tirisher kabider rabindrabichar* (Calcutta: Aruna Prakashani, 1987), p. 69.

34. Ibid., p. 23.

35. Edward Thompson, *Rabindranath Tagore: Poet and Dramatist* (Calcutta: Riddhi, 1979; first pub. 1926), pp. 315–316.

36. E. P. Thompson, *"Alien Homage": Edward Thompson and Rabindranath Tagore* (Delhi: Oxford University Press, 1993), p. 53.

37. Quoted in Ohadedar, *Rabindra-bidushan*, pp. 123, 125.

38. Benjamin, *Baudelaire*, p. 36.

39. "Chhander artha" (1917) in *RR*, vol. 14, p. 153.

40. "Gadyachhanda," quoted in Ujjvalkumar Majumdar, *E monihar* (Calcutta: Saibya Pustakalay, 1981), p. 64.

41. "Sristi" (1924) in *RR*, vol. 14, p. 319.

42. "Alashya o sahitya" (1887) in *RR*, vol. 13, p. 835.

43. "Shahityadharma" (1927), ibid., p. 327.

44. Bhattacharya, *Kabir chokhe*, p. 147. For Tagore's reply, see his *Chithipatra* (Calcutta: Visva Bharati, 1974), vol. 11, pp. 41–43.

45. *Kabir chokhe*, p. 163.

46. Ibid., p. 78.

47. Majumdar, *E monihar*, p. 223. For a statement by Jibanananda Das on Tagore, see his "Rabindranath o adhunik bangla kabita" in *Jibanananda daser prabandha shamagra*, edited by Faizul Latif Chaudhuri (Dhaka, 1990), pp. 24–29.

48. *Kabir chokhe*, p. 102.

49. Samar Sen, "Shvarga hote biday" (1937) in his *Kayekti kabita* (Calcutta: Anustup, 1989), p. 31. The title of the poem, "Banishment from Heaven" mimics the title of a poem by Tagore. For *Sheher kabita*, see *RR*, vol. 9, pp. 713–793.

50. Tagore to Chakravarty (1937), in *Chithipatra*, vol. 11, p. 201.

51. Quoted in Majumdar, *E monihar*, p. 243.

52. Cited in Bhattacharya, *Kabir chokhe*, p. 40.

53. For an historical account of the Bengal countryside in this period, see Sugata Bose, *Agrarian Bengal: Economy, Social Structure and Politics* (Cambridge: Cambridge University Press, 1986).

54. Seely's translation in *A Poet Apart*, p. 35.

55. "Joto durei jai" in *Subhash mukhopdhyayer sreshtha kabita* (Calcutta: Deys, 1976), p. 71–72.

56. See Sushilkumar Gupta, *Rabindrakabya prashanga: gadyakabita* (Calcutta: Indian Associated, 1966), pp. 52, 108. See also Sisir Kumar Ghosh, *The Later Poems of Tagore* (Calcutta, 1961).

57. Majumdar, *E monihar*, p. 65

58. For details of these debates, see Sengupta, *Kallolyug*; Shonamoni Chakrabarty, *Shanibarer chithi o adhunik bangla sahitya* (Calcutta: Aruna Prakashani,

1992); Jibendra Singha Ray, *Kalloler kal* (Calcutta: Deys, 1987); and Tagore's essay "Sahitye nabatva" (1927) in *RR*, vol. 14, p. 334.

59. There was some debate at the time about the status of this poem as *gadyakabita*. See Buddhdev Bose's remarks in Minakshi Datta, ed., *Budhhadev Bosu shompadito kabita*, vol. 1, p. 165; Mohitlal Mojumdar's critical opinions are given in his essay "Rabindranather gadyakabita" in his *Sahityabitan* (Calcutta: Bidyoday Library, 1962; first pub. 1942), pp. 53–63.

60. Vaikuntha: the celestial abode of the God Vishnu.

61. "Bansi" (1932) in *RR*, vol. 3, pp. 63–65.

62. See the essays "Chhander artha" in *RR*, vol. 14, pp. 153, 155–156; "Bastab," ibid., p. 295; "Kabir kaifiyat," ibid., p. 302, 305; "Sahitya," ibid., pp. 308–309; "Tathya o satya," ibid., pp. 312–316. Tagore's particular aesthetic theories did not persuade everybody. On these points, and also for a defence of Tagore, see Bhabanigopal Sanyal, *Rabindranather sahityatattva* (Calcutta: Modern Book Agency, 1974), part 2, pp. 38–40. See also Bimalkumar Mukhopadhyay, *Rabindranandantattva* (Calcutta: Deys, 1991), p. 296; Asitkumar Bandyopadhyay, *Sahityajijnashay rabindranath* (Calcutta: Karuna Prakashani, 1980), vol. 2; and Satyendranath Ray, *Sahityatattve rabindranath* (Calcutta: Sanskrita Pustak bhandar, 1972).

63. See Tagore's essay, "Kabir kaifiyat" (1915) in *RR*, vol. 14, p. 301.

64. Ibid. For an extended discussion, see Abu Sayeed Ayyub, *Tagore and Modernism*, translated by Amitava Ray (Delhi, 1995).

65. See his 1937 essay explaining the prose-poetry form, "Gadyachhander prakriti," in *RR*, vol. 14, p. 284.

66. Tagore's letter to Dhurjatiprasad Mukherjee, 17 May 1935, ibid., p. 280.

67. Ibid., pp. 312–313.

68. The tensions between romanticism and the eighteenth-century political-economic ideas of "utility" receives attention in James Chandler, *England in 1819: The Politics of Literary Culture and the Case of Romantic Historicism* (Chicago: University of Chicago Press, 1998), pp. 188–189, 231, 478.

69. See Eric Stokes, *The English Utilitarians in India* (Delhi: Orient Longman, 1989; first pub. 1959).

70. See John M. Robson, "J. S. Mill's Theory of Poetry," in J. B. Schneewind, ed., *Mill: A Collection of Critical Essays* (London: Macmillan, 1969), pp. 251–279; Jeremy Bentham, "Introduction to the Principles of Morals and Legislation" (1789) in Mary Warnock, ed., *Utilitarianism* (London: Fontana, 1969), p. 34.

71. Bankimchandra Chattopadhyay, "Kamalakanta" in *Bankimrachanabali*, edited by Jogeshchandra Bagal (Calcutta: Sahitya Samsad, 1974), vol. 2, p. 54. For an illuminating discussion of Bankim's writings in the context of colonialism, see Sudipta Kaviraj, *The Unhappy Consciousness: Bankimchandra Chattopadhaya and the Formation of Indian Nationalist Discourse* (Delhi: Oxford University Press, 1995).

72. See the essays "Sahitya" (1924) and "Tathya o satya" (1925) in *RR*, vol. 14, in particular pp. 308–309 and 312–313.

73. See his books on Bengali language, *Shabdatattva*, and on meter, *Chhanda*, included in *RR*, vol. 14. *Loka sahitya*, his book on folk literature, is included in *RR*, vol. 13.

74. "As it is, Bengali words have no weight, no accent as is customary with English, and no tradition, as in Sanskrit, of maintaning the long and short [vowel sounds]." Tagore, "Bangla chhande anuprash" in *RR*, vol. 14, p. 130.

75. See, for instance, "Phuljani" in *RR*, vol. 13, p. 943.

76. Satyajit Ray underscores this emphasis that Tagore placed on the words of his songs. Satyajit Ray, "Rabindrasangite bhabbar katha," in Abdul Ahad and Sanjida Khatun, eds., *Roilo tahar bani, roilo bhara shure* (Dhaka: Muktadhara, 1983), p. 157.

77. A handy source for discussions between Tagore and his interlocutors on his theories of music is Rabindranath Thakur, *Sangitchinta* (Calcutta: Visva Bharati, 1966).

78. Shankha Ghosh, *Kabitar muhurta* (Calcutta: Anustup, 1991), p. 14.

79. Binodbehari Mukhopadhay, "Chitrakar," *Ekshan*, annual number, 1978, pp. 201–202.

80. Prabhatkumar Mukhopadhyay, *Gitabitan: Kalanukramik shuchi* (Calcutta: Tagore Research Institute, 1992), gives 1905 as the date of composition of this song. For a comprehensive history of the Swadeshi movement, see Sumit Sarkar, *The Swadeshi Movement in Bengal, 1903–1908* (Delhi: People's Publishing House, 1973).

81. Edward Thompson, *Rabindranath Tagore*, p. 24. The poem was written about 1898. See Prabhatkumar Mukhopadhyay, *Rabindrajibani o sahityaprabeshak* (Calcutta: Visva-Bharati, 1960), vol. 1, p. 428.

82. Thompson, *Rabindranath Tagore*, p. 151.

83. Diana Eck's short book on *Darśan: Seeing the Divine in India* (Chambersburg, Penn.: Anima Books, 1985) is a useful introduction to the subject of *darshan* but falls back on anthropologizing gestures to make sense of the practice.

84. Raniero Gnoli, *The Aesthetic Experience According to Abhinavagupta* (Varanasi: Chowkhamba Sanskrit Series Office, 1968; revised version of the 1956 edition published from Rome), p. xlvi. See also the discussion in V. K. Chari, *Sanskrit Criticism* (Honolulu: University of Hawaii Press, 1990), pp. 44, 59–63; and Hari Ram Mishra, *The Theory of Rasa* (Chattarpur, M.P.: Vindhyachal Prakashan, 1964), pp. 412, 415.

85. Anderson, *Imagined Communities*, p. 15.

86. Chari, *Sanskrit Criticism*, p. 32.

87. Bimal Krishna Matilal, *Perception: An Essay on Classical Indian Theories of Knowledge* (Oxford: Clarendon Press, 1986), pp. 286–291, 311–312 draws attention to similarities between Hume's and Kant's use of the word "imagination" and the use of words like *kalpana* or *vikalpa* in Indian logic. In both cases,

says Matilal, "imagination" distinguishes between conception-free and conception-loaded perception in the work of memory. On Coleridge's "desynonimization" of "fancy" and "imagination," see Samuel Tylor Coleridge, *Biographia Literaria*, edited by Nigel Leask (London and Vermont: Everyman, 1997), chapter 4, pp. 55–56.

88. The famous chapter 13 of *Biographia Literaria* defines thus the "primary" and the "secondary" modes of imagination (p. 175): "The primary IMAGINATION I hold to be the living power and prime Agent of all human Perception, and as a repetition in the finite mind of the eternal act of creation in the infinite I AM. The secondary I consider as an echo of the former, . . . identical with the primary in the *kind* of its agency, and differing only in degree and the mode of its operation. It dissolves, diffuses, dissipates, in order to recreate. . . . It is essentially *vital*, even as all objects (*as* objects) are essentially fixed and dated." Coleridge's theories have spawned a huge literature. I have found the following works particularly helpful. Geoffrey Hartman, *The Unmediated Vision: An Interpretation of Wordsworth, Hopkins, Rilke and Valery* (New York: Harcourt, Brace & World, 1966); Geoffrey Hartman, "Reflections on the Evening Star: Akenside to Coleridge," Angus Fletcher, " 'Positive Negation': Threshold, Sequence and Personification in Coleridge," and Thomas McFarland, "The Origin and Significance of Coleridge's Theory of Secondary Imagination," all in Geoffrey Hartman, ed., *New Perspectives on Coleridge and Wordsworth: Selected Papers from the English Institute* (New York: Columbia University Press, 1972); James K. Chandler, *Wordsworth's Second Nature: A Study of the Poetry and Politics* (Chicago: University of Chicago Press, 1984); John Spencer Hill, ed., *Imagination in Coleridge* (London: Macmillan, 1978); Nigel Leask, *The Politics of Imagination in Coleridge's Critical Thought* (London: Macmillan, 1988); and Thomas McFarland, *Coleridge and the Pantheist Tradition* (Oxford: Clarendon, 1969). My thanks to David Lloyd, Jonathon Mee, and James Chandler for discussions on these points.

89. See Thomas McFarland, *Coleridge*, pp. 308–309.

90. Coleridge, *Biographia*, p. 57n1. Coleridge classifies this moment under eighteenth-century philosophies of "common sense."

91. As Massumi says in discussing the example of throwing a brick: "What is the subject of the brick? The arm that throws it? The body connected to the arm? The brain encased in the body? The situation that brought brain and body to such a juncture? All and none of the above. What is its object? The window? The edifice? The laws the edifice shelters? The class and other power relations encrusted in the laws? All and none of the above." Brian Massumi, *A User's Guide to "Capitalism and Schizophrenia": Deviations from Deleuze and Guattari* (Cambridge: MIT Press, 1992), p. 5; Massumi, "Which Came First? The Individual or Society? Which Is the Chicken and Which Is the Egg? The Political Economy of Belonging and the Logic of Relation," in Cynthia C. Davidson, ed., *Anybody* (Cambridge: MIT Press, 1997), pp. 175–188.

92. See Freud's essay, "The Uncanny" (1919) in Sigmund Freud, *Art and Literature*, translated under the general editorship of James Strachey, edited by Albert Dickson (Harmondsworth: Penguin, 1990), pp. 339–376.

93. S. Wajed Ali, "Bharatbarsha" in *Matriculation Bengali Selections* (Calcutta: Calcutta University Press, 1938), p. 322.

94. The episode is discussed in Partha Chatterjee, *Nationalist Thought and the Colonial World: A Derivative Discourse* (London: Zed, 1986), pp. 146–147.

95. Jawaharlal Nehru, *The Discovery of India* (New York: John Day, 1946), pp. 48–49, cited in Partha Chatterjee, *Nationalist Thought*, p. 146.

96. Homi K. Bhabha, "DissemiNation: Time, Narrative, and the Margins of the Modern Nation," in his edited volume *Nation and Narration* (London and New York: Routledge, 1990), pp. 291–322.

Chapter 7
Adda: A History of Sociality

1. Marshall Berman, *All That is Solid Melts into Air: The Experience of Modernity* (New York: Penguin, 1988; first pub. 1982), p. 5.

2. J. L. Mehta, *Martin Heidegger: The Way and the Vision* (Honolulu: University Press of Hawaii, 1976), p. 481n101.

3. Sunitikumar Chattopadhyay, "Hostel Life in Calcutta" (1913) appended to his *Jiban katha* (in Bengali) (Calcutta: Jijnasha, 1979), p. 210.

4. Try, for instance, "Calcutta Online" which offers the opportunity to subscribe to a site for "Bengali adda." The legendary nature of *adda* at the College Street Coffee House may also be seen in the fact that a news digest published from New York for immigrant and diasporia Bengalis in the United States carries news of the retirement of an "upcountry" working-class man, Ramuchacha, who for forty-five years served *addabaj* Bengalis at this coffee house. See *Udayan* (in Bengali), New York, 3 December 1997, p. 8: "The man who was inseparable from all the joys and sorrows, hopes and despair, poetry and *adda* of Coffee House over the last four decades, formally accepted farewell on last Saturday. . . . Ramuda alias Ramuchacha has now left behind forty-five of his seventy years of life in the main hall and in the balconies of Coffee House. . . . His white moustache moist with tears, Ramuchacha said in his slightly upcountry style: 'I am an ignorant man. I do not know the names of any of those whom I have seen here over the last forty years. But I can still recognise their faces. Students come, sip coffee, chat, write poetry—I only see them. Now I will return to my village and spend time in the company of my grand-children.' " Had it not been for the association Ramuchacha had with a space treated in Bengali middle-class memory as a sacred site in the history of Bengali literary modernism, the retirement of an "unknown" working-class person, who was not even a Bengali himself, would have seldom made news in the American-Bengali diaspora.

5. Nishithranjan Ray's "Preface" to Samarendra Das, ed., *Kolkatar adda* (Calcutta: Mahajati Prakashan, 1990).

6. Saiyad Mujtaba Ali, "Adda," in *Saiyad mujtaba ali racanabali* (Calcutta: Mitra o Ghosh, 1974/5), vol. 3, p. 396.

7. Sabitendranath Ray and Rabin Bal, "Bangla prakashanar panchash bochhor, 1947–97," in *Books in Print from West Bengal and Fair Directory 1997* (Calcutta: Publishers' Guild, 1997), p. xxxii.

8. On these questions, see Ranajit Guha, "The Migrant's Time," *Postcolonial Studies* 1, no. 2 (July 1998), pp. 155–160.

9. Arjun Appadurai, "Body, Property and Fire in Urban India," paper presented at the session on "Regimes of Value," American Anthropology Association meeting, Washington D.C., November 1997.

10. See "Addar darshan" in *Binay sarkarer baithake*, edited by Haridas Mukhopadhyay (Calcutta, 1942), p. 273.

11. Nishithranjan Ray, preface to Samarendra Das, ed., *Kolkatar adda*, p. 10.

12. Nripendrakrishna Chattopadhyay, "Adda," in his *Nana katha* (Calcutta: Deb Sahitya Kutir, 1978), pp. 2–3.

13. Saiyad Mujtaba Ali, "Adda passport" in his *Saiyad mujtaba ali rachanabali* (Calcutta: Mitra o Ghosh, 1974/5), vol. 3, pp. 404–411.

14. Nirad Chaudhuri, *The Autobiography of an Unknown Indian* (New York: Macmillan, 1989; first published 1951), p. 382.

15. All quotations from Chaudhuri are ibid., pp. 383–386.

16. Budhhadev Bose, "Adda" in Samarendranath Das, ed., *Kolkatar adda*, p. 13.

17. Chattopadhyay, "Hostel Life," p. 210, and Bose, "Adda," p. 13.

18. See Hirankumar Sanyal, *Porichoyer kuribochhor o onnanno smritichitra* (Calcutta: Papyrus, 1978), p. 145, and Gaurkishor Ghosh, "Bhumika" (Preface), *Saiyad mujtaba ali granthabali* (Calcutta: Mitra o ghosh, 1978), vol. 4.

19. *Samsad Bengali-English Dictionary* (Calcutta: Sahitya Samsad, 1968), entry for *adda*.

20. See Nishithranjan Ray's preface to *Kolkatar adda*, p. 9.

21. Pyarimohan Mukhopadhyay, *Amar dekha kolkata* (Calcutta, 1980/1), pp. 207–211, 222–224 describes such *addas* at the turn of the century.

22. *Mahasthabirer galpashamagra* (Calcutta, 1988), pp. 231. 364–365.

23. Lal Behari Dey, *Recollections of My School-Days* (along with *Bengal Peasant Life* and *Folk Tales of Bengal*), edited by Mahadevprasad Saha (Calcutta, 1969), p. 464. Unfortunately, Saha does not give the original date of publication of *Recollections*.

24. *Satik Hutom pyanchar naksha*, edited and annotated by Arun Nag (Calcutta: Subarnarekha, 1992), p. 52

25. Mukhopadhyay, *Amar dekha*, pp. 207–211.

26. See entries in the following Bengali dictionaries: Gyanendramohan Das, *Bangla bhashar abhidhan*, vol. 1 (Calcutta, Sahitya Samsad, 1988; first pub. 1916/

17); Haricharan Bandyopadhyay, *Bangiyo shabdakosh* (Calcutta: Sahitya Akademi, 1988; first pub. 1924/5); and Subal Chandra Mitra, *Saral bangala abhidhan* (Calcutta: New Age Publishers, 1984; first pub. 1906). Similar associations of the word are to be found in *Hutom*, pp. 63 and 105, and Sivanath Shastri, *Ramtanu Lahiri o tatkalin bangasamaj* (Calcutta, New Age Publishers, 1957; first pub. 1903).

27. *Hutom*, pp. 21, 23, 78–79, 87, 94, 102–103.

28. *Saral bangala abhidhan*, entry for *majlish*. It is not entirely clear whether Mitra is simply referring to the religious sect here.

29. Bose, "Adda," p. 14.

30. Parashuram [Rajshekhar Bosu], "Lambakarna" in his *Gaddalika* (Calcutta: M. C. Sarkar and Sons, 1974), p. 79.

31. Radhaprasad Gupta, "Amader jubakkaler adda: jhankidarshan," in *Kolkatar adda*, p. 27.

32. Parashuram [Rajshekhar Bosu], "Dakshinray" in *Kajjali* (Calcutta: M. C. Sarkar and Sons, 1969), pp. 65–66.

33. Peter van der Veer tells me that what is known in English or Australian as "going Dutch" or in American as "Dutch treat" is known to the Dutch themselves as "American party"!

34. Sagarmoy Ghosh, "Hirer nakchhabi," in *Kolkatar adda*, p. 52.

35. Jogindranath Bosu, *Michael Madhusudan Datter jibancharit* (Calcutta: Ashok Pustakalay, 1990), pp. 48–49, 51.

36. Bipinchandra Pal, *Sattarbatshar: atmajibani* (Calcutta: Jugajatri, 1957), pp. 202–203; Dineshchandra Sen, *Gharer katha o juga sahitya* (Calcutta: Jijnasha, 1969), pp. 95–98.

37. See Achintyakumar Sengupta, *Kallol jug* (Calcutta: M. C. Sarkar and Sons, 1960), pp. 6–16.

38. See Prasantakumar Pal, *Rabijibani* (Calcutta: Ananda Publishers, 1988), vol. 3, pp. 39, 60, 237, 268, 270.

39. Sarala Devi Chaudhurani, *Jibaner jharapata* (Calcutta: Rupa, 1982), p. 34. See also Pal, *Rabijibani*, vol. 3, p. 74.

40. Quoted in Amitrasudan Bhattacharya, *Bankimchandrajibani* (Calcutta: Ananda Publishers, 1991), p. 109.

41. Sachishchandra Chattopadhyay, *Bankim-jibani* (Calcutta: Pustak Bipani, 1989), pp. 283, 311.

42. *Hutom*, p. 41.

43. This sketch is entitled "Betaler baithake" (In the Parlor of Betal), and was used as a masthead for a regular column by "Betal" in the literary magazine *Prabashi*, first published in 1901 and resumed in the 1920s. I have reproduced it from an essay by Hirendranath Datta, "Sahityer adda" [Literary *Addas*] in *Desh*, special issue on literature, 1975, p. 49.

44. The sketch is reproduced from Chattopadhay, "Hostel Life," p. 199.

45. Ibid., pp. 198–199.

46. See the introduction to Jatindramohan Bhattacharya, *Bangla mudrita granthadir talika* (Calcutta: A. Mukherjee and Sons, 1990), vol. 1, p. ix.

47. Chattopadhyay, "Hostel Life," p. 201.

48. Sanyal, *Porichoyer*, p. 145.

49. Satyajit Ray, "Bhumika" (Preface) to Sukumar Ray, *Shamagra shishusahitya* (Calcutta: Ananda Publishers, 1977).

50. Jibendra Singha Ray, *Kolloler kal* (Calcutta: Deys, 1973), p. 5.

51. Ibid., pp. 2–3. Emphasis added.

52. See *Desh*, special issue on literature, 1975.

53. Nripendrakrishna Chattopadhyay, *Nana katha*, pp. 4–6.

54. Arun Das Gupta, "Three-B kalighat park south-e kanuda," in Manashi Das Gupta ed., *Kicchu chintakana, kichhu smriti: bimal ghosh smaranik patra* (Calcutta, 1987), p. 62

55. Debabrata Mukhopadhyay, *Kofir kaape shomoyer chhobi* (Calcutta: Communications and Media People, 1989), preface and p. 10.

56. Bipinbehari Gupta, *Puratan prasanga* (Calcutta: Bidyabharati, 1977; first pub. c. 1913/14)

57. Amiyabhusan Majumdar, "Rabindranath o bigyanacharya satyendranath," *Desh*, special issue on literature, 1975, p. 131.

58. Parimal Goswami, "Prabashir adda," Ibid., pp. 59–64. Ranajit Guha tells me that in the Calcutta of his youth (1930s), parks were indeed the place for *adda*, removed as they were from parental surveillance. Premankur Atarthi's writings explore these urban spaces in fictional and autobiographical forms and remain to be mined by a future historian of the city. For a captivating description of the social use made of terraced roofs in Calcutta in early and middle parts of the twentieth century see, for example, his short story "Chhate" in *Mahasthabirer granthabali*, pp. 354–363.

59. Unfortunately, nothing as interesting as Frank Conlon's essay "Dining Out in Bombay" in Carol Breckenridge, ed., *Consuming Modernity: Public Culture in a South Asian World* (Minneapolis: University of Minnesota Press, 1995), pp. 90–127, exists for Calcutta.

60. Muzaffar Ahmad, *Kazi nazrul islam smritikatha* (Calcutta: National Book Agency, 1965), pp. 277–278.

61. Susobhan Sarkar, "Bhumikar bodole," in Sanyal, *Porichoyer*, p. 9.

62. Radhaprasad Gupta, "Amader jubakkaler adda," in *Kolkatar adda*, p. 24.

63. Ibid.

64. Ibid., pp. 27–28.

65. Parashuram [Rajshekhar Bosu], "Ratarati" in *Hanumaner shapna ityadi galpo* (Calcutta: M. C. Sarkar and Sons, 1962), p. 79.

66. Bose, "Adda," p. 14.

67. Sanyal, *Porichoyer*, pp. 163–164.

68. Shyamalkrishna Ghosh, *Porichoyer adda* (Calcutta: K. P. Bagchi, 1990), p. 11.

69. Sushobhan Sarkar uses the word *galpagujob* (lit., tales and rumors) to describe the nature of conversation at an *adda*. Sarkar's preface to Sanyal, *Porichoyer*, p. 3.

70. Hemendrakumar Ray, *Jader dekhechhi* (Calcutta, 1948/9), vol. 1, pp. 112–114.

71. Sanyal, *Porichoyer*, p. 167.

72. The best modern study of *kathakata* to date is Gautam Bhadra, "Kathakatar nana katha," *Jogshutro*, October-December 1993, pp. 169–268.

73. Ibid., pp. 166–167.

74. Gupta, "Amader jubakkaler," p. 29.

75. See the essay "Meyeder adda" in *Kolkatar adda*.

76. Chattopadhyay, *Nana katha*, pp. 9, 16.

77. Ibid., pp. 4, 10. Darjeeling and Puri were among the favorite locations for holidays for Bengali middle-class families from Calcutta.

78. Parashuram [Rajshekhar Bosu], "Dvandik kobita," in his *Neel tara ityadi galpa* (Calcutta: M. C. Sarkar and Sons, 1962), pp. 121–126. The words italicized are in English in the original.

79. Srikumar Bandyopadhyay, *Bangasahitye upanashyer dhara* (Calcutta: Modern Book Agency, 1988), p. 148.

80. Mukhopadhyay, *Kofir kaape*, p. 16.

81. See Henri Lefebvre, *The Production of Space*, translated by Donald Nicholson-Smith (Oxford: Basil Blackwell, 1992), pp. 304–306 and *passim*.

82. Personal communication from Manashi Das Gupta.

Chapter 8
Family, Fraternity, and Salaried Labor

1. Rajnarayan Bosu [Bose], *Shekaal ar ekaal* [1874], edited by Brajendranath Bandyopadhyay and Sajanikanta Das (Calcutta: Ranjan Publishing House, 1976), pp. 39–41.

2. Anonymous *Naridharma* (Calcutta, 1877], p. 27.

3. Bosu, *Shekaal*, pp. 86–87.

4. Sumit Sarkar, " 'Kaliyuga,' 'Chakri,' and 'Bhakti': Ramakrishna and His Times," *Economic and Political Weekly* (hereafter *EPW*), no. 27–29 (18 July 1992), pp. 1,549–1,550.

5. See Partha Chatterjee, *The Nation and Its Fragments: Colonial and Postcolonial Histories* (Princeton: Princeton University Press, 1994); Meredith Borthwick, *The Changing Role of Women in Bengal 1849–1905* (Princeton: Princeton University Press, 1984); Ghulam Murshid, *Reluctant Debutante: Response of Bengali Women to Modernization* (Rajshahi: Rajshahi University Press, 1983); Tanika Sarkar, "Nationalist Iconography: Images of Women in Nineteenth Century Bengali Literature," *EPW* 22, no. 47 (November 1987), pp. 2,011–2,015; Malabika Karlekar, "Kadambini and the *Bhadralok*: Early Debates over Women's

Education in Bengal," *EPW* 21, no. 17, (26 April 1986), pp. WS–WS 31; Jasodhara Bagchi, "Representing Nationalism: Ideology of Motherhood in Colonial Bengal," *EPW* 25, nos. 42–43 (20–27 October 1990), pp. WS65-WS71; Srabashi Ghosh, "Birds in a Cage," *EPW* 21, no. 43 (October 1986) pp. 88–96; Bharati Ray, "Bengali Women and the Politics of Joint Family," *EPW* 28, no. 32, (28 December 1991), pp. 3,021–3,051; Hilary Standing, *Dependence and Autonomy: Women's Employment and the Family in Calcutta* (London: Routledge, 1991).

6. Tanika Sarkar, "The Hindu Wife and the Hindu Nation: Domesticity and Nationalism in Nineteenth Century Bengal," *Studies in History* n.s. 8, no. 2 (1992), p. 224.

7. Sarkar's argument in this essay is similar to that of Partha Chatterjee in his "The Nationalist Resolution of the Woman Question" in Kumkum Sangari and Sudesh Vaid, eds., *Recasting Woman* (New Brunswick, N.J.: Rutgers University Press, 1989), pp. 233–253.

8. See Mrinalini Sinha, *Colonial Masculinity: The "Manly Englishman" and the "Effeminate" Bengali in the Late Nineteenth Century* (Manchester: Manchester University Press, 1995).

9. John Locke, *Two Treatises on Government* (London, Melbourne, Toronto: Everyman's Library, 1978). Two commentaries especially influential for this analysis are C. B. Macpherson, *The Political Theory of Possessive Individualism: Hobbes to Locke* (Oxford: Oxford University Press, 1972), and Carol Pateman, *The Sexual Contract* (Stanford: Stanford University Press, 1988).

10. Macpherson, *Possessive Individualism*, chapter 5.

11. This complaint about having to eat "too early" was perhaps a reference to the way office attendance was forcing men to eat their midday meal as "breakfast" in the morning, what Bengalis eventually called *apisher bhat* or "office rice."

12. Bhabanicharan Bandyopadhyay, *Kalikata kamalalaya* (1823), edited by Brajendranath Bandyopadhyay (Calcutta: Ranjan Publishing House, 1952), pp. 8, 10–13. Hereafter, this text will be referred to as *KK*.

13. *KK*, pp. 8–9.

14. *KK*, p. 22. There is one word—*sarip* [?]—that I have left out of this list, as I could not understand it.

15. *Tattvabodhini patrika* (n.d.) cited in Sibnath Sastri, *Ramtanu Lahiri o tatkalin bangasamaj* (Calcutta: New Age, 1957), p. 58.

16. *KK*, p. 12.

17. *KK*, p. 22.

18. Ibid.

19. Kashinath Bosu, comp., *Darshandeepika* (Calcutta, 1848), p. 14.

20. See the minutes of the first meeting of this association: *Gauradeshiya samaj shangsthapanartha pratham sabhar bibaran* (Calcutta, 1823). The copy I consulted is in the British Library.

21. Bhudev Mukhopadhyay, *Achar prabandha* (Chinsurah, 1908), pp. 52, 60–61. Emphasis added.

22. Sumit Sarkar, " 'Kaliyuga' "; Partha Chatterjee, "A Religion of Urban Domesticity: Sri Ramakrishna and the Calcutta Middle Class," in Partha Chatterjee and Gyan Pandey, eds., *Subaltern Studies VII* (Delhi: Oxford University Press, 1992), pp. 40–68.

23. On Bengali adaptation of the idea of "improvement," see Ranajit Guha's essay, "Colonialism in South Asia: Dominance without Hegemony and Its Historiography," in his *Dominance without Hegemony: History and Power in Colonial India* (Cambridge: Harvard University Press, 1997), pp. 97–120.

24. Anonymous, *Streeshiksha* (Calcutta, 1877), vol. 1, pp. 28–29.

25. Mukhopadhyay, *Achar prabandha*, pp. 6, 12–13, 35.

26. Nagendrabala Saraswati, *Garhasthyadharma ba naridharmer parishista* (Jamalpur, Burdwan, 1904), pp. 1, 29.

27. Anukulchandra Datta, *Grihashiksha* [in Bengali] (Calcutta, 1906), p. 13.

28. Ibid., pp. 3–4, 34–39, 78, 80.

29. Ibid., pp. 55, 62; see also p. 65.

30. Chandranath Bosu, *Garhasthyapath* (Calcutta, 1887), pp. 15–16.

31. Datta, *Grihashiksha*, preface and title page.

32. Yogendranarayan Ray, *Bangamahila* (Chinsurah, 1881), pp. 87–88; Kailashbashini Devi, *Hindu mahilaganer heenabastha* (Calcutta, 1863), pp. 6–7, 63.

33. Quoted in Borthwick, *Changing Role*, p. 105.

34. *Streeshiksha*, vol. 1, pp. 84–87.

35. Yogindranarayan Ray, *Bangamahila*, pp. 87–88.

36. Radhikanath Thakur, comp. and trans., *Patripariksha* (Murshidabad, 1880), p. 17

37. Manmohan Bosu, *Hindu achar byabahar* (Calcutta, 1873), pp. 15–16, 58–60.

38. David Kinsley, *Hindu Goddesses: Visions of the Divine Feminine in the Hindu Religious Tradition* (Berkeley and Los Angeles: University of California Press, 1988), pp. 19–32. See also Manomohan Basu, *Hindu achar byabahar* (Calcutta, 1873), p. 60.

39. Paul R. Greenough, *Prosperity and Misery in Modern Bengal: The Famine of 1943–1944* (New York: Oxford University Press, 1982), pp. 12–41; Lina Fruzzetti, *The Gift of a Virgin: Women, Marriage and Ritual in a Bengali Society* (Delhi: Oxford University Press, 1990).

40. Upendranath Dhal, *Goddess Lakshmi: Origin and Development* (Delhi: Oriental Publishers and Distributors, 1978), p. 136.

41. Ibid., p. 141n20

42. I bought two such books from pavement-sellers in Calcutta: Baikunthanath Majhi, *Baromaser srisri lakshmidevir bratakatha o panchali*, revised by Madhusudan Bhattacharya (Calcutta, n.d.), and Pasupati Chattopadhayay, *Baromese srisri lakshmidevir panchali o bratakatha* (Calcutta, n.d.)

43. Bhikshuk [Chandra Sen], *Ki holo!* (Calcutta, 1876), p. 77.

44. Ronald B. Inden, *Marriage and Rank in Bengali Culture: A History of Caste and Clan in Middle Period Bengal* (Berkeley and Los Angeles: University of California Press, 1976), p. 96.

45. Ibid., p. 54n10.

46. Bhudev Mukhopadhyay, "Paribarik prabandha," in *Bhudev rachanashambhar*, edited by Pramathanath Bishi (Calcutta: Mitra o Ghosh, 1969), pp. 465, 471.

47. Ishanchandra Boshu, *Streediger proti upadesh* (Calcutta, 1874), pp. 8–11. See also Shibchandra Jana, *Patibratyadharmashiksha* (Calcutta, 1870), p. 35.

48. See the discussion and citation in Chapter 6.

49. This song was sung at the first Calcutta meeting of the Indian National Congress in December 1886. See Prabhatkumar Mukhopadhyay, *Gitabitan: kalanukramik shuchi* (Calcutta: Tagore Research Institute, 1992), p. 90.

50. Dwijendralal Ray, "Gaan," in *Dwijendrarachanabali*, edited by Rathindranath Ray (Calcutta: Sahitya Samsad, 1986), pp. 649–650.

51. Mukhopadhyay, "Paribarik prabandha," p. 470.

52. Ibid., p. 454.

53. Ibid., p. 465.

54. John Locke, *Two Treatises of Government* (London: Everyman's Library, 1978), chapters 5–8.

55. Ibid., p. 129.

56. Ibid.

57. Ibid., pp. 150, 152.

58. Pateman, *Sexual Contract*, chapter 4: "Genesis, Fathers, and the Political Liberty of Sons." Also Wendy Brown, *States of Injury: Power and Freedom in Late Modernity* (Princeton: Princeton University Press, 1995), chapter 6.

59. "Paribarik prabandha," p. 477.

60. See John Locke, "Some Thoughts Concerning Education" (1692) in *John Locke on Politics and Education*, introduced by Howard R. Penniman (New York: Walter J. Black, 1947), p. 235. Uday Singh Mehta, *The Anxiety of Freedom: Imagination and Individuality in Locke's Political Thought* (Ithaca: Cornell University Press, 1992), pp. 138–140.

61. See the essay on *jnatittva* (theories of kinship) in "Paribarik prabandha." Also the essay "Pashchatya bhab" [Western ways] in his *Samajik prabandha*, edited by Jahnabikumar Chakraborty (Calcutta: Pashchimbanga Rajya Pustak Parishad, 1981), pp. 125–130.

62. Tapan Raychaudhuri, *Europe Reconsidered: Perceptions of the West in Nineteenth Century Bengal* (Delhi: Oxford University Press, 1988), pp. 88–89.

63. Cited and translated by Tapan Raychaudhuri, ibid., p. 41.

64. For example, see some of the novels of Saratchandra Chatterjee (1876–1938): *Bindur chhele* (1914), *Baikunther will* (1916), *Nishkriti* (1917), *Mamlar phol* (1920), *Harilakshmi* (1926), and *Paresh* (1934).

65. Dayamayi Dasi, *Patibrata dharma* (Calcutta, 1870), pp. 1–2.

66. Ibid., pp. 1–2. I am grateful to Radhika Singha for alerting me to the possibility of a woman's personal presence in this passage.

67. Ibid., preface.

68. Sumit Sarkar, *The Swadeshi Movement in Bengal 1903–1908* (Delhi: People's Publishing House, 1973), p. 287.

69. Ibid.

70. Ibid.

71. See Sekhar Bandyopadhyay, *Caste, Politics, and the Raj* (Calcutta: K. P. Bagchi, 1990), and Masayuki Usuda, "Pushed towards the Partition: Jogendranath Mandal and the Constrained Namasudra Movement," in H. Kotani, ed., *Caste System, Untouchability, and the Depressed* (Delhi: Manohar, 1997), pp. 221–274.

72. Sudipta Kaviraj, "Filth and the Public Sphere: Concepts and Practices about Space in Calcutta," *Public Culture* 10, no. 1 (Fall 1997), p. 113.

73. See, for example, Ian Shapiro, "Resources, Capacities, and Ownership: The Workmanship Ideal and Distributive Justice," in John Brewer and Susan Staves, eds., *Early Modern Conceptions of Property* (London and New York: Routledge, 1996), pp. 21–42.

74. I quote these words from a relatively obscure Bengali publication to show how commonplace they are. Samarendrakrishna Bosu, "Bidyasagarer nastikata," in Ramakanta Chakrabarty, ed., *Satabarsha smaranika vidyasagar kolej* (Calcutta: Vidyasagar College, 1973), pp. 320–324. The quotation is from p. 322.

Epilogue
Reason and the Critique of Historicism

1. G.W.F. Hegel, *Phenomenology of Spirit*, translated by A. V. Miller (Oxford: Oxford University Press, 1979), pp. 329–349.

2. See, for instance, Barun De, "The Colonial Context of the Bengal Renaissance," in C. H. Phillips and Mary Doreen Wainwright, eds., *Indian Society and the Beginnings of Modernisation 1830–1850* (London: University of London Press, 1976). My purpose is not to single out Professor De. What he expressed was the "common sense" of Indian Marxism in the 1970s.

3. A. N. Bose, ed., *Modern Age and India* (Calcutta: Left Book Club, 1950).

4. Ibid., p. 13.

5. Ibid., pp. 144, 148.

6. Dilipkumar Ray, *Smriticharan* (Calcutta: Indian Associated Publishing, 1975), pp. 136–141.

7. Peter Burke, *The Renaissance Sense of the Past* (London: Edward Arnold, 1990), and J.G.A. Pocock, *The Ancient Constitution and the Feudal Law: A Study of English Historical Thought in the Seventeenth Century* (Cambridge: Cambridge University Press, 1990).

8. Much recent rethinking in anthropology was initiated by James Clifford, *The Predicament of Culture: Twentieth-Century Ethnography, Literature, and Art* (Cambridge: Harvard University Press, 1988), and James Clifford and George E. Marcus, eds., *Writing Culture: The Poetics and Politics of Ethnography* (Berkeley and Los Angeles: University of California Press, 1986). Kamala Visweswaran, *Fictions of Feminist Ethnography* (Minneapolis: University of Minnesota Press, 1994) extends the spirit of self-questioning to radical ends in feminist ethnography. See also Kirin Narayan, "How Native is a Native Anthropologist?" in *American Anthropologist* 95 (1993), pp. 671–686.

9. These basic terms of *Being and Time* have been explained in Chapter 2.

10. See Chapter 2.

11. Jomo Kenyatta, *Facing Mount Kenya: The Tribal Life of the Gikuyu* (New York: Vintage Books, 1965), pp. xix–xx. Emphasis added.

12. Ibid., p. 279.

13. B. Malinowski, "Introduction," ibid., pp. xii–xiii

14. For Kenyatta's expression, ibid., p. 223.

15. Kwame Anthony Appiah, *In My Father's House: Africa in the Philosophy of Culture* (New York: Oxford University Press, 1993), pp. 112–113.

16. D. D. Kosambi, *The Culture and Civilisation of Ancient India in Historical Outline* (Delhi: Vikas, 1975), p. 48. I can only notice here how Kosambi's texts constantly bring together the "archaic" and "women."

17. See Chapter 3.

18. Kosambi, *The Culture and Civilisation*, pp. 47, 48. I have discussed Kosambi's method in more detail in a Bengali essay: "Bharatbarshe adunikatar itihash o shomoy kalpana," *Aitihashik* 6, no. 2 (September 1997), pp. 121–128.

19. Marc Bloch, *The Historian's Craft* (Manchester: Manchester University Press, 1992; first pub. 1954) is still a classic on the subject.

20. Paul de Man, "Literary History and Literary Modernity," cited in Marshall Berman, *All That Is Solid Melts into Air: The Experience of Modernity* (Harmondsworth: Penguin, 1988), p. 331.

21. John Locke, *Two Treatises of Government* (New York: Everyman's Library, 1978), pp. 146–149.

22. Pocock, *The Ancient Constitution*, p. 235.

23. "The Eighteenth Brumaire of Louis Bonaparte" in Karl Marx and Frederick Engels, *Selected Works*, vol. 1 (Moscow: Progress Publishers, 1969), p. 398.

24. M. K. Gandhi, "A Vindication of Caste" (1936), reprinted in B. R. Ambedkar, *The Annihilation of Caste* (Jalandhar: Bheem Patrika Publications, n.d.), p. 137. Emphasis added.

25. B. R. Ambedkar, "Annihilation of Caste" (1936), ibid., pp. 92, 129, 131. For a recent study that skilfully brings out the many complexities—but also the historicism and decisionism—of Ambedkar's political and religious thought, see Gauri Viswanathan, *Outside the Fold: Conversion, Modernity, and Belief* (Princeton: Princeton University Press, 1998), chapter 7.

26. Gandhi, "A Vindication," p. 136.

27. Ambedkar, "Annihilation of Caste," pp. 131–132.

28. Ashis Nandy, "History's Forgotten Doubles," *History and Theory* 34 (May 1995), p. 61.

29. Ibid., p. 66. Emphasis added.

30. Ashis Nandy, "From Outside the Imperium," in *Traditions, Tyranny and Utopia: Essays in the Politics of Awareness*, pp. 147–148.

31. Ambedkar, "Caste in India," in *Annihilation of Caste*, pp. 20–21. Emphasis added.

32. The target of my criticism is my essay, "Postcoloniality and the Artifice of History: Who Speaks for "Indian" Pasts?" *Representations* 37 (Winter 1992) reproduced here as Chapter 1.

33. See Chapter 1 above.

34. This entire discussion is indebted to Heidegger's thoughts on the relationship between the structure of the "not yet" and the nature of Being in the chapter on "Dasein's Possibility of Being-a-Whole and Being-Towards-Death" in Division 2 of *Being and Time*. See Martin Heidegger, *Being and Time*, translated by John Macquarrie and Edward Robinson (Oxford: Basil Blackwell, 1985), pp. 276–289. Joan Stambaugh's recent translation of *Being and Time* (Albany: State University of New York Press, 1996), p. 225, replaces the expression "lack of totality" in the Macquarrie and Robinson edition with "constant fragmentariness." I should make it clear, though, that what I have borrowed (and tried to learn) from Heidegger here is a way of thought. My analysis remains at the level of what Heidegger called "historiological."

35. The two relevant chapters are chapters 4 and 5 of Division 2 of *Being and Time*.

36. Nandy, "History's Forgotten Doubles," p. 66.

37. In developing these ideas on futurity I am indebted to Michael Gelven, *A Commentary on Heidegger's "Being and Time"* (DeKalb: Northern Illinois University Press, 1989), chapters 8 and 9; and E. F. Kaelin, *Heidegger's Being and Time: A Reading for Readers* (Tallahassee: Florida State University Press, 1989), chapters 10 and 11.

38. Arunkumar Sarkar, *Tirisher kobita abong parabarti* (Calcutta: Papyrus, 1981), p. 2

39. Jacques Derrida, *Specters of Marx: The State of the Debt, the Work of Mourning, and the New International*, translated by Peggy Kamuf (New York and London: Routledge, 1994). See also Freud on "The Uncanny" (1919) in Sigmund Freud, *Art and Literature*, translated under the general editorship of James Strachey, edited by Albert Dickson (Harmondsworth: Penguin, 1990), pp. 339–376.

40. Henry Lefebvre, "Notes Written One Sunday in the French Countryside," in his *Critique of Everyday Life*, translated by John Moore (London: Verso, 1991), pp. xxiii, 213–214.

41. A. K. Ramanujan, "Is There an Indian Way of Thinking? An Informal Essay," in McKim Marriott, ed., *India through Hindu Categories* (Delhi: Sage Publications, 1990), pp. 42–43. But see also Fred Dallmayr's critical appreciation of this essay: "Western Thought and Indian Thought: Comments on Ramanujan," *Philosophy East and West* 44, no. 3 (July 1994), pp. 527–542.

42. See John F. Burns, "Science Can't Eclipse a Magic Moment for Millions," *New York Times*, 25 October 1995.

43. As one Indian philosopher wrote: "there is no other way open, to us in the East, but to go along with this Europeanization and to go *through* it. Only through this voyage into the foreign and the strange can we win back our own self-hood; here as elsewhere, the way to what is closest to us is the longest way back." J. L. Mehta, *Martin Heidegger: The Way and the Vision* (Honolulu: University of Hawaii Press, 1976), p. 466. Mehta echoes late Heidegger in a footnote (n101) in saying that the matter of being at home is always a question of homecoming, that is, of travel and journeying. Martin Heidegger, *Holderlin's Hymn "The Ister,"* translated by William McNeill and Julia Davis (Bloomington and Indianapolis: Indiana University Press, 1996), pp. 31–42; Fred Dallmayr, *The Other Heidegger* (Ithaca and London: Cornell University Press, 1993), p. 75.

Index

Althusser, Louis, 6, 12, 29
Ambedkar, B. R., 245–46
Amin, Samir, 5
Amin, Shahid, 106
anachronism, 238–39; and historical consciousness, 239, 243; and "the true present," 244
Anderson, Benedict, 149, 174
Ankersmit, F. R., 264n66
Appadurai, Arjun, 182
Appiah, Anthony, 239, 241–42
Aristotle, 51–52, 55
Arnold, David, 44

Bandyopadhyay, Srikumar, 154, 210–11
Bengali literature: and debates on realism, 159–63; and European romanticism, 167, 169; and formation of male intimacy, 194–95, 210–11; love and sexuality in, 134–41; widowhood in, 118, 133, 142
Benjamin, Walter, 23, 159, 265n68, 282n26
Berman, Marshall, 244; *All That is Solid Melts into Air*, 155–56, 180. *See also* modernism
Bernal, Martin, 5
Bhabha, Homi, 10, 40, 177, 264n58
Bhadra, Gautam, 85
Bhattacharya, Sukanta, 155, 161, 178
Bloch, Ernst, 12, 261n38
Bloch, Marc, 273n2
Bose, Budhhadev, 157, 160, 162, 183, 216; on *adda*, 185–86, 190–91, 204
Bose, Sugata, 283n53
Bosu, Rajsekhar (Parashuram), 191, 192–93, 203–4, 208–10
Bultman, Rudolf, 104–5
Burke, Peter, 40, 109

Carr, E. H., 106–7
Castoriadis, Cornelius, 53, 55
Chandler, James, 12, 261n37, 261n39, 284n68
Chatterjee, Partha, 33, 215, 268n46, 292n7
Chattopadhyay, Bankimchandra, 32, chapter 5 *passim*; *Bishabriksha*, 134, 136; on nature and beauty, 135–38, 139; on widowhood, 133
Chattopadhyay, Saratchandra: on widowhood, 133; on women as subjects, 139–40
Chattopadhyay, Sunitikumar, 187; on hostel-life and *adda*, 196–97
Chaudhuri, Nirad C., 35, 36, 187, 204; on *adda*, 183–85
civil society: Bengali critiques of, chapter 8 *passim*
Clifford, James, 296n8
Cohen, David, 106
Coleridge, Samuel Taylor: *Biographia Literaria*, 174, 286n88, 286n90
Collingwood, R. G., 272n2
Connolly, William, 35; on the subject of modernity, 130–31. *See also* modernity

Das, Jibanananda, 157, 160; *Rupashi Bangla*, 162
Dasgupta, Manashi, 142, 180, 207
Datta, Kalyani, 117, 118, 129, 141; chapter 5 *passim*
Datta, Sudhindranath, 162
Davis, Paul, 75
De, Barun, 295n2
Deane, Phyllis, 7
Dening, Greg, 106
Derrida, Jacques, 93, 95, 112
Dey, Bishnu, 160
Dirks, Nicholas, 267n39
domesticity: Bengali imaginings of, chapter 8 *passim*; and discipline, 224–25
During, Simon, 87, 88
Dutt, Michael Madhusudan, 33, 34, 126, 194–95

Eaton, Richard, 80, 87
Elster, Jon, 53
Ernst, Carl, 85, 86

Fanon, Frantz: on Enlightenment humanism, 5

Foucault, Michel, 6, 56, 82, 94, 148, 270n43; *Discipline and Punish*, 56; *History of Sexuality*, 144
Fraternal compact: in Bengali nationalism, 217–18, 229–32, 234–35; in Locke (*see* Locke)
Fukuyama, Francis: on the end of history, 3

Gadamer, H. G., 112; on prejudice, 127
Gandhi, Leela, 16
Gandhi, M. K., 34, 39–40, 245–46
Gelven, Michael, 89, 297n37
gender and public culture, 207–12
Grossberg, Lawrence, 7
Guha, Ranajit, 11, 12, 13, 14, 15, 101–4, 105, 106, 265n12, 267n38, 288n8, 290n58, 293n23
Gurevich, Aron, 109

Habermas, Jurgen, 35, 45
Haldane, J. B. S., 73
Harvey, David, 270n31, 270n45
Hegel, G.W. F.: *Logic*, 60–61; *Phenomenology of Spirit*, 237; *Philosophy of Right*, 130
Heidegger, Martin, 18, 19, 21, 22, 68, 112, 239, 241, 254, 262n51, 271n71; on "foreconception," 252; on "not yet" and the "fragment," 249–50, 251, 297n34; on "homecoming," 298n43
Henry, Michel, 91
historicism, 6–16, 22–23, 47, 49, 50, 73–74, 87, 88; and Bengali modernity, 235–36, 237; and "decisionism," 247–48; and the political, 178–79; postcolonial critiques of, chapters 1–4, Epilogue *passim*; and realism, 157; and romanticism, 12; and time, 243
Hobsbawm, Eric, 11–12, 13, 97, 99, 275n1
Horkheimer, Max, 67
Horton, Robin, 277n26
housewife: Bengali aestheticization of, chapters 5, 8 *passim*
Humboldt, Wilhelm von, 109, 113
Hume, David, 119, 174, 227n8, 278n23
Husserl, Edmund, 29, 30

Igger, George, 99
imagination: chapter 6 *passim*; in Adam Smith, 126; in Benedict Anderson, 149; and *darshan*, 173–76; in European romanticism, 174–75; 286n88; and Sanskrit aesthetics, 174, 285n87. *See also* Coleridge

Jameson, Fredric, 7, 42, 111

Kaviraj, Sudipta, 235–36
Kenyatta, Jomo, 239; *Facing Mount Kenya*, 240–41
Kierkegaard, Soren, 108
Kosambi, D. D., 239, 242–43, 268n6
Kracauer, Siegfried, 265n68

Lefebvre, Henry, 211, 252
Le Goff, Jacques, 101
literature: and sociality, chapter 7 *passim*
Lloyd, David, 111, 276n25
Locke, John, 141, 236; on fraternity, 217–18, 230–31, 244–45; *Some Thoughts Concerning Education*, 231; *Two Treatises of Government*, 217
Lyotard, J. F., 88

Macpherson, C. B., 130
Marx, K., 18, 29–30, 37, 47, 78, 88, 90, 91, 245, 254, chapter 2 *passim*; on abstract labor, 50–62; on capitalist discipline, 55–56, 59, 92; on formal and real subsumption, 268n7; on freedom, 59–60; on the history of modern machinery, 270n34; on living labor, 60–61; *On the Jewish Question*, 130; on plural histories of capital, 62–67; on productive labor, 68, 272n69; on real labor, 92, 94; on use value, 271–72n68
Marxist historiography, 12, 15, 17, 22, 23, 31–32, 96, 239, 245, 262n44; and historicism, 47–48, 50, 92; and the idea of uneven development, 12
Massumi, Brian, 286n91
Mehta, Deepak, 79–80
Mehta, J. L., 180, 298n43
Mehta, Uday Singh, 259n23, 260n27
memories: familial and public, 143–44, 280n59
Mill, J. S.: and Bengali romanticism, 169; on liberty and representative government, 8, 9
Mitchell, Timothy, 131
modernism: and Baudelaire, 156, 159; and Bengali literature, 155–61; definition of, 155–56; in Indian cities, 182. *See also* Berman

modernity: and Bengali kinship, 147; in Bengali literature, 134–42; fundamental themes of, 141; political, 4, 6; and the problem of interiority, 130, 133–34, 138–39, 140–41, 211–13; the subject of, 120–21, 129–31, 217; and the subject of suffering, 142–48. *See also* Fraternal compact; Locke
Morris, Meaghan, 39, 263n57
Mukherjee, Dhurjatiprasad, 168, 200
Mukhopadhyay, Bhudev, 223, 224, 231–32, 235; on natural rights, 229
Mukhopadhyay, Subhash, 163, 228–29

Nandy, Ashis, 248–49, 250
Nehru, Jawaharlal, 176–77
Nietzsche, Friedrich, 20, 148
nostalgia, 182, 250

Pandey, Gyan, 77, 78–80
Pateman, Carole, 42; on fraternal compact, 231. *See also* Fraternal Compact; Locke
Pollock, Sheldon, 258n13
Postone, Moishe, 53
Prakash, Gyan, 77, 81–82, 83, 267n39

Radhakrishnan, Sarvepalli, 10
Raphael, Vincente, 89
Raychaudhuri, Tapan, 4, 231
Rorty, Richard, 45
Rosdolsky, Roman, 271n65
Roy, Rammohun, 3, 32, 127, 221, chapter 5 *passim*; on compassion, 122–23; on rights of women, 120–21
Rubin, I. I., 53, 91

Sarkar, Sumit, 31, 214–15, 216, 224, 234, 285n80
Sarkar, Tanika, 215, 292n7
Sen, Asok, 278n9
Sen, Samar, 161
Sinha, Mrinalini, 216
Smith, Adam, 119; on productive labor, 272n69, 278n11; on sympathy, 126. *See also* Marx
Smith, Neil, 12, 261n37
Spivak, Gayatri C., 40, 41, 89, 270n32, 272n68
Subaltern Studies, 11, 21, 28, 31, 43–44, 101, 102, 103, 105, 261n33
sympathy, Bengali understanding of, 124–27; in Enlightenment thought, 127; in Sanskrit aesthetics, 126–27. *See also* Smith, Adam

uneven development, origins of the idea of, 12; and Marxist histories, 239, 261n37, 261n38. *See also* Marxist historiography
utilitarianism, romantic critiques of, 169–70, 284n68

Veer, Peter van der, 289n33
Veyne, Paul, 82
Vidyasagar, Iswarchandra, 120–21, 127, chapter 5 *passim;* on compassion, 122; on middle-class respectability, 131–33
Viswanathan, Gauri, 296n25

Wajed Ali, S., 175–76, 178
widowhood, literary representations of, 133–34; in Bengali society, 118; in colonial discourse, 118–19. *See also* Bengali literature

PRINCETON STUDIES IN CULTURE/POWER/HISTORY

High Religion: A Cultural and Political History of Sherpa Buddhism
by Sherry B. Ortner

A Place in History: Social and Monumental Time in a Cretan Town
by Michael Herzfeld

The Textual Condition *by Jerome J. McGann*

Regulating the Social: The Welfare State and Local Politics in Imperial Germany
by George Steinmetz

Hanging without a Rope: Narrative Experience in Colonial and Postcolonial Karoland *by Mary Margaret Steedly*

Modern Greek Lessons: A Primer in Historical Constructivism
by James Faubion

The Nation and Its Fragments: Colonial and Postcolonial Histories
by Partha Chatterjee

Culture/Power/History: A Reader in Contemporary Social Theory
edited by Nicholas B. Dirks, Geoff Eley, and Sherry B. Ortner

After Colonialism: Imperial Histories and Postcolonial Displacements
edited by Gyan Prakash

Encountering Development: The Making and Unmaking of the Third World
by Arturo Escobar

Social Bodies: Science, Reproduction, and Italian Modernity
by David G. Horn

Revisioning History: Film and the Construction of a New Past
edited by Robert A. Rosenstone

The History of Everyday Life: Reconstructing Historical Experiences and Ways of Life *edited by Alf Lüdtke*

The Savage Freud and Other Essays on Possible and Retrievable Selves
by Ashis Nandy

Children and the Politics of Culture *edited by Sharon Stephens*

Intimacy and Exclusion: Religious Politics in Pre-Revolutionary Baden
by Dagmar Herzog

What Was Socialism, and What Comes Next? *by Katherine Verdery*

Citizen and Subject: Contemporary Africa and the Legacy of Late Colonialism
by Mahmood Mamdani

Colonialism and Its Forms of Knowledge: The British in India *by Bernard S. Cohn*

Charred Lullabies: Chapters in an Anthropography of Violence
by E. Valentine Daniel

Theft of an Idol: Text and Context in the Representation of Collective Violence
by Paul R. Brass

Essays on the Anthropology of Reason *by Paul Rabinow*

Vision, Race, and Modernity: A Visual Economy of the Andean Image World
by Deborah Poole

Children in Moral Danger and the Problem of Government in
Third Republic France *by Sylvia Schafer*

Settling Accounts: Violence, Justice, and Accountability in Postsocialist Europe
by John Borneman

From Duty to Desire: Remaking Families in a Spanish Village
by Jane Fishburne Collier

Black Corona: Race and the Politics of Place in an Urban Community
by Steven Gregory

Welfare, Modernity, and the Weimar State, 1919–1933 *by Young-Sun Hong*

Remaking Women: Feminism and Modernity in the Middle East
edited by Lila Abu-Lughod

Spiritual Interrogations: Culture, Gender, and Community in Early African American Women's Writing *by Katherine Clay Bassard*

Refashioning Futures: Criticism after Postcoloniality
by David Scott

Colonizing Hawai'i: The Cultural Power of Law
by Sally Engle Merry

Local Histories/Global Designs:
Coloniality, Subaltern Knowledges, and Border Thinking
by Walter D. Mignolo

Provincializing Europe: Postcolonial Thought and Historical Difference
by Dipesh Chakrabarty

Engineers of Happy Land: Technology and Nationalism in a Colony
by Rudolf Mrázek